A Companion to the Works of
Elias Canetti

Edited by
Dagmar C. G. Lorenz

CAMDEN HOUSE

First published 2004
by Camden House

Camden House is an imprint of Boydell & Brewer Inc.
668 Mt. Hope Avenue, Rochester, NY 14620, USA
www.camden-house.com
and of Boydell & Brewer Limited
PO Box 9, Woodbridge, Suffolk IP12 3DF, UK
www.boydell.co.uk

ISBN: 1–57113–234–1

Library of Congress Cataloging-in-Publication Data

A companion to the works of Elias Canetti / edited by Dagmar C.G. Lorenz.
p. cm. — (Studies in German literature, linguistics, and culture)
Includes bibliographical references and index.
ISBN 1–57113–234–1 (hardcover : alk. paper)
    1. Canetti, Elias, 1905– —Criticism and interpretation. I. Lorenz,
Dagmar C. G., 1948–   II. Series: Studies in German literature, lin-
guistics, and culture (Unnumbered)

PT2605.A58Z644 2004
833'.912—dc22

                                                                2004005361

A catalogue record for this title is available from the British Library.

This publication is printed on acid-free paper.
Printed in the United States of America.

To Mohsin and Bennie with love and gratitude

Contents

Canetti's Principal Works   ix

Abbreviations of Works Frequently Cited   xiii

Introduction   1
Dagmar C. G. Lorenz

Canetti's Global Significance

Good-Bye to All That: Elias Canetti's Obituaries   25
William Collins Donahue

Writing and Language

"The Deeper Nature of My German":
Mother Tongue, Subjectivity, and the Voice of
the Other in Elias Canetti's Autobiography   45
Anne Fuchs

Elias Canetti's Attitude to Writers and Writings   61
Hans Reiss

Canetti and the Question of Genre   89
Julian Preece

The Works: Themes and Genres

"The Faultiest Expressions Have the Greatest Attraction":
Elias Canetti's Proverbial Aphorisms   107
Wolfgang Mieder

Canetti's *Aufzeichnungen*   123
Sigurd Paul Scheichl

Staging a Critique of Modernism: Elias Canetti's Plays   137
Helga Kraft

"Gute Reisende sind herzlos": Canetti in Marrakesh 157
Harriet Murphy

Space in Elias Canetti's Autobiographical Trilogy 175
Irene Stocksieker Di Maio

Philosophy and Social Thought

Canetti and Nietzsche:
An Introduction to Masse und Macht 201
Ritchie Robertson

Images of Male and Female in Canetti's Fictional,
Autobiographical, and Theoretical Work 217
Johannes G. Pankau

Canetti's Final Frontier: The Animal 239
Dagmar C. G. Lorenz

Historical Contexts

Canetti, Roustchouk, and Bulgaria:
The Impact of Origin on Canetti's Work 261
Svoboda Alexandra Dimitrova and Penka Angelova

Elias Canetti's Response to the Shoah: 289
Masse und Macht
Michael Mack

Works Cited 313

Notes on the Contributors 333

Index 337

Elias Canetti

Principal Works by Year of First Publication

When available in translation, English title and date of appearance are given.

1932   *Hochzeit.* Berlin: S. Fischer, 1932. (*The Wedding.* Translated by Gitta Honegger. New York: Performing Arts Journal Publications, 1986).

1935   *Die Blendung.* [Vienna: Herbert Reichner, 1935; Munich: Willi Weismann, 1948]. Munich: Hanser, 1963. (*Auto-da-Fé.* Translated by C. V. Wedgwood. New York: Stein and Day, 1946; also as: *The Tower of Babel.* New York: Knopf, 1947).

1950   *Komödie der Eitelkeit.* Munich: Weismann, 1950. (*Comedy of Vanity & Life Terms.* Translated by Gitta Honegger. New York: Performing Arts Journal Publications, 1983).

1955   *Fritz Wotruba.* Vienna: Rosenbaum, 1955.

1960   *Masse und Macht.* Hamburg: Claassen, 1960. (*Crowds and Power.* Translated by Carol Stewart. London: Victor Gollancz, 1962; New York: Viking, 1962).

1962   *Welt im Kopf.* Vienna: Stiasny, 1962.

1964   *Hochzeit, Komödie der Eitelkeit, Die Befristeten.* Munich: Hanser, 1964. (*Die Befristeten* translated as *The Numbered: A Play*, 1984. Translated by Carol Stewart. London: Martin Boyars, 1984).

       Der Ohrenzeuge: Fünfzig Charaktere. Munich: Hanser, 1964. (*The Earwitness.* Translated by Joachim Neugroschel. London: Deutsch, 1979).

1965   *Aufzeichnungen 1942–1948.* Munich: Hanser, 1965.

       Der andere Prozeß. Kafkas Briefe an Felice. Munich: Hanser, 1965. (*Kafka's Other Trial: The Letters to Felice.* Translated by Christopher Middleton. New York: Schocken, 1974).

1967   *Die Stimmen von Marrakesch: Aufzeichnungen nach einer Reise.* Munich: Hanser, 1967. (*The Voices of Marrakesh.* Translated by J. A. Underwood. London: M. Boyar, 1978; New York: Seabury, 1978).

1970   *Alle vergeudete Verehrung: Aufzeichnungen 1949–1960.* Munich: Hanser, 1970.

1972   *Die gespaltene Zukunft: Aufsätze und Gespräche.* Munich: Hanser, 1972.

         Macht und Überleben: Drei Essays. Berlin: Literarisches Colloquium, 1972.

1973   *Die Provinz des Menschen: Aufzeichnungen 1942–1972.* Munich: Hanser, 1973. (*The Human Province.* Translated by Joachim Neugroschel. New York: Seabury, 1978).

1976   *Das Gewissen der Worte: Essays.* Munich: Hanser, 1976. (*The Conscience of Words.* Translated by Joachim Neugroschel. New York: Seabury, 1979).

         Der Beruf des Dichters. Munich: Hanser, 1976.

1977   *Die gerettete Zunge: Geschichte einer Jugend.* Munich: Hanser, 1977. (*The Tongue Set Free: Remembrance of a European Childhood.* Translated by Joachim Neugroschel. New York: Seabury, 1979).

1980   *Die Fackel im Ohr: Lebensgeschichte 1921–1931.* Munich: Hanser, 1980. (*The Torch in My Ear.* Translated by Joachim Neurgroschel. New York: Farrar, Straus and Giroux, 1982).

1985   *Das Augenspiel: Lebensgeschichte 1931–1937.* Munich: Hanser, 1985. (*The Play of the Eyes.* Translated by Ralph Manheim. New York: Farrar, Straus and Giroux, 1986).

1987   *Das Geheimherz der Uhr: Aufzeichnungen 1973–1985.* Munich: Hanser 1987. (*The Secret Heart of the Clock: Notes, Aphorisms, Fragments 1973–1985.* Translated by Joel Agee. London: Deutsch, 1991).

1992   *Die Fliegenpein: Aufzeichnungen.* Munich: Hanser, 1992. (*The Agony of Flies: Notes and Notations.* Translated by H. F. Broch de Rothermann. New York: Farrar, Straus and Giroux, 1994).

1993   *Aufzeichnungen 1942–1985: Die Provinz des Menschen; Das Geheimherz der Uhr.* Munich: Hanser, 1993.

         Werke. Munich: Hanser, 1993–.

1994   *Nachträge aus Hampstead: Aus den Aufzeichnungen 1954–1971.*
        Zurich: Hanser 1994. (*Notes from Hampstead: The Writer's Notes,
        1954–1971.* Translated by John Hargraves. New York: Farrar,
        Straus and Giroux, 1998).

1999   *The Memoirs of Elias Canetti.* Translated by Joachim Neugroschel.
        New York: Farrar, Straus and Giroux, 1999.

2003   *Party im Blitz. Die englischen Jahre.* Eds. Kristian Wachinger and
        Jeremy D. Adler. Munich: Hanser, 2003.

Editions by Elias Canetti

Canetti, Veza. *Die gelbe Straße.* Munich: Hanser, 1989.

Canetti, Veza. *Der Oger.* Munich: Hanser, 1990.

Canetti, Veza. *Geduld bringt Rosen.* Munich: Hanser, 1992.

Translations by Elias Canetti

Upton Sinclair. *Das Geld schreibt.* Berlin: Malik, 1930.

Upton Sinclair. *Leidweg der Liebe.* Berlin: Malik, 1930.

Upton Sinclair. *Alkohol.* Berlin: Malik, 1932.

Abbreviations of Works Frequently Cited

A   *Das Augenspiel: Lebensgeschichte 1931–1937.* Munich: Hanser, 1985.

Aufz. 1942–48   *Aufzeichnungen 1942–1948.* Munich: Hanser, 1965.

Aufz. 1942–85   *Aufzeichnungen 1942–1985: Die Provinz des Menschen; Das Geheimherz der Uhr.* Munich: Hanser, 1993.

Aufz. 1949–60   *Alle vergeudete Verehrung: Aufzeichnungen 1949–1960.* Munich: Hanser, 1970.

Aufz. 1973–84   *Aufzeichnungen 1973–1984.* Munich: Hanser, 1999.

Aufz. 1992–93   *Aufzeichnungen 1992–1993.* Munich: Hanser, 1996.

Blendung   *Die Blendung.* Munich: Hanser, 1963.

DgZ   *Die gespaltene Zukunft: Aufsätze und Gespräche.* Munich: Hanser, 1972.

F   *Die Fliegenpein: Aufzeichnungen.* Munich: Hanser, 1992.

FO   *Die Fackel im Ohr: Lebensgeschichte 1921–1931.* Munich: Hanser, 1980.

Fritz Wotruba   *Fritz Wotruba.* Vienna: Rosenbaum, 1955.

GU   *Das Geheimherz der Uhr: Aufzeichnungen 1973–1985.* Munich: Hanser, 1987.

GW   *Das Gewissen der Worte: Essays.* Munich: Hanser, 1976.

GZ   *Die gerettete Zunge: Geschichte einer Jugend.* Munich: Hanser, 1977.

HEB   *Hochzeit, Komödie der Eitelkeit, Die Befristeten.* Munich: Hanser, 1964.

Marrakesch   *Die Stimmen von Marrakesch: Aufzeichnungen nach einer Reise.* Munich: Hanser, 1967.

MM   *Masse und Macht.* Hamburg: Claassen, 1960.

NH   *Nachträge aus Hampstead: Aus den Aufzeichnungen 1954–1971.* Zurich: Hanser, 1994.

Ohrenzeuge   *Der Ohrenzeuge: Fünfzig Charaktere.* Munich: Hanser, 1964.

PM   *Die Provinz des Menschen: Aufzeichnungen 1942–1972.* Munich: Hanser, 1973.

Prozeß   *Der andere Prozeß. Kafkas Briefe an Felice.* Munich: Hanser, 1965.

Welt im Kopf   *Welt im Kopf.* Vienna: Stiasny, 1962.

Introduction

Dagmar C. G. Lorenz

ELIAS CANETTI WAS A WITNESS TO the most cataclysmic events of the twentieth century; he was their analyst and their chronicler. A Sephardic Jew, born on the fringes of Europe in Roustchouk, Bulgaria, in 1905, he identified himself through European classical literature and the German language without forgetting his cultural roots. In his magnum opus *Masse und Macht* (1960), one of his prime examples of the survivor is the Jewish historian Flavius Josephus (37–ca. 100 A.D.), who became a Roman citizen and assistant to the Roman commander Titus. In *Die Stimmen von Marrakesch* (1967) Canetti's visit in the Jewish quarter is the highlight of his narrative.[1] Finally, Canetti's analysis about Franz Kafka's troubling relationship with his fiancée Felice Bauer is no less a chapter of Central European Jewish cultural history than it is the account of a prominent writer torn by his duties, desires, and sense of integrity.[2]

As was the case with Flavius Josephus and Franz Kafka, in Canetti's life, past and present, tradition and innovation, occidental and oriental influences represented equally strong forces. Faced by war and genocide perpetrated by those who spoke the language of his choice and were members of the culture he had come to love, Canetti did not disavow the German language and culture. Even while in exile in England he remained aloof, a cosmopolitan, and a critic of those who supported violence, regardless under which circumstances. "In Kriegen geht es ums Töten," he writes. "'Die Reihen der Feinde wurden gelichtet.' Es geht um ein Töten in *Haufen*. Möglichst viele Feinde werden niedergeschlagen; aus der gefährlichen Masse von lebenden Gegnern soll ein Haufen von Toten werden" (*MM*, 77). Identifying with more than one society, Canetti remained impartial to causes, programs, and ideologies. He took sides only against death itself, the misguided who killed on behalf of demagogues, and others who killed for the sheer pleasure of it.

Canetti was the oldest of three sons and the member of a minority among European minorities. He grew up a polyglot and a student of world cultures, including nations and groups that received little or no attention except perhaps from anthropologists and ethnographers — the Lele of Kasai, the Jivaros, the Pueblo Indians, the Shi'ites in Karbala, and the Xosas (*MM*, 151–58, 173–81, and 226–35). Disturbing to modern readers, he paralleled the seemingly barbarian customs of primitive peoples, "Naturvölker" (*MM,* 296), to accounts from Western culture and history, the supposed realm of civilization. For example, under the heading "Meute und Religion," the familiarity of Catholicism is discussed alongside the rain dances of the Pueblo Indians and the holy fire in Jerusalem (*MM,* 149–96). Canetti's extraordinary perspective of equality and diversity reflects the author's own multicultural upbringing. In addition, his confrontation with raw violent passion in interwar Europe, notably Austria, a country that prides itself with the highest cultural achievements, is fundamental to his writing.

Elias Canetti's father, the merchant Jacques Canetti, and his mother, Mathilde Canetti, née Arditti, were born in Bulgaria. His mother was a descendant of one of the oldest and wealthiest Sephardic families in Bulgaria, his father the son of a merchant from Adrianople, whom the Arditti family considered a parvenu even though he was a well-liked and successful businessman.[3] As a boy, Canetti was exposed to a great variety of cultural and linguistic influences, changes, and emotional traumata. His childhood, as described in his memoirs, was first dominated by the patriarchal, semi-rural culture in his grandparents' home in Roustchouk, where Ladino was spoken, and Jewish law and holidays were observed. In the first volume of his memoirs, *Die gerettete Zunge: Geschichte einer Jugend,* he describes how he was instilled with an inordinate pride of his origins as a Sephardic Jew: "Mit naiver Überheblichkeit sah man auf andere Juden herab, ein Wort, das immer mit Verachtung geladen war, lautete 'Todesco,' es bedeutete einen deutschen oder aschkenasischen Juden. Es wäre undenkbar gewesen, eine 'Todesca' zu heiraten, und unter den vielen Familien, von denen ich in Rustschuk als Kind reden hörte oder die ich kannte, entsinne ich mich keines einzigen Falles einer solchen Mischehe" (*GZ,* 12).

However, other influences were also present, including the Bulgarian language and Christian customs, to which Canetti and his brother Georges were exposed outside their parents' home and through the family's non-Jewish domestics. Moreover, Canetti's mother, who embraced cosmopolitan ideals and championed European high culture, tried to minimize the influence of her religious relatives and in-laws, although she could not prevent her father-in-law from enrolling Elias in a Talmud-Thora school during their stay in Vienna.[4] Having studied in Vienna, Canetti's parents loved German art and literature. They imparted their fascination to their young son by frequently reminiscing about Vienna and their uplifting cultural experiences in the Habsburg capital, most of all the *Burgtheater.* Canetti reports that his parents had dreamed of becoming *Burgtheater* actors. After returning to Bulgaria, they continued to speak German in their intimate conversations or when they wanted to prevent their children from following their conversation (*GZ,* 18, 37–38). The love Canetti's parents had for German, their literary interests, their nostalgia for Habsburg Vienna, and his family's ethical and intellectual positions, which Mathilde Canetti transmitted to her son, deeply influenced the philosophical views Canetti espoused in the course of his career. His pronounced individualism often placed Canetti at odds with his contemporaries and the popular trends of time, most of which, like socialism, communism, fascism, and National Socialism, involved collectivist ideas and demanded the subordination of the individual.

Elias Canetti's first four years were those of a pampered only child of whom both the parents and the extended family had the highest expectations. His special position was challenged little by the birth of his brothers Nissim (1909–) and Georges (1911–1971). Emotionally and intellectually Elias was the child closest to his mother, and when she became a widow, he assumed the role of her confidant and supporter. In 1911, when Elias was six years old, the Canettis relocated to England. Jacques Canetti defied his father's wishes by accepting an offer to join the business of his brothers-in-law in Manchester as a partner. The grandfather's disapproval overshadowed the move. Mathilde Canetti, whose desire it was to escape from her father-in-law's dominance, favored the relocation to England. She resented the patriarchal attitude of her husband's father as well as his strict religious observance. She welcomed the opportunity to lead an independent secular life in England, a nation she admired because of its democratic tradition (*GZ,* 49–50).

In Manchester, Elias took English lessons and later attended the local school. He enjoyed the social life at his parents' and relatives' homes and adjusted well until the summer of 1912 when his mother, for no apparent reason, fell ill and traveled to the Bavarian resort of Bad Reichenhall to recover. Shortly after her reluctant return to England, Jacques Canetti, a heavy smoker, died unexpectedly of a heart attack at the age of thirty. Possible factors contributing to this shocking event may have been a romantic entanglement Mathilde seems to have had with her physician in Reichenhall along with the news about outbreak of war on the Balkans and "the possibility of many casualties even within his family."[5]

In 1913 Mathilde, suffering from bouts of depression after her husband's death, decided to leave England, even though she appears to have been supported financially by her brother into whose house she had moved (*GZ,* 91). Canetti notes that during this time he went to school as usual without being treated like an orphan (*GZ,* 92). In the spring of 1913, Mathilde began to make preparations for a move to Vienna, be it that she wanted to return to the city of her first love, be it that she considered Austria a safer place than Bulgaria, where the military conflict continued to escalate. Mathilde and her sons first traveled to Lausanne via London and Paris and stayed in Switzerland for a few months. Here Elias received a crash course in German from his mother so that he would be able to enroll in Austrian schools. This experience turned out to be an extremely painful episode in

Canetti's life, and he discussed it at great length in his autobiography (*GZ,* 98–101). For example, listening in on a conversation between his mother and his English nanny, he hears the former referring to him as an idiot because she is dissatisfied with the progress he has made. "Das war sehr bitter, es war wieder das Wort, an dem es für mich hing" (*GZ,* 101).

In Vienna, with only limited funds available, Mathilde rented an apartment in the Second District, the so-called Leopoldstadt, the quarter close to the Danube Canal and the Prater. This affordable part of town was attractive to new arrivals from the provinces of the Danube Monarchy. Here, Elias attended elementary school, and his mother made plans to enroll him in a college preparatory school. However, the assassination of the Austrian heir apparent Franz Ferdinand and the beginning of the First World War, enthusiastically welcomed by the Viennese public, caused a change in plans. Following a visit to Bulgaria in 1915, during which his grandfather failed, as Canetti writes, "mir Interesse für meinen Geburtsort abzunötigen" (*GZ,* 138), Mathilde sought help in a sanatorium for serious depression. In 1916, she moved with her children to Switzerland. Although he had to adjust to an entirely new educational system, Canetti began to attend a Zurich college preparatory school (*GZ,* 191).

For the first time in his life, as he reports in his autobiography, Canetti had been confronted with anti-Semitism in Vienna (*GZ,* 116). Equally as enduring as the impression of the first such insult was his mother's rejection of it: ". . . sie nahm das Schimpfwort nicht an. Wir waren für sie etwas Besseres, nämlich Spaniolen" (*GZ,* 117). Mathilde shared her family's cultural biases. She was proud of her Sephardic heritage and looked down upon Ashkenazic Jews, who constituted the majority of Austro-Hungarian Jews. The elitist attitude often so evident in Canetti's writing may in part derive from the ingrained conviction of belonging to a lineage and tradition separate from that of Eastern European Jews, the traditional target of anti-Judaism and anti-Semitism. At the same time Canetti's apparent elitism can also be associated with the identification with High German and classical and avant-garde culture to which assimilated Jews, including Canetti's first idol and role model Karl Kraus (1874–1936), aspired. Indeed, throughout Canetti's writing, beginning with his novel *Die Blendung* (1935),[6] Austrian dialect as well as Yiddish-accented German, both associated with the lower classes and popular culture, are used in a derogatory manner and ascribed to more or less despicable characters.

The sense of his own importance as an intellectual and a writer was central to Canetti's attitude toward others and his career. His self-identification as one coming from a position of privilege allowed him to experience Vienna and Western Europe from a point of view different from that typically expressed in the writing of Eastern European Jews. Canetti's elitism neither involved, as it did with Karl Kraus and Egon Friedell (1878–1938), an overcompensation for his Jewish origins, nor was his world view colored by nostalgic memories of the *shtetl* as was the case with Josef Roth (1894–1939), Manès Sperber (1905–1984), and Isaac Bashevis Singer (1904–1991). The experience of Hasidic Jews, Jewish Socialists, or Zionists is not reflected in his writings, but it is essential to the works of his Ashkenazic contemporaries, such as Roth, Martin Buber (1878–1965), Sholem Aleichem (1859–1916), and Gershom Scholem (1897–1982).

In 1919, Mathilde moved back to Vienna. Canetti continued to live in a boarding house in Zurich, where he began to write. His mother's absence may have been a boon — he did not have to share his first attempts with her. In 1921, he moved to Frankfurt with his family, where he graduated from the Wöhler Realgymnasium in 1924. The experience of the economic crisis in the defeated country, the postwar trauma, and the horrors of unemployment and inflation made a deep impression upon him, and he later explored these phenomena in his writing. After his graduation he and his brother Georges moved to Vienna, again taking up residence in the Leopoldstadt. Canetti enrolled as a chemistry major at the University of Vienna. But his primary interests were literature and cultural criticism, which he pursued, spellbound by the charismatic critic, journalist, and satirist Karl Kraus, the legendary editor and author of the journal *Die Fackel*. At Kraus's 300th reading on April 1924, friends introduced Canetti to his future wife, the twenty-seven-year-old Venetiana (Veza) Taubner-Calderon (1897–1963), who enjoyed the reputation of being a beautiful and sophisticated woman of intellect.[7] Aside from the friends of his family, who likewise lived in the Second District, Canetti met persons of different outlooks and beliefs during his student years, including Fred Waldinger, a practicing Buddhist. He also studied twentieth century Viennese authors such as Otto Weininger (1880–1903), Sigmund Freud (1856–1939), and Arthur Schnitzler (1862–1931). Of all these Karl Kraus's monumental pacifist drama *Die letzten Tage der Menschheit* impressed him the most.[8]

In the summer of 1924, he traveled to Bulgaria. During a time of reflection in Sofia, he decided against a career in chemistry[9] but, encouraged by his cousin Bernhard, resolved to continue his studies as a subterfuge to mislead his mother, who "ist unter den Einfluß von gewöhnlichen Leuten geraten. Als sie krank war in Arosa, hat sie Leute kennengelernt, die 'im Leben stehen,' wie es so heißt, und Erfolg damit hatten" (*FO*, 107). Another problematic issue was his friendship with Veza Taubner-Calderon, of which his mother disapproved. In winter of 1924/25, he writes that he experienced an epiphany that directed him to the topic of his life's work, the phenomenon of the mass or crowd. "Was die Masse aber selbst wirklich war, das wußte ich nicht, es war ein Rätsel, das zu lösen ich mir vornahm, es schien mir das wichtigste Rätsel, jedenfalls das vordergründigste, unserer Welt" (*FO*, 141).

When Mathilde moved to Paris with Elias's brothers in 1927, he stayed in Vienna. The window of his new abode in Vienna-Hacking provided a panoramic view of the psychiatric hospital Steinhof, whose patients became a source of inspiration for his studies of the human mind and human aberrations and his new literary project, a cycle of novels á la Balzac titled "Comédie Humaine an Irren." Of these planned books *Die Blendung* was intended to be the first. Even more than the nearby soccer field did the riots of 1927 reveal to Canetti fundamental aspects of mass events. In *Die Fackel im Ohr* Canetti details his impressions of July 15, 1927, the fateful day after which a profound change in the political and social climate of the erstwhile socialist, "Red," interwar Vienna took place, a change that made the rise of Austrofascism possible (*FO*, 274).

Contrary to Veza Canetti, whose fictional works display a keen sense of politics and pro-socialist sentiments,[10] Elias Canetti focuses on his own perceptions of and reactions to the initially spontaneous mass demonstration caused by an apparent case of injustice against the working class. He recalls the sense of being taken up into the protesting mass, of forging ahead without consideration for material goods, and what is worse for Canetti, human life (*FO*, 275–82). Canetti's description of this momentous event reveals the way he deduces basic concepts in his theoretical work from his own perceptions of concrete events.

Inspired by his friend, the lyric poet Ibby Gordon, frustrated by his studies, and still under the impression of the 1927 riot, Canetti traveled to Berlin. He stayed with the publisher of the Malik publishing house, Wieland Herzfelde, who became Canetti's mentor in the German metropolis. Herzfelde suggested that Canetti undertake a biography of the Malik author Upton Sinclair (1878–1968), whose social critical fiction about the United States sold in record numbers in Weimar Germany. Moreover, Herzfelde knew every writer of note and generously shared his connections with his guest, who was introduced to painter George Grosz (1893–1953), Bert Brecht, and Isaac Babel (1894–1941).[11] Canetti was simultaneously attracted to and repulsed by Berlin's gaudy bohème, the corruption, and the lack of principle he perceived among the leading intellectuals, including Brecht, against whom he felt an intense animosity. "Bei seinem Anblick, ganz besonders aber bei seinen gesprochenen Sätzen packte mich jedesmal die Wut," Canetti writes, and admits denying him praise even for the work he admired, the *Hauspostille* (*FO*, 305).[12] With a sense of alienation Canetti left Berlin to complete his studies. In 1929 he received the degree Doctor of Chemistry from the University of Vienna and thereafter went to Berlin for the second time. Without being impressed with Sinclair's writings, Canetti did translate several of his works to support himself. Back in Vienna he worked on his own novel, a first draft of which he completed in 1931.[13]

Prior to *Die Blendung*, however, Canetti published his experimental dramas, the scathing satire *Hochzeit* (1932) and *Komödie der Eitelkeit* (1934).[14] In 1932, during a reading of *Hochzeit*, Canetti made the acquaintance of the Austrian-born novelist and mass-psychologist Hermann Broch (1886–1951), whose trilogy *Die Schlafwandler* (1931/32) Canetti had long admired.[15] A productive affinity between the two men ensued, and Canetti was introduced to Broch's friends. Steadily expanding his own circles of friends and acquaintances, Canetti came in contact with Alma Mahler (1879–1964), her daughters Manon and Anna, and her husband Franz Werfel (1890–1945), developing an especially close friendship with the sculptors Anna Mahler (1904–1988) and Fritz Wotruba (1907–1975).

Canetti's most significant acquaintance during the troubled years of 1933/34, when the National Socialists came to power in Germany, and Austria introduced a fascist regime, the so-called *Ständestaat*, a Catholic dictatorship, was a certain Abraham Sonne (1883–1950), referred to in Canetti's autobiography as Dr. Sonne. Like Canetti, Sonne was a patron of the Café Museum. Canetti reports that at the age of fifteen his friend had written Hebrew poetry under the name of Abraham ben Yitzchak.[16] More importantly, he admired his friend's encyclopedic knowledge, his emotional detachment, and his well-reasoned and balanced opinions. Without Sonne, he states, he would not have been able to distance himself from the influence of Karl Kraus who, in contrast to Sonne's rationality, came to represent to him passion and bias (*A*, 159).

Sonne's disposition, described in *Das Augenspiel* as "das Fehlen alles Persönlichen," differed from Canetti's in a fundamental way. Sonne became to his friend a "Sucht," an addiction (*A*, 145) as had been the case with Kraus and Broch in previous years. Overall, Canetti's own descriptions of his personal and professional relationships reveal an impetuousness that caused him to become completely enraptured, as for example in the case of Kraus, Veza, Anna Mahler, and Sonne, or too intolerant in the case of Brecht, Alma Mahler, and the strangers to whose conversations he listened with "Ingrimm," rage (*A*, 150). Little wonder that Veza "weigerte sich standhaft, Sonne anzuerkennen" (*A*, 153).

Until 1938 Canetti lived the life of a scholar of independent means in a circle of friends and foes, intellectuals, journalists, and scholars. The era prior to the "fall," first marked by the coup d'état that ushered in the fascist regime, and then by the invasion by Nazi Germany, was exceptional in that the most diverse forms of expression and thought intermingled in metropolitan Vienna, a city that attracted the most talented and accomplished artists and thinkers. After 1933, German exiles, including Brecht, fled to Vienna from National Socialism and brought new impulses to the Austrian capital. At this time Elias Canetti finalized his novel and the drama *Hochzeit*, and he worked on his major project involving crowds and crowd behavior.

Veza continued her charitable work and published some of her own works. However, she downplayed the importance of her own writing to encourage her future husband's creative efforts. From 1932 to 1934, she used different pen names including Veza Magd, Martha Murner, and Veronika Knecht. The extraordinary insight and talent obvious from the small number of her publications place her alongside the most respected authors of her time, including Canetti.[17] Yet, she did not succeed in publishing any of her works after she and Canetti, whom she married in 1934, took exile in England. And after 1945, except for the dedications in Elias Canetti's books, the author Veza Canetti was entirely forgotten until after her death in 1963. Only in the late 1980s did her husband start to edit and publish her works.

In 1935 the newlyweds moved to the suburb of Grinzing, where they lived next door to Ernst Benedikt, son of Moritz Benedikt, the legendary editor of the *Neue Freie Presse,* the most influential Viennese paper, and the arch enemy of Canetti's erstwhile idol Karl Kraus. Benedikt had to relinquish his position as editor and his share in the paper in 1934 due to the anti-Jewish climate. Interestingly, it is the proximity to the Benedikts, rather than the progressive radicalization of the public sphere and the problem of fascism, that Canetti problematized in his autobiography. His wife's posthumous novel *Die Schildkröten* (1999) reveals that the move to the idyllic vineyards of Grinzing must be considered a retreat from the increasingly problematic life in the capital, anti-Semitism, and the attacks on critical intellectuals.[18] Similar to Benedikt's career, Veza Canetti's activities as a publishing author also ended in 1934. Her works could no longer appear in Vienna, not even in the Social Democratic *Arbeiter-Zeitung,* because the editor-in-chief Otto König feared for his ability to continue publishing the paper if he continued to accept contributions by Jewish authors.

In 1935 Elias Canetti's novel *Die Blendung* was published, predated by a year. The book had been translated into Czech, and H. G. Adler (1910–1988), who after the Shoah made a name for himself because of his incisive studies about the ghetto Theresienstadt and Auschwitz, invited Canetti to a reading in Prague in 1937. The beauties of the ancient bohemian city made a deep impression on Canetti. Soon after his return to Vienna, he was called to his mother's deathbed in Paris. She died in her small apartment in the Rue de la Convention with Canetti and his brother at her side (*A,* 350).

In March 1938 Nazi Germany invaded Austria. The Canettis stayed in Grinzing until they received the necessary documents to leave the country. They departed for Paris in 1938 and then London, where they arrived in January 1939. They took up residence in a modest place in the London suburb of Hampstead. In the following decades, Elias Canetti devoted most of his energies to his life's work on crowds and power. In 1942 he began writing his *Aufzeichnungen,* notes or aphorisms, to counterbalance the all-consuming effort that went into his anthropological and sociological studies. The *Aufzeichnungen* of that time reveal that he was preoccupied with the war, the devastation and suffering caused by it, and the consequences, about the extent of which one could only speculate at the time. Canetti, who so closely identified with German culture clearly faced a double bind. An exile from Nazi-controlled Austria living in Great Britain, he felt that he owed loyalty both to his country of residence and to the culture to which he owed much of his creativity and his language. Canetti, who had learned German under almost traumatic circumstances, became the self-proclaimed protector of the German language. In his *Aufzeichnungen* he wrote:

> Die Sprache meines Geistes wird die deutsche bleiben, und zwar weil ich Jude bin. Was von dem auf jede Weise verheerten Lande übrig bleibt, will ich als Jude in mir behüten. Auch *ihr* Schicksal ist meines; aber ich bringe noch ein allgemein menschliches Erbteil mit. Ich will ihrer Sprache zurückgeben, was ich ihr schulde. Ich will dazu beitragen, daß man ihnen für etwas Dank hat.[19]

Canetti continued to adhere to the German language as his language of publication even though during and after the war he was virtually unknown "im Raum der von ihm gewählten 'Muttersprache.'"[20] His emotional ties to German and Austrian culture also remained strong, albeit ambivalent. Unlike other exiles from German-speaking countries, he did not publish during the war years let alone get involved in propaganda — doing so would have compromised his position as a neutral arbiter, which he struggled to establish for himself. Even after Germany's defeat when he had learned of the extent of the destruction of war and the devastation of the Holocaust, he did not indict his culture of choice. Rather, his observations in these years reveal the agony that resulted from the author's attempt to preserve his neutral stance. He was preoccupied with death, paranoia, and the figure of the pathological leader of masses in universal rather than specific terms.[21] Moreover, he repeatedly stated his compassion for all those who had suffered, including the Germans who would have tried to murder him had he stayed in Vienna. Yet Canetti avoided addressing the topics of Nazi anti-Semitism and the Holocaust directly even though aspects of both are implied in his crowd studies and his writings about the paranoid leader. On the other hand, he wrote with great sensitivity and compassion about the plight of the victims of Hiroshima in his review" of a Japanese survivor's account, "Dr. Hachiyas Tagebuch aus Hiroshima" (1975).[22]

From 1946 to 1949 translations of *Die Blendung* were published under the titles *Auto-da-Fé* (1946) in England, *The Tower of Babel* (1947) in the United States, and *La Tour de Babel* (1949) in France. Canetti was awarded the Prix International, and in 1948 a new edition of *Die Blendung* appeared in German, published by the Willi Weismann Verlag in Munich. In 1950 the same publisher began to set *Komödie der Eitelkeit* to print but did not go through with the project. In 1952 Canetti became a British citizen, but his primary publishers were prominent West German companies, the Hanser and Fischer publishing houses, As his reputation grew, scholars and journalists from German-speaking countries, including Marcel Reich-Ranicki and John Patillo-Hess, who organized the annual Canetti symposium at the Vienna Urania in the 1980s, were among his guests in Hampstead. So were British scholars and intellectuals. His circle of friends and associates included the British scholar Idris Parry, and the philosopher and novelist Iris Murdoch (1919–1999), who was the later wife of the Oxford professor and writer John Bayley (1925–).[23]

In 1952, Canetti worked on the drama *Die Befristeten,* but the opportunity to travel to Morocco in the company of a film team interrupted his writing. The experience of a North African Arab society with a rich Sephardic history and subculture proved highly productive. It resulted in the "Moroccan Memoirs," a travel narrative published in 1968 as *Die Stimmen von Marrakesch: Aufzeichnungen nach einer Reise* (1967). In 1955 the biography of the prominent sculptor Fritz Wotruba, one of Canetti's closest friends from the interwar period, appeared[24] and at the same time, Canetti's *Die Befristeten* (1964) was produced at the Oxford Playhouse in English translation. As his monumental study *Masse und Macht* neared completion, Canetti traveled to France (1957) and Italy (1959). Finally, in 1960 after more than three decades of work, Hamburg publisher Claassen published *Masse und Macht.*

Canetti went on a tour to Greece in 1961 and published a selection of his essays and literary works through the small Viennese Stiasny publishing company in the following year.[25] Negotiations with the Hanser publishing company concerning a new publication of *Masse und Macht* and his following writings were well underway in 1963 when Veza Canetti died. Her death during one of the most prolific and successful periods of his life affected Canetti deeply. "Seit dem Tod meiner Frau war ich mit ganz anderen Dingen beschäftigt, wenn man das so nennen kann. Es wird wohl noch Wochen und vielleicht Monate dauern, bevor ich mich den auch objektiven geistigen Interessen meines Lebens wieder zuwenden kann," he wrote to Hans Bender.[26]

The debates caused by *Masse und Macht* among critics contributed greatly to Canetti's international profile. So did his contract with Hanser, who had Canetti's works appear in short succession. In 1964 *Hochzeit, Komödie der Eitelkeit,* and *Die Befristeten* were published in a volume of collected dramas, followed by *Aufzeichnungen 1942–1948.* The performance of *Hochzeit* at the Staatstheater Braunschweig in the same year ended in a scandal as did that of *Komödie der Eitelkeit.* Prior to the events of 1968 and the following years, the student movement and the worldwide anti-Vietnam war demonstrations, the German middle-class audience was not ready for experimental dramas such as Canetti's and did not approve of his provocative themes and caustic satire. Suddenly Canetti, a representative of the prewar generation, became as controversial as the postwar avant-garde, Peter Handke (1942–), and the Vienna Actionists.

Considered an Austrian author by the Austrian literary establishment, Canetti was awarded the *Literaturpreis der Stadt Wien* in 1966, the year that he also received the *Deutscher Kritikerpreis*. A similarly charismatic reader of his own texts as Karl Kraus, his former idol, Canetti released successful recordings of his readings through the Deutsche Grammophongesellschaft in 1967. These include the disturbing chapter "Der gute Vater" from *Die Blendung*, a story about domestic violence and child abuse, as well as excerpts from *Die Stimmen von Marrakesch*. In the following decades Canetti's travels to Vienna often included readings, which drew enthusiastic audiences. In 1968, the year that the German premiere of *Die Befristeten* in Bonn gave rise to another theater scandal, Canetti was awarded the coveted Großer Österreichischer Staatspreis and *Die Stimmen von Marrakesch* appeared in print.

One of Canetti's most intriguing works, his edition of Franz Kafka's letters to his fiancée Felice Bauer, *Der andere Prozeß: Kafkas Briefe an Felice*, was published in 1969 and awarded the *Literaturpreis der Bayerischen Akademie der Schönen Künste*. Canetti's analysis of Kafka's torturous relationship with a clearly incompatible woman reveals much about Canetti's own views on gender relationships. In 1971, following the publication of *Alle vergeudete Verehrung*, his *Aufzeichnungen* of 1949–1960, Canetti began writing his autobiography.[27] The death of his brother Georges in Paris and his marriage to Hera Buschor were two momentous events that called for a project that would force the author to take a close and subjective look at his own history and that of twentieth-century European society. In 1972, the year his daughter Johanna was born, Canetti published *Macht und Überleben* (Power and Survival), a volume that contains three major essays and *Die gespaltene Zukunft*, a collection of essays and reviews, and was awarded the Büchner Prize of the city of Darmstadt. Additional volumes of short prose, aphorisms, essays, and satires appeared in the following years: *Die Provinz des Menschen: Aufzeichnungen 1942–1972* (1973), *Der Ohrenzeuge* (1974), fifty satirical physiognomies, and his collected essays titled *Das Gewissen der Worte* (1975), and *Der Beruf des Dichters* (1975).[28] In 1975 he received two major awards, the Franz Nabl Prize and the Nelly Sachs Prize. That same year, he was awarded honorary doctorate degrees by the universities of Munich and Manchester.

In 1977 the first volume of Canetti's autobiography appeared, titled *Die gerettete Zunge: Geschichte einer Jugend*. This work, which was devoted to his experiences between 1904 to 1921, earned him the Gottfried Keller Prize. Following his autobiography, the *Komödie der Eitelkeit* was produced in Basel, Switzerland in 1978, and productions of his other plays in Vienna and Stuttgart took place in the following years. In 1979 Canetti was invited to the order "Pour le Mérite," one of the highest distinctions for an intellectual. In 1980 the second volume of his autobiography, *Die Fackel im Ohr,* a narrative of the years 1921 to 1937, was published. Canetti then received the Italian Europa Prato Prize and the Johann Peter Hebel Prize, followed by the Kafka Prize in 1981.

In 1981 Canetti's lifetime achievements were honored by the Nobel Prize in Literature. In spite of the many distinctions and honors he had received, Canetti remained relatively unknown up until this point. Unlike the members of the Frankfurt School, his works were not part of the academic curricula, and his influence was limited to academics or "alternative" scholarship such as Klaus Theweleit's provocative two-volume treatise *Männerphantasien* (1977–78).[29] The surprise that an obscure author from Bulgaria writing in German would receive the Nobel Prize calls to mind the reaction to Nelly Sachs and Isaac Bashevis Singer achieving the same distinction. Also in 1981 two cassettes of *Die Befristeten* read by Canetti were released by the Hanser Verlag. In 1983 Canetti received the Große Verdienstkreuz der Bundesrepublik Deutschland. In 1985 he published *Das Augenspiel* (1985), his autobiography dealing with the years 1931 to 1937. *Das Geheimherz der Uhr* (1985), Canetti's notebooks from 1973 to 1985, and *Die Fliegenpein* (1992), containing his most recent, most misanthropic and apocalyptic *Aufzeichnungen,* were also published.[30] Canetti's wife Hera Buschor, to whom he had dedicated the third part of his autobiography, died in 1988. In 1994 Elias Canetti died in Zurich, where he had maintained a second residence since the 1970s. His grave is close to that of James Joyce, who as a writer stood similarly apart from the crowds as did Canetti.

Throughout his career Canetti had never been a part of the intellectual mainstream. Rather than being carried by a group or school of intellectuals, he relied on his observations and inspirations from other outsiders to the literary scene, including his mother, Mathilde Canetti, an avid reader although not a writer, and his wife, Veza Canetti, a powerful but virtually unknown author. The role model of his youth, Karl Kraus, was as famous as he was controversial, a lonely spirit, maligned by many and described as a case study in *Der jüdische Selbsthaß* (1930) by Theodor Lessing.[31] Hermann Broch, another major figure in Canetti's life, attained an excellent reputation as a fiction writer, but his mass psychology remained largely unknown, and Anna Mahler, the artist featured in *Das Augenspiel,* never attained the prominence of a Käthe Kollwitz and, as Marlene Streeruwitz reveals in her novel *Nachwelt* (1999), ended up in relative obscurity in California.[32] There is also little information to be found about the much admired Abraham Sonne.

Canetti deliberately steered clear of the trends of his age and literary and ideological movements. Even his early works, e.g. his novel, contain much of the philosophical and anthropological ideas of his later notes and treatises, his dramas and his autobiographical writings. Indeed, he began conceptualizing his great theoretical work *Masse und Macht* as early as 1925, when he wrote an outline for a book on mass psychology.

The unmistakable character of Canetti's oeuvre is in part the result of the author keeping his distance from party politics and popular ideologies in an era dominated by ideologies and collectivism — nationalism, communism, Zionism, and fascism. Instead, he trusted on his own observations and assessments and chose his friends and role models not by the acclaim they achieved in the general public but because of how they appealed to him. In addition, Canetti watched the phenomena that shaped his time closely: mass events such as the party rallies and demonstrations of the interwar era, political murders, and acts of terrorism, and could ignore the power that these phenomena had over his fellow Europeans.

For this reason he was far from celebrating the individual and individualism in his writings. He recognized the frailty of the individual person as well as the lack of character and integrity in the majority of those around him. He was keenly aware of the innate cruelty and ruthlessness of *homo sapiens,* which he watched coming to the fore after the rise of the Nazis in Germany and Austria, and during Stalinism. He also was aware of the individual's corruptibility and greed. Contrary to Marxist, humanist, and Christian authors, Canetti did not believe in the good, let alone, the perfectibility, of mankind, and he never championed man as the crown of creation. For that reason he rejected the concept of revolution or the notion of a just war, even if this war was directed against Nazi Germany. He never tired of emphasizing the atavistic elements of war, and denied specific causes and political goals, thereby reiterating his mother's assessment of the First World War: "Sie nannte den Krieg nie anders als 'das Morden.' Ihr Haß gegen den Krieg hatte etwas Elementares" (*GZ,* 178). Familiar with numerous languages and cultures, Canetti looked beyond the claims of greatness on the part of any given civilization or person and rejected the complacency of nationalism or national pride, regardless of which nation or ethnic group. He subscribed to no dogma offered to him by thinkers and politicians ancient and modern, endorsed no culture or political system, aware of the pitfalls and merits of each, and he became ever more attached to the language of his choice, the German language, because it was shunned by the international community and Jews worldwide. To be sure, there were some other notable exceptions such as Berthold Viertel (1885–1953) and Ernst Waldinger (1896–1970), German-speaking Jews in exile, who expressed their love for their German mother tongue despite the negative associations it had acquired during the Nazi regime.[33] In his notebook of 1942–1945, Canetti describes his position as follows:

> Heute, mit dem Zusammenbruch in Deutschland, hat sich das alles für ihn geändert. Die Leute dort werden sehr bald nach ihrer Sprache suchen, die man ihnen gestohlen und verunstaltet hatte. Wer immer sie

rein gehalten hat, in den Jahren des schärfsten Wahns, wird damit herausrücken müssen. Es ist wahr, er lebt weiter für alle, und er wird immer allein leben müssen, sich selber als höchster Instanz verantwortlich:
aber er ist jetzt den Deutschen ihre Sprache schuldig; er hat sie sauber
gehalten, aber jetzt muß er damit herausrücken, mit Liebe und Dank,
mit Zins und Zinseszinsen.[34]

This love for the German language is the reason that in his writings on
power, crowds, killing, survival, gender relations and divisions, humans and
non-humans, Canetti avoided touching on certain topical subjects. In the
1930s and 1940s he did not comment on National Socialism and the Holocaust, even though his works *Masse und Macht* and his notebooks are clearly
informed by these events. Neither does he tackle the issue of Stalinism and
human rights abuses in the Soviet Union, or enter into an explicit debate
with authors who do, for example Hannah Arendt (1906–1975). Undoubtedly familiar with the phenomenon of the authoritarian personality discussed
by Wilhelm Reich (1897–1957), author of *Massenpsychologie des Faschismus*
(1934) and Theodor Adorno (1903–1969), he refrains from applying this
knowledge to proponents of war and violence and the criminals of his time
such as Hitler and Eichmann but rather contextualizes his own theses about
the paranoid leader personality with a historical figure such as Daniel Paul
Schreber (1842–1911).[35] The same applies to his autobiography, where the
major players of the early to mid-twentieth century are conspicuously absent
although lesser known, even obscure persons are introduced to elucidate
issues and problems central to his era and beyond.

This new volume of Canetti scholarship reveals how fresh and important
Canetti's thoughts and writing still are at the beginning of a new millennium. Indeed, several of the authors represented here underscore that Canetti may have been less well-known and appreciated in his own time than
he is today precisely because his works were *unzeitgemäß* in the sense of
being apart from their time; their representational style and unsystematic
thought finds a greater resonance with postmodern audiences than they did
with previous generations.

The first section of the companion volume, "Canetti's Global Significance," features William Collins Donahue's essay "Good-Bye to All That:
Canetti's Obituaries," which reveals Canetti's intellectual influence in light
of the wide range of reactions to his death in 1994. The large number of
obituaries in leading journals and by well-known critics attest to the growing
fascination with an author who, at the time he received the Nobel Prize, was
considered an outsider and an oddity by critics worldwide. Despite Canetti's
global appeal, Donahue does take exception to the essays and shorter obituaries that wanted to make Canetti the "avatar" of European culture. Rather,
he points to *Masse und Macht,* a work that criticizes culture, particularly

European culture, in the most radical terms imaginable. Yet, Donahue argues, the image of Canetti as "*the* enlightened European" is likely to be perpetuated by critics in search of cultural icons and intellectual heroes. For many who seek validation from the point of view of their vastly different tenets and attitudes, Canetti provides a fertile ground, indeed. Donahue points out that Canetti was a self-critical moralist, a skeptical and flawed system-builder, a mystical secularist, and a poet, who turned to literature for social analysis. Last, but not least, he was "a great European who stood European culture on its head."

The next section, "Writing and Language," features essays examining Canetti's relationship to language, writing and literary traditions, and authors in his changing intellectual environment. These are fundamental issues in every author's work, particularly one who defines himself, as did Canetti, primarily through his intellectual affinities and antipathies. The three essays in this section explore the underlying assumptions and fabric of Canetti's work.

The first essay, Anne Fuchs's "'The Deeper Nature of My German': Mother Tongue, Subjectivity, and the Voice of the Other in Elias Canetti's Autobiography," deals with Canetti's attitude to writing, representation, and textual strategies in light of the author's relationship to other people, primarily individuals in his immediate family and circle of friends. Fuchs describes the way Canetti's autobiographical texts implicitly question the very notion of autonomy on which they seems to be based. Central to Fuchs's discussion is Canetti's relationship with his mother, on which, according to her, all his future relationships depended. She scrutinizes the symbiotic yet conflict-ridden mother-son relationship and Canetti's oft-repeated claim to intellectual independence and originality. It appears surprising that he would write, as Fuchs phrases it, "a story about the son's painful and largely unsuccessful struggle to set himself free from a stifling maternal hold" and yet insist so staunchly on his autonomy. Even more intriguing is that the site of the battle between mother and son is the German language, Canetti's chosen language as a thinker and literary writer. Fuchs argues that German is in the truest sense of the word Canetti's "mother tongue" because it is imbued with struggles and conflicts deeply rooted in his family of origin.

Hans Reiss's "Elias Canetti's Attitude to Writers and Writings" explores the relationship that the *poeta doctus* Canetti establishes with his intellectual ancestors, the great writers and poets of the European tradition, world religions, and world literature. Reiss maintains that Canetti deliberately placed himself into the tradition of classical literature, tracing his own intellectual lineage all the way back to Homer. It seems that through the proximity with "immortals," Canetti, who despised death, sought to affirm his own immortality. In his own works he mentioned only those whom he considered truly great writers, who in his mind conquered death because their work became timeless, for example Aristophanes, Büchner, Cervantes,

Dickens, Dostoyevsky, Kleist, and Tolstoy. Reiss is also interested in establishing which authors Canetti rejected and why, for example Thomas Bernhard. Canetti's attractions and dislikes are important as a key to Canetti's creative process.

In his essay "Canetti and the Question of Genre," Julian Preece analyzes Canetti's choice of genre in the context of the three creative periods, the first ranging from the 1930s to the publication of *Die Blendung*, the second from the early exile years to *Masse und Macht*, with *Die Befristeten* (1952) and *Fritz Wotruba* (1955) as his only publications during this period, and his third and most prolific period devoted to his own experiences and perceptions recorded in *Aufzeichnungen* and his autobiographical works. Preece's analysis reveals the lack of "coherence" in Canetti's oeuvre, manifest in the shifts in genre and forms of expression. Yet Preece also notes recurring patterns, for example neither in Canetti's novel nor in his autobiography is the protagonist led to an integrated and productive role in society in the traditional sense. Canetti's novel ends with the protagonist's self-destruction and the destruction of his intellectual and mental home — his library, and the autobiography ends with the death of the author's mother at the time when he is forced to leave Austria. Being a Jew, Canetti was unable to remain in the cultural sphere he had chosen for himself. Preece points to the lack of social integration expressed throughout Canetti's oeuvre that mirrors the dilemma of being uprooted several times. Indeed, Canetti's exile and his "failure" to create a closed narrative calls to mind Heinrich Heine (1797–1856), who a century earlier died an exile in Paris, and who left his "Jewish" novel *Der Rabbi von Bacherach* a fragment.[36]

In the third segment of the Companion volume, "The Works: Themes and Genres," individual works and texts are discussed as representative of their particular genre — drama, aphorism, prose. Wolfgang Mieder's "'The Faultiest Expressions Have the Greatest Attraction': Elias Canetti's Proverbial Aphorisms" examines Canetti's art of the aphorism and his textual strategies. Mieder holds that, similar to his great precursors Lichtenberg and Kraus, Canetti was concerned with the proper use of language, and as was also the case with them, the correct term is at the heart of his moral messages. By exposing the unreflected use of proverbs and clichés, Canetti exposes the crudeness of speakers who thrive on stock phrases. The notion that language characterizes the speaker in an intellectual as well as a moral sense connects Canetti to traditional and contemporary "Sprachkritiker" such as Elfriede Jelinek and Marlene Streeruwitz. In "Canetti's *Aufzeichnungen*" Sigurd Scheichl traces the wide intellectual and emotional range of Canetti's aphorisms. The expansiveness of Canetti's thought and linguistic gestures may be the reason why critics often avoid these highly dense, suggestive, and elusive texts. Scheichl demonstrates that Canetti considered his aphorisms a central part of his work and shows them to be great works of art.

Helga Kraft's essay, "Staging a Critique of Modernism: Elias Canetti's Plays," discusses the reception of Canetti's dramas and analyzes the actual texts. The essay takes a fresh approach to the author's most controversial works and reveals the innovative, even revolutionary, character of Canetti's plays. Kraft argues that Canetti challenges social systems that hold everyone in bondage, whether the persons in question are victims or victimizers. By refusing to present solutions to uncomfortable problems such as the preeminence of property over the individual, the conflict between personal and collective interests, and the question of what society is able to do to bestow meaning upon life even though human beings are aware that they will die, Canetti brought new, radically unsentimental perspectives to the world of theater.

Harriet Murphy's essay "'Gute Reisende sind herzlos': Canetti in Marrakesh" raises doubt that Canetti, who so carefully observed the reactions of the masses and the plight of the weak, is indeed a *critic* of the masses. She scrutinizes his approach to a foreign culture in *Die Stimmen von Marrakesch*, a travelogue, which thematizes, as she maintains, the clash between East and West. To define this clash, Murphy holds, proper tools are still missing despite the work of Edward Said, Peter Scholl-Latour, and other Middle Eastern "experts." Emphasizing the almost sensual gratification Canetti derives from his observations of life in Marrakesh, even though it appears atavistic and primitive in his description, Murphy proposes that the seemingly simple text is more than a travel account; it is a poetic rapprochement to the Other.

In her meticulous analysis of the function of space in Canetti, "Space in Elias Canetti's Autobiographical Trilogy," Irene Stocksieker Di Maio reveals the vast intellectual and emotional distances Canetti covers in his intellectual and psychic journey with regard to the past and the present. Movement in Canetti's works seems a positive force, as it leads to powerful experiences and insights and releases creative energies. Di Maio maintains that, without attempting to create a false harmony, Canetti acknowledges discomfort, turbulence, even chaos as he encounters them in his wanderings, and rejects "anything provincial, confining, restricting, cramped, narrow, or closed." Obviously he demands for himself and others space that accommodates diversity and the full range of the human experience.

The essays in the fourth section, "Philosophy and Social Thought," revolve around Canetti as philosopher, anthropologist, and social critic. Foregrounding central intellectual issues of the early to mid-twentieth century, they analyze Canetti's contribution to the culture of the Occident and discuss him in the context of Western discourse. In his essay "Canetti and Nietzsche: An Introduction to *Masse und Macht*," Ritchie Robertson explores *Masse und Macht* in light of Nietzsche's philosophy, placing Canetti into the tradition leading from Darwinism to naturalism and, via Nietzsche and Freud, to contemporary sociobiological literature. Canetti himself often obscured his indebtedness to this tradition in his own writings. Robertson, focusing on the significance of the body in Canetti's cross-cultural representation of crowds and crowd psychology, foregrounds commonalities between human and non-human animals as revealed in Canetti's treatise. Canetti views social structures as the products of the drive to survive and dominate and, Robertson argues, he endorses none of the great political systems of his era: neither capitalism, liberalism, socialism, nor fascism.

Johannes G. Pankau's focal point is Canetti's depiction of gender relationships and gender in his essay "Images of Male and Female in Canetti's Fictional, Autobiographical, and Theoretical Work." He approaches his admittedly "tricky task" by examining major works of different eras, *Die Blendung, Masse und Macht, Der andere Prozeß,* the drama *Hochzeit,* and Canetti's autobiographical writings and statements about himself. Pankau also probes into the intellectual environment of Canetti's works, the misogynist Viennese discourse of the notorious Otto Weininger, and then calls for a more differentiated assessment of Canetti's gendered universe than the one offered by late twentieth-century feminist scholarship. Feminist scholars, in Pankau's view, often display a hostile attitude toward the author of *Die Blendung,* but he observes that Canetti's representation of gender varies according to the respective genre. In his autobiographical writings, he renders more subtle descriptions of women than he does in his dramas and in his novel. In the literary works he plays with types and stereotypes because his primary interests are abstract issues and abstract problems.

In "Canetti's Final Frontier: The Animal," Dagmar C. G. Lorenz presents a reading of Canetti in light of discourses questioning the Cartesian view of the world and human supremacy. Lorenz shows that Canetti's images of animals are influenced by ideas emerging in the late nineteenth century, ranging from *Tierschutz,* animal protection, to Buddhist thought (with which Canetti was familiar). In conjunction with the author's own misanthropic and culturally critical statements in his autobiographical writings and notebooks, Canetti's works are replete with provocative animal images and statements that call for a fundamental revision of the way humans think about themselves and other species.

The fifth section, "Historical Contexts," examines Canetti from the perspective of the past, the author's origins in fin-de-siècle Roustchouk; Canetti's present, the monstrous era of National Socialism, the Shoah, and exile, of which he was a survivor; and the future, the posthumous reception of his work, which demonstrates his importance for future generations. "Canetti, Roustchouk, and Bulgaria: The Impact of Origin on Canetti's Work" by Svoboda Alexandra Dimitrova and Penka Angelova explores Canetti's roots in Bulgaria. Even though there is relatively little that seems to connect the mature Canetti, who adopted the German language as his literary tool, and who lived in England and Switzerland, to his hometown Roustchouk, the authors argue that almost every motif touched upon in the Bulgaria episodes of *Die gerettete Zunge* (1977) recurs in later chapters of his autobiography, and more importantly, becomes a central theme in the author's works. The essay evokes a vivid impression of Roustchouk, a multicultural, multilingual place apt to inspire a young author with the ideals of cosmopolitanism and pacifism, and it reveals the importance of site and geography in the works of a self-declared cosmopolitan.

Michael Mack's essay "Elias Canetti's Response to the Shoah" positions Canetti's oeuvre within the context of Shoah literature. He maintains that precisely because of its conspicuous absence in the works of an author, who like any Central European Jew had experienced the cruelty of the Nazi regime first hand, the term Holocaust or Shoah assumes a powerful significance within Canetti's writing. Mack observes that Canetti's outlook on humanity is bleak, almost shocking, albeit tempered by the author's self-censorship, which leads him to an ethical rather than academic or artistic agenda. This said, Canetti often comes close to representing humanity as a "killing machine." In comparison to the approach of his friend Franz Baermann Steiner, who insisted on a third model, the depiction of the humane, Canetti appears cynical and disillusioned.

The essays in this Companion volume to Canetti provide a scholarly introduction to Canetti's works by leading international Canetti experts. The references to the primary texts follow the first Claassen or Hanser editions, which appeared during Canetti's lifetime, or, when appropriate, the more recent Hanser edition of *Werke* (1993), because Canetti's prewar publications, *Hochzeit* (1932) and *Die Blendung* (1935) are virtually inaccessible. Note that the *Aufzeichnungen* in the 1993 *Werke* edition are not in all cases identical with the earlier versions. From one edition to the next Canetti made slightly different selections and occasionally changed the wording. The editions referred to and the abbreviations used to cite them in this volume are found in the Works Frequently Cited list preceding this introduction. Canetti's papers are housed in the Zentralbibliothek Zurich; his daughter, Johanna Canetti, holds the rights to his unpublished writings.

New publications by and about Canetti keep appearing, including the third part of the autobiography, *Party im Blitz* (2003, Party during the Blitz), discussing Canetti's life in England. Written in 1990, the work provides in the author's partly sweeping, partly aphoristic style insight into his views on and encounters with British society and his reactions to global events including his intellectual and personal aversions and predilections.[37]

Notes

[1] Elias Canetti, *Masse und Macht* (Hamburg: Claassen, 1960), 276–85. Cited hereafter as *MM; Die Stimmen von Marrakesch,* "Die Stimmen von Marrakesch. Aufzeichnungen nach einer Reise." *Die Stimmen von Marrakesch: Das Gewissen der Worte* (Munich: Hanser, 1995), 9–89; Flavius Josephus, *The Jewish War* (New York: Penguin Viking, 1984).

[2] Franz Kafka, *Der andere Prozeß: Kafkas Briefe an Felice* (Munich: Hanser, 1965). Translated by Christopher Middleton as *Kafka's Other Trial; the Letters to Felice* (New York: Schocken, 1974).

[3] Elias Canetti, *Die gerettete Zunge* (Munich: Hanser, 1977), 37. Cited as *GZ.*

[4] Gerald Stieg, "Canetti, Elias." *Metzler Lexikon der deutsch-jüdischen Literatur,* ed. Andreas B. Kilcher (Stuttgart: Metzler, 2000), 99–102. Here: 100. With some ambivalence Canetti describes his grandparents' visits in Vienna and his less than flattering memories of the religious school in *Die gerettete Zunge.* "In dieser Schule ging es eher jämmerlich zu, das hing damit zusammen, daß der Lehrer lächerlich schien, ein armer krächzender Mann, der so aussah, als stünde er frierend auf einem Beine, er hatte gar keinen Einfluß auf die Schüler, die taten, was ihnen beliebte" (*GZ* 101).

[5] Thomas H. Falk, *Elias Canetti* (New York: Twayne Publishers, 1993), 10–11.

[6] Elias Canetti, *Die Blendung* (Munich: Hanser, 1963).

[7] "'Eine wunderschöne Person mit einem spanischen Gesicht . . . Die hat mehr gelesen als wir alle zusammen,'" he remembers the Asriels, friends of his mother's, describing his future wife. Elias Canetti, *Die Fackel im Ohr* (Munich: Hanser, 1980), 80. Cited hereafter as *FO.*

[8] Karl Kraus, *Die letzten Tage der Menschheit; Tragödie in fünf Akten* (Munich: Kösel, 1957). Original: 1926.

[9] Elias Canetti, *Die Fackel im Ohr. Lebensgeschichte 1921–1931* (Munich: Hanser, 1980), 107. Cited as *FO.*

[10] Veza Canetti, *Die gelbe Straße* (Munich: Hanser, 1990). Originally published sequels in the Vienna *Arbeiter-Zeitung* in 1934.

[11] Veza Canetti's short story, *Geduld bringt Rosen,* ed. Elias Canetti (Munich: Hanser, 1992), was first published by Wieland Herzfelde in the anthology *Junge deutsche Autoren* (Berlin: Malik, 1932).

[12] Bertolt Brecht, *Hauspostille* (Berlin, Propyläen, 1927).

[13] Elias Canetti translated Upton Sinclair's, *Leidweg der Liebe* (Berlin: Malik, 1930), *Das Geld schreibt* (Berlin: Malik, 1930), and *Alkohol* (Berlin: Malik, 1932).

[14] Elias Canetti, *Hochzeit, Komödie der Eitelkeit, Die Befristeten* (Munich: Hanser, 1964).

[15] Hermann Broch, *Kommentierte Werkausgabe, vol. I, Die Schlafwandler,* ed. Paul Michael Lützeler (Frankfurt: Suhrkamp, 1995).

[16] Elias Canetti, *Das Augenspiel. Lebensgeschichte 1931–37* (Munich: Hanser, 1985), 160. Cited as *A.*

[17] Before his death in 1994, Canetti edited Veza Canetti's novel *Die gelbe Straße* (Munich: Hanser, 1989), which had first been published in 1933/34 in the Vienna *Arbeiter-Zeitung,* her drama *Der Oger* (Munich: Hanser, 1990), and her collected short prose under the title *Geduld bringt Rosen* (Munich: Hanser, 1991). The title story had been included in Wieland Herzfelde's anthology *Junge deutsche Autoren* (Berlin: Malik, 1932).

[18] Veza Canetti, *Die Schildkröten* (Munich: Hanser, 1999).

[19] Elias Canetti, *Aufzeichnungen 1942–1948* (Munich: Hanser, 1965), 73.

[20] Carol Petersen, *Elias Canetti* (Berlin: Colloquium Verlag, 1990), 60.

[21] Similarly, the German exile authors of *The Authoritarian Personality* (New York: Harper, 1950) by Theodor W. Adorno, Else Frenkel-Brunswik, Daniel J. Levinson, and Newitt R. Sanford also focused on more general traits and psychological profiles.

[22] Elias Canetti, "Dr. Hachiyas Tagebuch aus Hiroshima," *Das Gewissen der Worte* (Munich: Hanser, 1975), 57–65.

[23] Iris Murdoch dedicated her book *The Flight from the Enchanter* (New York: Viking Press, 1956) to Canetti.

[24] Elias Canetti, *Fritz Wotruba* (Vienna: Rosenbaum, 1955).

[25] Elias Canetti, *Die Welt im Kopf* (Vienna: Stiasny, 1962).

[26] September 9, 1963. Quoted by Petersen, 61.

[27] Elias Canetti, *Der andere Prozeß: Kafkas Briefe an Felice* (Munich: Hanser, 1976); *Alle vergeudete Verehrung: Aufzeichnungen 1949–1960* (Munich: Hanser, 1970).

[28] Elias Canetti, *Die Provinz des Menschen: Aufzeichungen 1942–1972* (Munich: Hanser, 1973); *Der Ohrenzeuge* (Munich: Hanser, 1974); *Das Gewissen der Worte* (Munich: Hanser, 1975); *Der Beruf des Dichters* (Munich: Hanser, 1975).

[29] Klaus Theweleit, *Männerphantasien* (Frankfurt: Roter Stern, 1977–78).

[30] Elias Canetti, *Das Augenspiel* (Munich: Hanser, 1985); *Das Geheimherz der Uhr* (Munich: Hanser, 1985); *Die Fliegenpein* (Munich, Hanser, 1992).

[31] Theodor Lessing, *Der jüdische Selbsthaß* (Berlin: Jüdischer Verlag, 1930).

[32] Marlene Streeruwitz, *Nachwelt* (Frankfurt: Fischer, 1999).

[33] About Viertel's, Waldinger's, and Canetti's loyalty to the German language, see Dagmar C. G. Lorenz, *Verfolgung bis zum Massenmord* (New York: Peter Lang, 1992), 311–12.

[34] Elias Canetti, *Aufzeichnungen 1942–1948* (Munich: Hanser, 1965), 87–88. See also Dagmar C. G. Lorenz, "Schweigen und Entfremdung. Canettis Reaktion auf Exil und Krieg." *Das Exilerlebnis,* ed. Donald G. Daviau and Ludwig M. Fischer (Columbia: Camden House, 1982), 181–91.

[35] Wilhelm Reich, *Massenpsychologie des Faschismus* (Frankfurt: Fischer, 1974).

[36] Heinrich Heine, *Historisch-kritische Gesamtausgabe der Werke,* vol. 5 (*Almansor; William Ratcliff; Der Rabbi von Bacherach; Aus den Memoiren des Herren von Schnabelewopski; Florentinische Nächte*), ed. Manfred Windfuhr (Hamburg: Hoffmann und Campe, 1994).

[37] Elias Canetti, *Party im Blitz. Die englischen Jahre,* eds. Kristian Wachinger and Jeremy D. Adler (Munich: Hanser, 2003).

Canetti's Global Significance

Good-Bye to All That:
Elias Canetti's Obituaries

William Collins Donahue

I BEGAN COLLECTING CANETTI'S OBITUARIES the morning I learned of his death. I was headed to the Stuttgart train station, where one can easily find a whole array of European papers. I bought an armful, even in languages I couldn't read. In the United States it is still too rare a pleasure to find anyone outside of German Studies familiar with Canetti's work. But in Europe his death had made the front pages, not to mention fairly extensive coverage in the arts and culture sections, of virtually all the major papers. When I first planned my errand to the Stuttgart Hauptbahnhof, I did so with the intention of visiting Canetti in the Klosbachstrasse, not of gathering his death notices, or as the Germans more poetically put it, his "Nachrufe."

Contrary to the posthumous claim that his death was completely unexpected,[1] I knew (or thought I did) that Canetti was ill. He had written to discourage my visit, saying that he expected to be under a doctor's care. Yet I was also familiar with the rumors about his vaunted love of privacy, his reclusiveness, and sometime misanthropy. Erich Fried and Claudio Magris both tell how Canetti, before the age of the answering machine, would screen his Hampstead phone by mimicking the voice of the housekeeper. Others recount how Canetti would simply pretend not to be home if he didn't want to answer the door. So I wasn't sure if the brief note I received was a ploy to evade the intrusions of an overeager academic, or if he was dead serious. I was determined to try my luck, but to no avail: By the time we heard of his death, Canetti had already been buried, as all the newspapers reported, in a Zurich cemetery plot adjacent to James Joyce's grave.

I remember thinking what a coup this was: Canetti had posthumously continued his autobiographical endeavor by arranging an affiliation that would be picked up in even the briefest obituary, thereby ensuring that he would be associated once again with perhaps the century's best known modernist author. Canetti had begun his career to critical notices that frequently associated *Die Blendung* with Joyce's novels — an observation justified only in the general sense that both Joyce and Canetti are strikingly non-traditional and frankly sometimes demanding.[2] And now Canetti managed to end his career with this prestigious association firmly reinstated. But

had he really orchestrated it, as for example the Mexican *La Jornada* asserts?[3]
Is it fair to assume — as I first did — that this amounts to a kind of "Selbst-
Nachruf"? Is this Canetti's effort to manipulate his reception from the grave?

Very quickly one concludes that there are competing views of Canetti
abroad, and that these disparities can hardly be resolved by referring to the
obituaries, which themselves are responsible for some of the confusion. The
point here is not to get at the "real" Elias Canetti. To the extent that is
possible, it would clearly be the task of the critical biographer, rather than
that of the sometimes partisan obituarist, and we now have reason to believe
that this fundamental desideratum of Canetti scholarship may soon be met.[4]
Yet the obituaries do provide a fascinating glimpse of how Canetti is remembered — and appreciated — by a group largely outside the academic
establishment. Indeed, the Canetti of academic criticism is rather a different
creature — and Canetti would not have minded the animal nomenclature —
than the one presented in the more popular feuilleton. Subsequent to an
overview of the obituary corpus, I want to propose three points that arise
from this reading. First, Canetti's death inaugurates a more independent
and, I believe, more fruitful phase of criticism. Second, I will lay out the
disparity between certain aspects of Canetti scholarship and what I am calling "the feuilleton perspective," with the suggestion that the former may
have something crucial to learn from the latter. Finally, while the obituaries
clearly perpetuate some fantasies about Canetti — such as his improbable
embodiment of a grand era in European letters — they form on balance an
instructive and intriguing guide to his viability. In valorizing the "feuilleton
Canetti" as the Canetti with the most life left in him, I am in part, I must
admit, taking the obituaries as an opportunity to reflect on the current state
of Canetti scholarship with the unabashed goal of promoting future directions. There is something inescapably ironic about turning to obituaries to
get a better picture of Canetti. Is this famed "enemy of death" — an appellation no obituary omits — now to be approached from the perspective of
death? Not only that, but by someone — and I trust I am not alone in
this — curiously addicted to obituaries? It may well be that an appetite for
this genre merely confirms Canetti's notion that the experience of *survival*
implicit in this illicit reading practice provides a covert pleasure that constitutes an expression of power. So be it.

In combing through what has become a fairly exhaustive collection, including every German-language newspaper or magazine of note as well as a
rich sampling from the British, American, French, Spanish, Italian, Mexican,
and Israeli press, I do not pretend to have escaped the inevitable snares of
reception criticism. Often caricatured as mere bean-counting, this distinctly
unfashionable critical pursuit certainly does not supplant our need to interpret. Even in restricting myself to an exploration of Canetti's appeal to a
broader readership, I remain cautious. For whom do these cultural elites

stand besides themselves? I do not stake a major claim on their representative status. For my purposes, their value lies more in the challenge — and sometimes the solution — they pose to the academic agenda. To fundamental questions of method, some obituaries, precisely in their attempt to come to grips with what is worth holding on to in the Canetti oeuvre, offer productive answers. And even when they fail — they are, for example, notoriously unreliable and inconsistent on certain facts — these weaknesses can be turned to the good; for we thereby learn what needs to be set aright. Canetti himself warned against a static, mechanistic positivism: "Für manche Leute wird die Bemühung um die Wahrheit zu einer Art von Käfersammlung. Ihre Käfer sehen sich gleich, grau und bedenklich."[5] This evocation of a dreary natural history museum exhibit — Canetti's collection of gray bugs — need not of course characterize our current pursuit.

Of course, not all obituaries are equal or of equal interest. The leading American and Canadian newspapers took dutiful notice of the Nobel laureate's death, but uniformly relied on the bare bones data provided by the Associated Press, and typically printed a brief story in the obituary pages only. *The New York Times,* which typically publishes well-researched and well-written obituaries, reported that *Masse und Macht* (1960) was published in 1935, an error repeated here and there throughout the North American press.[6] The only North American publication to run any substantial remembrance — the small-run literary journal *Salmagundi* — lifted the bulk of its article from the Italian *La Repubblica,* and even then got Canetti's age wrong by two years. The obituaries of substance are without exception European. Indeed, almost every major European newspaper, and many a lesser one, judged Canetti's death worthy of front-page coverage — the *Süddeutsche Zeitung* even gave it a banner headline — and also provided extensive treatment, in some cases four or five separately authored entries, in the arts and culture sections. *Le Monde* gave Canetti full front-page coverage, including fairly detailed discussion of his works. With few exceptions, these authors — obituarists, as I will dub them here — evince an intimate and impressive familiarity with the Canetti oeuvre and at this level alone are more compelling than many derivative academic articles. Frequently these newspapers commissioned short reminiscences by other poets such as Robert Schneider and Friederike Mayröcker, publishers and editors such as Egon Ammann, Michael Krüger, and Mario Muchnik,[7] friends such as Claudio Magris and Gerald Stieg,[8] or those connected in some professional way to Canetti such as Hans Hollmann, who directed each of the author's three plays. In conjunction with the obituaries, one often finds a collection of Canetti's aphorisms — usually from the then unpublished *Nachträge aus Hampstead* — which I assume were provided by the Hanser Verlag.

Extensive coverage in all the major French dailies reflects the fact that Canetti, who was compared to activist writers Sartre and Simone de Beauvoir, "zu den wenigen Autoren deutscher Sprache gehörte, die in den französischsprachigen Gebieten Gewicht hatten."[9] Italy was no less thorough in its coverage (and homage), providing depth and commentary far beyond the curious notice (in *La Repubblica*) of the author's "strangely Italian appellation" (Peter Winkler). Similar in scope, though more likely to stress Canetti's actual heritage (in particular the etymology of his family name, which derives from the village of Cañete in the province of Cuenca[10]) was the Spanish press, where most national newspapers immediately dedicated two or more pages to the author's life and work (Beat Ammann). Although the British papers took no less notice of the author's passing, they were less gushing, noting that while Canetti rates as an "original thinker and author," he remains one of the most "puzzling figures of world literature."[11] These obituaries did not demur recalling the bafflement with which the British press first greeted *Auto-da-Fé*.

Reviewing the German-language press, Hoffmann observes, "Eindrucksvoller können Nachrufe auf einen Dichter kaum sein." His title, "Ganzseitige Verbeugungen" (Whole-page Obeisances), is typical of the Swiss coverage, where the *Neue Züricher Zeitung* undoubtedly led the way. The Austrians were hard put not to claim Canetti as one of their own.[12] Though he accepted the status of honorary citizen of Vienna in 1986, Canetti steadfastly refused all attempts to repatriate him, retaining the British passport he received as a refugee from fascist Austria. Chancellor Vranitzky remarked candidly on this, but still found reason to celebrate Canetti's important connection to Austria.[13] Other Austrian obituarists strained to situate this "großer Autor deutscher Zunge" — as the *Frankfurter Rundschau* deemed him — within a specifically Austrian "literarische Heimat."[14] Like numerous other obituarists, Vice Chancellor Busek fêted Canetti as the last representative of the brilliant Viennese modernist movement, the "Wiener Moderne," taking his cue perhaps from Canetti himself, who remarked at the Nobel ceremony that he accepted the honor on behalf of those great Austrian writers, such as Kraus, Broch, and Musil, who never received it.[15] Precisely as "der erklärte Nicht-Österreicher," Canetti may have made his most valuable contribution to Austrian cultural life.[16]

Although some of the essays are clearly inflated (in line with genre expectations), the bulk are balanced assessments of the author's life and work, including a few openly negative pieces.[17] Approaching Canetti from beyond the grave, so to speak — with neither gratuitous animus nor obsequious affirmation — is a distinctly salutary critical practice strongly associated with the obituary phase of critical response. To put it a bit polemically, one could say that Canetti scholarship divides, at its worst, into two parties: the largely uncritical celebrants of the Canetti scripture, on the one hand; on the other hand, those clever critics who think they have beaten Canetti at his own game — catching him in some apparent contradiction in *Masse und Macht* (which is frankly child's play) or convicting him of covertly deploying the very power he claims to deplore. We know these two groups: the former are the Canetti acolytes — the "Canetti-ologen" as one Viennese wit puts it — of the *Canetti Gesellschaft*. The latter can easily be found between the pages of that unfortunate book *Experte der Macht*.[18]

Tongues Set Free

Although there have always been saner voices that refreshingly defy such a simplistic dichotomization (and did so even prior to 1994) — here the names Susan Sontag, Ritchie Robertson, and Walter Sokel spring to mind — I want to suggest that Canetti's death has set us free from the pressure of belonging to either one camp or the other. Of course Thomas Bernhard, too, famously managed to break free well before Canetti's actual demise — recall Bernhard's maliciously entertaining *Leserbrief*. But for those of us dependent on the author for access, for interviews (actual or hoped for), for correspondence, or to simply be connected by the bonds of friendship or admiration, Canetti's death has proven liberating. Surely such a thought is anathema to orthodox Canetti disciples — how could the arch *Feind des Todes* approve such a notion? Yet I find it confirmed in my own experience. Having received Canetti's imprimatur for my book on *Die Blendung*, I came under his sway and began to write with this approval in mind. Although I don't think it was wrong to defend his novel against facile and anachronistic charges of misogyny — such as those that reduce the novel to Kien's transparently misogynistic ranting — one needn't do so, as one critic pointed out, by portraying Canetti as a poster boy of the post-1968 feminist agenda. My lack of distance, at least in the early drafts, caused me to sacrifice critical nuance for what now appears to be an obviously misguided notion of loyalty.

From today's perspective this attitude may seem exceedingly slavish, but it was not perceived so at the time. Recall that the first monograph on *Die Blendung* — Dieter Dissinger's *Vereinzelung und Massenwahn* of 1971[19] — opens with the author's proud declamatory preface title "Statt eines Vorworts," which introduces a letter from Canetti that praises the book in some detail. Alfred Doppler took similar delight in showing me a letter in which Canetti expresses gratitude and approval for the manner in which Doppler defends the author's autobiography against critics who find it insufficiently self-reflective and philosophically naïve.[20] Although Doppler, who is, I believe, in any event right about the autobiography, composed his essay independently of Canetti's imprimatur, the point remains that Canetti's approval counted a great deal. This pride in "getting it right" is understandable, for we found ourselves in the difficult — though not impossible — position of commenting upon an author whose erudition often vastly exceeded our own. Iris Murdoch begins her 1962 review of *Masse und Macht* with this humble confession: "I am not the polymath who would be the ideal reviewer of this remarkable book. To deal adequately with *Crowds and Power* one would have to be, like its author, a mixture of historian, sociologist, psychologist, philosopher and poet."[21] Now, even though there may have been additional reasons for Murdoch's deference to Canetti, as John Bayley's memoir seems to suggest,[22] the point remains that in this early stage of scholarship, we as a guild were cowed by Canetti. If a novelist and philosopher of the caliber of Murdoch felt outflanked intellectually, how much more so many of us. Then, too, there was Canetti's wrath with which we might have had to contend. As Erich Fried relates in *Ein Dichter gegen Macht und Tod*, the German television documentary made in the wake of Canetti's receipt of the Nobel Prize, Canetti could be harsh and voluble with those who dared to criticize — or as Canetti deemed it, to "misunderstand" — his work. Fritz Arnold, who served for many years as Canetti's editor at Hanser and only twice succeeded in getting him to change his text, puts it plainly: "War einer so unvorsichtig, Einwände zu äußern, und sei es auch noch so behutsam, dann mußte er damit rechnen, verbannt zu werden."[23]

But no longer. Dagmar Barnouw, as is well known, provided the first comprehensive treatment of Canetti's oeuvre, the immensely useful 1979 Metzler handbook.[24] This volume depended primarily, as the author reveals in her introduction, on interviews and correspondence with her subject, and I think this shows in what today appear to be rather cautious if not uniformly affirmative assessments of the individual works. In her post-1994 work, however, one notices a more sovereign, less reverential attitude. Here Barnouw more decisively challenges Canetti's rendition of his break with Karl Kraus, and more freely confronts the performability of his dramas than ever before.[25] Canetti's death has made us better critics.

One can trace this development logically enough to the obituaries. Claudio Magris, professor of literature and philosophy, and long-time Canetti friend, wrote eloquently in 1983 of the fundamental break between the formally more radical early works — he especially loves the novel — and the later best-selling autobiography. Though he makes no bones about the "gentle and smooth surface of the autobiography, which stands in such contrast to the angularity of *Die Blendung* and which deceptively appears to tell all," Magris goes to some lengths in this essay "The Writer in Hiding" to *justify* these more popular texts, telling us that the autobiography, when properly considered, harbors the same "via negativa" that is characteristic of the earlier works. At this juncture Magris appears almost ready to baptize the autobiography as modernist:

> At the center of the [autobiography] is a void, a vortex, an implosion that sucks up its own innards and that appears to destroy the ordered material of the narrative. [. . .] *Auto-da-Fé* also contains this void. In-

deed this dizzying absence has been identified as the central absence, as the insanity of life hidden beneath a credible and conciliatory gesture of dissimulation that attempts to assure us that everything is all right. Like every book of real substance, Canetti's autobiography must be read with both fascination and suspicion; it must be examined for what it says and also for what it does not say. In a splendid passage from *The Torch in My Ear* Canetti remarks that in the face of reality we all resemble Samson, blinded and shattered, as he looks upon the world for the last time, a world that is fading and sinking. Perhaps Canetti also feels this fear, but he masters it brilliantly in his autobiography.[26]

Here Magris is unmistakably sanguine about the autobiography, even if we sense him straining semantics in his attempt to equate it with the "void" figured in *Die Blendung*. Just over a decade later, however, writing on the occasion of Canetti's death for the *Süddeutsche Zeitung,* he alters his assessment considerably: "Ohne die Autobiographie hätte er den Nobelpreis nicht erhalten; bei aller Faszination erreicht sie nicht die 'unerträgliche' Größe der *Blendung,* zu harmonisierend geht sie mit den Dingen um. Sie ist eine Schrift über viele Abgründe, aber sie trägt die Erfahrung des Abgrundes nicht in sich."[27]

Magris claims to have communicated these thoughts to Canetti, harvesting disapproval and rejection for his efforts: "Ich glaube, das sich sein Gesicht verfinsterte, als ich ihm dies sagte, auch deswegen, weil er ein eifersüchtiger, geradezu tyrannischer Wächter des Bildes war, das er von sich geben wollte. [. . .] Vielleicht hat uns dies ein wenig voneinander entfernt"[28] While Magris may have related this critique to Canetti privately, at no point prior to this obituary had he expressed himself *in print* so unambiguously on this matter. It was indeed Canetti's death that set free his tongue. In 1991, three years before Canetti's death, Ritchie Robertson observed, "We still need to distinguish what is living and what is dead in Canetti's thought."[29] The obituarists are, I think, the first group of critics to fulfill this injunction broadly, albeit partially. Indeed, they evince a laudable and balanced sovereignty in considering the relative merits and potential future of the novel, dramas, aphorisms, and social thought. They honor Canetti by taking him seriously, rather than uncritically.

Two Canettis?

If Magris is to be credited with the original "two Canettis" thesis — the more radical and uncompromising young author of *Die Blendung, Hochzeit,* and *Masse und Macht* as opposed to the elderly, crowd-pleasing author of the autobiography — the obituaries suggest, as I have indicated above, a rather different division, namely the Canetti of academic literary criticism versus the feuilleton Canetti. This bifurcation is perhaps best exemplified in the contrasting treatments of *Masse und Macht*, beginning with the question of reception. Whereas it appears to be taken as an article of faith among academics that *Masse und Macht* fell upon deaf ears when it appeared in 1960,[30] the obituaries paint a more differentiated picture. While some observers grant that "es fand bei Fachleuten wenig Beifall," as *Der Spiegel* put it,[31] others, including the Austrian author Robert Schneider, remember it quite differently. Roland Jaccard, writing the front page article for *Le Monde*, refers to *Masse und Macht* as "one of the cult classics of the century," and he is joined by numerous other commentators in remarking on this work's ongoing appeal and relevance.[32] The impression one gleans from these essays — the obituarist for the Mexican *La Jornado* for example pronounces it "Canetti's masterpiece"[33] — is that there is a persistent if unquantifiable interest in *Masse und Macht*, a life I would not have suspected given the gloomy picture one gleans from many academic treatments. Of course both parties may be correct to some extent since it depends greatly upon whose attention is deemed to count. *Masse und Macht* has indeed failed to gain a bridgehead among mainstream sociologists and anthropologists,[34] yet it has garnered the fascination and admiration of journalists and cultural commentators. Peter von Matt, writing for *Die Zeit*, explains that this inverse relationship is perhaps no accident.[35]

For von Matt the true measure of *Masse und Macht* lies not in its ability to conform to established academic inquiry, but precisely in its capacity to challenge the over-specialization and effeteness of these disciplines. Though he refers to the autobiography in the following remark, von Matt's impatience with what he deems sterile academic paradigms is centrally relevant to the discussion of *Masse und Macht*: "Dabei schrieb [Canetti] hier genau so, wie alle Germanisten sagten, daß man heutzutage keinesfalls mehr eine Autobiographie schreiben könne. Er regiert das Buch als genau jenes unerschütterliche Ich, das es nach der heiligen Überzeugung zahlloser akademischer Seminarbeiwohner keinesfalls mehr geben darf, übrigens auch gar nie gegeben hat und das überhaupt, wenn man vom eigenen Privatfall einmal absieht, eine abscheuliche Illusion ist. Daß das Ich das Produkt des Denkens sei und nicht umgekehrt, hat der späte Nietzsche kurz und bündig festgestellt."[36]

Given this assessment, it is not surprising that von Matt — and others like him — constructs his valorization of *Masse und Macht* in conscious *opposition* to systematic academic inquiry. Interestingly, he not only defends Canetti, but is equally eager to demonstrate his full knowledge of the epistemological issues at stake. In portraying Canetti as a supra-disciplinary intellectual, von Matt is joined by Martin Halter of *Der Tages-Anzeiger*, who celebrates the hallmarks of Canetti's work as "seine universale Neugier, sein Hang zum Fragmentarischen und Unfertigen," which, in turn, amount to "die radikale Abkehr von einer 'Mechanik des Denkens,' die falsches Pathos und fixe ideologische Gewissheiten verabscheut."[37] In a similar vein, Uwe

Schweikert salutes *Crowds and Power* specifically for its dismissal of "das Schubkastendenken aller universitären Disziplinen."

This might well remind us of the hilarious spoof on academic overspecialization contained in *Die Blendung,* where Peter Kien insists that real discipline-specific learning depends on excluding everything else in the world. Yet von Matt goes beyond this clichéd critique of academia; indeed, he is well aware that classifying the author of *Masse und Macht* as a poet, as numerous observers have done, can easily backfire.[38] Viewing *Masse und Macht* as a "novel," as does David Constantine (*The Guardian*),[39] or more precisely, an "anthropological novel or novelistic anthropology," as Italo Chiusano does (*La Repubblica*),[40] draws proper attention to the work's fundamental literary quality, but introduces another problem: "Solange man ihn als Dichter abtun kann," he observes, "geht es noch an. Man rettet sich deshalb in der Regel auch so rasch wie möglich in die These, daß alles, was er geschrieben hat, im Grunde Dichtung sei, Fiction, als solche ganz kurzweilig, aber weiter nicht relevant für Philosophie oder Geschichte, für Soziologie oder Anthropologie."

For von Matt, the value of Canetti's study resides in its ability to interrogate other disciplines. He demonstrates this point with reference to an aphorism from *Die Fliegenpein* that asserts "Die chinesische Geschichte wimmelt von *fetten* Rebellen."[41] In a reflection that I cannot fully recount here, he argues that such unexpected observations — and here he explicitly finds this process apposite of *Masse und Macht* — are meant to function as gadflies to conventional wisdom and that they possess a parasitic, but ultimately salubrious, relationship to received truth. Obese rebels do not make any sense in the face of the typical conception of revolutionary motivation deriving from the French Revolution and taught in the standard Western school curriculum. And thus we are forced to rethink fundamental assumptions about society and power: "So geschieht es," von Matt explains, "daß die blitzartige Evokation eines Zeitalters, das von fetten Rebellen wimmelt, altgewohnte Auffassungen von den Abläufen der Macht leise, aber nachhaltig angreift. So geschieht es, daß ein einziger Canetti-Satz, der als bloße Information durchaus im Leeren hängt, ein politisch-geschichtliches Denkbild stiftet, mit dem man selber wieder Ordnung schaffen und arbeiten kann."[42] This view seeks to justify Canetti in terms more of intellectual process than any particular argument. We are implicitly told not to worry so much about the precise status of the study's various and sundry truth claims, for this perspective treasures Canetti's "universal curiosity" as a way of transcending and dissolving the particularities and limitations of the social sciences.[43]

Now, one might object that this "feuilleton Canetti," if constructed in studied opposition to academia, is in fact ignorant of its adversary. Scholars have long wrestled with the tension between Canetti the poet and Canetti the intellectual. Neither do we lack, thanks to Hansjakob Werlen's Stanford

dissertation of 1988, a systematic study of the rich array of narrative strategies deployed in *Masse und Macht*. The implicit dispute between these two
groups, who sometime appear to be talking past each other as ineffectively
as any two parties in Canetti's *Hochzeit*, has more to do with the scholarly
assumption that readers need to be protected, so to speak, from the work's
deceptive narrative strategies. For example, in his more recent study "Destiny's Herald," Werlen goes to some length to explain that, despite the
author's self-assured tone, *Masse und Macht* does not really have the authority of science.[44] What is more — and worse, from the point of view of the
feuilleton writers — Werlin concludes his analysis not by celebrating the
plurality of methods, but rather by indicting Canetti for failing to show us
the way out of "the closed system of power." Canetti unmasked.

The feuilleton writers suggest that this kind of warning misses the
mark.[45] That Canetti takes considerable liberties with academic procedures
and collides with accepted leftist social critique (as, for example, represented
by the Frankfurt Institute for Social Research) comes as no surprise to
them.[46] Theirs, one might be tempted to assert, is a postmodern Canetti, an
enticement quite encouraged by Hanser editor Michael Krüger, when he
declares that Canetti is the "enemy of any systematic thought."[47] This is at
best a half truth, the danger of which is quite evident: it would make Canetti
a moving target, never holding him responsible for the many and quite
adamant truth claims he makes in *Masse und Macht*. The "obituary view,"
however, suggests that the Canetti with real longevity is not one who ele-
vates anti-systematic thinking, pastiche, and playfulness to first principles —
though all this is to be found in Canetti — but one who works with an
open, evolving, and self-critical system. In one of Canetti's last reflections,
first published in conjunction with the *FAZ* obituary, one sees that the
system-builder is present until the very end, only overwhelmed and humbled
by his frankly unmanageable topic. Here Canetti compares himself to the
great theorist of power, Machiavelli, commenting: "Ich muß viel mehr lesen
als er, seine Vergangenheit ist die Antike, Rom hauptsächlich, meine Vergangenheit ist alle, von der es ein Wissen überhaupt gibt. Aber ich glaube,
daß wir auf eine ähnliche Weise lesen: zerstreut und konzentriert zugleich
und die verwandten Erscheinungen von überallher zusammenspürend."[48]
The obituarists provide on the whole a rounded view, admonishing us to see
both the moral(izing) "Weltverbesserer" as well as the epistemological
skeptic, to put Canetti's thinking in the context of his total oeuvre,[49] and
thus not to isolate *Masse und Macht* from the later aphorisms, some of which
explicitly reflect upon and revise that work.[50] Even that vaunted and central
concept of "Verwandlung," von Matt reminds us in his Zurich memorial
address, remained a fundamental mystery to Canetti to his dying day.[51] This
diachronic approach provides the latitude necessary to assess more accurately
the development in Canetti's thinking.

There is a further aspect of the "feuilleton Canetti" that, I think, discourages the indiscriminate application of the postmodern epithet, namely the continued importance accorded to a literary reading of the world. The obituarists tend to endorse this practice, for example, when Günter Kunert places Canetti within a tradition of Jewish thought that consciously eschews abstract theory in favor of a "bildhaftes Denken."[52] When Canetti sees a crowd image in a field of grain or fire, it is never merely an ad hoc icon — never just a visual aid to his theory — but rather a discovery of something that is somehow inherently related to the crowd phenomenon itself. His catalogue of national symbols — the German forest (Wald) as intrinsically militaristic, for example — lays claim to this same privileged semiotic status. This literary function is never made fully explicit — even in Canetti's theoretical writings — yet it would be a great mistake to take any one of these images as mere illustration of a fully elaborated theory. For Canetti they demonstrate but also extend in some inexplicit manner a prior thesis; as such, they do not simply supply explanation, but also demand interpretation. In endorsing the prospect of achieving a relatively more integrated view of culture by means of the literary, these critics are telling us that they understand and accept the fundamentally provisional, provocative, and speculative nature of Canetti's social analysis. Writer Hugo Loetscher confesses in a reminiscence: "*Masse und Macht* wurde für mich nie zu einem geschlossenen Werk, zu einem Ganzen. Es blieb ein Buch einzelner Kapitel."[53]

To say all this, however, is by no means to protect *Masse und Macht* from the rigorous attention it still requires. Ritchie Robertson's masterful explication of Canetti's reliance on the outmoded paradigm of evolutionary anthropology is exemplary in this regard. Appreciating Canetti as a useful gadfly to academic criticism — who can sore above disciplinary boundaries and yet dive in for a well-targeted sting — need not impede our progress toward finding Canetti's place within twentieth-century intellectual history. Despite von Matt's binary — and entertainingly inflammatory — rhetoric, we should view this "feuilleton Canetti" as complementary rather than opposed to scholarly endeavors. It can serve as a corrective to the needless compartmentalization and arid reductionism characteristic of some Canetti scholarship; but it cannot replace scholarship at its best. One could conceivably make progress toward overcoming this dichotomy simply by keeping this broader cultivated feuilleton readership in mind as the target audience of our own scholarly pursuits. Ultimately the "academic/ feuilleton" dichotomy is of course not ontological, but rather one of mood and style; Magris, to be sure, is first and foremost a professor of literature, as is Stieg. Furthermore, we can not credit the obituaries exclusively with this more capacious approach to Canetti. Earlier wide-ranging retrospective essays by William Gass and Roger Kimball,[54] both penned well before Canetti's demise, as well as David Denby's 1999 *New Yorker* essay "Learning

to Love Canetti," all perform the same salubrious function of placing Canetti in richer and broader intellectual contexts.[55] There are also encouraging
signs on the academic horizon: Michael Mack's recent study, *Anthropology
as Memory: Elias Canetti's and Franz Baermann Steiner's Responses to the
Shoah,* is one of the very few scholarly treatises that boldly — and by no means
uncritically — inserts Canetti into the very intellectual, philosophical, and
religious debates that his work engages and provokes.[56] If this is a sign of
things to come — that is, of a fundamental paradigm shift away from current
insular practices — then Canetti scholarship has reason indeed to rejoice.

The *Europa* Myth

Canetti was remembered in many ways, but above all for possessing a perhaps idealized image of the feuilletonists themselves. In the great feuilleton
tradition, Canetti's oeuvre juxtaposes a rich array of styles, topics, genres,
and often with enviable erudition, usually with a sense of urgency, and not
infrequently with a dose of wicked humor. There is a hint of nostalgia in
many of the obituaries, owing in part to the fact that Canetti was the last of
a great generation of authors, poets, and artists — "the last son of that
central European culture," according to Giorgio Pressburger (*Corriere della
sera*).[57] "Ein Ohr ist taub geworden," laments Gustav Seibt (*FAZ*), "das
noch der durchdringenden Stimme von Karl Kraus gelauscht hatte, ein
Mund verstummte, der mit Robert Musil und Hermann Broch, Isaak Babel
und Bertolt Brecht geredet hat, ein Auge sieht nichts mehr, das mit pani-
schem Entsetzen und forschender Nachdenklichkeit zum Zeugen beispiello-
ser historischer Umbrüche wurde." In this remark, not untypical, by the
way, we see Canetti valued as the synthesizing witness to the greatness of
others rather than for any of his own particular accomplishments.

And yet these writers are also bidding farewell to the last thinker who seriously used the term "Dichter," to one who cared deeply about vastly
disparate issues, read widely and in numerous languages, and mastered
almost every literary genre. "Elias Canetti's Werk," opines Verena Auffermann in the *Süddeutsche* "ist ein Dokument des zersprengten 20. Jahrhunderts."[58] Canetti's biography — a life story that zigzagged all over Europe —
paints the picture of the cultivated European with catholic interests if not
universal knowledge in many of these narratives. Zurich city president Josef
Estermann was moved to assert: "Er will durch die Geschichte seiner Kindheit Europa vereinigen."[59] One writer casts Canetti as a polyglot pan-
European in didactic opposition to the disturbing "Fremdenhass" (xenophobia) that was making German headlines in the early and mid-nineties.[60]

In their efforts to make Canetti the avatar of European culture, some
writers seem however to have forgotten the author of *Masse und Macht*, who
so mercilessly took this culture to task.[61] In the 1990s — which began with

the Gulf War that divided Europeans over support for Israel and later witnessed the explosion of violence in the Balkans — I assumed that the enthusiastic evocation of Canetti's childhood served perhaps as a counter-image to the present, a golden-tinged recollection of international European harmony affiliated with a sanitized recollection of the Austro-Hungarian empire. But globalization was already then afoot, the bipolar world already dissolved, and a united Europe already high on the political agenda. So the image of Canetti as *the* enlightened European may belong as much to the future as to the past. Whatever illusions and self-gratifying images contained in the obituaries, one finds among them a Canetti who was cherished for who he in fact was: a self-critical moralist, a skeptical and flawed system-builder, a mystical secularist, a poet who believed in the importance of literature for social analysis, and a great European who stood European culture on its head.

Notes

My sincere gratitude to Geoff Baker and Daniel Skibra for patiently and relentlessly gathering these many obituaries and related materials from disparate sources and for providing many crucial translations. The bulk of the German-language essays were provided by the Innsbrucker Zeitungsarchiv.

[1] This claim, rife in the obituaries, has its source, I believe, in a press release from the Zurich mayor's office. See for example: Gisela Hoyer, "Dasein als Einspruch," *Leipziger Volkszeitung*, August 19, 1994, and "Letzte Ruhstätte neben Joyce," *Neues Deutschland*, August 19, 1994.

[2] Elias Canetti, *Die Blendung* (Munich: Hanser, 1963). Canetti, in a 1969 interview with Swiss writers Paul Nizon and Ippolita Pizzetti, denied the possibility of any direct influence; he would not read Joyce until later. Nevertheless, one senses the possibility that he is flattered by the comparison. Joyce makes an appearance in volume three of the autobiography, *Das Augenspiel: Lebensgeschichte 1931–1937* (Munich: Hanser, 1985), 187–94, ("Joyce ohne Spiegel"). Canetti relates here that Joyce attended one of his readings in Zurich, but left early because he couldn't understand the Viennese dialect (Canetti read from *Hochzeit* and *Die Blendung*). The interview is reprinted along with the obituary in *Corriere della sera*, August 19, 1994, 21.

[3] The article "Elias Canetti — Seine Heimat war die deutsche Sprache" contains an excerpt of a letter in which Canetti apparently requests to be buried in Zurich.

[4] Hanser Verlag has announced that Sven Hanuschek will take up this all important challenge; see *Fachdienst Germanistik*, April 2001.

[5] Originally published in the *Frankfurter Allgemeine Zeitung* 191, August 18, 1994, 23; later included in Canetti's posthumous *Nachträge aus Hampstead* (Zürich: Hanser, 1994). Subsequent references to the *Frankfurter Allgemeine Zeitung* are cited in the text using the abbreviation *FAZ*.

[6] Elias Canetti, *Masse und Macht* (Hamburg: Claassen, 1960).

[7] See "Krüger, il suo editore tedesco: 'L'ultima volta mi parlò dell'Italia,'" *Corriere della sera,* August 19, 1994, 23; Mario Muchnik, "El custodio de la metamorfosis," *El País,* August 19, 1994, 23; Beat Ammann, "Ein verlorenes Paradies: Cañete in spanischer Sicht," *Neue Züricher Zeitung,* August 24, 1994.

[8] Claudio Magris, "Fu premio Nobel: Morto Canetti poeta della vita," *Corriere della sera,* August 19, 1994, 1; Gerald Stieg, "Canetti zum Gedächtnis: Die Geschichte eines sehr persönlichen Nachrufs," *Profil,* August 22, 1994.

[9] Barbara Villiger Heilig, "Ein deutschsprachiger Autor mit Gewicht: Stimmen aus Frankreich und der Romandie," *Neue Züricher Zeitung,* August 14, 1994.

[10] Vivian Schnitzer, "Muere Elías Canetti, la conciencia de Centroeuropa: El premio Nobel fallecío a los 89 años el pasado fin de semana en Zúrich, cuando escribía sobre la inmortalidad," *El País,* August 19, 1994, 22.

[11] Charles Ritterbrand, "England — Ort der Kindheit und des Exils: Ambivalentes Verhältnis des Autors," *Neue Züricher Zeitung,* August 24, 1994.

[12] Karl Graber, "Canetti — ein osteuropäischer Schriftsteller: Meinungen in Österreich," *Neue Züricher Zeitung,* August 24, 1994.

[13] See "Die deutsche Sprache war seine Heimat," *Wiener Zeitung,* August 19, 1994.

[14] Hans Haider, "Das Gewissen des Wortes: Nobelpreisträger Elias Canetti starb 89 jährig in Zürich. Sein Werk ist stark von Wien geprägt," *Die Presse,* August 19, 1994, 1; 3.

[15] See "Reaktionen." *Vorarlberger Nachrichten,* August 19, 1994.

[16] Michael Cerha, "Der Wiener Dialekt der Diaspora," *Der Standard,* August 19, 1994.

[17] James Kirkup, "Elias Canetti," *The Independent,* August 19, 1994, 28; Willi Winkler, "Zykop, Monomane, Narziß: Warum man mit Elias Canetti hierzulande meist doch so recht nichts anfangen konnte," *die tageszeitung,* August 22, 1994.

[18] Kurt Bartsch and Gerhard Melzer, eds., *Experte der Macht: Elias Canetti* (Graz: Droschl, 1985).

[19] Dieter Dissinger, *Vereinzelung und Massenwahn: Elias Canettis Roman "Die Blendung"* (Bonn: Bouvier, 1971).

[20] Alfred Doppler, "Vor- und Gegenbilder (Gestalten und Figuren als Elemente der Zeit- und Lebensgeschichte in Canettis autobiographischen Büchern)." *Elias Canetti: Londoner Symposium,* ed. Adrian Stevens and Fred Wagner (Stuttgart: Verlag Hans-Dieter Heinz/Akademischer Verlag Stuttgart, 1991); concurrently: *Publications of the Institute of Germanic Studies* (University of London, 1991), 48:33–44.

[21] Iris Murdoch, "Mass, Might and Myth," *The Spectator,* September 6, 1962.

[22] John Bayley, *Elegy for Iris* (New York: Picador/St. Martin's, 1999). *Elegy for Iris* refers to the affair but remains fairly coy. A more explicit account of Canetti's relationship with Iris Murdoch can be found in Peter J. Conradi, *Iris Murdoch: A Life* (New York: W. W. Norton, 2001). After this article went to press, Hanser published the posthumous *Party im Blitz* (Munich: Hanser, 2003), in which Canetti gives (among many other things) his account of the affair with Murdoch, including a rather harsh judgment of her intellectual accomplishments.

[23] Fritz Arnold, "Die fremde Zunge gerettet," *Frankfurtur Rundschau,* December 23, 1995. I once sent Canetti a seminar paper in which I suggested that the "episte-

mological critique" of *Die Blendung* was less radical than in Kafka. I never received an acknowledgement. Of course Canetti may have had other reasons for disregarding this essay.

[24] Dagmar Barnouw, *Elias Canetti* (Stuttgart: Metzler, 1979).

[25] Compare for example Dagmar Barnouw, "Utopian Dissent: Canetti's Dramatic Fictions," in *Critical Essays on Elias Canetti*, ed. David Darby (New York: G. K. Hall, 2000), 121–34 and Barnouw's essay of 1987 "Elias Canetti — Poet and Intellectual," ibid., 15–34.

[26] Claudio Magris, "The Writer in Hiding," in *Critical Essays on Elias Canetti*, ed. David Darby (New York: G. K. Hall, 2000), 279–91. Here: 290.

[27] Claudio Magris, "Eine Stimme aus Mitteleuropa," *Süddeutsche Zeitung*, August 19, 1994, 11.

[28] Ibid. Magris also expresses some of the same ideas in an interview with Antonio Gnoli of *La Repubblica*, August 19, 1994, 26; this interview appears in English in *Salmagundi*.

[29] Ritchie Robertson. "Canetti as Anthropologist," in *Critical Essays on Elias Canetti*, ed. David Darby (New York: G. K. Hall, 2000), 158–70. Here: 158.

[30] See, for example, Ritchie Robertson, "Canetti as Anthropologist," in *Critical Essays on Elias Canetti*, 158, as well as Martin Halter, "Den unerschütterlichen Hass gegen den Tod gepredigt: Das Paradies war für Canetti im Diesseits angesiedelt, in den Büchern," *Tages-Anzeiger*, August 19, 1994, 11, who writes that *Masse und Macht* "irritierte 1960 die Spezialisten und liess das Publikum kalt." Although Hansjakob Werlen, "Destiny's Herald: Elias Canetti's *Crowds and Power* and Its Continuing Influence," in *Critical Essays on Elias Canetti*, 171–85, here: 184, begins his essay by documenting Canetti's general current appeal in places like Mexico City and Paris, as indicated by recent public exhibitions, he asserts flatly "in 1960, the publication of his massive work *Crowds and Power* elicited scarcely a reaction, and the silence that greeted the book, whose research and writing occupied Canetti for more than 30 years, left the author stunned and deeply disappointed" (172; see also 174–75).

[31] "Elias Canetti: 1905 bis 1994," *Der Spiegel* 34 (1994).

[32] Jaccard, Roland. "Elias Canetti ou le territoire de l'homme: Le Prix Nobel de littérature 1981 est mort Dimanche 14 août à Zurich, à l'âge de 89 ans," *Le Monde*, August 19, 1994, 1. For example, Hansres Jacobi, "Bildhaftigkeit des Denkens," *Neue Züricher Zeitung*, August 29, 1994 assesses *Crowds and Power* as "das Lebenswerk [. . .], das bis heute bedrängend aktuell geblieben ist." See also Fritz Arnold, "Die fremde Zunge gerettet," *Frankfurter Rundschau*, December 23, 1995; Gerald Stieg, "Canetti zum Gedächtnis: Die Geschichte eines sehr persönlichen Nachrufs," and *profil*, August 22, 1994.

[33] "Elias Canetti has died," *La Jornada*. August 19, 1994, 1.

[34] A notable exception is Sibylle Tönnies's analysis of philo-Semitism in post-unification German society; see her "Die Klagemeute: Warum sich Deutsche den Opfern aufdrängen," *Frankfurter Allgemeine Zeitung*, April 23, 1996.

[35] Peter von Matt, "Der weise Komödiant," *Die Zeit*, August 26, 1994.

[36] Ibid.

[37] Martin Halter, "Den unerschütterlichen Hass gegen den Tod gepredigt: Das Paradies war für Canetti im Diesseits angesiedelt, in den Büchern," *Tages-Anzeiger,* August 19, 1994, 11.

[38] See for example Gerald Stieg's formulation "ein soziologisch-anthropologisches Gedicht." Gerald Stieg, "Nimm und lies!" *profil,* August 22, 1994.

[39] David Constantine, "Alone in a Crowd: Obituary: Elias Canetti," *The Guardian,* August 19, 1994, sec. G, p. 2.

[40] Italo A. Chiusano, "Elias, ultimo grande," *La Repubblica,* August 19, 1994, 23.

[41] von Matt, "Der weise Komödiant," *Die Zeit.* August 26, 1994. "Die chinesische Geschichte wimmelt von *fetten* Rebellen." Quoted from Canetti's *Fliegenpein: Aufzeichnungen* (Munich: Hanser, 1992).

[42] von Matt, ibid.

[43] This point is made in various ways by Urs Marti, "Die Sehnsucht nach Unversehrt-heit," *Wochenzeitung* 34, August 26, 1994; Fritz Arnold, "Die fremde Zunge geret-tet"; Gerald Stieg, "Canetti zum Gedächtnis: Die Geschichte eines sehr persönlichen Nachrufs," and also "Nimm und lies!" *profil,* August 22, 1994.

[44] See Werlen, "Destiny's Herald: Elias Canetti's *Crowds and Power* and Its Continu-ing Influence," in *Critical Essays on Elias Canetti.*

[45] Michael Cerha, "Der Wiener Dialekt der Diaspora," *Der Standard,* August 19, 1994, for example, clearly grasps that *Masse und Macht* contravenes conventional academic conventions.

[46] Peter Iden, "Mich brennt der Tod: Fernere Erinnerungen an das dramatische Werk Elias Canettis," *Frankfurter Rundschau,* August 24, 1994; Willi Winkler, "Zyklop, Monomane, Narziß: Warum man mit Elias Canetti hierzulande meist doch so recht nichts anfangen konnte," *die tageszeitung,* August 22, 1994.

[47] In: "Krüger, il suo editore tedesco: 'L'ultima volta mi parlò dell'Italia,'" *Corriere della sera,* August 19, 1994, 23. *Corriere della sera,* August 19, 1994, 21.

[48] "Ich mißtraue dem Nachruhm, und am meisten mißtraue ich dem Erfolg: Anmer-kungen zu Macht, Tod und Unsterblichkeit / Die letzten Aufzeichnungen von Elias Canetti," *Frankfurter Allgemeine Zeitung,* August 18, 1994, 23.

[49] For example, Gustav Seibt, "Das verworfene Paradies: Wer sich vor der Wirklich-keit drückt, verdient es nicht zu leben: Zum Tode des Schriftstellers und Nobel-preisträgers Elias Canetti," *Frankfurter Allgemeine Zeitung,* August 18, 1994, 23, writes: "Der späte Essay 'Hitler nach Speer,' die tiefgründigste Analyse des Unge-heuers, hat auch *Masse und Macht* neu zugänglich gemacht."

[50] In a posthumously published reflection, Canetti observes: "Was die Masse selbst anlangt, so habe ich meine früheren Vorurteile verloren, sie ist für mich weder gut noch schlecht, sondern *da,* und die Blindheit, in der wir bis jetzt über sie gelebt haben, ist mir unerträglich." This first appeared in *FAZ* (*Frankfurter Allgemeine Zeitung*), August 18, 1994, 23; and later in *Nachträge aus Hampstead.*

[51] "Dennoch deutet einiges daraufhin, dass der Begriff der Verwandlung, das Schlüs-selwort seines Lebens, für Canetti selbst nie bis zum letzten durchschaubar wurde . . ." See Peter von Matt, "Aus einem elementaren Vertrauen in die Sprache: Eine

Gedenkrede auf Elias Canetti," *Neue Züricher Zeitung* (Fernausgabe) 230, October 4, 1994.

[52] Günter Kunert, "Der letzte Europäer," *Die Woche,* August 25, 1994. Kunert goes on to compare Canetti with Walter Benjamin, though in the process his remarks regarding Jewish intellectuals may generalize too greatly: "Am Jahrhundertbeginn gingen aus dem europäischen Judentum Denker und Philosophen hervor, die in einer Tradition standen, welche sich durch den mündlichen Diskurs, durch den Triumph der Eloquenz auszeichneten. Es fehlte die Blässe des Gedankens, das Grau der Theorie. Es dominierte ein bildhaftes Denken, dessen Großartigkeit und Grazie wir beispielsweise von Walter Benjamin kennen." See also Jacobi.

[53] Hugo Loetscher, "'Du darfst keinen Satz vergessen': Stimmen zum Tod von Elias Canetti," *Neue Züricher Zeitung,* August 21–22, 1994. W. G. Sebald, Iso Camartin, Urs Widmer, Gerhard Neumann, Hugo Loetscher, Jochen Hörisch, and Manfred Schneider also contributed to the article.

[54] William H. Gass, "The Road to the True Book: A Portrait of Elias Canetti," *The New Republic,* November, 8, 1982, 27–34. Roger Kimball, "Becoming Elias Canetti," *New Criterion* 5.1 (1986): 17–28.

[55] David Denby, "Learning to Love Canetti: The Autobiography of a Difficult Man," *New Yorker,* May 31, 1999, 106–13.

[56] Michael Mack, *Anthropology as Memory: Elias Canetti's and Franz Baermann Steiner's Responses to the Shoah. Conditio Judaica* 34 (Tübingen: Niemeyer, 2001).

[57] Giorgio Pressburger, "Fino all'ultimo con Karl Kraus cittadino della Grande Vienna," *Corriere della sera,* August 19, 1994, 21.

[58] Verena Auffermann, "Die Toten als die Überlebenden: Nachruf auf den Schriftsteller Elias Canetti," *Süddeutsche Zeitung,* August 19, 1994, 11.

[59] Luzie Küng, "Vertrauen in das Wort: Züricher Grabreden für Canetti." *Basler Zeitung,* September 27, 1994.

[60] Reinhold Tauber, "Der Rebell ist unterlegen," *Oberösterreichische Nachrichten,* August 19, 1994.

[61] For example, when Vivianne Schnitzer asserts that "Canetti was the writer who represented like no other the continuity of central European culture . . .," she seems to forget how thoroughly Canetti had challenged the fundamental notion of *Kultur* in *Masse und Macht.* Saverio Vertone, "Come un profeta errante nella civiltà europea," *Corriere della sera,* August 19, 1994, 21, waxes even more rhapsodic, making Canetti into the very incarnation of the European ideal: "Canetti perhaps carried with him as well the key to a great secret of European civilization, his mysterious capacity to reconcile origins and ends, antiquity and modernity, the West and the Middle East, the Mediterranean and the Central European, the Bible and Quevedo, Ibn Gabirol and Voltaire."

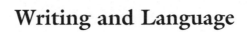

Writing and Language

"The Deeper Nature of My German": Mother Tongue, Subjectivity, and the Voice of the Other in Elias Canetti's Autobiography

Anne Fuchs

> Ich will sie [die Erinnerung] so intakt belassen, wie sie dem Menschen, der für seine Freiheit besteht, zugehört, und verhehle nicht meinen Abscheu vor denen, die sich herausnehmen, sie chirurgischen Eingriffen so lange auszusetzen, bis sie der Erinnerung aller übrigen gleicht. Mögen sie an Nasen, Lippen, Ohren, Haut und Haaren herumoperieren, soviel sie mögen, mögen sie ihnen, wenn es denn sein muß, andersfarbige Augen einsetzen, auch fremde Herzen, die ein Jährchen länger schlagen, mögen sie alles betasten, stutzen, glätten, gleichen, aber die Erinnerung sie sollen lassen stân.[1]

THIS REFLECTION ON the nature of memories is perhaps one of the most frequently cited passages of Elias Canetti's *Die Fackel im Ohr*. Dismissing all analytical approaches to the process of remembering — especially the psychoanalytic version — as some kind of unnecessary surgical operation, the narrator makes the case for the integrity of all memories. As many readers have noticed, the final exclamation "die Erinnerung sie sollen lassen stân" refers to a verse from Martin Luther's *Eine feste Burg ist unser Gott* (God is our Fortress) of 1527, whose fourth stanza opens with "das Wort sie sollen lassen stahn" — just let the word be. By transposing Luther's invocation of the sacred nature of the word onto the remembering process, the narrator assumes a defiant posture that aims at safeguarding the authenticity of the individual's memories in the age of multiple and fragmented identities.

The confessional and slightly heroic tone of this passage has had considerable influence on many of Canetti's critics who write about him as if they needed to defend an anachronistic narrative that appears out of step with most leading paradigms that have shaped the reflection on self and other in the latter half of the twentieth century. A case in point is Martin Bollacher's analysis of the above-mentioned passage from *Die Fackel im Ohr*. Bollacher reads it as a prime example of Canetti's authoritative poetics, which aims to defend both the unbroken power of the poetic word that makes the world legible and the individual's right to favor a literal reading of one's life.[2] The fact that the above-cited passage has become a topos in much Canetti criticism suggests that Canetti has actually succeeded in exercising considerable authority over the reception of his works,[3] thus canonizing a model of subjectivity that appears to favor the power of the autonomous subject.[4]

This essay argues, however, that through the depiction of the relationship between mother and son as an unrelenting "Kampf auf Leben und Tod" (*FO*, 144), the autobiography implicitly questions the very notion of autonomy. What appears to be a traditionally closed narrative that tells the story of the genesis of the self is in fact a story about the son's painful and largely unsuccessful struggle to set himself free from a stifling maternal hold. The site of this battle between mother and son is the German language that — as we will see — is in quite a literal sense his mother tongue.

Canetti dramatizes this battle in his three-part autobiography, which consists of *Die gerettete Zunge* (1977), *Die Fackel im Ohr* (1982), and *Das Augenspiel* (1985). While the first part relates the profound effect of the acquisition of German as mother tongue, *Die Fackel im Ohr* and *Das Augenspiel* (1985) tell the story of the son's attempted liberation. In this process the German language is turned from a site of love into the site of a contest that concerns the boundaries between the self and the other, the mother. The son must free himself from the mother to develop a proper sense of self.

Language, particularly the German language, becomes the battleground in this painful struggle for selfhood. The self that arises from this drawn-out battle attempts to salvage a space of its own by means of a split between the spoken and the written word, between *parole* and *écriture*.

Focusing on shifting images of orality and reading in *Die gerettete Zunge,* the essay explores first the eroticization of the German language. German is a highly libidinized object in the parental relationship and, as such, the object of the child's Oedipal envy. Forcing the boy to learn German after the father's sudden death, the mother also forces him into a symbiotic relationship from which the son later struggles to escape. Second, this essay then analyzes the various stages of the son's struggle for independence in *Die Fackel im Ohr* and *Das Augenspiel*. Here I will attempt to demonstrate that the son's decision to become a writer does not resolve the deadly battle against and for the mother. Conceived as the site of liberation from the maternal hold, the son's writing only traps him further in a classic double bind where each work is the simultaneous expression of the son's rebellion and obedience.

Language as a veritable battlefield where self and other thrash it out enmeshes not only mother and son but all representatives of divergent social forces. We will see how *Das Augenspiel* portrays a compromise between maternal demands on the one hand and the need for independence on the other. Canetti's struggle for independence involves the mapping of a utopian space that is not defined by ownership of the mother, the primary other.

This is a central concern of the final part of *Das Augenspiel,* in which the narrator develops the utopian notion that the pure voice embodied in Dr. Sonne can transcend social and linguistic antagonisms. Against the backdrop of the social satire of Karl Kraus, which is a central theme in *Die Fackel im Ohr,* the narrator now conceives the voice of the other as the domain of alterity and reciprocity. In contrast to the Canetti of *Die Blendung* and the early plays who uses the human voice for satirical purposes, the Canetti of the autobiography celebrates the elusive quality of the pure voice as a way of transcending battles for power, success, and knowledge. Toward the end of the trilogy he envisages a utopian kind of orality that is devoid of all desire, in other words a new language that transcends the deadly battle between mother and son. What amounts to a split between *Stimme* and *Schrift* allows the son to continue to serve his mother and, at the same time, create a space that is other than mother. The fact that this is at best a precarious compromise that is divorced from concrete reality makes Canetti a complex modern writer whose works display the very cracks and fissures that they attempt to cover up.

That the tongue is a dominant leitmotif in *Die gerettete Zunge* is so self-evident that many critics have stopped short of a more detailed analysis of its symbolism. The opening scene, which, with its powerful iconography, re-enacts the existential threat of castration, a threat that is even more powerful by virtue of its deferral, is the first in a series of childhood memories that deal with sexual aggression and the fear of being devoured.[5] There is, for instance, the story of the mother's winter journey when the sleigh is attacked by a pack of wolves. The narrator tells us that the red tongues of the wolves come so close to her that the mother is haunted by this memory for years (*GZ,* 16).[6] And so is the son who, only a little later, is terrified when a wolf appears at his bedside with his red tongue hanging dangerously out of his mouth. When the father who is the sheep in wolf's skin, takes off his mask and tries to explain that both wolf and threat were imaginary, the child is inconsolable (*GZ,* 29). For weeks, we are told, the wolf returns in his sleep.

The overtness of the iconography of these episodes has acted as an effective smoke screen that has prevented critical engagement with Canetti's founding myth. In all three episodes the red tongue is clearly associated with a male threat that is deferred from the boy to the mother and then back to the boy. The scenario is, however, further complicated by virtue of the complex cross-stitching of opposing functions of the tongue: although in the first episode the tongue is the direct target of a phallic threat, in the ensuing wolf episodes it is its very agent. As both target and agent of the threat, the tongue is a highly libidinized object, a site of desire that, however, paralyzes its speech function: we learn at the end of the first chapter that the child could not talk about this original threat for ten years — his tongue was effectively cut off from the function of speech (*GZ,* 10).

But it is important to note how Canetti resolves this threat in the third episode: when the father takes off the wolf's mask, explaining the difference between role-play and reality, he introduces the idea of make-believe and fiction that, as the later chapters show, is the very cornerstone of the parental relationship. This is fully brought to the fore in the chapter titled "Die Zaubersprache," the magic language, which introduces not only the motif of German as the parental secret code but also the notion that language can be a powerful carrier of desire (*GZ,* 33–36). In clear contrast to the aggressively sexualized images of the early passages, the narrator depicts the relationship between husband and wife as a magical discourse that is only temporarily interrupted by the demands of the mundane world. We are told that when the father came home from work, he would instantly speak to his wife in German. These talks revolve around their happy school days, the world of the Vienna *Burgtheater,* and their unfulfilled passion for acting (*GZ,* 33). For Canetti's parents, talking and loving are not only inseparable, but the world of fiction is also the very core of their relationship. Feeding their secret love at first through endless conversations in German, their marriage eventually legitimizes this continuous role-play. The narrator even implies that their marriage was an act of compensation for their missed careers on stage. For the boy who at this point has no word of German, the sound and intonation of the ongoing parental babble is so fascinating that he associates the language with a world of magic:

> Ich hörte ihnen mit der größten Anspannung zu und fragte sie dann, was dies oder jenes bedeute. Sie lachten und sagten, es sei zu früh für mich, das seien Dinge, die ich erst später verstehen könne. Es war schon viel, daß sie mir das Wort "Wien" preisgaben, das einzige. Ich glaubte, daß es sich um wunderbare Dinge handeln müsse, die man nur in dieser Sprache sagen könne. Wenn ich lange vergeblich gebettelt hatte, lief ich zornig davon [. . .] und sagte mir die Sätze, die ich von ihnen gehört hatte, her, im genauen Tonfall, wie Zauberformeln, ich übte sie oft für mich, und sobald ich allein war, ließ ich alle Sätze oder auch einzelne Worte, die ich eingelernt hatte, hintereinander los, so rasch, daß mich sicher niemand verstanden hätte. Ich hütete mich aber davor, die Eltern das je merken zu lassen, und erwiderte ihr Geheimnis mit meinem. (*GZ,* 34)

Canetti rewrites the Oedipal drama here in that the passage transposes the child's anger at being excluded from the parent's love for each other into his sense of exclusion from the code of this love. The result of this transference of love to language is the libidinization of the German language, or to be more precise, the libidinization of the non-semantic quality of spoken German. As pure sound without meaning, the language acquires an erotic quality that the boy registers as magic. It is therefore not surprising that the son imitates this magical sound pattern in secret: through this mimicry of the parental love code the son symbolically announces that one day he will usurp the paternal place by producing the same magic formulas. This symbolic dimension is reinforced at the end of the episode where he succeeds in duping his mother by imitating his father's voice, calling her "Mädi" (*GZ*, 34). Insofar as the entire episode revolves around the transference of desire onto language, it highlights that within the parental relationship desire is, to a large extent, desire for the libidinized word.

It is the parental identification with German and Austrian literature that prepares the groundwork for the famous episode in which Canetti's mother teaches the boy German after her husband's sudden death. Her brutal teaching method with its emphasis on the spoken word and a reign of terror that involves the verbal degradation of her son whenever he makes a mistake has been commented on by generations of readers. Reflecting on the impact of this episode, the narrator points to his mother's profound need to speak German with her son after her husband's sudden demise. Because her marriage had taken place in German, she attempted to substitute this loss of intimacy as fast as possible by putting the son in his father's place:

> Der furchtbare Schnitt in ihrem Leben, als sie 27jährig das Ohr meines Vaters verlor, drückte sich für sie am empfindlichsten darin aus, daß ihr Liebesgespräch auf deutsch mit ihm verstummt war. In dieser Sprache hatte sich ihre eigentliche Ehe abgespielt. Sie wußte sich keinen Rat, sie fühlte sich ohne ihn verloren, und versuchte so rasch wie möglich, mich an seine Stelle zu setzen. [. . .] So zwang sie mich in kürzester Zeit zu einer Leistung, die über die Kräfte jedes Kindes ging, *und daß es ihr gelang, hat die tiefere Natur meines Deutsch bestimmt, es war eine späte und unter wahrhaftigen Schmerzen eingepflanzte Muttersprache.* (*GZ*, 90)

The narrator's final observation that German was a late and painfully implanted mother tongue should be taken quite literally. What is at stake here can be explored by comparison with the opening scene in which the boy's ability to speak was symbolically threatened by the man with the knife. Here, however the mother induces a second language by forcing the son to swallow her tongue. Remember that in the previous episode the son perceived the parental love talk as some magical babble that derived its desirability from the purity of the sound pattern. Forcing these sounds down his throat, the mother commits a brutal act that violates the boundaries between self and mother to such an extent that it is doubtful that the violated boy can ever occupy a space of his own. From now on mother and son are not only inextricably linked, but the mother will, as a kind of ventriloquist, speak through her son. We can see how the introjection of the mother tongue leads to a fateful maternalization of the German language: because the son has actually internalized the mother's tongue, the German language has, to a large extent, lost its potential to emancipate this struggling self. Furthermore, the brutal implantation of what is literally a mother tongue results in a symbolic matrix that both desymbolizes language and fictionalizes desire. As we will see later on, from the mother's point of view, the ensuing literary conversations between mother and son allow her to continue her relationship with her husband.

To explore this further, it may be useful to remember the significance of accession to the symbolic order. Before we are speaking subjects in a world of coherent objects, we all inhabit a space without proper boundaries and borders. Kristeva refers to this space as the *chora*, "a self-contemplative, conservative, self-sufficient haven" that is shared by mother and child and precedes the mirror stage.[7] Eventually, the young child begins to demarcate boundaries between self and mother. It needs a third party, the father or the "paternal metaphor," to pursue this struggle to demarcate and divide, and to ensure that the subject will find its place in the symbolic order. The paternal metaphor enables the struggling "not-yet-I" to make the transition and to give up the "good maternal object"[8] in favor of finding its place within the symbolic order. The implication here is that the symbolic order as the domain of language, reason, positions, rules, and so forth functions only because of the repression of the maternal. Elizabeth Grosz comments that "civilization, the symbolic order, the coherent text, then are possible only at the cost of the silencing, the phallicization, of the maternal *chora*."[9]

According to psychoanalytic theory, the acquisition of language implies a breaking away from the mirror identifications that bind mother and child. Canetti's autobiography, however, reverses this process through the story of his dramatic rebirth in German. Instead of freeing the child from the devouring mother, the German language locks him even further into a narcissistic dependence that will eventually result in a battle for life and death.

One might argue, however, that the actual resolution of the teaching episode runs somewhat counter to my interpretation: we are told that this period of suffering ends through the cunning intervention of the nanny. When Miss Bray notices that the son lives in a constant state of terror, she plots to save the boy from a crazy teaching method that relies exclusively on an aural technique. This method involves the reproduction of a limitless number of German sentences as well as their translations without any aide-mémoire. It is hardly surprising that, after some initial success, the son cannot remember all the sentences the mother has taught him. Whenever he makes a mistake, she spits verbal abuse on him, calling him an idiot. Eventually, Miss Bray ends his suffering by suggesting to the mother that he would like to learn Gothic script (*GZ*, 88). The argument that he will need to both speak German and write Gothic script when he enters school in Vienna persuades the mother to give him at last the much coveted grammar book.

With the help of the book, the son now manages the lessons and the tirades of abuse stop. The resolution of the teaching episode suggests that the world of books can provide a safe haven from the violence of the maternal grip. Reading would thus reinstate the symbolic order and achieve the eventual repression of the maternal. However, since the world of literature has already been associated with the eroticized love babble of the parents, this solution is doomed to failure. This is borne out by the ensuing "Leseabende" — evenings spent reading — where the boundaries between loving and reading are constantly blurred, and the mother confuses son and husband. Instead of opening up a space for the third other, reading reinforces the maternal hold.

From the safe distance of old age Canetti comments on the maternalization of German as follows:

> Immerhin, in Lausanne [. . .] wurde ich unter der Einwirkung der Mutter zur deutschen Sprache wiedergeboren und unter dem Kampf dieser Geburt entstand die Leidenschaft, die mich mit beidem verband, mit dieser Sprache und mit der Mutter. Ohne diese beiden, die im Grunde ein und dasselbe waren, wäre der weitere Verlauf meines Lebens sinnlos und unbegreiflich. (*GZ,* 94)

This overt identification of the language and the mother is the foundation of the mother's and son's frenzied narcissistic co-dependence, which results in the violent rejection of all potential agents of the Law of the Father. Canetti, who detested psychoanalysis more than any other paradigm of the twentieth century, seems to write a text book of psychoanalysis when he describes the boy's violent hatred of the *Herr Dozent* who courts the mother in Vienna. Watching how the mother and *Dozent* take tea on the balcony of their apartment, he fantasizes that the balcony collapses and buries the rival. The murderous fantasy ends with the proud admittance of the deed: "Ich habe ihn heruntergestürzt [. . .] er hat meiner Mutter die Hand geküßt" (*GZ,* 151). When the rival is finally defeated, mother and son celebrate the return to their dyadic unity by falling into each other's arms (*GZ,* 161).[10] Again it is the transparency of this textbook Oedipal rivalry that has prevented critics from examining the underlying structure of the mother-son relationship.

What has rarely been commented on is that this literal definition of the mother tongue cuts language effectively off from the symbolic order that allows the individual to negotiate a compromise between the excessive demands of the self and those of the other. From now on mother and son indulge in a series of powerful narcissistic projections that are channeled through literature. Reading Shakespeare and Schiller with her son, the mother returns to her "alte Liebe," the world of the stage and the memory of her dead husband. Although these evenings begin with a didactic exploration of their reading, they eventually turn into an imaginary dialogue that blurs the boundary between husband and son: "Ich fühlte, dass sie zum Vater sprach, wenn sie auf diese Weise ergriffen war, und vielleicht wurde ich dann selbst, ohne es zu ahnen, zu meinem Vater" (*GZ,* 103). The point is not so much that Canetti keeps recasting the Oedipal scene, but that this folie-à-deux between mother and son effectively fictionalizes desire. Instead of introducing the space for the third other, literature is unwittingly turned into a narcissistic fetish that feeds into projections of grandeur and the eroticization of language. The price for this undisturbed unity between mother and son is the derealization, or vice versa, the fictionalization of sexual desire. As a result of this configuration, literature becomes the only permitted locus of desire. Reflecting on the mother's great sacrifice for her children, the narrator states: "Ich sah das Opfer darin, daß sie soviel Zeit an uns wandte, während sie doch immerzu *gelesen* hätte" (*GZ,* 200). The taboo of sexuality is extremely powerful (*GZ,* 202): not only does it affect the adolescent but it translates itself into Canetti's lifelong revulsion at bodily processes and drives and, as we will see, the conception of the voice as the organ of utopian purity.

Although the title *Die gerettete Zunge* points the reader to the iconography of the opening scene, the ensuing chain of images runs counter to its powerful symbolism: ironically, the myth of an original phallic threat turns out to be a screen memory that barely disguises a far more deadly battle between mother and son that fully erupts in *Die Fackel im Ohr.* But the maternalization of language that is at the heart of the mother-son relationship also means that the son's tongue has not been set free.

Die gerettete Zunge ends with the image of the expulsion from paradise. This prepares the ground for the full-scale battle for independence in *Die Fackel im Ohr,* at the core of which is the son's recognition of the social dimension of language against the mother's continued hold over his life. The transition from the stifling dyadic relationship toward the social sphere is already implied in the title's reference to the great Viennese social satirist Karl Kraus.

The remaining pages will not once again stress the importance of literary figures such as Kraus, Musil, and Broch for the development of Canetti the writer; instead they will focus on two episodes of central importance for the eventual freeing of the son's tongue: the dramatic money episode in the chapter "Ausbruch" (*FO,* 131–36) and his meeting with Veza in *Die Fackel im Ohr* (*FO,* 72–74). Finally, I shall explore Canetti's idealization of the voice with reference to the figure of Dr. Sonne in *Das Augenspiel* and *Die Stimmen von Marrakesch* (1967).

The blowup referred to in the chapter title is caused when his mother refuses to allow Canetti to go on a long-planned hiking tour in the Karwendel Mountains. She declares that she does not have enough money for such luxury and tells the son that he should deem himself happy that he would be able to attend a university (*FO*, 135). The son, however, understands very well that the mother uses an artificially induced economic pressure as a pretext to maintain a firm hold over his life. Grabbing a note pad, he begins to frantically fill one sheet after the other with the words "Geld, Geld und wiederum Geld," until the floor is covered with paper. This frantic activity is only interrupted when the family doctor appears and prescribes the desired walking trip as an appropriate cure.

What is striking about this episode is not so much the vehemence of his counter-attack but the medium through which it is carried out. By choosing the written word and thus evoking the world of writing that was at the heart of the symbiotic relationship between mother and son, he repudiates the notion that his mother and his language are one and the same. I agree with Waltraut Wiethölter who argues that this frantic writing act demonstrates the great effort of the writer to liberate his self from the maternal hold by claiming writing as an activity that belongs to the paternal sphere.[11] But, according to Wiethölter, Canetti ultimately loses this battle for life and death because his writing remains wedded to the maternal hold.[12] In her view, figures such as Karl Kraus and later Veza simply replace the maternal figure with Veza providing new grand visions of Canetti the writer.[13]

Because Wiethölter pitches Canetti's autobiography against the overtly deconstructing narratives of Thomas Bernhard, Peter Weiss, and Christa Wolf, she dismisses the narrative, arguing that the narrator rattles it off like clockwork as if there had never been a crisis of subjectivity.[14] In my view this reading misses the split between *Stimme* and *Schrift* that emerges as Canetti's ultimate response to the deadly maternal hold. What appears to be a traditionally closed narrative is in fact a story about the self's struggle to salvage a space of its own. The third part of the autobiography indicates the possibility of such a space by prioritizing the voice over all writing. Strange as this may sound — after all Canetti was a writer — Canetti's poetics favors the human voice for its capacity to create a space for reciprocity between self and other. This is most evident in his relationship with Veza and, in *Das Augenspiel,* his conversations with Dr. Sonne.

Let me first turn to Veza: many readers of Canetti have noticed that the portrait of his wife-to-be remains strangely abstract and ephemeral. Comparing her twice to a Persian miniature (*FO*, 72, 120), the narrator introduces her as a precious and exotic figure that has hardly a bodily existence. Having observed her from a distance in Karl Kraus's lectures, he eventually musters up his courage and visits her at home. Interestingly, their first extended conversation revolves around the figure of Shakespeare's Lear: while Canetti makes his claim on eternity by stating that the old king should have lived forever, Veza speaks in favor of renewal of life and acceptance of death, a point-of-view that is informed by her experience of the tyranny of her ninety-year-old stepfather. The young man is most impressed with how she managed to establish a quiet but determined sense of authority over the old tyrant who never dares to invade her territory. The demarcation of a space of her own demonstrates that Veza, unlike Canetti, has succeeded in mapping the boundaries that are necessary for the constitution of the self and the other. This is further underlined in their ensuing literary conversations, where Veza demonstrates her superior intellectual independence: unlike Canetti, who is a slavish follower of Karl Kraus, Veza preserves her right of judgment by, for instance, defending Heine against Kraus's scathing attacks. Examples like this are numerous — they all show that in Veza's asylum Canetti finds more than a simple refuge from the mother. Through Veza he discovers that real dialogue is based on the recognition of the difference between self and other.

Interwoven in this portrait of Veza is, however, a curious episode in which the narrator relates how Veza speculates as to whether Canetti's mother is a secret writer. For the informed reader who knows that Venetiana Taubner-Calderon published her own works in the early thirties under a variety of pseudonyms and that she was writing for the *Arbeiter-Zeitung* in Vienna, this inquiry about the mother's writing must appear like a willful displacement through which Canetti disavows Veza as a writer.[15] The fact that Canetti fails to mention her writing clearly smacks of the machismo of a misogynist ego. Although this may play a role in the omission, I believe that there is more to this displacement: by having Veza speculate about his mother's secret writing career, the narrative reveals that the domain of writing remained locked in this deadly battle against and for the mother. That the written word is the site of an ongoing contest between mother and son can be shown with reference to her reception of *Die Blendung*: early on in *Die gerettete Zunge* the narrator relates how, after the publication of the novel, the mother writes an enthusiastic letter, celebrating the book in the following way:

> Das Buch, das sie gelesen hatte, sei Fleisch von ihrem Fleisch, sie erkenne sich in mir, so wie ich Menschen darstelle, habe sie immer gesehen, so, genau so, hätte sie selber schreiben wollen. (*GZ,* 77)

The curious formulation that the book and not the son is flesh of her flesh reveals her claim that she has actually authored both the son and his writing. It is relevant to note here that the son uses the subjunctive when relaying what amounts to a classic projection that she would have liked to write exactly like that. The subjunctive opens up a certain distance from a claim that reflects the mother's inability to distinguish between self and writing. She is clearly unable to accept any kind of symbolic agency and the notion of representation. As a result of this disavowal of the symbolic, the mother views writing as "flesh of her flesh," in other words as a domain that is completely non-transcendental.

It is against this threat of continued ownership that Canetti eventually pitches the spoken word: by making Veza the ideal reader, listener, and conversationalist, he creates an alternative space where another type of language can flourish: that of the free exchange of ideas, one that is driven by passion for the subject matter. In *Das Augenspiel* the narrator explains that this led to regular confrontations which both of them loved as a token of their mutual truthfulness and integrity (*A*, 14–18).[16] The reciprocity of their relationship is emphasized again in a chapter in *Die Fackel im Ohr*, titled "Schule des Hörens" (*FO*, 201–9) in which the narrator also deals with Karl Kraus's pervasive influence.

At this point it may be helpful to say a few words about the interdependence of the school of hearing and Karl Kraus, a crucial connection that is already highlighted in the book's title *Die Fackel im Ohr*. When in the above-mentioned chapter the narrator describes Kraus as a satirist whose mastery consisted in accusing people with their very own words, he introduces the notion of the acoustic mask (*FO*, 208). As a keen listener of Karl Kraus's famous public lectures, Canetti develops the idea that it is the spoken word with its variations in pitch, tone, rhythm, and other paralinguistic modes of expression that forms a person's acoustic mask. For Canetti, the acoustic mask betrays a person's true character without any reference to the content of the speech act; it therefore becomes an essential satirical tool in many of his writings. The characters of *Die Blendung* are a good example of this in that they expose themselves and their social origins through the way in which they speak. But satire presupposes a superior moral point of view and, by implication, a hierarchical relationship between self and other. This raises the question of how Canetti's concept of the acoustic mask sits with the idea that the voice can transcend the sphere of representation, ownership, and social contest. Isn't there a basic contradiction between satirical exposure on the one hand and the notion of a non-hierarchical, reciprocal relationship on the other? In order to address this question, I would like to analyze the figure of Dr. Sonne in *Das Augenspiel*.

Through Veza, Canetti already experienced dialogue as a mode of communication that is passionate but free from dominance. The portrait of Dr. Sonne radicalizes this idea substantially. What Canetti presents here is an extended apotheosis that turns the figure of Dr. Sonne into the paradigm of pure voice that disavows or — from Canetti's point of view — transcends the physicality of life. The first thing we learn about Dr. Sonne is that he never talks about his personal life (*A*, 131). Unlike Musil who, according to the narrator, maintains a connection to the world through his own strong physical presence, Sonne has renounced all such worldly attachments. A man without personal qualities, he is all mind and no body. Separating him from any attachment to physical reality, the narrator even confesses that he forgot that Sonne was a human being (*A*, 129). A voice without bodily needs, he solely consists of the sentences that he produces in the free flow of speech:

> Ich wußte nichts über Sonne, er bestand aus seinen Sätzen und er war so sehr in ihnen enthalten, daß man davor zurückgeschreckt wäre, etwas von ihm außerhalb seiner Sätze zu finden. Es lag nichts von ihm herum, wie bei allen anderen Menschen, auch keine Krankheit und Klage. [. . .] Ich hätte Broch oder Musil nach seiner Adresse fragen können. Ich tat es nicht, es schien mir angemessener, daß er keine habe. (*A*, 134)

Clearly, this apotheosis of a voice that does not need to be housed in a body is founded on Canetti's willful disavowal of the murky underside of life, of the body's physical needs and desires that make life terminable.

It may be fruitful at this point to dwell a little longer on Canetti's strong aversion to the physical demands of the body, in particular the need to eat, which is the theme of several of his aphorisms and annotations. Three entries in *Die Provinz des Menschen* (1973) are of particular interest in that they point to a connection between Canetti's aversion to food and his fear of incorporation. Reporting that he has seen a human stomach and that it looked exactly like a lump of meat, in fact a "Schnitzel," the self of the annotations wonders why the incorporation of flesh (Fleisch) is the condition of life (*PM*, 138).[17] A few entries later the diarist returns to the subject by imagining a human being that would not have to eat, an idea that in his view would constitute the highest possible moral experiment that would help to overcome death (*PM*, 140). A third entry develops this theme further with reference to the dual function of the mouth as a shredder of foodstuffs and the speech organ. It is worthwhile to quote the entire entry:

> Wie ist es möglich, das man Zerrissenes in den Mund tut, es lange darin weiterzerreißt und daß dann aus demselben Munde Worte kommen? Wäre es nicht besser, man hätte eine andere Öffnung für die Nahrung und der Mund wäre für die Worte allein da? Oder ist in dieser intimen Verquickung aller Laute, die wir bilden, mit Lippen, Zähnen, Zunge, Kehle, eben den Gebilden des Mundes, die dem Nahrungsgeschäft dienen, — ist in dieser Verquickung ausgedrückt, daß Sprache und Fraß für immer zusammengehören müssen, daß wir nie etwas Edleres und Besseres werden können, als wir sind, daß wir im Grunde, in allen Verkleidungen, eigentlich dasselbe Schreckliche und Blutige sagen, und daß sich der Ekel in uns nur meldet, wenn mit dem Essen etwas nicht stimmt. (*PM*, 140)

Drawing upon the conventional opposition of mind and body, Canetti clearly re-inscribes himself here in the Western philosophical tradition. While mind is correlated with reason and spirituality as a measure of human achievement, the body is perceived as a brute animalistic force that stands in the way of human progress. However, it seems to me that the powerful iconography of the passage, with the detailed images of the human cavity, exceeds a simple binary opposition between mind and body. The fact that the mouth is not just an organ of speech but also an apparatus that devours other organisms defiles for Canetti the purity of language. His psycho-social horror at the body's need for nourishment is a classic example of what Kristeva calls the abjection of the maternal. Having had to swallow the mother's tongue as a boy, he now projects his fear of introjection onto food as something that violates the boundaries between self and other, purity and impurity, the sublime and the abject. Oral disgust is an expression of the self's refusal to accept its own mortality since the need to incorporate food keeps reminding the self that it is housed by a body that will die. Recoiling from the body as a living organism, Canetti attempts to sublimate his oral disgust by poeticizing a pure voice that is detached from all bodily manifestations of life.

It is in line with this — and this brings me back to the autobiography — that Sonne is a writer who has transcended writing. Toward the end of the chapter, we eventually learn that the figure of Sonne refers to Abraham ben Yitzchak, a poet who had helped to regenerate Hebrew poetry but had stopped writing after the publication of a small number of refined poems. The narrator evaluates this as an act of pure renunciation:

> Jetzt wußte ich aber, daß er auch als Dichter gegolten und diese Geltung von sich abgeworfen hatte, während ich daran war, mir diese Geltung, die ich noch nicht hatte, zu gewinnen. (*A,* 141)

Bernd Witte reads Sonne as an allegory of discourse that allows Canetti to realize his utopia of metamorphosing life into language.[18] In contrast to this, Joseph Strelka has argued that Canetti only idealizes Sonne to such an extent because, as a passive reader of newspapers, he no longer posed a threat to Canetti the up-and-coming writer.[19] What at first may appear as two diametrically opposed readings turns out to be complementary interpretations that point to the splitting between the spoken and written word that characterizes Canetti's poetics. The marriage of writing and "Geltung" — recognition — in the above-cited passage underlines once more that for Canetti writing is enmeshed in the sphere of representation, social recognition, and ownership, in short, the world of power that had been defined for him by the ongoing battle for and against his mother. Set against this is the notion of the voice that cracks open the unity, certainty, and closure associated with the discursive word.

While in *Das Augenspiel* Dr. Sonne still talks about things, thus remaining tied to the world of discourse and power, Canetti takes this idealization of the pure voice a step further in *Die Stimmen von Marrakesch.* This narrative, which evokes an abundance of sounds and aural impressions, celebrates the voice as an agency that releases language from the constraints of the symbolic order. Borne by vocalic and kinetic differences, the voice with its transient quality transcends discursive language in favor of a utopian receptiveness that for Canetti recovers the dignity of all life. The title *Die Stimmen von Marrakesch* reflects the primacy that Canetti attaches to the non-semantic dimension of experience. It emphasizes those prelinguistic sensual impressions that appeal to an intuitive understanding but ultimately preserve a sense of strangeness. Favoring auditory over visual impressions, Canetti detaches himself from the politics of ethnography that has systematically privileged the eye as the primary agent in the discovery and colonization of the other. In contrast to this, Canetti favors the aural sense, which, because the traveler does not understand Arabic, is cut off from the semantic dimension of language and thus from the power relations implied in the symbolic order. I will finish with the call of "the unseen" in the final chapter of *Die Stimmen von Marrakesch*. Here the voice is reduced to a singular sound emitted by a brown bundle that cannot be discerned behind a shield of cloth. At the same time as interpreting the bundle as a symbol of life, Canetti voices his respect for its dignity and otherness:

> Der Sinn seines Rufes blieb mir so Dunkel wie sein ganzes Dasein: Aber es lebte und war täglich zu seiner Zeit wieder da. Ich sah nie, daß es Münzen aufhob, die man ihm hinwarf; man warf ihm wenig hin, nie lagen mehr als zwei oder drei Münzen da. Vielleicht besaß es keine Arme, um nach den Münzen zu greifen. Vielleicht besaß es keine Zunge, um das "l" in "Allah" zu formen, und der Name Gottes verkürzte sich ihm zu "ä-ä-ä-ä." Aber es lebte, und mit einem Fleiß und einer Beharrlichkeit ohnegleichen sagte es einen einzigen Laut, sagte ihn Stunden und Stunden, bis es auf dem ganzen weiten Platz der einzige Laut geworden war, der Laut, der alle anderen Laute überlebte.[20]

With this bundle that cannot be properly seen, Canetti radicalizes the notion of the pure voice: the one and only sound that this bundle emits over and over again is not only quite disembodied, but it is a sound which is no longer produced by the tongue. So in the end Canetti arrives at a utopian vision where it is not the tongue that is set free but the voice that is liberated from the dominance of the tongue. Because the mother of the autobiography had force-fed her son with her tongue, the son now rids himself of this introjected ventriloquist by authoring a voice that does not need a mother tongue. In a manner of speaking, by cutting the tongue off the voice, the son reintroduces the transcendental dimension of all language and writing that his mother had so forcefully tried to repress.

Although *Die Stimmen von Marrakesch* is an expression of Canetti's poetics of otherness, the three-part autobiography traces the genesis of his poetics back to the deadly battle between mother and son. In an ironic twist

Canetti rewrites the founding myth of the autobiography by envisaging a voice without a tongue. However, the question that remains is to what extent this conception of a disembodied voice can liberate the son. Clearly, the utopian idea of the pure voice as an agent of another language that escapes the deadly power play of discourse can only be realized in and through poetic fiction.

Notes

¹ Elias Canetti, *Die Fackel im Ohr. Lebensgeschichte 1921–1931* (Munich: Hanser, 1993), 289. Further references are abbreviated as *FO* and page number in parentheses.

² Martin Bollacher, "'[. . .] das Weitertragen des Gelesenen': Lesen und Schreiben in Canettis Autobiographie," in *Canetti als Leser,* ed. Gerhard Neumann (Freiburg: Rombach Litterae, 1996), 41.

³ The following publications are examples of the dominant tradition of Canetti criticism: Dagmar Barnouw, *Elias Canetti zur Einführung* (Hamburg: Junius, 1996); Claudio Magris, "The Writer in Hiding," in *Critical Essays on Elias Canetti,* ed. David Darby (New York: G. K. Hall, 2000), 279–91; Bernd Witte, "Der Einzelne und seine Literatur. Elias Canettis Auffassung vom Dichter," in *Experte der Macht: Elias Canetti,* ed. Kurt Bartsch and Gerhard Melzer (Graz: Droschl, 1985), 14–27.

⁴ Bollacher, "'[. . .] das Weitertragen des Gelesenen': Lesen und Schreiben in Canettis Autobiographie," in *Canetti als Leser,* 38. In recent years a more critical strand of commentary has emerged that attempts to challenge Canetti's self-representation by exposing the power play in the narrative. For example, while Joseph Strelka engages with Canetti's portraits of male writers, Gerhard Melzer focuses on Canetti's implicit rhetoric of power that, according to Melzer, silences and devalues otherness. This is also a theme in Friederike Eigler's book that provides, among other things, a critical analysis of Canetti's misogynist portraits of women, ranging from his scathing attack on Alma Mahler-Werfel to his representation of Frau Weinreb and Ruzena in the tradition of Weininger. Compare: Joseph Strelka, "Betrachtungen zu Elias Canettis autobiographischem Band 'Das Augenspiel,'" in *Autobiographie zwischen Fiktion und Wirklichkeit: Internationales Symposium, Russe Oktober 1992* (St. Ingbert: Röhrig Universitätsverlag, 1997), 233–48; Friederike Eigler, *Das autobiographische Werk von Elias Canetti: Verwandlung, Identität, Machtausübung* (Tübingen: Stauffenburg, 1988), 149–97; and Gerhard Melzer, "Der einzige Satz und sein Eigentümer. Versuch über den symbolischen Machthaber Elias Canetti," in *Experte der Macht,* 58–72.

⁵ According to Waltraut Wiethölter, the opening scene cites the iconography of the Madonna with the child. For Wiethölter it is a product of Canetti's imaginary omnipotence that compensates for the threat of castration and indicates right from the start that one day the son will overcome the mother. See Waltraut Wiethölter, "Sprechen — Lesen — Schreiben: Zur Funktion von Sprache und Schrift in Canetti's Autobiographie," in *Deutsche Vierteljahresschrift* 64/1(1990/1): 149–71.

⁶ Elias Canetti, *Die gerettete Zunge: Geschichte einer Jugend* (Munich: Hanser, 1997). Abbreviated as *GZ* and page number in parentheses.

[7] Julia Kristeva, *Powers of Horror: An Essay on Abjection* (New York: Columbia UP, 1982), 14.

[8] Kristeva, *Powers of Horror: An Essay on Abjection*, 45.

[9] Elizabeth Grosz, *Sexual Subversions: Three French Feminists* (Sydney: Allen & Unwin, 1989), 49.

[10] This theme is continued a little later when relatives try to persuade the mother to marry the Dozent. Rejecting this proposition the mother explicitly equates her own with her son's desire: "Die Mutter sagte zärtlich: 'Du kommst mich beschützen. Du bist mein Ritter. Jetzt wißt ihr's hoffentlich,' wandte sie sich an die beiden: 'Er *will* nicht! Ich will's auch nicht!'" (*GZ,* 167).

[11] Wiethölter, "Sprechen — Lesen — Schreiben: Zur Funktion von Sprache und Schrift in Canetti's Autobiographie," 158.

[12] Wiethölter, 171.

[13] Wiethölter, 158.

[14] Wiethölter, 166.

[15] Hannelore Scholz, "'Keine Angst geht verloren, aber ihre Verstecke sind rätselhaft': Frauen im autobiographischen Wahrnehmungsspektrum von Elias Canetti," in *Autobiographie zwischen Fiktion und Wirklichkeit,* 263.

[16] Elias Canetti, *Das Augenspiel: Lebensgeschichte 1931–1937* (Munich: Hanser, 1994). Abbreviated as *A* and page number in parentheses.

[17] Elias Canetti, *Die Provinz des Menschen: Aufzeichnungen 1942–1985* (Munich: Hanser, 1993).

[18] Bernd Witte, "Der Einzelne und seine Literatur. Elias Canettis Auffassung vom Dichter," *Experte der Macht: Elias Canetti,* 23.

[19] Joseph Strelka, "Betrachtungen zu Elias Canettis autobiographischem Band *Das Augenspiel,*" *Autobiographie zwischen Fiktion und Wirklichkeit,* 245.

[20] Elias Canetti, *Die Stimmen von Marrakesch: Das Gewissen der Worte* (Munich: Hanser, 1967), 104.

Elias Canetti's Attitude to Writers and Writings

Hans Reiss

For Idris Parry

E LIAS CANETTI WAS A MOST LEARNED MAN, a genuine *poeta doctus*. He was a compulsive book buyer, who owned more books than he was able to read, and an ardent reader, who was always looking forward to reading more. He was, however, far too interested in other people, as any great writer has to be, to be a mere bookworm. Yet he was well aware of all writers' indebtedness to the tradition of books. Therefore, this essay will seek to explore his account of what other writers' work meant to him. Canetti's own writings will inevitably provide most of the evidence for his views. But I also shall quote from or refer to letters which he wrote to Idris Parry, Professor Emeritus of German at the University of Manchester. Parry, who is a perceptive Canetti critic and scholar and knew Canetti well, has kindly put these extracts at my disposal.[1] I shall also quote or refer to what Canetti wrote or said to me. I saw him on several occasions, not only in England, but also in Switzerland, mainly in the house of my close Zurich friend, Dr. Hans-Ruedi Müller-Steiger, who became his doctor on my recommendation, and in whom he had "ein unerschütterliches Vertrauen," as he wrote to me on December 26, 1981.

Canetti had a remarkable gift for conjuring up the world in which writers lived and for portraying what they were like as people. His portrayal of Hermann Broch proves it.[2] He also knew how to cast a spell. Although I spent my formative years in Ireland, where the art of conversation is much, often even dizzily, practised, I never came across anyone whose conversation was so completely enthralling. When I first met him, he had come to Bristol at my invitation to read from his work, followed by a university dinner. Afterwards we went into the street where I was surprised to be in Bristol and not in the Vienna of the thirties that he had brought to life during the evening. We also talked about Arthur Schnitzler and Hugo von Hofmannsthal. Whereas he spoke of Schnitzler with respect but detachment, he dismissed Hofmannsthal, much to my surprise, as insubstantial. When I pressed him for an explanation, it was decisive: "Er war wie ein Fürst." Canetti had, rightly or wrongly, in Hofmannsthal detected pretence and false pride, features of character that he found repellent since for him they covered up evil attitudes.

Canetti admired clarity and precision as well as imaginative power in writing, but detested pretentiousness and excessive self-esteem in writers. Only good writing is able to bring to life the moral and cultural significance of intellectual activity. Imaginative literature is *the* weapon with which a writer can fight the enemies of mankind, of which the first and foremost, for Canetti really the sole one, is death. For death is "die erste und älteste, ja man wäre versucht zu sagen: die einzige Tatsache" (*GW,* 15) that really matters. It is the purpose of all religions, as he said, to cope with it, but, in his view, all have failed: "alle Versuche sich mit ihm abzufinden, und was sind die Religionen sonst, sind gescheitert" (*GW,* 15). Therefore, a writer has to fight death in his writings with all his might. This fight is thus a religious one. By the strength of his writing, he can make his readers aware of the need to hate and fight death.

> Seine eigene Angst, und wer hätte sie nicht vor dem Tode, muß zur Angst aller werden. Sein eigener Haß, und wer haßt den Tod nicht, muß zum Todeshaß aller werden. Dies und nichts Anderes ist sein Widerspruch zur Zeit, die von Myriaden und Abermyriaden Toden erfüllt ist.
>
> Damit ist dem Dichter ein Erbteil des Religiösen zugefallen, und sicher das beste Stück aus dem Erbe. (*GW,* 15)

Death constitutes the framework for Canetti's autobiography. At the beginning of the first volume, *Die gerettete Zunge,* the maid's lover threatens to cut off Canetti's tongue and thus confronts the small boy with the death of speech, which is for a writer the very essence of life. The sudden, unexpected death of his father was the decisive event of his life, which deeply affected his later experiences and thought.[3] The work also ends with death, that of his mother. It had to end in that way, as he told me in a letter of June 16, 1985. After all, she had, after his father's death, moulded his life for years. Against her influence and tyranny he had to defend himself to become independent in mind and spirit. Yet while he has to accept her physical death, he feels at the same time that death did not conquer his spirit; it was unable to defeat him. The last words of the autobiography are devoted to his younger brother Georg, the physician, because their mother will live on in him.

Canetti even felt that writers really ought to be able to prevent war and thus killing; he jotted down on August 23, 1939, when the outbreak of the Second World War appeared inevitable, a remark by an anonymous writer with which he agreed, "Wäre ich wirklich ein Dichter, ich müßte den Krieg verhindern können" (*GW,* 258). By writing, a writer can defeat death; his writings, if they are really good, will survive him and make him live on beyond his own physical death. Canetti was convinced that, in view of the world wars, mass murders, and the genocide in the twentieth century, it was even more urgent to fight and overcome death.

Death is however brought about primarily by evil, which, in Canetti's view, is identical to death.[4] Therefore, he sought to expose evil relentlessly in his work, and he did so powerfully. And he knew he was not alone, for a writer writes within a tradition; he has ancestors:

> Ein Dichter braucht Ahnen, Einige von ihnen muß er namentlich kennen, Wenn er am eigenen Namen, den er immer trägt, zu ersticken vermeint, besinnt er sich auf Ahnen, die ihre eigenen, glücklichen, nicht mehr sterblichen Namen tragen. Sie mögen seine Zudringlichkeit belächeln, doch sie stoßen ihn nicht weg. Auch ihnen ist an anderen, nämlich an Nachkommen gelegen. Sie sind in tausend Händen gewesen: niemand hat ihnen etwas angehabt, sie sind darum zu Ahnen geworden, weil sie sich kampflos der Schwächeren zu erwehren vermögen, an der Kraft, die sie verleihen, werden sie selber stärker. Es gibt aber auch Ahnen, die sich ein wenig ausruhen wollen. Diese schlafen für ein-, zweihundert Jahre ein. Sie werden geweckt, darauf kann man sich verlassen, plötzlich wie Fanfaren tönen sie von überall und sehnen sich schon zurück in die Verlassenheit ihres Schlafes.[5]

Thus, he saw great writers as his predecessors to whose company he wanted to belong.

Inevitably, his main themes, death and the exposure of evil, of the malignant power of the crowds as well as his desire for clarity and precision of writing, and his belief in the value of great literature, to which he aimed to belong, mark his attitude to other writers. He usually wrote far more about their personalities than about their work, which, however profoundly, determined his attitude to them. What mattered to him were the feelings that writers and their works aroused in him. He hardly ever engaged in literary criticism. Even when he wrote about an author at length in an essay, in a speech, or in his autobiography, as he did about Bertolt Brecht, Hermann Broch, Georg Büchner, Confucius, Johann Peter Hebel, Franz Kafka, Karl Kraus, or Leo Tolstoy, he set out to depict the person, his attitude to life and to people, his habits and emotions, anxieties and sufferings, but he did not analyze his works. Only by implication can something about them be culled from his remarks. Rarely does he analyze a work in detail. His comments on *King Lear*[6] are virtually an exception. There he points out how the older sisters' language unmasks their evil character at the very beginning and how the intriguer Edmund, Gloucester's natural son, is "sehr schwarz" and how the "Vollkommenheit seiner Verstellung," the only conventional element in the play, links him to these sisters who fight about him and thus all three of them become "ein recht eigener Kern, ein glaubwürdiger Teil des

Ganzen." He contrasts Cordelia's language with that of her sisters; she is incapable of speaking like them and is eventually reduced to silence. He also notes how the play is characterized by "vielerlei Verstellungen [. . .] auch solchen von >Guten<." He loves this play because "über die Verhinderung von Selbstmord durch seine scheinbare Ausführung gibt es nichts Weiseres." Finally, he remarks:

> Der Tod in diesem Stück ist unverhüllt er selbst. Cordelia, die Gute, stirbt unmittelbar nach ihren bösen Schwestern. Es wird kein Unterschied gemacht und niemand bleibt am Leben, bloß weil er es verdient hätte. Als letzter stirbt der Älteste, Lear selbst. Das Furchtbarste hat er so lange ausgehalten, nach allem, was vorangegangen ist, hat sein Tod etwas Friedliches. Die Bösen haben einander zuvor gegenseitig vernichtet, das einzige Vorrecht der Guten ist, daß sie es vor ihrem Ende noch erfahren. (*GU*, 91)

Since books mattered so much to him, it is not surprising that Peter Kien, the hero of his great novel *Die Blendung* (1935), owns a huge library. Kien, in the end, sets fire to the books and brings about his own suicide as a result. At the beginning of *Das Augenspiel,* the third volume of his splendid autobiography, Canetti describes that he almost felt relief when Kien committed suicide after suffering so much throughout the novel, but he himself had been emotionally and spiritually shattered at allowing Kien's library to be burned. He felt as if he had burnt his own books as well as all the books of the world, for Kien's library had contained all the important books of both the Western and Eastern world, of all religions, of all thinkers who retained any kind of life. But in the novel he did not make any attempt to save them:

> zurück blieb eine Wüste, es gab nun nichts mehr als Wüste und ich selbst war an ihr schuld. Denn es ist kein bloßes Spiel, was in einem solchen Buch geschieht, es ist eine Wirklichkeit, für die man einzustehen hat, viel mehr als jeder Kritik von außen, sich selbst gegenüber und wenn es auch eine Angst sehr großen Ausmaßes ist, die einen zwingt, soche Dinge niederzuschreiben, so bleibt immer noch zu bedenken, ob man nicht durch sie eben das mit herbeiführt, was man so sehr fürchtet. (*A*, 9)

The last words may be an allusion to Nazi book burning. Be that as it may, Canetti felt lost in a spiritual desert created by himself, even though he had destroyed only a fictional library. But the reading of books, of Büchner's work, which he had not known before, saved him from despair. He believed that good books are sources of knowledge and insight, and thus sheet-anchors for life, and as real as the everyday world. In his childhood his mother read with him and talked to him again and again about her enthusiasm for writers. As he told Rudolf Hartung: "Ich merkte, daß Dichter meiner Mutter die wichtigsten Menschen auf der Welt waren — und so beschloß ich, ihr zuliebe auch einer zu werden."[7] He decided to become a German writer, because German was the secret language of his parents in which they talked about literature and especially about the performances in the Viennese Burgtheater, which they had seen before they had met. After his father's death, his mother forced him to learn German. Because he loved her and feared her criticism, he did learn it speedily. Thus, "Deutsch ist also meine Muttersprache im eigentlichen Sime des Wortes."[8] And, therefore, he decided not to become a Spanish, English, or French writer, although he had learned these languages earlier than German. His friendship with writers in Vienna in the twenties and thirties confirmed him in the conviction that it was his task to be a German writer.[9]

Canetti's attitude to world literature knew no frontiers. As he told me, his mother did not read Spanish literature since Spanish was her native tongue (her family and his father's spoke the late medieval Spanish to which the descendants of Jews expelled from Spain in 1492 had clung, and so she presumably associated Spanish with her family to whom literature was of no account). However, Canetti appreciated the great Spanish writers, too. Cervantes's *Don Quixote* was a major inspiration.[10] For him, it was the greatest of all novels. And he thought of Quevedo as one of his literary ancestors (*A,* 319).

In his autobiography he mentions the names of many authors, one hundred eleven in all,[11] but is reticent about their work. Of this list, he regarded the following as important: Aristophanes, Babel, Broch, Büchner, Cervantes, Defoe, Dickens, Dostoyevsky, Gogol, Gorky, Gotthelf, Hebel, Wieland Herzfelde, Homer, Gottfried Keller, Kleist, Karl Kraus, Lenz, Heinrich and Thomas Mann, Conrad Ferdinand Meyer, Mörike, Musil, Pascal, Poe, Quevedo, Gustav Schwab, Shakespeare, Stendhal, Swift, Tolstoy, Trakl, and Robert Walser. None of them, except perhaps Schwab, surprises. But Schwab is a special case: his account of Greek mythology fired Canetti's imagination as a boy. In other works he speaks of his admiration for, or esteem of, authors such as Aubrey, Dante, Flaubert, Goethe, Hebbel, Alexander Herzen, Thomas Hobbes, La Bruyére, Lichtenberg, Gérard de Nerval, Abraham Sonne, Theophrastes, and Villon, to mention only a few. But he is distrustful of, or dismisses as intolerable or insignificant, writers such as Altenberg, Blei, Borchardt, Brecht, Heine (for a while), Hofmannsthal, Emil Ludwig, Scott, Friedrich Stoltze, Wedekind, Werfel, Zuckmayer, and Stefan Zweig. Some of them are ephemeral figures, but others still belong to the literary canon. Not surprisingly, when writing about other writers he always singles out the central themes of his own work: the discernment of evil and the awareness of death.

In this essay it is pointless to consider his comments on all the many writers whom he mentions in his work. To concentrate on only a few writers, first of all on Thomas Hobbes and Stendhal, who for very different reasons were pivotal figures for him, and only briefly on some others who were important for him, is therefore necessary.

Hobbes is an English seventeenth-century writer. Canetti knew English history of that period well; he talked at length in my presence about Clarendon's famous *History of the Great Rebellion*. Canetti greatly admired Hobbes and took him much more seriously because he understood the nature of political life better than any other thinker; at the same time, he had to fight him as *the* enemy:

> *Hobbes.* Unter den Denkern, die nicht durch eine Religion gebunden sind, können mich nur die beeindrucken, die extrem genug denken. Hobbes gehört zu ihnen; im Augenblick ist er mir der wichtigste . . .
>
> Nur wenige seiner Gedanken erscheinen mir richtig. Er erklärt alles durch Selbstsucht, und obwohl er die Masse kennt — er erwähnt sie des öfteren —, hat er eigentlich nichts über sie zu sagen. Meine Aufgabe aber ist es gerade zu zeigen, wie zusammengesetzt die Selbstsucht ist; wie das, worüber sie herrscht, ihr gar nicht zugehört, es enstammt anderen Bezirken der menschlichen Natur, eben jenen, für die Hobbes blind ist.
>
> Warum beeindruckt mich dann seine Darstellung so? Warum freue ich mich über seinen falschesten Gedanken, wenn er nur extrem genug gefaßt ist? Ich glaube, ich habe in ihm die geistige Wurzel davon gefunden, wogegen ich am meisten ankämpfen will. Er ist der einzige Denker, den ich kenne, der die Macht, ihr Gewicht, ihre zentrale Stellung in allem menschlichen Gebaren nicht verhüllt; er verherrlicht sie aber auch nicht, er läßt sie einfach stehen. [. . .]
>
> Er weiß, was Angst ist; seine Rechnung enthüllt sie. [. . .]
>
> Er unterschätzt nicht das furchtbare Gewicht des Staates. Wie kläglich wirken, gemessen an ihm, viele politische Spekulationen späterer Jahrhunderte. Rousseau scheint neben ihm ein kindlischer Schwätzer. Die früheste Periode, die uns, die wir heute sind, wirklich schon enhält, ist das 17. Jahrhundert. Hobbes hat diese Periode bewußt und denkend erlebt. [. . .]
>
> Er steht wirklich allein als Denker. [. . .] Er hat, wie ich schon sagte, sehr viel Angst gekannt und diese Angst offen zur Sprache gebracht wie alles übrige, mit dem er sich auseinandersetzte. Sein religiöser Unglaube war ein Glück ohnegleichen; mit billigen Verheißungen war seiner Angst nicht beizukommen. [. . .]
>
> Seine Abneigung gegen den Schrei der Masse hat er nicht erklärt, aber verzeichnet. Man kann von niemand erwarten, daß er alles erklärt.

Machiavelli, aus dem so viel Wesen gemacht wird, ist kaum wie die eine Hälfte, die klassische Hälfte von Hobbes. [. . .] Von Religionen hat Machiavelli, der mit Kardinälen umging, überhaupt nichts verstanden. Die Erfahrung der religiösen Massenbewegungen und Kriege in den gut hundert Jahren zwischen ihm und Hobbes, konnte er sich nicht mehr zu nutze machen. Seit es Hobbes gibt, hat es nur noch historische Bedeutung, sich mit Machiavelli zu befassen.[12]

That Canetti speaks in those terms of Hobbes will surprise most readers not familiar with the history of political thought. Surely, Machiavelli is the writer who has in *The Prince* uncovered the true springs of political action; his understanding of what prompts politicians at any time to seek to conceal their motives and intentions to gain or to keep power is generally held to be most profound. Canetti's attitude may be unorthodox, at least for a German writer. But Hobbes's work, in particular the *Leviathan*, which he had just been studying, belonged to his "Denk-Bibel, meine Sammlung der wichtigsten Bücher- und damit meine ich besonders die Bücher der Feinde." These are the books "an denen man sich schärft und nicht die, an denen man erlahmt, weil sie schon längst ausgesogen und erschöpft sind. Zu dieser 'Bibel' werden, das weiß ich gewiß, weder die 'Politik' des Aristoteles noch der 'Principe' des Machiavelli noch Rousseau's 'Contrat Social' gehören" (*PM*, 147). Two years later, in 1951, he was still attracted to Hobbes:

Noch immer zieht mich an *Hobbes* alles an: sein geistiger Mut, der Mut eines Mannes voll von Angst; selbstherrliche Gelehrsamkeit, die mit einem Instinkt ohnegleichen spürt, was sie *in sich* zu konfrontieren hat und was sie als leer und ausgesogen seitab liegen lassen soll; seine Zurückhaltung, die ihm erlaubt, reife und kräftige Gedanken jahrzehntelang zurückzubehalten, ihren Augenblick allein, unbeeinflußt und erbarmungslos zu bestimmen; die Freude an diesem geschlossenen Ring von Feinden um ihn, — er seine eigene Partei, der zwar manche im Glauben seiner Verwendbarkeit beläßt, aber sich doch gegen Mißbrauch zu wehren weiß, und ohne auf niedere Macht je aus zu sein, nur das tut, was seinen Gedanken Gehör verschafft; seine Konstanz bei so viel Lebendigkeit und Frische seines Geistes; sein Mißtrauen vor Begriffen — was ist sein Materialismus anderes? — und sein hohes Alter. (*PM*, 170)

Since Hobbes is rarely read by students of German or of twentieth-century literature in general, it is probably appropriate briefly to consider those salient points of his work with which Canetti may have taken issue. Like Canetti, Hobbes does not harbor illusions about human nature. We need to live in a commonwealth; if we do not, justice cannot prevail. In the state of nature, the war of all against all prevails. As Hobbes writes in chapter XIII of the *Leviathan*, in the state of nature "every man is enemy to every man;

[. . .] no arts; no letters; no society; and which is worst of all, continual fear, and danger of violent death; and the life of man, solitary, poor, nasty, brutish, and short." Because we fear sudden violent death more than anything else, our inborn desire to preserve our life requires that a commonwealth be established to prevent this war of self-interest. That commonwealth must be based on a contract that places all under the power of a sovereign whose duty it is to enact laws that will preserve the peace for everyone, for that is what everyone desires. The powers of the sovereign are unlimited, provided he secures peace for everyone. The individual citizen may disagree with the sovereign's decisions and the laws enacted by him, but it is his duty to obey, as Hobbes obeyed Charles I, Cromwell, and Charles II in turn. In a state in which peace prevails, the individual has no coercive rights against the sovereign. However, if peace is no longer preserved, the sovereign has failed to exercise power properly. Moreover, since this social contract it is based on self-preservation, a citizen cannot be expected to submit to any threat to or to any interference with his right to defend himself against death and thus to protect his liberty to seek felicity. Similarly, his sovereign cannot force opinions or beliefs, including religious ones, on individuals. They are solely their own. And anything that the law does not forbid, an individual may do.

Hobbes is undoubtedly an authoritarian. Admittedly, the sovereign ought not to commit deeds or to enact laws that are arbitrary or inequitable, but Hobbes does not say who has a right to decide on that issue. The importance of Hobbes can be gauged by Kant taking him very seriously; for Kant in a famous essay *On the Common Saying, this may be true in Theory, but does not apply to Practice* (1793) devotes its most important section, the second one, to a rebuttal of Hobbes ("On the Relationship of Theory to Practice in Political Right. Against Hobbes"). According to Hobbes (*De Cive*, chapter 7, § 14), the head of state has no contractual obligations towards the people; he can do no injustice to a citizen, but may act towards him as he pleases. Kant finds this proposition, in its general form, quite terrifying.[13] Doubtless Canetti would have sided with Kant. He is bound to have felt that Hobbes is willing to accept tyranny, even if he does allow a citizen to defend his liberty and life if the ruler threatens to destroy it.

Canetti was, however, impressed by the honesty of Hobbes's appraisal of life: "Ich *traue* ihm; die Prozesse seines Lebens und Denkens scheinen mir unverfälscht. Er ist der Widersacher, den ich höre; er langweilt mich nie und ich bewundere die Gedrungenheit und Kraft seiner Sprache" (*PM*, 170). He agreed with Hobbes's analysis of self-interest as the psychological source of human action, which entails the need to secure self-preservation. Hobbes took a sombre view of life. Canetti, too, was well aware of the dark sides of life, but he held a different view of mankind. Just as his mother disliked, even despised, almost all members of her family, but retained her pride in her family itself, so he detected human shortcomings in profusion, but thought well of mankind: "Die Menschheit überhaupt empfinde ich wie ein unversehrtes weißes Licht, aber damit es unversehrt bleibt, will ich es in seinen Brechungen untersuchen."[14]

Canetti would certainly have shared Hobbes's belief that "one should not do to others what one would not wish to have done to oneself." He would also have agreed that none of us has to consent to a contract that deprives us of our life or does any other injury to us or prevents us from enjoying or having access to all that is necessary for life, namely the open air, food, and in general the liberty to seek to achieve our felicity to the best of our ability and knowledge. Hobbes also stipulates that we do not prevent others from having the same rights and that they must be willing to accept the same obligations. Canetti would have shared that view.

Canetti's intensive study of power occupied him for years and culminated in his important sociological work *Masse und Macht*. Crowds and power for him were the sources of evil. Hobbes, however, accepts power — hence he is *the* enemy. But power has not merely to be fought in the public sphere, as Swift, for instance, did in his satires, but also in the private sphere, where Canetti had witnessed the awesome power that his grandfather exercised over his father, where he had to defend himself against his Manchester uncle Salomon, the "Oger," of whom his father had said "er geht über Leichen,"[15] and where his mother had forced him to learn German as a boy and had driven him out of his Zurich paradise after the First World War. However, although from the "Anschluß" of March 1938 until he fled in November of that year soon after the "Kristallnacht" he had studied National Socialism at first hand almost daily by listening and talking to people everywhere in Vienna — in the streets, restaurants, and cafés[16] — he refrained from explicitly commenting on the political tyrannies that devastated Central Europe during his lifetime. This failure to write explicitly about these dreadful issues is surprising, especially because the last book which his father had given him before his sudden early death was about Napoleon, the very example of a tyrant to be abominated, and because Canetti had to experience the bitterness of exile. Only when writing his essay on Speer's account of Hitler did he depict the latter's megalomania as a central feature of his power complex (*GW*, 163–77); there may well be an implicit attack in his imaginative works on National Socialism, as for instance in *Komödie der Eitelkeit*.[17]

For both Hobbes and Canetti death is the ultimate evil. Yet their attitude about death is basically different. Here may indeed be the deepest reason why Canetti fought against Hobbes. Hobbes merely acknowledges death, but by not attacking it, he minimizes its power and accepts that it will prevail in the end. Canetti wants to be victorious. To defeat death is the only victory that he desires. For him, freedom is the refusal to exercise the power that is inextricably linked with death. But for Hobbes death is merely to be temporarily avoided by giving power to the sovereign.

Canetti's hatred of death made him fight the prophets and harbingers of nihilism, both those who admired death during his lifetime and Nietzsche, who claimed that the strong have a right to rule and that it is right for the weak to perish. Canetti felt inured against Nietzsche since his late twenties when he read the letters of Nietzsche's mother and became overcome by anger: "am kranken Nietzsche habe ich den 'Willen zur Macht' durchschaut und nie habe ich mich seither zu einer Konzession an Nietzsche verführen lassen" (*GU*, 169). He was convinced:

> Nietzsche kann mir nie gefährlich werden: denn jenseits von aller Moral ist in mir ein ungeheuer starkes, ein allmächtiges Gefühl von der Heiligkeit jedes, aber wirklich auch jedes Leben. Daran prallt der roheste wie der raffinierteste Angriff ab. Eher gebe ich mein eigenes Leben ganz und gar auf, als ein irgendeines andern auch nur im Prinzip. [. . .] Ich anerkenne keinen Tod. [. . .] Nietzsches Attacken sind mir wie eine giftige Luft, aber eine, die mir nichts anhaben kann. Ich atme sie stolz und verächtlich wieder aus und bedaure ihn für die Unsterblichkeit, die seiner wartet.[18]

Yet Nietzsche, like Hobbes and de Maistre, was for him also an important thinker because his ideas were diametrically opposed to his own. All three thinkers wrote clearly — though, as Canetti rightly remarked, Nietzsche is not as clear as he seems — and maintained their ideas as if they were true beyond contradiction.[19] Therefore, Canetti hated them, but was also stimulated to fight them constantly.

In contrast, Canetti felt indebted to Jakob Burckhardt, whom he admired as a historian on account of "seinen Widerstand gegen Nietzsche, früh für mich eine Warnung" (*GU*, 8). Burckhardt put him on guard against Nietzsche so that he was able to see him as a "Philosoph zum Aufblähen" (*GU*, 17). He owed him also "die Weigerung gegen jedes System aus der Geschichte; seinem Gefühl, daß nichts *besser* geworden war, im Gegenteil eher schlechter: seinem Respekt vor allem *Gestalteten;* im Gegensatz zum Begrifflichen, seiner Wärme für wirklich gelebtes Leben, von der Zartheit seines Verzichts genährt"(*GU*, 8). Canetti also fought the nihilists among his contemporaries. Without mentioning his name, he attacked Thomas Bernhard in his speech *Die Aufgabe des Dichters,* which he delivered in the University of Munich in 1976 when receiving an Honorary Doctorate, because Bernhard had glorified death. Bernhard realized that this implicit criticism was meant for him and wrote a nasty letter to *Die Zeit* in which he descended to personal abuse — for instance, he called Canetti "a Spätlingsvater." Bernhard's outrageous words led me to write a letter to *Die Zeit* in Canetti's defence, in which I deplored Bernhard's descending to personal abuse in lieu of a reasoned argument. It was duly printed, and I was greatly surprised when I saw Canetti some months later, he showed no anger towards Bernhard. He told me that he understood the reason for Bernhard's polemic: he knew that Bernhard was bound to have been deeply hurt by having his convictions assailed. He had earlier, on March 30, 1976, written to me in most generous terms about my letter and explained why he had attacked Bernhard:

> Bernhard ist mit seiner schrecklichen Natur geschlagen, ich kenne ihn gut. Er war — verzeihen Sie das Wort, er war seines — einer meiner grössten "Verehrer" und pflegte überall zu sagen, wie viel er von der "Blendung" gelernt hat. Die harte Kritik an ihm in meiner Rede hat ihn offenbar schwer getroffen. Es zeigt in seiner Reaktion, daß er nichts gelernt hat. Meine Kritik war eine prinzipielle und richtete sich gegen die gewissenlosen Lobhudler des Todes, die sich in der neueren Literatur immer breiter machen. In einem Interview vor einigen Jahren hat B. sich den Ausspruch geleistet: "Der Tod ist das Beste, was wir haben": Dagegen <u>musste</u> ich mich wenden.

However much Canetti admired, and fought against, Hobbes, his praise of Stendhal is unreserved. He writes: "Ich gestand, daß das mein liebster französischer Autor sei, ich hätte ihn als meinen Meister betrachtet und mich bemüht, von ihm zu lernen" (*A,* 198) and said:

> La vie de Henry Brulard de Stendhal [. . .] fut sans doute mon modèle, un exemple de ce que je voulais tenter en écrivant l'histoire de mes debuts dans la vie. Je crois que c'est l'unique autobiographie qui soit absolument vraie [. . .]. Stendhal a eu aussi le courage d'aller très loin dans l'expression de ses haines et de ses amours. Comme lui, je crois que les sentiments extrêmes que l'on a éprouvés enfant vous accompagneront toujours. If faut le courage de faire encore mal à ceux que l'on a détestés et de dire l'allocation que nous ont inspiré certaines personnes.[20]

And in 1971 he gives some detailed reasons for his attitude to Stendhal:

> Stendhals dreifaches Vorbild in seiner Kindheit: der skeptische Großvater, der sich immer etwas dachte; die stolze Tante mit ihrer spanischen Noblesse; der Genießer Romain Gagnon, sein Onkel, ein Frauen- und Augenblicksmensch. Aber stärker noch die *Gegenbilder* seiner Jugend: der berechnende Vater, die keifende andere Tante, die ihn mit Haß verfolgt, und der >Jesuit< Raillane, sein Lehrer. Diese Aufspaltung in Liebe und Haß, in Vor- und Gegenbilder ist deutlicher und erregter dargestellt als in jeder anderen Autobiographie. (*PM,* 333)

These words recall Canetti's own telling comments on his family:

> In meiner Familie und besonders in ihrer [der meiner Mutter] sah ich, was Menschen durch Geld geschah. Ich fand die am schlechtesten, die sich am willigsten dem Gelde hingaben. Ich lernte alle Übergänge von Geldgier zu Verfolgungswahn kennen. Ich sah Brüder, die einander durch ihre Habgier in jahrelangen Prozessen zugrunde richteten und die weiter prozessierten, als kein Geld mehr da war. (*GZ*, 13)

This insight into the dark side of human nature also prevails in Tacitus, who, as Canetti told me, had greatly influenced him, and to whom he also owed precision and economy of means. As he wrote in a letter to Idris Parry on February 21, 1963, he also learned the virtue of precision from Stendhal. He also states: "Stendhal verdanke ich die Überzeugung, daß jeder Mensch, — wenn es ihm gelänge, sich vollständig aufzuschreiben —, erregend und staunenswürdig und auch unersetzlich wäre" (*PM*, 333). Doubtless he was also much impressed by Stendhal's attempt to write about his life objectively, with detachment and self-criticism, which gives his work an air of authenticity. Moreover, as his description of the Great Inflation in post-1918 Germany reveals, he, too, like Stendhal in his account of the battle of Waterloo in *La Chartreuse de Parme,* records historical events as events *felt* by him. Stendhal had sought to write a new type of autobiography. So did Canetti, who agreed with me when I suggested that it had been his intention. In other respects their autobiographies differ profoundly. The structural differences between them are striking. *Vie de Henry Brulard* remained a fragment, whereas Canetti created a carefully arranged, fully completed work. Of course, all autobiographies, like all histories, have to be selective. But Canetti's is fundamentally discontinuous, whereas Stendhal's provides a more continuous narrative. Canetti's omissions may seem surprising. But, as he told me, he was writing only about that which had made an impact on him as a writer. His writing was what mattered to him above all, and not the events of daily life. Not that they did not affect him — they patently did. Yet he writes remarkably little even about his first wife Veza; he hardly speaks of his brothers, except at the end of the autobiography, and even then he is virtually silent about their life and character. Yet, as he wrote to me in a letter dated December 2, 1985, he admired and deeply loved his younger brother Georg. He also does not talk explicitly about the political and economic developments in Germany and Austria, except by implication in his conversations with Dr. Sonne and in his description of the Great Inflation of the early twenties in Germany or the storming of the "Justizpalast" in Vienna, cardinal political events in Germany and Austria in the interwar years, neither of which he sets in the political context. Nor does he explain why his mother moved with her sons to Switzerland in the middle of the First World War. (One of the reasons was, as he told me, the impossibility of transferring money from Britain to Austria, though doubtless her hatred of war and the warlike atmosphere in Vienna was another.) He also states that his awareness of crowd psychology, a vital concern of his, began in 1922 when he saw a demonstration in Frankfurt protesting against the assassination of the German Foreign Minister Walter Rathenau. But he does not describe the important political context itself at all. There is no need to list the many omissions. However, his gift of storytelling is such that they are not noticed on first reading. It was rather Stendhal's style and his whole commitment to culture that were examples that Canetti addressed. Thus, he writes in *Nachträge aus Hampstead:*

> Stendhal ist mir so wichtig geworden, daß ich mich alle fünf oder sechs Monate ihm zuwenden muß. Es kommt gar nicht darauf an, welches Werk es ist. Wenn es nur Sätze sind, die seinen Atem haben. Manchmal lese ich zwanzig oder dreißig Seiten von ihm und glaube, daß ich ewig leben werde. (*NH,* 37)

Canetti also liked Stendhal's novels, particularly his two great masterpieces, *Le Rouge et Le Noir* and *La Chartreuse de Parme* (*NH,* 29), the latter a novel that, as he told Idris Parry in a letter on January 31, 1979, "one can never exhaust." While writing *Die Blendung,* he daily read a few sentences from *Le Rouge et le Noir* before starting to write because it was a model of "Dichte, Klarheit" and "schlackenlose Duchsichtigkeit" for him.[21] Thus, of all writers it is only Stendhal whom he both loved and envied (*NH,* 29); as he notes, "Stendhal belebt mich zu jeder Zeit, in jeder Verfassung" (*GU,* 19).

However, Canetti was also alive to Stendhal's shortcomings. For instance, Canetti's comment on his inability to match Stendhal's descriptions need hardly be taken literally:

> Die Lust an topographischer Zeichnung, der Stendhal in seinem >Henry Brulard< mit leichter Hand frönt, ist mir nicht gegeben, und zu meinem Leidwesen war ich immer ein schlechter Zeichner. So muß ich die Art, wie die Wohngebäude um unseren Gartenhof in Rutschuk angelegt waren, kurz beschreiben. (*GZ,* 19–20)

Vie de Henry Brulard contains many drawings by Stendhal of houses and rooms about which he writes, but they are hardly of any value in themselves. Surely, Canetti's comment here is ironic. Canetti's verbal descriptions, though, are of high quality, as are Stendhal's. But Canetti never slavishly modelled his writing on Stendhal; instead, he always sought to preserve his independence of mind, even if he owed Stendhal his freedom to breathe and thus to write:

> Stendhal war nie meine Bibel, aber er war unter den Schriftstellern mein erlösender Mensch. Ich habe ihn keineswegs ganz oder immer wieder gelesen. Aber ich habe nichts von ihm aufgeschlagen, ohne mich leicht und hell zu fühlen. Er war nie mein Gesetz. Aber meine Freiheit

war er, und wenn ich am Ersticken war, fand ich sie bei ihm. Ich bin ihm viel mehr schuldig als allen, die mich beeinflußt haben. Ohne Cervantes, ohne Gogol, Dostojewski, Büchner wäre ich nichts: ein Geist ohne Feuer und Kanten. Aber leben konnte ich nur, weil es Stendhal gibt. Er ist meine Rechtfertigung und Liebe zum Leben. (*NH*, 90)

Canetti's mother adored Shakespeare and read his plays with him when he was a young boy. Canetti shared her admiration for Shakespeare. What is however of note is his mother's exceptional enthusiasm for *Coriolanus*. In this play, as in many of Shakespeare's plays, power is at issue. Shakespeare's remarkable ability to depict crowds and their power comes particularly to the fore in *Coriolanus*, whose hero impresses by his insistence to stand apart from the Roman crowd, by his refusal to bow to its moods, even though his attitude leads to his ruin. Perhaps it was *Coriolanus* that planted in Canetti the first seed of his fascination with crowds and their power, whose study occupied him for decades and culminated in *Masse und Macht*.

Great writers endowed him with strength of mind. Thus Goethe, whose achievement is unattainable, as Canetti told me, inspired his will to survive:

Wenn ich trotzdem am Leben bleiben sollte, so verdanke ich es *Goethe*, wie man es nur einem Gott verdankt. Es ist nicht ein Werk, es ist die Stimmung und Sorgfalt eines erfüllten Daseins, das mich plötzlich überwältigt hat. Ich kann ihn aufschlagen, wo ich will, ich kann Gedichte hier und Briefe oder ein paar Seiten Bericht dort lesen, nach wenigen Sätzen erfaßt es mich und ich bin so voll Hoffnung, wie sie keine Religion mir geben kann. (*PM*, 49–50)

Goethe also liberated Canetti from the despotism to which he had submitted himself by seeing the French Revolution as a kind of model and by seeing life as something that was "eine unaufhörliche, nimmersatte, von jähen und unberechenbaren Augenblicken erhellte Revolution" (*PM*, 50). That conception of the French Revolution had produced "Unruhe und Heftigkeit" in him, misled him in many ways. Goethe gave him the feeling that "alles, was ich unternehme, legitim und natürlich [ist]. [. . .] Er gibt mir mein Recht: Tue, was Du mußt, sagt er, auch wenn es nichts Tobendes ist, atme, betrachte, überdenke" (*PM*, 51). Canetti felt at one with Goethe's refusal to allow death a part in his life and work, and he greatly appreciated the scope, depth, and fullness of experience they conveyed.

Canetti also wrote warmly about quite a few other writers. Thus, on expressing his thanks for receiving the Johann Peter Hebel Prize, Canetti spoke not only of his debt to Hebel, but also of Kafka's praise for the Alemannic writer.[22] He greatly valued Hebel's language:

Seine Sprache ist so, als wäre sie um seinetwillen entstanden. Ihre Frische sucht in der Literatur ihresgleichen. Er kennt keine müden Worte, sie erschlaffen, wie sie vor Hochmut bersten, und was man von der Sprache überhaupt denken möchte, bei ihm ist es Wahrheit geworden. Jede Geschichte, die man von ihm lies, erfüllt und entlässt einen mit *Erwartung*.[23]

Hebel's *Schätzkästlein* gave him the feeling that "jeder zählt, weil jeder sein Leben hat,"[24] but otherwise he is once again economical in his comments on Hebel's work itself. So is he also when writing about Dickens, Dostoyevsky, and Gogol, all of whom he greatly admired. As a boy he read Dickens with greater enthusiasm than he did any writer's works later on (*GZ*, 218; see also his letter to Idris Parry, March 23, 1977). To Gogol he owed, as he told Idris Parry in a letter of February 21, 1963, "die Unbekümmertheit und Freiheit der Erfindung." He was very pleased when I told him that the portrayal of evil in his work reminded me of Dostoyevsky, but he remained silent about the Russian novelist's work.

Canetti's *Aufzeichnungen* owe much to Aubrey, La Bruyére, Lichtenberg, and Hebbel. He recorded that, when he had not read the diaries of Lichtenberg and Hebbel for some time, he experienced a "Gefühl der Verarmung."[25] It is possible here only to note the significance that these writers had for his aphoristic writing. He was particularly struck by the inquisitiveness that he found in the writings of John Aubrey, a not very well-known seventeenth-century English writer (*GU*, 63). "Bei Aubrey blieb alles frisch. Jede Nachricht steht für sich selbst. Man spürt die Neugier, mit der sie aufgenommen wurde. Auf dem Papier noch erregt sie Neugier" (*GU*, 64). But above all he was deeply indebted to Lichtenberg, whom he read again and again in his London exile;[26] he believed that Lichtenberg "wirft Licht, er will treffen, aber nicht töten, kein mörderischer Geist." Canetti admired him because:

> Er ist nicht mit sich unzufrieden, weil ihm zuviel einfällt. Ein wimmelnder Geist, aber im Gewimmel ist immer Platz. Daß er nichts abrunden mag, daß er nichts zu Ende führt, ist sein und unser Glück: so hat er das reichste Buch der Weltliteratur geschrieben. [. . .] Er weicht Theorien nicht aus, aber jede Theorie ist ihm Anlaß zu Einfällen. Er kann mit Systemen spielen, ohne sich in sie zu verwickeln. Das Schwerste kann er wie ein Stäubchen vom Rock wegflitzen. (*PM*, 304)

Canetti's aim was to achieve a limpidity of style equal to Lichtenberg's.[27] He admired aphoristic writing but appears to have been generally critical of most philosophers who produced systematic works. He mistrusted concepts; he thought that concepts could not be tested because all that they do is to refer to other concepts. Hence, it is not surprising that he disliked Plato (*Aufz.1973–84*, 58) and that, in his view, Hegel and Freud had poisoned language (*Aufz. 1973–84*, 88). However, he admired the pre-Socratic philosophers (*GU*, 182; *PM*, 312), especially Heraclitus (*PM*, 249, 253; *GU*, 49), Democritus (*PM*, 239, 299, 323), and Theophrastus (*PM*, 283), as well as Chinese thinkers, such as Confucius, Hsün-Tse, and Laotse (*GU,* 182; *PM,* 249, 312). He also esteemed Giordano Bruno (*PM,* 299).

When being awarded the Nobel prize in Stockholm, Canetti singled out four authors, Karl Kraus, Kafka, Musil, and Broch, but added that only the first three made an impact on his work.[28] Therefore, a few comments on his attitude to them are appropriate, and by way of contrast, a word about Brecht may be useful, too. On hearing Kraus's public reading of his own writings Canetti fell under his spell and modelled not only his own reading but also his literary judgments on him. He accepted Kraus's view of language unquestioningly for a long time. Kraus was always deliberately polemical and uncompromisingly quoted inadequate writing to attack those who had composed it. The power of Kraus's reading made his attack hit home. Canetti believed what Kraus said and, in his wake, condemned those authors whom Kraus condemned — and Kraus condemned more authors than he praised — "Jedes Urteil war auf der Stelle vollstreckt. Einmal ausgesprochen, war es unwiderruflich. Wir alle erlebten die Hinrichtung" (*GW,* 41). In this context, his 1942 note about Swift, another satirist of stature, is revealing:

> *Swifts* zentrales Erlebnis ist die Macht. Er ist ein verhinderter Machtha-ber. Seine satirischen Urteile stehen für Todesurteile. In seinem Leben waren sie versagt, sie sind in seine Satire geraten. So ist diese im eigent-lichsten Sinne des Wortes die furchtbarste, die einem Schriftsteller je zu Gebote stand. (*PM,* 27)

Kraus also taught him to treat language with a due sense of responsibility so that he could be on his guard against its misuse, against a flowery style or any kind of mendacious or meaningless writing; "Karl Kraus, dessen Gefühl für den Mißbrauch der Sprache aufs feinste verschärft war, hatte die Gabe, die Produkte dieses Mißbrauches *in statu nascendi* aufzufangen und nie wieder zu verlieren. Für den, der ihn hörte, war dadurch eine neue Dimension der Sprache eröffnet, die unerschöpflich ist" (*GW,* 45). Kraus's satirical readings of contemporary Viennese books and newspapers, but especially his readings of Nestroy, opened Canetti's ear to Viennese speech. If he had not heard them he would hardly have gone into "Wiener Volkslokale" to listen for hours to how people spoke there.[29] Before Kraus, ordinary speech had been only sporadically satirized. Nestroy was the great exception; Kraus had learnt much from him. So did Canetti, even if he hardly ever wrote about Nestroy's impact on him. But he did admit his debt to Nestroy when in 1980 he told Gerald Stieg: "ich müßte mich, rein sprachlich schon, zur Literatur Wiens zählen: Nestroy und Kraus."[30] Like Stendhal and Tacitus, Kraus also taught him precision:

> Es gehört dazu, die Gliederung der Sätze selbst, die Unerbittlichkeit ih-rer Längen, die Zahllosigkeit, die Unabsehbarkeit, das Fehlen eines Ge-samtziels, jeder Satz ist sich selber Ziel, und wichtig ist nur, daß man

ihre Gleichmäßigkeit so lange auf sich einwirken läßt, wie es einem möglich ist, die Erregung zu fühlen. (*GU,* 25)

Canetti also shared Kraus's hatred of war (*GU,* 26; *GW,* 237), especially after he became aware in Switzerland that peace did not spell weakness. But in Berlin he discovered that Kraus, too, had feet of clay; Kraus liked Brecht, whom Canetti detested. Finally, Ludwig Hardt, the actor, cured him of Kraus's condemnation of Heine as summed up in Kraus's wrong-headed essay *Heine und die Folgen* and revealed to him that not all of Kraus's judgments were correct (*FO,* 331). Apparently, Kraus had merely been in tune with the then-prevailing ideas of the German nationalist literary historians who mistook Heine's criticism of Romantic illusions and "sacred" German myths for corruption of thought and style, a view fortunately no longer in favour in Germany and never held in England.

Thus, Canetti eventually became disillusioned with Kraus. He was appalled when Kraus supported Dollfuss, who destroyed democracy and waged war on the Social Democrats in Austria, foreshadowing the Anschluß of 1938. In the end, Canetti realized that he had been living under Kraus's tyranny for years: "Ich habe damals wirklich erlebt, was es heißt, unter einer Diktatur zu leben. Ich war ihr freiwilliger, ihr ergebener, ihr leidenschaftlicher und begeisterter Anhänger: Ein Feind von Karl Kraus war ein verwerfliches, ein unmoralisches Wesen" (*GW,* 48). He was glad at long last to be liberated, having become aware how easy it is to fall prey to political misapprehension: "Ich hätte die Macht nie wirklich kennen gelernt, wenn ich sie nicht ausgeübt und nicht selbst das Opfer dieser eigenen Übung geworden wäre. So ist mir die Macht dreifach vertraut: ich habe sie beobachtet, ich habe sie ausgeübt, ich habe sie erlitten" (*PM,* 112). He even stated as late as 1984: "Manchmal denke ich — heute noch — daß Karl Kraus mich zerstört hat" (*Aufz. 1973–84,* 117).

Canetti devotes a whole section of his autobiography to Brecht (*FO,* 302–9), written when Brecht's reputation was still largely unimpaired. Brecht struck him as the opposite of what a writer should be. He disliked Brecht because of his arrogance, pretence, and interest in money; he felt repelled by his haughtiness and lack of empathy for a young aspiring writer like himself. As he told me, when they first met in Berlin, Brecht had just bought a car and contemptuously looked down on anyone who, like Canetti, did not own one. He thought little of Brecht's plays, which were highly successful soon after the war. As he wrote to Idris Parry on November 3, 1971, he greatly preferred Horváth to Brecht as a playwright; "Brecht is castrated by his theories and can be at times as dull as his pupil Peter Weiss." But Canetti valued Brecht's lyric poetry and wrote enthusiastically about *Die Hauspostille:* "Von diesen Gedichten war ich hingerissen, ich nahm sie, ohne an ihn zu denken, in einem Zug auf" (*FO,* 304–5).

Kafka mattered greatly to Canetti. When writing about Kafka's doomed love for Felice Bauer in *Der andere Prozeß: Kafkas Briefe an Felice,* his striking psychological analysis affords an insightful entry into Kafka's works, in particular *Das Urteil* and *Der Prozeß,* both written under the impact of this unhappy relationship. However, about the works themselves he again remains silent, although his admiration for Kafka was boundless. Appropriately, in his Stockholm speech he specifically referred to his debt to Kafka. What was important to him was that Kafka completely lacked vanity and detested power:

> *Kafka* geht wirklich die Eitelkeit des Dichters ab, nie prahlt er, er kann nicht prahlen. Er sieht sich klein und geht in kleinen Schritten. Wo immer er den Fuß aufsetzt, spürt er die Unsicherheit des Bodens. [. . .] So verzichtet er auf die Täuschung und das Blendwerk der Dichter, [. . .] auf Predigt . . . Er ist von allen Dichtern, der einzige, den Macht in keiner Weise angesteckt hat; es gibt keine wie immer geartete Macht, die er ausübt. (*PM,* 129)[31]

Kafka is thus never on the side of the powerful but of those who are humiliated (*GW,* 130). In his radio conversation with Idris Parry, Canetti expressed this view vividly:

> Kafka described in his work every possible form of humiliation, of fear of power, of avoidance of power, and by doing that he has shown power in a much fuller way than we usually think of it. When we say "power" we just think of a strong person exerting power and what this power looks like, but we tend to forget that power is displayed in a number of situations all the time in our lives, not only politically or in dramatic events. If one wants to know what power really is, one can't refer to the great stormy things, to thunder and lightning or the things treated in history, one has to show it in everyday life, in hundreds of different situations, and these situations Kafka not only explored. I think he felt them.[32]

Kafka's work reveals "a strong dislike" of power exerted by "small bureaucratic officials." On reading Kafka we are reminded of "the dangerous powers we can't control, and the most dangerous powers in the world are mysterious things." Indeed, Kafka's "great originality as a writer is his gift for transformation into small things and small beings."[33] He agreed with Idris Parry's perceptive insight that "the striking thing about Kafka's writings [is that] they are concrete images."[34]

Canetti shared Kafka's admiration for Robert Walser. He read Walser's "short pieces, the most beautiful things in modern German literature" again and again. He was one of his favourite writers (letter to Idris Parry, May 12, 1972; see also letter to Idris Parry, September 30, 1968). He writes that "he [Walser] is becoming more and more important to me. I am convinced that without him Kafka would not have come into existence, and in any way I hope one day to explain he means as much to me as Kafka" (letter to Parry, March 23, 1977). In comparison to Walser, says Canetti, "all these slick and immensely successful German writers today make me sick" (letter to Parry of May 12, 1972).

Canetti also greatly respected Thomas Mann and Robert Musil. Canetti regarded Musil highly, probably even above Mann, but he was not entirely uncritical of both writers, as his comment from 1980 proves: "Das Glück Musils als Dichter, das, was ihn weit über Thomas Mann z.B. hebt, ist seine Freiheit von Musik. Doch ist es ein zweifelhaftes Glück, was bei ihm Musik ersetzt: Nietzsche. Immerhin ist es Nietzsche ohne Wagner" (*Aufz. 1973–84*, 62). He never met Mann, who had attempted to see him in Vienna, but was unable to get in touch with him, so Canetti told me. He also told me he was grateful to Mann for enabling him to escape from Austria. He was dejected when Mann understandably did not have the time to read the manuscript of *Die Blendung*, but he was overjoyed when Mann, after reading the published novel, wrote him a letter on November 14, 1935, in which he said that he was "aufrichtig angetan und freudig bewegt von seiner krausen Fülle, dem Debordierenden seiner Phantasie, der gewissen Großartigkeit seines Wurfes, seiner dichterischen Unerschrockenheit, seiner Traurigkeit und seinem Übermut." Canetti's joy was so great that he incautiously told Musil of Mann's letter when he saw him that very morning in a café. Before he did so, Musil had said to him most friendly and perceptive words about his novel. But Musil reacted sharply to Canetti's account because he thought of Mann as a "Großschriftsteller" who did not deserve the fame that he had won but had eluded Musil himself. Musil immediately left the café and did not speak to Canetti for a long time after that. Although he later on relented a little, their old relationship was never properly restored: Musil's feelings about Mann were far too strong for that. Canetti was convinced that *Der Mann ohne Eigenschaften,* which Musil was writing when he saw him frequently in Vienna, was bound to be a great work, even though it remained a fragment. But Musil was right in believing in his own stature, only barely recognized at the time, and Canetti admired not only Musil's steadfastness in continuing to write his great novel under adverse circumstances, but also the clarity, decisiveness, and precision of his writing, which he sought to emulate. He compared Musil most favourably with James Joyce and wrote about him with compassion:

> Alles an Joyce widerstrebt ihm, und wäre es nicht um der Blindheit willen, er würde ihn für zu wenig respektieren. [. . .]

> Aber warum dann Musil? War er weniger menschenfeindlich, weniger rücksichtslos? Weniger wegweisend?

Er ist in Not und Demütigung gestorben. [. . .]

Er ist nie wirklich gefeiert worden, als große Entdeckung, wie Joyce in Paris.

Für sehr wenige, zu Lebzeiten wurde er die >höchste Instanz<. Wenn er's wurde, gewahrte er's nicht. Er ist eine tragische Figur *und* einer der schärfsten Geister. Als Geist hatte er sich trotz seinem Schicksal allem zuwenden können. Er blieb bei seinem Unternehmen. Es war unvollendbar. Was mehr läßt sich sagen?[35]

Like Musil, Canetti was moved by moral concerns; yet the works of neither writer read like moral tracts. Nor were they meant to be. Canetti told me explicitly almost a year before his death that, of course, his writing had a moral core, but it was his aim to create works of imaginative literature that would enthrall his readers.

Canetti's main moral concern was, in the last resort, his fight against death, the great enemy of mankind. However powerful death was and however much evil it brought about, he felt mankind deserved to survive: Canetti believed in the value of his work because he succeeded in exposing evil and in fighting death. The following anecdote, which he related to me, confirms this conviction: in 1951 Jack Isaacs, who later became Professor of English literature at Queen Mary College, University of London and was a senior colleague of mine for some years, had just given a series of highly successful BBC Third Program talks that were first published in *The Listener* and then as a book called *An Assessment of Twentieth Century Literature*. These radio talks drew for the first time the attention of the English literary public to Musil and Canetti, both of whom were hitherto virtually unknown in England. Isaacs singled out both writers for high praise. He writes about Canetti with the sure touch of a fine literary critic:

> The finest book of this kind [a man fighting against, or experiencing, the power of evil, as, for instance, evidenced by Camus's *The Plague* (*La Peste*)], that I ever read is Elias Canetti's masterpiece *Auto da Fé*. [. . .] It has been hailed as one of the great novels of this century, and yet it is hardly known here. It is a book of giant stature, one of those books whose multitudinous intensity sweeps us along in a torrent like the first reading of the *Brothers Karamazov* and Joyce's *Ulysses,* leaving the richness of the detail to be savoured at leisure. Its theme is the disintegration of culture and the degeneration of man. In the treatment of evil, compared with Canetti, Francois Mauriac is a mere amateur and Graham Green as innocent as a babe newborn.[36]

Understandably, these words were bound to please Canetti. So he went to the Institute of Contemporary Arts on Dover Street, Mayfair, to listen to a public lecture by Isaacs, at that time at the height of his fame. Isaacs had a distinguished audience. T. S. Eliot sat in the first row. Isaacs was conscious of Eliot's august presence; Eliot had at that time been a dominant figure in English literary criticism for quite a few decades. In the course of his lecture Isaacs, not surprisingly, repeatedly paid tribute to Eliot. Suddenly, Canetti noticed unrest at the end of the lecture hall. Because Isaacs was a Jew, he assumed, mistakenly as he discovered later, that it was caused by anti-Semitism. After the lecture Canetti wandered down the street and entered a pub, where a friend of his, the literary critic Sir John Squire, saw him and asked him to join him and others, including Graham Greene, all of whom had caused the unrest because they were tired of Isaacs's continuous references to Eliot. When the pub closed Graham Greene invited all those present to join him for more drinks in his nearby flat. While they were talking and drinking there, someone mentioned Isaacs's book and asked Greene whether he owned a copy. Greene went looking for it and found it at the very bottom of some bookshelves, hidden behind a piece of furniture, where, according to Canetti, books are kept that one would rather not notice. The book was handed around. Understandably, Canetti looked for the above-mentioned passage in which Isaacs had written about him. The words referring to Greene and himself were underlined, and a line with an arrow pointed to the margin, where a picture of a gallows had been drawn. A very corpulent man (Isaacs was very corpulent, indeed) was hanging from it. Patently, Greene had not been pleased by Isaacs's words. Envy among writers is not unknown. Doubtless Canetti understood Greene's feelings because he himself had felt that his writings were not properly appreciated for most of his life. In the end, critics agreed with his self-assessment: thirty years later, in 1981, it was he, and not Greene, a much better-known and far more widely-read writer, who was awarded the Nobel prize.

In *Party im Blitz: Erinnerungen an England,* Canetti's posthumously published memoirs about his life in England, he writes about many contemporary English writers whom he met. However, his comments about most English writers are so cursory that only a few are worth relating, except that it should be mentioned that he was fascinated by three men whom he met: by Bertrand Russell (*PA,* 104–5) on account of his conversational gifts; and by William Empson (*PA,* 10–12) and Enoch Powell (*PA,* 117–21) because of their learning and independence of mind. When he was invited to literary parties, he found them permeated by courteous, detached conversation that lacked vitality.[37] No interest was ever shown in others and their work; he found only academics different since they were spurred on by inquisitiveness (*PA,* 69). However highly he thought of English literature of earlier centuries, in the twentieth century it had declined, he believed, and by 1945 that decline had become starkly obvious. Above all, he blamed T. S. Eliot for its impoverishment (*PA,* 8, 204). That charge is of course most controversial in view of the esteem accorded to Eliot in English and American criticism and elsewhere. He accuses Eliot of having exercised an undue influence as a director of the publishing house Faber & Faber and having been influenced by Hegelianism. Admittedly, Eliot wrote a Harvard Ph.D. dissertation on F. H. Bradley, a Hegelian philosopher whose writings are at least free from the obscurities of German Hegelianism. Yet Eliot's criticism, though not always just, is clear, subtle, and free from jargon. Canetti rightly indicts Eliot for being unfair to Dante, Goethe, Blake, and the English Romantic poets (*PA,* 204), though in later years Eliot revised his views on Goethe[38] and also came to appreciate the Romantic poets. In 1950, Eliot accorded to Dante the same status in Italian literature that Shakespeare enjoyed in English literature.[39]

Of course, Eliot's main concern was with poetry and drama and not with novels. Thus, he does not appear to have read *Die Blendung,* though, if he had done so, Canetti admits in mitigation that he would have appreciated it (*PA,* 8). But in Canetti's view Eliot's reputation is overrated; his minimal output of poetry did not deserve the Nobel Prize (*PA,* 8–9). He disapproves of Eliot's later dramas because he wrote them to make money (*PA,* 8–9). They were of course overestimated at the time, but are now no longer much esteemed. Canetti, who hardly knew Eliot, found him most detached, which he, frequently almost a recluse, apparently was, and implies surprise that he was a friend of Virginia Woolf. He condemns Eliot's conceit and calls him "abgrundschlecht" (*PA,* 204). But his own words, a tirade of contempt, if not hatred, convey his attitude far more forcefully than a summary could and are worth quoting in full:

> Ich denke an die großen Dichter seit Shakespeare, die noch in dieses 17. Jahrhundert hinüber reichen: ein Ben Jonson, John Donne, Milton, Dryden, und an den jungen Swift. Welche Prosa in der ersten Hälfte! Burton, Sir Thomas Browne, John Aubrey, nie werde ich genug von ihnen gelesen haben. Bunyan, George Fox, Hobbes, dieses allein ist schon unermüdlich. Wie kümmerlich ist Deutschland damit verglichen! Spanien mehr. Frankreich genug, aber die größte Literatur in diesem Jahrhundert ist die englische. Sie ist auch im nächsten mehr als die aller andern. Im 19. Jahrhundert immer noch. Ich hatte in England gelebt, als sein Geist zerfiel. Ich war Zeuge des Ruhmes eines Eliot. Wird man sich je genug dessen schämen? Ein Amerikaner bringt einen Franzosen mit aus Paris, der jung verschwand (Laforgue), träufelt seinen Lebensekel auf ihn, lebt wahrhaftig als Bankangestellter, während er alles Frühere taxiert, verringert, was immer mehr Atem hat als er, läßt sich von seinem verschwenderischen Landsmann, der die Größe und Spannung eines Verrückten hat, beschenken und rückt mit dem Ergebnis heraus: seiner Impotenz, die er dem ganzen Lande mitteilt, ergibt sich jeder Ordnung, die alt genug ist, sucht jeden Elan zu verhindern, ein Wüstling des Nichts, Ausläufer Hegels, Schänder Dantes

(in welche Höllenregion würde ihn dieser sperren?), dünnlippig, kalt-
herzig, frühalt, Blakes unwürdig wie Goethes und jeder Lava, erkaltet
bevor er heiß war, weder Katze noch Vogel noch Kröte, schon mehr
Maulwurf, gottgehorsam, nach England gesandt (als wäre ich zurück
nach Spanien), mit kritischen Spitzen und Zähnen, von einer manns-
tollen Frau gequält — seine einzige Entschuldigung —, so sehr gequält, daß ihm die "Blendung" eingegangen wäre, wenn er sich an sie
gewagt hätte, einen höflichen Ton in Bloomsbury, von der edlen Virginia [Woolf] erlaubt und eingeladen, *allen,* die ihn zu Recht gerügt haben, entronnen und schließlich durch einen Preis ausgezeichnet, den
nicht Virginia [Woolfe], nicht [Ezra] Pound, nicht Dylan [Thomas], den
niemand, der ihn verdient hätte — außer Yeats — bekam. (*PA,* 8–9)

Less controversially, Canetti wrote warmly about the refugee poet Franz
Baermann Steiner (*PA,* 123–32). He deeply regretted Steiner's early death,
thinking him a poet of rank, whose his anthropological work he greatly
valued. In 1972, at dinner with a common friend, the late Donald MacRae,
professor of sociology at the London School of Economics, I learned how
both men, who had known and greatly appreciated Steiner, much deplored
that his anthropological work in Oxford had not been properly recognized
for years, and regretted that recognition finally came only just before his death.

Canetti does write about Iris Murdoch's novels as well as her philosophical writings, neither of which he liked (*PA,* 173–89). He thought her
writings were permeated by philosophical twaddle bred in the Oxford school
of philosophy, which, not surprisingly, struck him as sterile (*PA,* 174, 204).
He found her work and that of her Oxford colleagues wanting in comparison with that of earlier English philosophers, especially those of the sixteenth
and seventeenth centuries. Murdoch's novels breathed for him an empty
Oxford atmosphere that he did not care for, although he liked Oxford itself.
For her as a woman he, who knew her intimately, appears to have felt pity
rather than liking, let alone love.

Canetti also appears to have respected earlier English historians. For instance, he spoke warmly about Clarendon's *History of the Rebellion.* He also
singled out *Brief Lives* by John Aubrey. However, he disliked most contemporary English historical writings, except that he found warm words for
Veronica Wedgwood, the distinguished historian of the seventeenth century
(*PA,* 121–23), who translated *Die Blendung* He was greatly impressed by
Arthur Waley's knowledge of and translations from the Chinese (*PA,* 104–
10) from which, as from Steiner's work, he learned much that he applied to
his work on *Masse und Macht* (1960), the major enterprise of the first two
decades of his life in England. Regrettably, he did not write about his enthusiasm for Wales and the Welsh language, aroused by a week's walking tour
through the principality with my friend and Manchester colleague Idris

Parry. He told me in Zurich that he fell in love with the language and even decided to learn five hundred words of Welsh.

Canetti felt that his work belonged to the great literary tradition. Great Writers had succeeded in conquering death because their work survived their physical life. He harked back to Homer, the first great European writer of stature. No lesser figure would do as his first literary ancestor. Thus, before starting to write *Die Blendung,* he read the whole *Odyssey* out loud to his wife because it gave him "den <u>Atem</u>" for his book, as he told Idris Parry in a letter dated February 21, 1963.

Thus, all great writers were his ancestors. Since he was convinced that his work would still be read after his physical death, he believed he would in this way survive, too. That is why the works of those writers that had survived mattered so much to him:

> [Literarische Unsterblichkeit] bedeutet, daß man da sein wird, wenn alle andern, die zur selben Zeit gelebt haben, nicht mehr da sind . . . Man tritt erst in hundert Jahren in die Schranken, wenn man selbst nicht mehr lebt und so nicht mehr töten kann. Es ist Werk gegen Werk, was sich dann mißt, und es ist zu spät etwas dazu zu tun . . . Ihre [der Dichter] Unsterblichkeit kommt den Lebenden zu gute: in dieser Verkehrung des Todesopfers fahren alle wohl. Das Überleben hat seinen Stachel verloren, und das Reich der Feindschaft ist zu Ende.[40, 41]

Notes

[1] See for instance Idris (F.) Parry, "Elias Canetti's Novel 'Die Blendung," *Essays in German Literature,* I, ed. F. Norman (London: University of London Institute of Germanic Studies, 1965), 145–66.

[2] Elias Canetti, *Das Gewissen der Worte: Essays* (Munich: Hanser, 1976), 9–22. Subsequent references to this work are cited in the text using the abbreviation *GW* and the page number.

[3] Ruprecht Slavko Baur, "Gespräch mit Elias Canetti. Zagreb, 15 May 1972," *Literatur und Kritik,* 65 (1972): 272–79. Here: 273.

[4] Baur, "Gespräch mit Elias Canetti. Zagreb, 15 May 1972," 277.

[5] Elias Canetti, *Das Augenspiel: Lebengeschichte 1921–1931* (Munich: Hanser, 1985), 319. Subsequent references to this work are cited in the text using the abbreviation *A* and the page number.

[6] Elias Canetti, *Das Geheimherz der Uhr: Aufzeichnungen 1973–1985* (Munich: Hanser, 1987), 89–91. Subsequent references to this work are cited in the text using the abbreviation *GU* and the page number.

[7] Rudolf Hartung, "Gespräch mit Elias Canetti," in *Elias Canetti: Ein Rezipient und sein Autor: Eine Dokumentation,* ed. Bernhard Albers (Aachen: Rimbaud, 1992), 94.

[8] Baur, "Gespräch mit Elias Canetti. Zagreb, 15 May 1972," 272.

[9] Hartung, "Gespräch mit Elias Canetti," *Elias Canetti: Ein Rezipient und sein Autor: Eine Dokumentation,* 89–90.

[10] See Christine Meyer, "Don Quichotte dans l'Auto-da-fé," 85–97, *Ein Dichter braucht Ahnen: Elias Canetti und die europäische Tradition, Jahrbuch für Internationale Germanistik* 44, ed. Gerald Stieg and Jean-Marie Valentin. Reihe A, Kongreßberichte Akten des Pariser Symposiums/Actes du colloque de Paris. (Bern etc.: Lang, 1997). This book contains other useful essays on Canetti's attitude to some of other authors such as: Françoise Kenk, "Goethe, le premier ancêtre," 123–43; Heide Helwig, "Canetti und Nietzsche," 145–62; Walerij Susman, "Canetti und Kafka," 163–71; Adrian Stevens, "Aufzcichnungen, Menschen und Fragmente. Zur Poetik der Charakterdarstellung bei Canetti, Aubrey und La Bruyére," 207–24; Peter von Matt, "Canetti und Hebbel," 253–63; Gerald Stieg, "Die Fackel und die Sonne. Karl Kraus in Elias Canettis Autobiographie," 267–81. Some other most interesting essays on authors, such as Aristophanes, Joubert, La Bruyére, Pascal, and Theophrastes, to whom Canetti was, to some extent or other, indebted, are also found in this volume. Lack of space regrettably prevents me from listing the authors, titles, and page numbers of these essays.

[11] I owe this piece of information and some of the following remarks to the thorough research recorded in the useful article by Beatrix Kampel, "Ein Dichter braucht Ahnen. Canettis Begegnungen mit Literatur und Literaten im Spiegel seiner Autobiographie," in *Experte der Macht,* ed. Kurt Bartsch and Gerhard Melzer (Graz: Droschl, 1985), 102–15.

[12] Elias Canetti, *Die Provinz des Menschen: Aufzeichnungen 1942–1972* (Munich: Hanser, 1973), 150–51. Subsequent references to this work are cited in the text using the abbreviation *PM* and the page number.

[13] Hans Reiss, ed., *Kant: Political Writings,* trans. H. B. Nisbet. Cambridge Texts in the History of Political Thought (Cambridge: Cambridge UP, 2nd enlarged ed. 1991), 84.

[14] Hartung, "Gespräch mit Elias Canetti," in *Elias Canetti: Ein Rezipient und sein Autor: Eine Dokumentation,* 99.

[15] Elias Canetti, *Die gerettete Zunge: Geschichte einer Jugend* (Munich: Hanser, 1977), 74. Subsequent references to this work are cited in the text using the abbreviation *GZ* and the page number.

[16] Baur, "Gespräch mit Elias Canetti. Zagreb, 15 May 1972," 274.

[17] See Barbara Bauer, "'Unter dem Eindruck der Ereignisse in Deutschland,' Ideologiekritik und Sprachkritik in Elias Canettis *Komödie der Eitelkeit,*" in *Canetti als Leser,* ed. Gerhard Neumann (Freiburg im Breisgau: Rombach, 1996), 77–111. Elias Canetti, *Komödie der Eitelkeit* (Munich: Weismann, 1950).

[18] Elias Canetti, *Die Fliegenpein: Aufzeichnungen* (Munich: Hanser, 1992), 51–52.

[19] Gerald Stieg, "Questions à Elias Canetti" ("Homage à Canetti"), *Austriaca* 6/11 (1950): 24.

[20] Raphael Sorin, "Elias Canetti l'irréducibe," *Le Monde,* June 13, 1980, a passage from an interview that is quoted by Christine Meyer, "La Vie de Henry Brulard comme modèle pour l'autobiographie de Canetti," *Austriaca* 16 (1991): 98. I am much indebted to this fine article.

[21] Elias Canetti, *Die Fackel im Ohr: Lebengeschichte 1921–1931* (Munich: Hanser, 1980), 407. Subsequent references to this work are cited in the text using the abbreviation *FO* and the page number.

[22] Ortrun Huber, ed., *Wortmasken: Texte zu Leben und Werk von Elias Canetti* (Munich: Hanser, 1995), 140–42.

[23] Huber, *Wortmasken: Texte zu Leben und Werk von Elias Canetti*, 140.

[24] Ibid.

[25] Elias Canetti, *Aufzeichnungen 1973–1984* (Munich: Hanser, 1999), 58. Subsequent references to this work are cited in the text using the abbreviation *Aufz. 1973–84* and the page number.

[26] See Dieter Lamping, "'Zehn Minuten Lichtenberg.' Canetti als Leser anderer Aphoristiker," in *Canetti als Leser,* ed. Gerhard Neumann (Freiburg im Breisgau: Rombach, 1996), 113–25.

[27] "J'ai recherché une langue qui soit aussi limpide que celle de Lichtenberg," Gerald Stieg, "Questions à Elias Canetti," 25.

[28] Huber, *Wortmasken: Texte zu Leben und Werk von Elias Canetti*, 143–44.

[29] Stieg, "Questions à Elias Canetti," 25.

[30] Stieg, "Questions à Elias Canetti," 29. Manfred Durzak and Elias Canetti, "Akustische Maske und Maskensprung. Materialien zu einer Theorie des Dramas. Ein Gespräch," in Manfred Durzak, ed., *Interpretationen zu Elias Canetti*, LWG Interpretationen 63 (Stuttgart: Klett, 1983), 17–30. Here: 18–19. For Canetti's remarks on Nestroy's impact on his work, see the very informative article by Gerald Stieg, "Canetti and Nestroy," *Nestroyana: Blätter der Internationalen Nestroy-Gesellschaft* 20/1–2 (2000): 51–64.

[31] See Idris Parry, "Attitudes to Power. Canetti, Kafka, Crowds and Paranoia," *Times Literary Supplement* 15/1 (1971): 67–68; also as: "Haltungen gegenüber der Macht: Canetti, Kafka, Massen und Paranoia" in *Canetti Lesen: Erfahrungen mit seinen Büchern,* ed. Herbert G. Göpfert (Munich: Hanser, 1975), 69–77, for a perceptive account of Canetti's analysis of power in his whole work, especially with reference to Kafka.

[32] Idris Parry, "Canetti on Kafka," *PN Review,* 31 (1983): 13–17. Here: 16.

[33] Ibid.

[34] Ibid., 15.

[35] Elias Canetti, *Aufzeichnungen 1992–1993* (Munich: Hanser, 1996), 32.

[36] Jack Isaacs, *An Assessment of Twentieth-Century Literature: Six Lectures Delivered in the B.B.C. Third Programme* (London: Martin Secker & Warburg, 1951), 60–61.

[37] Elias Canetti, *Party im Blitz: Erinnerungen an England* (Munich: Hanser, 2003), 68–69, 123–25. Subsequent references to this work are cited in the text using the abbreviation *PA* and the page number.

[38] Eliot's attitude to Goethe is rather complex. It is well analysed by Nicolas Boyle in his thoughtful essay "T. S. Eliot and Goethe," *London German Studies* II (1983): 50–75, where some other scholars' writings on T. S. Eliot and Goethe are also cited.

[39] T. S. Eliot, "Dante," in *Selected Prose,* ed. by John Hayward (Harmondsworth: Middlesex, 1953), 99–101.

[40] Elias Canetti, *Masse und Macht* (Hamburg: Claassen, 1960), 318–19.

[41] My thanks are due to Raymond Chapman, John Hibberd, and Dagmar C. G. Lorenz, editor of the *Canetti Companion,* for their advice; to Idris Parry for providing me with extracts from Canetti's letters to him; to Elisabeth Mayer and Andrea Rauter of the Austrian Cultural Forum, London, for their help in obtaining a copy of the Canetti number of *Austriaca;* and to Kristian Wachinger for sending me a proof copy of *Party im Blitz* as well as providing me with valuable information. Finally, I have to thank Canetti's daughter Johanna Canetti for permission to quote from and refer to Canetti's unpublished letters.

Canetti and the Question of Genre

Julian Preece

> *Ich nehme jede der Gattungen, in denen*
> *ich mich versuche, sehr ernst und wünsche*
> *mir, etwas zustande zu bringen, was so*
> *vorher noch nicht da war.*
> — Elias Canetti[1]

WHEN ELIAS CANETTI DIED in 1994 at the age of eighty-nine he left behind one novel, completed more than sixty years earlier at the age of twenty-six; three plays; several books of "Aufzeichnungen" — mixtures of notes, reminiscences, mini-essays, and aphorisms that cover more than fifty years from 1942 — an account of a journey to Marrakesh he made at the age of forty-nine but published thirteen years later; a volume of essays written largely in his sixties; a book of character portraits published shortly before he turned seventy; and a three-volume autobiography, the ripe product of his old age. Somewhere in between is the work of his middle years, which he began at twenty, which absorbed him completely from thirty, and which he published when he was fifty-five, *Masse und Macht* (1960), "the only masterpiece of crowd theory," according to one historian of writing on the crowd.[2] In an interview from 1965, Canetti mentions another novel, two more plays, and, of course, the second volume of *Masse und Macht*, long and often heralded, which he still intended to publish as late as 1972.[3] These are all presumably found in his "Nachlaß," along with his diaries, which promise to be voluminous.

We might divide Canetti's long creative life into three phases, each one associated with a big book. The first covers the 1930s and includes the first two plays, *Die Komödie der Eitelkeit* (1934) and *Hochzeit* (1931) and the novel *Die Blendung* (1935); the second extends to *Masse und Macht*, during which he wrote little else and published less — *Die Befristeten* (1952) and *Fritz Wotruba* (1955)[4] are his only publications, although he did begin writing Aufzeichnungen and also completed the account of his Moroccan journey.[5] All the rest belongs to the third phase, when he discovered what is arguably his greatest subject — himself. For, as he wrote in "Dialog mit dem grausamen Partner": "Wer wirklich alles wissen will, lernt am besten an sich."[6] In this essay on diaries he distinguishes between "Merkbücher," where he notes down for his own benefit on what particular day what particular books or people made an impact on him, "Aufzeichnungen," of which we only know selections, and "Tagebücher," which, like the "Merkbücher," "gehen niemand etwas an" (*GW, 59*).

Other essays in *Das Gewissen der Worte* (1976) form the basis of chapters in *Die Fackel im Ohr* (1981) and *Das Augenspiel* (1985) (those on Broch, Kraus, Büchner, and *Die Blendung*). *Die Stimmen von Marrakesch* (1967) comprises — to paraphrase Goethe — several more fragments in his greater autobiographical "confession," and the latter volumes of "Aufzeichnungen" are more personal than those collected in *Die Provinz des Menschen.*[7] He writes of *Der Ohrenzeuge* (1974) that the fifty characters are more autobiographical sketches than sketches for novel characters:[8] "So reich ist man zusammengesetzt und so sähe man jeweils aus, wenn ein einziges dieser Elemente, aus denen man besteht, konsequent auf die Spitze getrieben wurde."[9] The three volumes of autobiography in turn teem with portraits of people the author has encountered.

Indeed, it would be a revealing exercise to explore how many figures in his life match up with types in *Der Ohrenzeuge*. Many reflect, after all, an aspect of Canetti, who grows through interaction with them. The variety of narrative, discursive, and dramatic genres he tried out make Canetti's position in twentieth-century German writing quite unique. Perhaps Kafka is the only other writer of German to essay so many different forms, which is surely one reason Canetti so admired him. Kafka, according to Canetti, "ist mit nichts zu Ende, es ist dasselbe, was ihn vom Anfang bis zum Schluß beunruhigt. Er kehrt es immer wieder um, er umschreibt es, er begeht es mit anderen Schritten" (*GW, 69*) — words Canetti would surely like to hear applied to his own work. As a result we can read most of Canetti's books in the terms of most of the others; overlaps in theme, methodology, style, and fields of metaphor make the whole into a coherent oeuvre. One could argue, for instance, that the first-person narrator of the autobiography — the heroized, transmogrified Elias Canetti himself — is a reincarnation of *Die Blendung*'s intellectually myopic hero, Peter Kien. Canetti challenges us to consider him in this light in the chapter "Simsons Blendung" from *Die Fackel im Ohr* (*FO*, 109–14), which in turn invites an autobiographical reading of the novel.

Canetti planned for the long term and wrote for posterity. In 1965, he explained to Horst Bienek why he had published relatively little at that point:

> Ich hatte mir schon vorgenommen, nie ein Buch zu veröffentlichen, das nicht Anspruch auf Bestand hat . . . Ich möchte meine Leser ernst nehmen. Mein größter Wunsch wäre es, noch in hundert Jahren gelesen zu werden. (*DgZ*, 103)

He wrote of and for his time, as all true writers must (which meant in his case the era that ended with the defeat of Hitler), but as a writer he could appear out of his time. In *Masse und Macht* he might possibly have penetrated deeper into the psyche of German totalitarianism than any other critic or historian, but he spends more time on the Australian Aborigines and the Bushmen of the Kalahari than he does on the Nazis. This mammoth work of typology is the most difficult to classify generically and — for that reason — has not had the wider acclaim, or popular success, enjoyed by most of Canetti's other books. His approach to the causes of the twentieth-century catastrophe is quite at odds with that adopted by any other writer on the subject, making *Masse und Macht* truly *sui generis,* a work that establishes its own genre. For related reasons, *Die Blendung* is the most peculiar major novel in the twentieth-century German canon, owing perhaps its greatest debt to Karl Kraus, who wrote no novels. In his presentation of everyday speech, Canetti is closer to the plays of Ödon von Horváth than to the novels of any of his contemporaries. There is also something of the modernist stage set about the settings for most of the episodes. He holds locations, usually interiors, for the whole length of an action; both the positioning of furniture and the layout of rooms in Kien's flat are highly significant.

Die Blendung's plot and central character recall *Don Quixote* — and indeed it is populated by a series of inverted Don Quixotes —; its grotesques are cousins to Gogol's satirical creatures, but in its desolate imagery of human abandonment it is quintessentially modernist. Elsewhere Canetti is perhaps more a revivalist. The "Aufzeichnungen" (the lack of an English term is significant) breathe new life into modes of writing more practiced among the *moralistes* of seventeenth-century France. With *Der Ohrenzeuge* he returned to a tradition of prose character portraits that had blossomed in the last decades of *le grand siècle* at the court of Louis XIV. It would be easy to call the book an anachronism; apart from a handful of references to modern technology and modern forms of travel, there appears little that attaches it to the late twentieth century. Until the autobiography, *Die Stimmen von Marrakesch* was possibly his most conventional book, but while fulfilling some of the requirements of the travel genre he could not help calling its assumptions into question at every turn. In his literary criticism it goes without saying that he pays no attention to academic trends. As he explains with respect to Büchner and Kafka, he founds his approach to the elucidation of literary texts in his own emotional and intellectual experience of reading them. This is biographical criticism with a difference because the biography of the critic, the moment in his life when he reads the texts in question, is the deciding criterion. The same applies to both seeing pictures and meeting people. Reading the works of other writers and writing his own works are linked through Canetti's all-encompassing notion of transforma-

tion. His autobiography is then the account of his own multifarious transformations. One thing that he means by transformation is seeing the world
from other points of view: reading is one way of doing this; writing in different genres is another. Canetti hates systems because they are complete,
ideologies because they are pre-formed, and clichés because they indicate
borrowed thinking. At best, he wants to say something new, in a new way,
in each sentence he writes.

In all his writings except *Masse und Macht,* Canetti built on traditions
and extended them. What he wanted to be his life's work, however, stands
alone. It can hardly count as a work of anthropology because he undertook
no research in the field, however extensively he quotes at times from anthropological sources. It is not a work of history as so much of his material is
secondhand, and he crisscrosses centuries and continents in an apparently
ahistorical or at least anti-historical manner. There is occasionally a sense of
immediacy when, writing suddenly in the first person, he reveals that he is
in pursuit of the secret of the twentieth-century catastrophe. In the epilogue
he announces that the era of what he has defined as "Klagereligionen" has
come to an end, but such insights are rare. Historians and anthropologists
have seldom taken note of the book; standard works on Hitler and the Third
Reich rarely include Canetti's name in their bibliographies, and it is rarer still
that their authors engage with its contents.

One exception is J. S. McClelland, who makes it clear that Canetti's apparent failure to deal with other writers on the subject or to write in such a
form as to acknowledge their contributions is, from the point of view of
genre, no failure at all. Nowhere is Canetti more eccentric than in *Masse und
Macht,* but his eccentricity is purposeful because he is writing against the
grain of all previous writing on the crowd. That he supplies a typology of
crowds without referring to crowd leaders is highly significant, for instance.
McClelland does not have to refer to the chapter titled "Die Rechtfertigung" in *Die Fackel im Ohr* to realize that Canetti knows Freud and Le Bon
(*FO,* 136–46).[10] Canetti's non-engagement with their ideas is part of his
elaborate tease, as well as a way of establishing the freshness and originality
of his own approach.

Masse und Macht is difficult to read not because the concepts are difficult, though sometimes they are, and the sentences resist easy assimilation,
but because the work is still, more than forty years later, so new, so different.
It is hardly surprising that themes and motifs from *Masse und Macht* should
feature in the autobiography, which, like everything else he wrote, stands in
its shadow. The personal nature of the subject matter is thereby underlined.
The organization of the book, the imaginative jumps are Canetti's own, the
pursuit of his two twin subjects and the metaphors and keywords — call
them what you will — that encircle them in all their possible manifestations
requires no less patience in the reader as it did dedication in the author. The

architecture of *Masse und Macht* is not immediately significant, but it can be dipped into, insights can suddenly grab the reader.

When considering where *Die Blendung* belongs, we can do worse than refer to Canetti's own essay on it, most of which he reproduced in *Die Fackel im Ohr*. He admits a debt to Stendhal but only on account of stylistic clarity, the uncluttered manner of his writing. The Renaissance painter Grünewald was another inspiration but only because he devoted four years to completing the Isenheimer Altar.[11] It is otherwise the uniqueness of his own achievement that Canetti wants his readers to appreciate. Uniqueness is a useful term to set out with and can be outlined through comparison. Canetti read Thomas Mann's *Der Zauberberg* and sent his finished manuscript of *Die Blendung* to Mann, who returned it unread, although he reacted positively to its publication four years later.

The discussion between Peter and Georges Kien in Canetti's penultimate chapter, "Listenreicher Odysseus" (*Blendung*, 464–98), recalls the great dialogues between Naphta and Settembrini. Yet while Mann's theme, which Canetti takes to be death, made a great impression on him, he held "Trotzdem [. . .] starke Einwände gegen seine Art von Roman."[12] He had not read, however, either Broch's *Die Schlafwandler* or Musil's *Der Mann ohne Eigenschaften* because they had yet to be published, though he met both authors shortly after finishing his own novel.[13] In *Das Augenspiel* he records Musil's resentment of what he regarded as Broch's inferior achievement, which he — Musil — had inspired (*A*, 166), which brings both novels close to Canetti's own. All three take the disintegration of Habsburg culture as their subject, all three expand the novel form to do so, but Canetti, very much the others' junior and the pioneer, writes what one could call the purest novel because of its plot and sub-plots, structure and characterization, leitmotifs, imagery, and novelistic devices, such as surprise and suspense, and absence of essayistic digression. Canetti addresses his theme through imagery and metaphor.

While *Der Mann ohne Eigenschaften* follows the course of a very specific year in Austrian and European contemporary history, the last year of peace under the Habsburgs, 1913–14, and preparations for Emperor Franz Josef's Diamond Jubilee in 1916 are one major narrative strand, *Der Zauberberg* ends with a vision of Hans Castorp stumbling through the trenches on the Western Front.[14] Broch in each of his three volumes concentrates on an epoch he defines exactly. Canetti, however — like Kafka — mentions no dates. One of the nearest clues to the date and indeed the location is to be found in an exchange between the porter and the chambermaid in one of the hotels Kien stays in after leaving Therese. His favor having been bought by Kien, who has just given him an outrageously generous tip, the porter wants to impress on the chambermaid the importance of their guest by telling her: "Besitzer der Hofbibliothek ist er!" Yet he has made up this "fact" to impress her, and, like all the other characters in the novel, immediately forgets that he has invented something before re-interpreting reality in the light of his invention: "er begriff, *wie* fein der Herr oben sein müsse, weil er "Hof" auf dem Meldezettel weggelassen hatte." The absence of evidence thus becomes evidence. The chambermaid, more astute than he expected, challenges him:

> "Es gibt doch eh keinen Hof."

> "'Aber die Hofbibliothek gibt's! So was Dummes! Glauben S', die Leut' haben die Bücher aufgefressen!?'" (*Blendung*, 182)

We must deduce that there *has* been a court and a court library, but the issue is of no interest to Kien. As for designation of place, apart from the speech of the less educated figures only incidental details tell us we must be in Vienna. Paris is named, however, as are England, America, and Jews, the latter repeatedly with respect to the dwarf hunchback, Fischerle. His last hours, his plan to emigrate to the United States, the condescension he encounters in buying a book to teach himself English, and his awful death are not the only intensely moving episodes in the novel. His life and fate are something of an allegory of Jewish history.[15]

It is sometimes claimed that it is impossible for a reader to identify with Canetti's collection of grotesque monomaniacs (the same has been said too of the obsessives in Günter Grass's *Die Blechtrommel*),[16] which would make *Die Blendung* a very strange novel indeed. It is at moments where pity is called for — and not given by any of the novel characters — that Canetti's diagnosis of what is wrong with his world is most plangent. Kien's retreat to the bathroom where he quietly sobs after his unsuccessful attempt to seduce his bride on his wedding night shows us, in case we had forgotten, that Canetti is depicting people and not caricatures. In this very cerebral novel, bodies would appear to take second place and it is easy to overlook them. But Kien's height and build are mentioned repeatedly; Fischerle's size and disability determine his character. Kien's increasing thinness after leaving his flat at the end of the first book is a sign of his self-destructiveness, his meals and his neglect of them a leitmotif. When he is undressed in the police station in the chapter "Privateigentum" (*Blendung*, 321–53), his fragile physicality alarms the undressing officers and both underlines his objectified status while undermining it by revealing his humanity. Both the police officers and Therese see in him what they want to see, a common thief from the underclass or the murderer of his first wife, just as Kien is convinced that the Therese he sees is a hallucination because the Therese he married is dead. Bodies are often assumed to be corpses in this novel. Both Kien and Therese believe the other to be dead and treat the still living body as if it were a corpse.

Although there are no dates, we are told repeatedly that Peter Kien is forty years old and that Therese is fifty-six, though she believes herself to appear — and thus to be — ten years Kien's junior. In terms of generic affiliation these symbolic ages may be significant. *Die Blendung* is about marriage and courtship, marital strife, infidelity, and thoughts of conjugal murder. In novels the age of thirty is the time when men should turn their thoughts to marrying and settling down to family life. Kien has missed out, something is not right. He has only books to guide him and his judgements of reality are misjudgements.

Die Blendung begins *in medias res*, on what turns out to be a turning point in Kien's life. After the opening dialogue between Kien and the young boy interested in reading some of his books, there follows an assured unfurling of Kien's circumstances as the narrative eye accompanies him back to his flat. The first chapter takes as long to read as it does to happen, a narrative technique Erich Auerbach associated with "stream of consciousness," but Canetti eschews the methods of a Woolf, Joyce, or Schnitzler.[17] Instead he uses narrative focalization to shift his perspective and to achieve different effects. When a passerby asks Kien the way to the Mutstraße, the narrative situation replicates Kien's own perception of the incident — but he does not let on that they were standing in the Mutstraße and that the passerby noticed this after a while and grew more angry because of his foolishness, not because of Kien's refusal to answer. He delays telling us this until he is back in his flat and writes up the incident. Kien's perception is the source of much comedy. There is often no explanation and no reflection on what is happening. Information is passed on when it crops up and not before because the individual characters can only see the portion of the world that they want to see. Canetti explains in his essay on *Die Blendung* that this came about after he realized "daß die Welt nicht mehr so darzustellen war wie in früheren Romanen' because "die Welt war *zerfallen*, und nur wenn man den Mut hatte, sie in ihrer Zerfallenheit zu zeigen, war es noch möglich, eine wahrhafte Vorstellung von ihr zu geben" (*GW*, 249). He understands his method to be realist.

Die Stimmen von Marrakesch is a minor work and possibly a minor masterpiece that has enjoyed renewed attention since the renaissance in travel writing in the 1980s. Because travel is an autobiographical genre, Canetti begins with a sentence in the first person: "Dreimal kam ich mit Kamelen in Berührung und es endete jedesmal auf tragische Weise," which promises a mock-heroic Oriental anecdote (*Marrakesch*, 7). He does not disappoint, and in the first two sections concentrates on two conventional points of interest for Western travelers to Arab lands: after "Begegnung mit Kamelen" (*Marrakesch*, 7–16) comes "Die Suks" (*Marrakesch*, 16–21) — which still might leave one wondering why he did not take himself to the steam baths to produce "Die Hamams" — a shyness of bodies perhaps. If he does not tell us conventional details about how he got there, how long he stayed, why he went or where he went afterwards, about who he traveled with and who he left behind, his "ich" is nevertheless at the center of his text. It is Canetti's own gaze, his relationship with the objects of his gaze, the people he encounters, whom he can only understand if they have learnt French, the language of the colonial power, which concern him. The third of the fourteen titled sections, "Die Rufe der Blinden" (*Marrakesch*, 21–25), then begins with a page of methodological rumination where he realizes the limits language can impose on perception. He turns his inability to understand Maghrebian Arabic or any of the Berber languages spoken in the shadow of the Atlas Mountains into an advantage and claims he had deliberately not read up on Morocco before leaving London. He wants to perceive what he encounters in a purer, more original way than language — the bearer of ideologies, prejudices, and preconceptions — allows: "nichts durch unzulängliches und künstliches Wissen abschwächen" (*Marrakesch*, 22).

This tells us something too about genre and Canetti's repeated failure to meet genre expectations; he places image over explanation, metaphor over narrative. In *Das Augenspiel* he recalls that he first practiced listening to sounds he could not understand when he visited Prague in May 1937, to the bafflement of his host, H. G. Adler. Listening to how people speak had become a preoccupation of the original "ear-witness" and collector of "acoustic masks" years earlier in Vienna ("Hudba. Bauern tanzend," *A*, 289–99).

Canetti wants his perception to be new and places himself as the traveler-perceiver at the center of his short travelogue. In "Der Speichel des Marabu" (*Marrakesch*, 25–30) he realizes after gazing uncomprehendingly on what for him is a mysterious sight, but for his hosts something they might see every day, that "Das erstaunliche Geschöpf war ich, der ich so lange nicht begriff" (*Marrakesch*, 28). A few pages later he notices that he is attracting more attention from passersby than the object of his curiosity, an unveiled woman standing behind a barred first-story window emitting strange noises that sound to him like terms of endearment (*Marrakesch*, 35–36). Moroccan women, either veiled or hidden altogether, fascinate him, but the women, like the blind men, like the battered donkey that suddenly surprises him with evidence of its vitality, do not answer his gaze.

It is not on account of revelation or reflection that *Die Stimmen von Marrakesch* belongs to Canetti's autobiographical corpus. Like his other work, it can be read too in terms of categories and metaphors that he elaborates on in *Masse und Macht*. In the travelogue the handful of details he reveals about himself and his background all concern his identity. He mentions that he has lived among the English for fifteen years and become in certain respects like them, and also that he had returned to Vienna in the previous year for the first time since the war (*Marrakesch*, 22). It emerges also that he is Jewish and that his encounter with the Sephardic community in the Jewish quarter of Marrakesh, which takes up the two longest sections in the middle of the book, is a journey back to his roots.[18] This complicates his own status: he is outsider as ex-insider. He does not know the prayers or rituals of worship and would be embarrassed if led into circumstances where he would be expected to participate in them. Embarrassment is a recurrent emotion. He is embarrassed when a young Moroccan asks him for help or wants to be his guide; ill at ease when trying to get a glimpse of the interior of a Jewish house. He relies on being able to say that he is working with some filmmakers to justify his presence in the city at all, which makes us feel he is there under false pretenses. The film project might be the reason he came to the city, but it is not the reason he stayed.

The year 1954, when Canetti traveled to Morocco, is the year of Dien Ben Phu, when the French lost their grip on Indo-China, and the year when the war of liberation in Algeria began. By 1967, when he published *Die Stimmen von Marrakesch*, the French had been driven out of the Magrheb altogether, the United States was entrenched in a hopeless neo-colonialist war in Vietnam. Other contemporary German writing on countries of the Third World is devoted to liberation struggles.[19]

As in *Die Blendung* and *Masse und Macht*, Canetti gives us no history although he writes primarily about a moment in history. Yet in the section "Die Verleumdung" (*Marrakesch*, 84–90) he tells us all we need to know about colonial attitudes — and all the more effectively for not calling them such. In this section he learns from a French restaurant owner that the little Moroccan children who throng around him every day begging for money and whose theatrical face pulling he admires are available to Westerners for sex. The source of this information is not reliable and may well be trying turn Canetti against the local urchins whose hungry expressions the restaurateur fears might ruin the appetites of his wealthy diners. In other words make them embarrassed that they can eat so well while children all around them have so little. His Rabelaisian reminiscence of helping to fool a prostitute out of her fee for sleeping with one of his friends compounds Canetti's distaste for the French custom of referring to all Moroccan women as *fatma*, which deprives them, among other things, of their individuality, their uniqueness. The man awakens nothing but revulsion in Canetti, who ends the section with a passage of regulated rage that condemns the Frenchman in terms familiar from *Masse und Macht:*

> Er, der mit solcher Verachtung für [die Kinder] begonnen hatte, hatte sich in kürzester Zeit selber verächtlich gemacht. Ob er sie verleumdete oder ob er die Wahrheit über sie sprach, was immer die Bettelkinder taten, er stand nun tief unter ihnen und ich wünschte mir, daß es doch eine Art der Strafe gäbe, wo er auf *ihre* Fürsprache angewiesen wäre. (*Marrakesch*, 89–90)

Nowhere is Canetti a sterner moralist than when he sees abuses of power.

The 1960s and 1970s are Canetti's most varied decades. True, he does not return to writing either novels or plays, and he had begun writing the "Aufzeichnungen" while working on *Masse und Macht*. It is true also that *Die Stimmen von Marrakesch* came about after a visit in 1954, and it would seem we have little reason to doubt that he wrote down his impressions straight away. What became the first and final sections appeared in their final form in a volume edited by Erich Fried in 1962, which, we now know, was planned and selected by Veza Canetti to enhance her husband's reputation in the wake of *Masse und Macht*.[20] *Der Ohrenzeuge* is new, however, and is one of his most intriguing publications. The absence of a first-person narrative voice makes it unique among the books published after 1960. But it belongs unmistakably to a tradition of "character portraits," a tradition that began in antiquity with Theophrastus but had been mostly dormant since La Bruyére in the age of French classicism. Canetti wrote very deliberately within this generic tradition, which made the book stand out on publication in 1974.[21] La Bruyére had painted a portrait of his age, the morals at the Court of Louis XIV, a satire on pretensions and pretentiousness that mocks human folly. Canetti is satirical too, but he is highly eccentric in his choice of types, each with a made-up name. Each is greatly exaggerated: we are unlikely in reality to find an individual who resembles his portrait, but there might be a little of many portraits in each of us. He had followed a similar principle in his typology of crowds in *Masse und Macht*. No single crowd exactly corresponds to a single type, but most have elements of several. We can recognize ourselves or people we know in *Der Ohrenzeuge*, but we perhaps have not registered the behavior he portrays until we read the portrait. There then follows a moment of recognition. This is surely why he invents new types that he designates with strange neologisms. *Der Ohrenzeuge* too can be read in terms of *Masse und Macht*.[22]

Two of Canetti's three major works are essentially essayistic. Readers can dip into *Masse und Macht* to pick out discrete chapters that make sense out of context; all three volumes of the autobiography contain episodic chapters, not only those on the famous figures in his life that call out for anthologization. All of these chapters have a place in his overarching narrative; it is of immense importance that he notes at what point in his life he had certain experiences and encounters because everything stands in a dynamic relation with everything else. But the episodes or narrative fragments have an independent life of their own. *Das Gewissen der Worte* is a structured volume too and not just a compilation. There are several pieces he has missed out: where is his introduction to Fritz Wotruba or his commentary on Alfred Hrdlicka's illustrations to *Masse und Macht*?[23] There are thematic links with his literary works and also an impression of what they might have looked like boiled down to their essentials or, in the case of "Hitler, nach Speer," if the ideas had been applied and explained by the author. If you do not have the strength to read *Masse und Macht*, then read "Hitler, nach Speer," ostensibly a review of Speer's memoirs (*GW*, 175–204). It stands comparison with Mann's "Bruder Hitler" or anything written on Hitler by Brecht, but it is mere prose after the poetry of the major work.

Of all the genres Canetti worked in, the essays as essays have received least attention, apparently transparent, purely informative or expository.[24] Perhaps it is easiest to begin by saying what the essays are not: journalism. As the last of the gentleman scholars, Canetti, though far from wealthy, chose not to make a living turning out weekly reviews. He explains their autobiographical basis by saying that they are "wie eine Rechenschaft über die geistigen Stationen meines ganzen erwachsenen Lebens" (*GW*, 9). A comparison of his comments on Brecht in the essay on his first novel with the portrait he paints in *Die Fackel im Ohr* show one basic distinction between memoir and autobiography: in autobiography the empirical facts of recollected history make way for the poetic truth of fiction. The fictionalized Brecht is a vain, self-seeking hypocrite whose posturing and love of material things repel the young Canetti, who contrasts his attitudes with those of the modest and open Isaac Babel. In the essay, which appeared twelve years before *Die Fackel im Ohr*, Canetti appears in retrospect to sympathize with Brecht, "der meine Naivität sofort erkannte und dem meine 'hohe Gesinnung' begreiflicheweise auf die Nerven ging." He recognizes that Brecht tried to provoke him with his cynical comments while Babel liked him for his innocence (*FO*, 247). There is more self-knowledge in the essay because there is not, contrary perhaps to first impressions, a controlling reflective voice in the autobiography that looks back at Canetti's succession of past selves from a fixed point in the narrative present. He gives barely a hint, for instance, on what happened to him after 1937 when he breaks off his narrative.

Canetti wrote what became the centerpiece of *Das Gewissen der Worte*, "Der andere Prozess: Kafkas Briefe an Felice," his most substantial piece of literary criticism, as a review essay that appeared in two parts in *Die Neue Rundschau* (1968). He explains that he was moved to write it because of the impact the letters had made on him, "wie ich sie seit Jahren bei keinem literarischen Werk erlebt habe" (*GW*, 78). It is a phenomenal experience, an unexpected encounter with something new, which immediately becomes a part of him and he writes in order to rationalize his reaction. From the autobiography we know of the effects that new reading experiences, like new people, can have on him — there is a right moment for a new author. But the autobiography stops shortly after he reaches thirty, at which age he might feel he has got somewhere. For new books to have such effects on someone well into his sixties is remarkable. That is the starting point of his comments: "Ich für mich kann nur sagen . . ." (*GW*, 79).

It is power, Kafka's attempt to control Felice, but also his self-abasement in his wish "sich der Macht in jeder Form zu entziehen" (*GW*, 137), which interests Canetti. Contrary to the view of Canetti as incorrigible chauvinist, he is alert to Kafka's manipulativeness and shows sympathy for Felice. His scholarly eye notes the recurrence of a statement on his inner personality that he first wrote in the mammoth penultimate letter to Felice: "Der ist ihm gut gelungen, er gehört in die Literatur; er gefällt ihm so gut, daß er ihn für einen Brief an Max Brod wortwörtlich abschreibt, und dann noch einmal wortwörtlich in sein Tagebuch" (*GW*, 126). This leads Canetti to accuse Kafka of bad faith.

It would be easy to list observations both on Kafka's work in general and the letters to Felice in particular that, while they might have been contested since, Canetti made first and that have become points of reference in Kafka criticism. What interests us more now is his method because that is linked to the genre question: the genre being criticism as autobiography, the method being that of transformation. Also important is Canetti's interest in each living person and his willingness to get himself underneath that person's skin. In a brief methodological statement that begins his discussion of power a third of the way through the second part of "Der andere Process" (*GW*, 78–169), Canetti makes the surprising claim that "Der Mensch, der sich für den Maßstab aller Dinge hält, ist beinahe noch unbekannt, seine Fortschritte in der Kenntnis von sich sind minimal, jede neue Theorie verdunkelt von ihm mehr, als sie erleuchtet." He insists that "Nur die unbefangen konkrete Erforschung einzelner führt allmählich weiter," which makes Kafka "ein Glücksfall ohnegleichen" because he presents himself "in solcher Vollkommenheit zur Erkenntnis" (*GW*, 137). Daniel Paul Schreber's *Denkwürdigkeiten eines Nervenkranken* is another such case, which is why an essay on it concludes *Masse und Macht*.

Perhaps the relative shortage of decent material is the reason Canetti eventually turned to himself. His last great work is his autobiography, published in three discrete installments between 1977 and 1985, and now available in a single English volume, titled simply, and perhaps misleadingly, *Memoirs*.[25] Canetti had made his name internationally before the appearance of *Die gerettete Zunge* (1977) and no longer needed a Nobel Prize in 1981 to stimulate interest in his work. Yet sales for the autobiography soon began to exceed those for any of his other books, even *Die Blendung* and *Die Provinz des Menschen*. For *Die Fackel im Ohr* and *Das Augenspiel*, this may have something to do with the rich variety of literary celebrities he knew in Vienna and Berlin in the 1920s and 1930s; for *Die gerettete Zunge*, his evocation of a "magic childhood." Historical and family circumstances make the first thirty-odd years of Canetti's life rich in incident: that a German writer could have been brought up in the Balkans seemed exotic by the standards of the 1970s, that he could move as a child from Bulgaria to

Manchester to Vienna, Zurich, and Frankfurt, learning so many languages as he went, was astounding in the post-Holocaust era of the Cold War. It would have been a dull person indeed who did not grow up with a tale to tell, a bad writer who could not order his memories and Canetti has the tricks of a novelist up his sleeve. In addition he relates an account of intellectual growth, of great battles with an overbearing mother, whose death concludes the last volume, and of his disregard for money and material things in favor of haughty intellectualism that develops in parallel with a series of encounters with sadistic sexuality. Power and transformation are two overarching themes. His freeing himself from the influence of Karl Kraus is all the more powerful for his not having realized Kraus's debilitating hold on him, for instance. But are the three volumes important as literary autobiography, or are they really memoirs as his American publishers would have us believe?

Some readers have felt that the narrative self is too commanding and self-assured, that the author of such a radically destabilizing novel as *Die Blendung* was now ignoring contemporary reality with this throwback to a past age of certainty. These readers claim there is a telos to the three volumes, an end point of finished development, from which the finally rounded self reviews his past life and interprets it in terms of what he has become. Yet we have no sense at all of the location of the author in the present. Canetti appears to revive the notion of an integrated self in the age of fractured identity and the de-centered subject; and the view that he is emulating the structure of the classical German *Bildungsroman* is quite widespread.[26] In fact he presents a case of contrafacture: the narrative voice is only apparently stable. Canetti's self — the self that he projects in his autobiography — is a temporal construct, never identical with itself because it is always evolving and always set in relation to one or more of its past manifestations. It is true that the unsuspecting Canetti is confronted with unappealing aspects of himself and is forced to address both them and his inability to perceive them, but in a *Bildungsroman,* self and society are finally integrated and at the end the hero is set to play a useful role in the world. This is not the case with *Das Augenspiel,* which ends with the death of his mother on the eve of his departure from Austria. Although reconciliation between mother and son offers some closure and the last section began with a chapter where his reunion with Ludwig Hardt forced him to reflect fully on his volte-face from Kraus, there is no sense that he has finished his growth, become integrated, or reached the stability that would underpin a stable narrative voice. On the contrary, the chapter on the Spanish Civil War is about failure. As a Jew, Canetti is forced to flee Vienna, the cultural home he had chosen after hearing his parents speak in what was then a secret language he could not comprehend. This lack of social integration is refracted in his work and is perhaps one more reason that over such a long and productive life he essayed so many genres.

Notes

[1] Elias Canetti, "Gespräche mit Horst Bienek" (1965), in *Die gespaltene Zukunft: Aufsätze und Gespräche* (Munich: Hanser, 1972), 93–103. Here: 101. Cited hereafter as *DgZ*.

[2] Elias Canetti, *Masse und Macht* (Hamburg: Claassen, 1960) cited hereafter as *MM*; J. S. McClelland, "The Sanity of Crowds and the Madness of Power: Elias Canetti's *Crowds and Power*," in *The Crowd and the Mob: From Plato to Canetti* (London: Unwin Hyman, 1989), 293–96. Here: 293.

[3] Canetti, "Gespräch mit Horst Bieneck," [*Die gespaltene Zukunft: Aufsätze und Gespräche*], 101; and "Gespräch mit Joachim Schickel" (1972), *Die gespaltene Zukunft*, 104–31.

[4] Elias Canetti, *Fritz Wotruba* (Vienna: Rosenbaum, 1955).

[5] Elias Canetti, *Hochzeit, Komödie der Eitelkeit, Die Befristeten* (Frankfurt: Fischer, 1964).

[6] Elias Canetti, "Dialog mit dem grausamen Partner," in *Das Gewissen der Worte: Essays* (Munich: Hanser, 1976), 54–71. Here: 55. Cited hereafter as *GW*.

[7] Elias Canetti, *Die Fackel im Ohr: Lebensgeschichte 1921–1931* (Munich: Hanser, 1981), 136–46, cited as *FO; Das Augenspiel* (Munich: Hanser, 1985), cited as *A; Die Stimmen von Marrakesch: Aufzeichnungen nach einer Reise* (Munich: Hanser, 1967), cited as *Marrakesch; Die Provinz des Menschen* (Munich: Hanser, 1973).

[8] Elias Canetti, *Der Ohrenzeuge: Fünfzig Charaktere* (Munich: Hanser, 1974).

[9] *Das Geheimherz der Uhr: Aufzeichnungen 1973 bis 1985* (Frankfurt: Fischer, 1990), 23.

[10] Sigmund Freud, *Massenpsychologie und Ich-Analyse* (Leipzig: Internationaler Psychoanalytischer Verlag, 1921); Gustave Le Bon, *The Crowd: A Study of the Popular Mind,* with a new introduction by Robert A. Nye (New Brunswick: Transaction, 1997). First published 1897.

[11] Canetti, "Das erste Buch: Die Blendung," *Die gespaltene Zukunft: Aufsätze und Gespräche,* 214–53. Here: 250–51.

[12] Elias Canetti, "'Die Welt ist nicht so darzustellen wie in früheren Romanen.' Gespräch mit Elias Canetti," interview by Manfred Durzak, in *Gespräche über den Roman: Formbestimmungen und Analysen* (Frankfurt: Suhrkamp, 1976), 86–102. Here: 98.

[13] Hermann Broch, *Die Schlafwandler: Romantrilogie* (Zurich: Rhein-Verlag, 1931/32); Robert Musil, *Der Mann ohne Eigenschaften,* ed. Adolf Frisé (Reinbek: Rowohlt, 1978).

[14] Thomas Mann, *Der Zauberberg* (Berlin: Fischer, 1925).

[15] For a more nuanced reading, see Ritchie Robertson, *The 'Jewish Question' in German Literature 1749–1939* (Oxford: Oxford UP, 1999), 338–45.

[16] Günter Grass, *Die Blechtrommel* (Luchterhand: Darmstadt and Neuwied, 1959).

[17] Erich Auerbach, "The Brown Stocking," in *Mimesis: The Representation of Reality in Western Literature,* trans. Willard Trask (New York: Doubleday, 1957), 463–88.

[18] See Gunther Steussloff, "Der Reisende auf der Suche nach seiner jüdischen Vergangenheit," in *Autorschaft und Werk Elias Canettis: Subjekt-Sprache-Identität* (Würzburg: Königshausen & Neumann, 1994), 198–207.

[19] Predictably *Die Stimmen von Marrakesch* does not feature in accounts of this writing. See Arlene A. Teraoka's otherwise excellent, *EAST, WEST, and Others: The Third World in Postwar German Literature* (Lincoln: U of Nebraska P, 1996).

[20] Elias Canetti, *Welt im Kopf,* ed. Erich Fried (Vienna/Graz: Stiasny, 1962). On Veza Canetti's contribution, see Angelika Schedel's "Nachwort" to Veza Canetti, in *Der Fund: Erzählungen und Stücke* (Munich: Hanser, 2001), 317–18.

[21] The generic history appears to be the main reason *Der Ohrenzeuge* has attracted academic attention. See Adrian Stevens, "Aufzeichnungen, Menschen und Fragmente. Zur Poetik der Charakterdarstellung bei Canetti, Aubrey und La Bruyere," in *"Ein Dichter braucht Ahnen." Elias Canetti und die europäische Tradition,* Proceedings of the Paris Symposium, 16–18.11.1995, *Jahrbuch für internationale Germanistik,* vol. 44, eds. Gerald Stieg and Jean-Marie Valentin (Bern: Lang, 1997), 207–24; and Wendelin Schmidt-Dengler, "Theophrast, La Bruyére, Canetti und die Komödie," *"Ein Dichter braucht Ahnen." Elias Canetti und die europäische Tradition,* 225–33. In his other book of characters, published too late to be discussed in this essay, it is Aubrey's *Brief Lives* which is his model; see *Party im Blitz. Die englischen Jahre* (Hanser, 2003).

[22] See Guoqing Feng, *Kreisel für Erwachsene: Zur Kurzprosa in der Gegenwartsliteratur in Österreich: Thomas Bernhard, Elias Canetti und Erich Fried* (Lang: Bern, 1993), 73–128.

[23] Alfred Hrdlicka, "Das Chaos des Fleisches," in *Graphik* (Frankfurt: Ullstein, 1973), 176–77.

[24] Maja Razbojnikova-Frateva, "Die Essays von Elias Canetti — Eine Biographie des Geistes. Versuch einer Annäherung," in *Autobiographie zwischen Fiktion und Wirklichkeit,* Proceedings of the International Symposium held at Russe, October 1992, *Schriftenreihe der Elias Canetti Gesellschaft* (St. Ingbert: Röhrig, 1997), 63–73.

[25] Elias Canetti, *The Memoirs of Elias Canetti* (New York: Farrar, Straus, Giroux, 1999).

[26] See, for example, Jiri Stromsik, "'Das Eigentliche der Welt.' Menschen und Figuren in Elias Canettis Autobiographie," in *Ist Wahrheit ein Meer von Grashalmen? Zum Werk Elias Canettis* (Bern: Lang, 1993), 97–108. Here: 108.

The Works: Themes and Genres

"The Faultiest Expressions Have the Greatest Attraction": Elias Canetti's Proverbial Aphorisms

Wolfgang Mieder

ONE YEAR BEFORE HIS DEATH in 1994, Elias Canetti republished his observations, reflections, thoughts, sketches, and aphorisms that he had composed over a period of more than four decades under the title *Auf-zeichnungen 1942–1985: Die Provinz des Menschen; Das Geheimherz der Uhr* (1993).[1] Like his two acclaimed precursors Georg Christoph Lichtenberg (1742–1799) and Karl Kraus (1874–1936), Canetti also took considerable delight in confronting his contemporaries with short satirical prose texts based on linguistic analyses of their speech. He did so in his important novel *Die Blendung* (1935), in the philosophical work *Masse und Macht* (1960), as well as in his plays and essays. However, he made use of this pointed and argumentative decoding of language primarily in his *Aufzeichnungen,* where he combines sociolinguistic awareness with a sincere commitment to what has been characterized as "radikaler Humanismus."[2]

The aphorisms of this hefty volume are not arranged in any particular order other than the year of their formulation. As is customary for books of aphorisms, the individual texts are presented without rhyme or reason, enabling their authors to celebrate free and spontaneous thought processes.[3] Canetti characterized this open form of reflection in two self-analytical aphorisms that clearly show his desire to be anything but cohesive in his short texts: "Die Gedanken mit Gewalt auseinanderhalten. Sie verfilzen sich zu leicht, wie Haare" (1948; 15); and "Angst vor der Aristotelisierung meiner Gedanken; vor Einleitungen, Definitionen und ähnlichen leeren Spielereien" (1955; 207). It is, in fact, his intention to keep his thoughts apart from each other, consciously avoiding any systematization or adherence to a logical plan. Whatever enters Canetti's keen mind can become a written "Aufzeichnung" (annotation or commentary) and thus be exposed to critical scrutiny, no matter how trivial or obscure the observation might be. The broad spectrum of Canetti's aphorisms extends from everyday banalities to utopian ideals.

Quite often Canetti begins with real situations or concrete facts that subsequently lead him to expanded "Denkprozesse[n] und Assoziationsreihen."[4] Again and again he also confronts single words or phraseologisms in the form of idioms, proverbial expressions, and proverbs. He regards such pre-formulated and frequently repeated phrases as a linguistic mirror of human and social conditions and ills. Thus the critic of society is at the same time an interpreter of language and vice versa. How much Canetti is predisposed toward this critical analysis of normal speech can be seen in the following texts from *Aufzeichnungen 1942–1985*. They contain an interpretive key for those aphorisms that are consciously based on proverbial expressions and proverbs. Such verbal clichés represent to Canetti an obvious danger in human communication. They not only hinder individual thought, but they also reduce interpersonal relations to mindless patterns void of sincere feelings or significant messages:

> Manchmal glaube ich, die Sätze, die ich höre, seien dreitausend Jahre vor meinem Dasein von anderen für mich ausgehandelt worden. Höre ich genauer hin, so werden sie immer älter. (1942; 15)

> Der Mensch hat die [sprichwörtliche] Weisheit all seiner Vorfahren zusammengenommen, und seht, welch ein Dummkopf er ist. (1942; 15)

> Zuviel Straßen in der Sprache, alles [phrasenhaft] vorgebahnt. (1958; 236)

> Die Worte [Phrasen] sind nicht zu alt, nur die Menschen sind es, die die selben Worte zu häufig gebrauchen. (1970; 336)

> Ein Mann aus [phrasenhaften] Redeteilen. (1985; 521)

Repetition of the same vocabulary without conscious word or phrasal choice not only leads to empty talk, it also reflects thoughtlessness, if not stupidity. But the real danger comes from the repetitive and indiscriminate use of phraseological and proverbial language. The automatic use of such readymade clichés and metaphors ignores the real and often cruel origin of these phraseologisms. After all, one forgets too quickly that the expressions "die Daumenschrauben anziehen" and "Salz in offene Wunden streuen" go back to medieval torture practices. In fact, Canetti argues, the intent of such phrases says a great deal about the mentality of their users:

> Im Gebrauch ihrer Lieblingswendungen und -worte sind die Menschen geradezu unschuldig. Sie ahnen nicht, wie sie sich verraten, wenn sie am harmlosesten daherplappern. Sie glauben, daß sie ein Geheimnis verschweigen, wenn sie von anderen Dingen reden, doch siehe da, aus den häufigsten Wendungen baut sich plötzlich ihr Geheimnis drohend und düster auf. (1942; 17)

Wenn die Menschen vom Leben und Treiben in ihnen auch nur die lei-
seste und unverbindlichste Ahnung hätten, würden sie vor vielen Wor-
ten und Redensarten zurückschrecken wie vor Gift. (1942; 19)

Die falschesten Redensarten haben den größten Reiz, solange es noch
irgendwelche Leute gibt, die sie ernsthaft anwenden. (1945; 90)

These three revealing texts against the naïve use of phrases and proverbial
expressions, all written during the early 1940s, mirror the linguistic analysis
of Nazi phraseology that Victor Klemperer undertook in his acclaimed book
L[ingua] T[ertii] I[mperii]: Notizen eines Philologen (1947).[5] And even
more so, Klemperer attacked the vicious and criminal use of traditional
phrases in his invaluable diary *Ich will Zeugnis ablegen bis zum letzten: Tagebücher 1933–1945* (1995).[6] As he describes the linguistic terror of Nazi
Germany, he coins the anti-proverb "In lingua veritas" to claim that the
language of National Socialism will reveal the ugly truth of victimization and
destruction.[7]

Neither Klemperer nor Canetti mention the proverbial expression "etwas bis zur Vergasung tun" or the proverbs "Arbeit macht frei" and "Jedem
das Seine," three popular phrases that should not be used today after the
horrors of the Holocaust. Alfred Andersch in his novel *Efraim* (1967) exposed the inappropriateness of the "Vergasung" phrase,[8] and the sadistic misuse
of the two proverbs on concentration camp gates has been discussed as well.[9]
Whoever employs such proverbial language today does indeed reveal a linguistic and moral insensitivity toward the victims of Nazism. Canetti the satirical
moralist did well to warn modern readers of the pitfalls of "favorite" expressions that *nolens volens* expose the inhumanity of their thoughts if not actions.

The exposure of language as a codified system in which phrases and
proverbs become signs of invalid rules and dangerous stereotypes is certainly
part of Elias Canetti's aphoristic modus operandi. As such, he follows, as has
been mentioned, in the footsteps of Lichtenberg and Kraus. However, the
aphorisms of Marie von Ebner-Eschenbach (1830–1916) are also precursors
of this satirical type of language analysis. In more modern times the critical
texts of Erwin Chargaff (1905–2002), Stanisław Jerzy Lec (1909–1966),
Felix Pollak (1909–1987), Arthur Feldmann (born 1926), Gerhard Uhlenbruck (born 1929), Werner Mitsch (born 1936), and Elazar Benyoëtz (born
1937) readily come to mind.[10] Little wonder that Canetti, like most aphoristic writers, at times felt that other authors had already expressed some of his
ideas in similar ways: "Die großen Aphoristiker lesen sich so, als ob sie alle
einander gekannt hätten" (1943; 53). Without doubt Canetti was especially
thinking of Lichtenberg and Kraus. He learned a great deal from both of
them, notably regarding the "konventionelle Abnutzung von Sprache, die
Erfahrung von Sprache nicht als Mittel der Kommunikation, sondern als
Ausdruck eines monologisierenden verbalen Leerlaufs [. . .] und [das] Wört-

lichnehmen [. . .] der zur Phrase verformten Alltagssprache."[11] And yet, there are considerable differences between Kraus and Canetti, particularly with regard to the aphorisms critical of language and their users. Even if Canetti acknowledges in one of his essays about "Karl Kraus, Schule des Widerstands" (1965) that he owes his interest in the "Mißbrauch der Sprache"[12] to this satirist par excellence, he nevertheless does not follow or imitate Kraus in his "merely" brilliant and punning wordplays based on proverbial expressions and proverbs, which can, of course, also be ruthlessly satirical. Most certainly Canetti had his intellectual "father" Kraus in mind when he wrote this aphorism: "Auch an den besten Satirikern stört mich ihre Vernünftigkeit, der schale Teich, dem ihre ungeheuerlichen Einfälle entsteigen" (1950; 166). Although Kraus made the satirical play with proverbial language at least in part the raison d'être of his aggressive and bitter morality, Canetti is more concerned with a positively enlightened and hopeful criticism of humankind. He too wants to uncover, expose, and alienate, but he does so with a sincere and compassionate understanding for human existence that cannot easily be forced into a preconceived corset of virtues.

For this reason Canetti is hardly ever clever or humorous in his fifty-odd phraseological and proverbial aphorisms (most aphoristic writers use proverbial language much more frequently as a starting point of their aphorisms). The Second World War and the ensuing Cold War were too serious for him — so much so that Uwe Schweikert, in a revealing article on Canetti's *Aufzeichnungen,* speaks with much justification of the "Ernst eines leidenschaftlichen Humanisten."[13] As a moralist, Canetti feels called upon to awaken the conscience of his fellow human beings, to show them their inhumanity, and to try to convert them to better ways. This becomes obvious from the following unnerving aphorism that Canetti wrote in the middle of the war during his exile in London: "Man hat kein Maß mehr, für nichts, seit das Menschenleben nicht mehr das Maß ist" (1942; 22). Clearly Canetti is alluding to the proverb "Der Mensch ist das Maß aller Dinge," which can be traced back to classical antiquity. However, he actually takes the original meaning one step further to a deeper insight. For Canetti it is no longer the human being that is of highest value but rather human life, a most appropriate alteration of the traditional proverb in light of the inhumanity of the Nazi regime with its mass killings.

In another aphorism from this time, Canetti juxtaposes the two proverbial expressions "die Maske fallen lassen" and "das wahre Gesicht zeigen" to reveal the insincerity and dishonesty of people during this terrible period: "Ob du die Verwandlungen der anderen nicht überschätzt? Es gibt so viele, die immer die gleiche Maske haben, und wenn man sie herunterreißen will, merkt man, es ist ihr [wahres] Gesicht" (1943; 55). Obviously people cannot be trusted to show their true face when insincerity and deceit have become their character. From that same time of dictatorial power, when scientists placed their knowledge and expertise into the service of mass destruction and thus turned the metaphorical proverb "Wissen ist Macht" into gruesome reality, stems a revealing aphorism that accuses and condemns such action. This time the underlying proverb is not changed, but the implied intellectual power is now interpreted as a brutal and murderous force:

> Die Wissenschaft hat sich verraten, indem sie sich zum Selbstzweck gemacht hat. Sie ist zur Religion geworden, zur Religion des Tötens, und sie will weismachen, daß von den traditionellen Religionen des Sterbens zu dieser Religion des Tötens ein Fortschritt ist. Man wird die Wissenschaft sehr bald unter die Herrschaft eines höheren Antriebs bringen müssen, der sie zur Dienerin herabdrückt, ohne sie zu zerstören. Für diese ihre Unterjochung ist nicht mehr viel Zeit übrig. Sie gefällt sich als Religion und beeilt sich, die Menschen auszurotten, bevor man den Mut hat, sie zu entthronen. So ist Wissen wirklich Macht, aber rasend gewordene und schamlos angebetete Macht; ihre Anbeter begnügen sich mit Haaren oder Schuppen von ihr; wenn sie nichts anderes ergattern können, mit den Abdrücken ihrer schweren künstlichen Füße. (1943; 36)

There is a third, somewhat shorter phraseological aphorism from the year 1943 that also discusses the perversion of power that had gotten into the manipulated heads of many people: "Die Macht steigt auch denen zu Kopf, die keine haben, doch verraucht sie hier rascher" (1943; 43). Indeed, at the end of the war and of the Nazi regime, the "normal" citizens forgot only too quickly that they too succumbed to the obsession with total power.

The texts just discussed might be of some help in an attempt to interpret a rather cryptic aphorism with which Canetti quite typically forces the reader into a challenging thought process: "Sie konnten die Köpfe einziehen und lugten durch ein winziges Loch in der Brust" (1956; 211).[14] Here the proverbial expression "den Kopf einziehen" is changed into a grotesque image. The retracted head with its "rationality" is now located in the chest of humankind, and perhaps the reader is now to assume that people look with a bit more feeling or compassion on their compatriots and the world. There is a similar aphorism that in its absurd imagery is once again reminiscent of a Hieronymus Bosch painting: "Dem bluten die Augen, aber nie das Herz" (1969; 324). This short text might be saying that inhuman coldness does not permit the proverbial bleeding heart to occur. Canetti seems to use this linguistic "Verfremdungseffekt"[15] to indicate that compassion and help for a fellow human being must come from a feeling heart. Just seeing social ills with "bleeding eyes" is not a remedy, but heartfelt compassion might result in corrective action. Such texts are anything but mere puns or wordplays based on linguistic manipulations.

Canetti, quite different from a straightforward moralist like Jeremias Gotthelf (1797–1854), whom he admired and whose novella *Die schwarze Spinne* (1842) he very much appreciated,[16] never presents any obvious solutions. In fact, people are quite a conundrum to him, and it is difficult to follow their proverbial tracks: "Wer wirklich wüßte, was die Menschen miteinander verbindet, wäre imstande, sie vor dem Tode zu retten. Das Rätsel des Lebens ist ein soziales Rätsel. Niemand ist ihm auf der Spur" (1960; 257). But even though life is a social riddle, the following aphorism is not to be interpreted as negatively as it sounds: "Deute nichts, erkläre nichts. Gib denen etwas zu tun, die sich den Kopf zerbrechen möchten" (1977; 412). Canetti as an intellectual is hardly asking for an abandonment of enlightened rationality in this text. What he wants to say once again is that rationality alone cannot comprehend the complex nature of the human being. Phraseological racking of one's brain ("head" in German) does not suffice if the results are nothing but insensitive platitudes or rigid rules. But critical thought is definitely necessary, and for this reason Canetti does not provide pre-digested interpretations for people in his thought-provoking aphorisms.

This is shown splendidly in yet another aphorism in which the proverbial expression "sich in den Schwanz beißen" metaphorically circumscribes the limitations of every formal system of thought:

> Die Früheren lachen mich aus. Ihnen genügt es, daß ihre Gedanken sich fest in den Schwanz beißen. Sie glauben, damit haben sie etwas wirklich begriffen, und es ist doch nur ihr einzelner Gedanke, der sich schon wieder in den Schwanz beißt! Je öfter er es tut, um so richtiger, denken sie, ist er, und wenn er sich gar nährt von seinem eigenen Leib, dann schnappen sie über vor Entzücken. Ich aber lebe in der einzigen Angst, daß meine Gedanken zu früh stimmen, und auch darum lasse ich ihnen Zeit, ihre ganze Falschheit zu entlarven oder sich wenigstens zu häuten. (1943; 43–44)

Canetti tries to go beyond the apparent "truth" of proverbial language and wisdom, which is too inflexible and too limiting. He wants to expose the often false claims to universal principles of proverbs or at least "skin" them like a snake of such falsehood. The last thing Canetti would have wanted is to provide his readers with prototypes of expressions that could turn into proverbial clichés. Nevertheless, Canetti would surely have accepted the wisdom of the proverb "Die Gedanken sind frei" — but even that text is missing among the liberating aphorisms of this free thinker!

As Canetti sees it, the task of the modern author is to be a "Hüter der Verwandlung."[17] In this ability to change or transform, Canetti sees hope for humanity because a conscious and responsible metamorphosis could lead to a more humane world. Spontaneous action as well as "Häutungen" (shedding of skins) are necessary to even attempt to bring about meaningful social change. This can be seen from two telling aphorisms that once again are based on well-known proverbial expressions: "Es wäre die Frage, was einer kann, der nicht bereit ist, es für etwas Besseres sofort aufs Spiel zu setzen" (1965; 282); and "Räume wie eine falsche Haut, in denen man aus ihr fahren möchte" (1979; 434). It must be noted, however, that Canetti does not present any ready-made solutions or answers. In the first aphorism he argues for the importance of taking the proverbial risk no matter what. This is, although indirectly, another reminder of the necessary process of change. In the second text the proverbial expression "aus der Haut fahren" is deprived of its metaphorical meaning by transposing it into the world of human reality. In addition, Canetti does not have the type of "Aus-der-Haut-Fahren" in mind that characterizes an explosive outburst of anger. Rather, he interprets the shedding of the skin, as in the case of a snake, as a necessity of life itself.

Animal metaphors play a significant role in Canetti's oeuvre.[18] He insists on the right to life for all animals in the modern world. In his aphorisms Canetti often juxtaposes animals and humans, or he reverses their normal roles. The results are experimental texts "des Grotesken, des Hypothetischen, vor allem des Spekulativen,"[19] as for example in the two following proverbial aphorisms: "Die Fliege, der er kein Haar krümmen könnte, ist inzwischen gestorben" (1967; 304); and "Der Hund nahm seinem Herrn den Maulkorb ab, behielt ihn aber an der Leine" (1970; 342). Regarding such texts, Thomas Lappe has spoken of a "symbolischen Umkehrung"[20] of the generally accepted reality and its norms. Canetti's interest in metamorphoses goes so far that literally everything is possible in his experimental and hypothetical "Denkmodelle."[21]

To see things and relationships from an entirely new and different perspective is also the main thrust of an animal aphorism that is formulated around the common proverbial expression "Katz und Maus mit jemandem spielen." Basing his critical thoughts on the literary and iconographic motif of the world-upside-down,[22] Canetti, in 1942, made this metaphorical and yet most telling statement: "Mein größter Wunsch ist es zu sehen, wie eine Maus eine Katze bei lebendem Leibe frißt. Sie soll aber auch lange genug mit ihr spielen" (1942; 13). Most likely Canetti is alluding to the crimes that the Nazi perpetrators were inflicting on their innocent victims. The text in its gruesome expressiveness is original enough, yet it might have been influenced by a short prose text by Franz Kafka (1883–1924) that Canetti is likely to have known:

Kleine Fabel

"Ach," sagte die Maus, "die Welt wird enger mit jedem Tag. Zuerst war sie so breit, daß ich Angst hatte, ich lief weiter und war glücklich, daß ich endlich rechts und links in der Ferne Mauern sah, aber diese langen Mauern eilen so schnell aufeinander zu, daß ich schon im letzten Zimmer bin, und dort im Winkel steht die Falle, in die ich laufe." "Du mußt nur die Laufrichtung ändern," sagte die Katze und fraß sie.[23]

But while Kafka in typical fashion emphasizes the impossibility of escape and survival of the mouse, Canetti offers a new intellectual orientation with his role reversal of cat and mouse, albeit only by employing the world-upside-down motif of letting the victim come out on top.

In yet another text in which human behavior is seen as parallel to that of the cat and mouse, Canetti again draws a grotesque picture, but this time, one that shows matters in a more pessimistic light: "Die Gefangenen bewundern ihre Häscher, um am Leben zu bleiben. Je dankbarer und respektvoller sie von ihnen sprechen, desto mehr Hoffnung haben sie, ihnen zu entkommen. 'Du bist wunderbar! Laß mich los!' sagte die Maus zur Katze und leckte ihr die Krallen" (1969; 331).[24] This proverbial mini-fable could be referring to the psychology of human behavior, as victims in utter despair deal with their inhuman torturers by idolizing them. Totalitarian Nazi Germany and the Holocaust come readily to mind. It should also be noted that Canetti makes use here of the traditional proverbial genre of the wellerism and its triadic structure, for example, a statement (often a proverb or a proverbial expression), a speaker, and a situation that places everything into a humorous or satirical light.[25] Most aphoristic writers have on occasion structured texts on this folkloric form, and even Canetti could not escape this inviting structure, as can be seen from three additional examples:

Ich will sterben, sagte sie, und trank zehn Männer herunter. (1967; 301)

Eitel bin ich nicht, sagte der Eitelste, ich bin empfindlich. (1981; 467)

Das ist ein Aphorismus, sagt er, und klappt den Mund rasch wieder zu. (1973; 381)

The last example is an ironic statement about the shortness of most aphorisms that do not tolerate contradiction, a sort of aphoristic definition in the traditional form of a wellerism. This is not to say that Elias Canetti wants to cut off critical thought or intellectual discussion, but he is clearly stating that aphorisms can stand alone without any careful explanations by their authors. They are there for the readers to reflect upon as free and provocative thoughts expressed in terse language.

Regarding actual folk proverbs, it is interesting to note that Canetti uses these traditional bits of wisdom in his novel *Die Blendung* to show "das ziel- und endlose Geschwafel, dieses völlige Aneinander-Vorbeireden, das sinn- und inhaltslose Reden"[26] of certain people. In contrast, he utilizes proverbs and their structures only four times in his *Aufzeichnungen,* a fact that differentiates him considerably from many other writers of aphorisms.[27] There is first of all the socially critical short aphorism, "Was dem Armen die Hoffnung, ist dem Reichen der Erbe" (1942; 32), which is a telling variation of the proverb "Wat den eenen sin Uhl, dat is den annern sin Nachtigall." Although the proverb is simply stating that people have their preferences, the aphoristic anti-proverb maintains the formulaic structure while pointing out the world of difference between the poor and the rich. While the poor have to live on hope, the rich worry about how to get their wealth distributed to their heirs (preferably without inheritance tax). By implication Canetti is saying that the world could be a better place if the haves shared their fortune with the have-nots. It is this communication by indirection that makes Canetti's social aphorisms so poignant. The reader is forced to read between the proverbial lines to understand the hidden message of these texts.

The equally concise aphorism "Die Hölle des Diebs ist die Angst vor Dieben" (1951; 178) might well be a varied loan translation of the English proverb "The thief thinks that everyone else is a thief," but this proverb is also current in German in a quite similar wording: "Der Dieb meint, sie stehlen alle." Canetti's text is thus only a slight variation of both the English and German proverbs, but by employing the "hell" of knowledge and perhaps even that of the guilty conscience, he is able to add a psychological depth to the social wisdom of the folk proverb.

With the remaining two proverbial aphorisms, things are much clearer regarding the German proverbs that Canetti must have had in mind when formulating them. There can be no doubt that his aphorism "Der Feind meines Feindes ist nicht mein Freund" (1971; 346) is a conscious reversal of the proverb "Die Feinde unserer Feinde sind unsere Freunde." Once again Canetti is saying that life and human relations are not as clear-cut and simple as some proverbs would have us believe. A similar message is contained in Canetti's manipulation of the classical proverb "Steter Tropfen höhlt den Stein" to the provocative query "Aus jedem Jahr zwölf Tropfen. Steter Tropfen? Welcher Stein?" (1983; 506). Here the author seems to be asking what could possibly be executed in such a determined fashion that by simple persistence a meaningful result might be achieved. The complexity of the modern world does not offer such obvious solutions to human life.

Of interest is also a short note, which at the outset is identified as nothing more than an unchanged proverb: "'Eine Traube, die eine andere sieht, wird reif,' *Byzantinisches Sprichwort*" (1982; 490). This is most likely a traditional proverb that Canetti encountered in his vast readings and simply noted down as an interesting bit of international wisdom. Probably he was struck by its underlying thought that in nature one thing is influenced by another and that consequently metamorphoses do take place. The metaphor of the proverb might have been understood by Canetti in such a way that a person becomes psychologically "reif" (mature) through the good example of another person. This proverb can be traced back to the Roman satirical writer Juvenal (ca. A.D. 60 to after A.D. 127). It was loan translated into many languages and is known in German as "Eine Traube sieht die andere an und wird dabei faul (reif; schwarz)."[28] The variants with "faul" and "schwarz" indicate that the proverb was also current with a negative connotation, since people can learn from bad examples as well. But clearly Canetti was impressed by the positive version in this case, attesting to his basic belief in the principle of hope for humankind.

Humankind and mass society were of major concern to Elias Canetti, and it should not come as a surprise that "der Mensch" was at the center of his observations and reflections. Owing to the masculine gender of the German noun "Mensch," Canetti makes use of its equivalent masculine pronoun "er" in many aphorisms, referring to both male and female genders with this generic concept. Consequently there is a whole group of aphorisms in which one person "er" (he) is brought together with a concrete situation and a metaphorical expression, usually implying humans of both sexes. These texts are doubtlessly "Gedankenexperimente,"[29] whose innovative messages are grounded in satirical "Sprachentlarvungen."[30] It is precisely such unexpected use and interpretation of well-known proverbial expressions that, after considerable critical thought, lead to an enlightening "Erkenntnis-Ruck."[31] These aphorisms are hardly ever mere puns, as is often the case with lesser aphoristic writers, and at times also with Karl Kraus. Canetti, on the other hand, connects his innovative reversals and questioning manipulations of proverbial expressions "mit dem satirischen Motiv der verkehrten Welt, die erst die richtige wäre. Daß es anders sein müßte, als es ist: dieser Verdeutlichung dient die Umkehrung."[32] Canetti's concise reversals of metaphorical language have been referred to as a type of "Minimal-Sprache,"[33] and this linguistic minimalism is part of the intellectual challenge of his proverbial aphorisms.

It is truly remarkable what satirical expressiveness Canetti achieved by structuring his short aphorisms around proverbial language. He twists and integrates this preformulated language in such a way that unexpected insights result concerning various social concerns and ills, while the pronoun "er" for the most part refers to "der Mensch," that is, people in general. Thus two texts ridicule militarism from different points of view. The first aphorism criticizes the mindless enlistment in the armed forces that implies unquestioning obedience: "Er geht unter die Soldaten: er will nicht mehr wissen, was geschieht; er will nicht mehr wissen, was er tut" (1942; 22).

Without doubt Canetti is alluding to Christ's forgiving words on the cross here: "Father, forgive them; for they know not what they do" (Luke 23:34). Canetti wrote this aphorism in 1942, and it is clear that he is speaking of exuberant and blind soldiers who don't even want to know what is happening around them and what they are doing. After the Second World War and the Holocaust such soldiers were only too willing to declare that they had only followed orders in anything they had done, and thus had no moral responsibility for the crimes they had committed. The second aphorism attacks the military-industrial complex of the Cold War: "Er hat so viel Geld, daß ihm die Bomben aus der Hand fressen" (1950; 167). Monetary control and the construction of weapons clearly go hand in hand.

Two other aphorisms comment on the blasphemous confrontation with God by people whose hubris has driven them far away from humility and decency: "Er braucht Gott, um ihm auf die Schulter zu klopfen und ihm zu sagen, wie er's hätte machen sollen" (1968; 322); and "Er hängt es an die große alte Glocke Gott. Aber sind die neuen großen Glocken besser?" (1979; 434). Modern humankind in its arrogance is even of the opinion that the sun can be controlled: "Wenn die Sonne herauskommt, sagt er sich verächtlich: auch sie werden wir bald am Gängelband haben" (1969; 329). There appears to be no more measure or control: "Er fühlt sich geeicht, doch er kennt nicht das Maß" (1964; 279); and there is concern that the world might just blow up altogether: "Als gütiger Erzähler erwarb er sich das Vertrauen der Menschheit, zwei Monate bevor sie in die Luft ging" (1982; 484). Modern life is full of lies: "Er entlief der Binsen-Gegenwart in jede alte Lüge" (1966; 293); and everything seems to be preoccupied with senseless news flashes: "Er führt zwei zeitungslose Tage der Woche ein und siehe da, es bleibt alles beim Neuen" (1973; 381). People worry about persecution: "Er ist mir auf der Spur. Aber es stört ihn, daß ich seinen Spuren von mir auf der Spur bin" (1983; 501); and they even fear themselves: "Er steht vor dem Spiegel und zeigt sich die Zähne. Er fürchtet nur noch sich" (1984; 515). And yet, despite of this pessimism, Canetti also includes a proverbial aphorism that declares positively that perhaps everything in life is not in vain after all: "Er kriegt's nicht aus dem Kopf; daß es *alles* vielleicht umsonst ist. Nicht etwa nur er allein, alles. Er kann trotzdem nur so weiter-leben, als ob es nicht umsonst wäre" (1982; 489).

A number of such "er" or "Mensch" aphorisms center around Canetti's major theme of language and communication. In one of them Canetti simply shows how someone who is used to acting out the proverbial expression of "den Mund voll nehmen" all of a sudden has to learn to deal with the loss of the accustomed power base: "Ach, er nahm immer den Mund so voll und jetzt soll er einfach reden" (1985; 526). Perhaps something has finally touched the heart of this person, even if it is still difficult to admit to this human reaction to the world: "Sätze, die ihn ins Herz getroffen haben,

Sätze, die er sich [noch] nicht zugeben kann" (1978; 422). But there is always hope in Canetti's view of the world, and a clear sign of this is when people finally recognize that their arrogant and thoughtless communication is void of sincere and humane feelings. They can then stop this dangerous talk, as can be seen from these two last proverbial aphorisms referring explicitly to social use of language: "Er erkannte die Wirkung seiner Worte und verlor darüber die Sprache" (1973; 377); and "Bevor die Worte zu strahlen beginnen, fällt er sich in die Rede" (1985; 531). In the first text someone recognizes the negative effects of language and literally loses the ability to speak. The second aphorism indicates that it is possible to interrupt one's uncontrolled and dangerous talk before the words have the chance to hurt others.

The proper use of language is clearly at the heart of Canetti's moral messages in his proverbial aphorisms. The mindless use of proverbial expressions and proverbs exposes the mental brutality of those who employ them without being conscious of their often questionable character. Those who become aware of the power of clichés and stereotypes will be more careful in choosing the words and expressions that are needed for communication. Because people expose their thoughts and feelings through their language in general and through proverbial utterances in particular, Canetti repeatedly pointed out his contemporaries' use of such stock phrases in order to reveal their inhumanity. In this sense "[haben] die falschesten Redensarten den größten Reiz" for Canetti, for they give him the welcome opportunity to refer his fellow human beings to the possibility of change and metamorphosis. That in turn might lead to more humanity and responsibility based on a moral value system uncompromised by rigid thinking in the form of proverbial expressions and proverbs.

Notes

[1] Elias Canetti, *Aufzeichnungen 1942–1985: Die Provinz des Menschen; Das Geheimherz der Uhr* (Munich: Hanser, 1993). The two parts of this volume had previously been published in 1973 and 1987. References to this volume will be indicated in the text of this essay by year of composition and page number.

[2] Ingo Seidler, "Bruchstücke einer großen Konfession. Zur Bedeutung von Canettis Sudelbüchern," *Modern Austrian Literature* 16/3–4 (1983): 1–21. Here: 16. Elias Canetti, *Masse und Macht* (Hamburg: Claassen, 1960) and *Die Blendung* (Munich: Hanser, 1963), cited as *Blendung*.

[3] See Carol Petersen, *Elias Canetti* (Berlin: Colloquium, 1990), 63; and also Jürgen Jacobs, "Elias Canetti," in *Deutsche Literatur der Gegenwart,* vol. I, ed. Dietrich Weber (Stuttgart: Kröner, 1976), 93–109. Here: 104.

[4] Stefan H. Kaszyński, "Im Labor der Gedanken. Zur Poetik der Aufzeichnung von Elias Canetti," in *Elias Canettis Anthropologie und Poetik,* ed. S. Kaszyński (Munich: Hanser, 1984), 151–62. Here: 157–58.

5 Victor Klemperer, *LTI: Notizbuch eines Philologen* (Cologne: Röderberg, 1987).

6 Victor Klemperer, *Ich will Zeugnis ablegen bis zum letzten: Tagebücher 1933–1945*, 2 vols., ed. Walter Nowojski (Berlin: Aufbau Verlag, 1995).

7 See Wolfgang Mieder, *"In lingua veritas": Sprichwörtliche Rhetorik in Victor Klemperers Tagebüchern 1933–1945* (Vienna: Edition Praesens, 2000), 20–27. For the misuse of proverbial language, see also W. Mieder, "Proverbs in Nazi Germany: The Promulgation of Anti-Semitism and Stereotypes through Folklore," in *Proverbs Are Never Out of Season: Popular Wisdom in the Modern Ages* (New York: Oxford UP, 1993), 225–55.

8 Alfred Andersch, *Efraim* (Munich: Deutscher Taschenbuch Verlag, 1971), 124–26.

9 See Wolfgang Brückner, *"Arbeit macht frei": Herkunft und Hintergrund der KZ-Devise* (Opladen: Leske & Budrich, 1998); and Karin Doerr, "'To Each His Own' (*Jedem das Seine*): The (Mis-)Use of German Proverbs in Concentration Camps and Beyond," *Proverbium: Yearbook of International Proverb Scholarship* 17 (2000): 71–90. See also Wolfgang Mieder, "'As If I Were the Master of the Situation': Proverbial Manipulation in Adolf Hitler's *Mein Kampf*," in *The Politics of Proverbs: From Traditional Wisdom to Proverbial Sterotypes* (Madison, Wisconsin: U of Wisconsin P, 1997), 9–38.

10 See Wolfgang Mieder, *Sprichwörtliche Aphorismen: Von Georg Christoph Lichtenberg bis Elazar Benyoëtz* (Vienna: Edition Praesens, 1999); and W. Mieder, *Aphorismen, Sprichwörter, Zitate: Von Goethe und Schiller bis Victor Klemperer* (Bern: Peter Lang, 2000). The first book mentioned contains a German version (see 182–91) of the present English essay.

11 Manfred Durzak, "Elias Canetti," in *Deutsche Dichter der Gegenwart*, ed. Benno von Wiese (Berlin: Erich Schmidt, 1973), 195–209. Here: 204–5.

12 Elias Canetti, "Karl Kraus, Schule des Widerstands" (1965), in *Das Gewissen der Worte: Essays* (Frankfurt: Fischer, 1982), 42–53. Here: 49. See also Gerald Stieg, "Elias Canetti und Karl Kraus. Ein Versuch," *Modern Austrian Literature* 16/3–4 (1983): 197–210; and Detlef Krumme, *Lesemodelle: Elias Canetti, Günter Grass, Walter Höllerer* (Munich: Hanser, 1983), 51–53.

13 Uwe Schweikert, "Der Weg durch das Labyrinth: Versuch über Elias Canettis Aufzeichnungen," *Neue Rundschau* 85 (1974): 154–63. Here: 158.

14 For an interpretation of this aphorism see Peter von Matt, "Der phantastische Aphorismus bei Elias Canetti," *Merkur* 44 (1990): 398–405. Here: 401–2.

15 Christiane Altvater, *"Die moralische Quadratur des Zirkels": Zur Problematik der Macht in Elias Canettis Aphorismensammlung "Die Provinz des Menschen"* (Bern: Peter Lang, 1990), 125.

16 See Wolfgang Mieder, "'Spuren der schwarzen Spinne': Elias Canetti und Jeremias Gotthelf," *Sprachspiegel* 50/5 (1994): 129–35. Jeremias Gotthelf, *Die Schwarze Spinne* (Kreuzlingen/Bern: Erpf, 1988).

17 Elias Canetti, "Der Beruf des Dichters" (1976), in *Das Gewissen der Worte: Essays* (Frankfurt: Fischer, 1982), 279–90. Here: 283–85.

[18] See Harry Timmermann, "Tierisches in der Anthropologie und Poetik Elias Canettis mit Beispielen aus dem Gesamtwerk," *Sprache im technischen Zeitalter* 94 (1985): 99–127.

[19] Thomas Lappe, *Elias Canettis "Aufzeichnungen 1942–1985": Modell und Dialog als Konstituenten einer programmatischen Utopie* (Aachen: Alano, 1989), 29.

[20] Lappe, *Elias Canettis "Aufzeichnungen 1942–1985,"* 135.

[21] Lappe, *Elias Canettis "Aufzeichnungen 1942–1985,"* 131.

[22] For many references of the use of proverbial language in the depiction of this motif in literature, art, and the mass media see Wolfgang Mieder and Janet Sobieski, *Proverb Iconography: An International Bibliography* (New York: Peter Lang, 1999).

[23] Franz Kafka, *Beschreibung eines Kampfes: Novellen, Skizzen, Aphorismen* (New York: Schocken, 1946), 121.

[24] See the similar aphorism that also expresses a role reversal between cat and mouse: "Die Katze behängte die Maus mit ihren Krallen und entließ sie ins Leben" (1970), *Aufzeichnungen 1942–1985: Die Provinz des Menschen; Das Geheimherz der Uhr* (Munich: Hanser, 1993), 342.

[25] For Wellerisms see Lutz Röhrich and Wolfgang Mieder, *Sprichwort* (Stuttgart; Metzler, 1977), 11–14. See also W. Mieder and Stewart A. Kingsbury, eds., *A Dictionary of Wellerisms* (New York: Oxford UP, 1994).

[26] Alfons-M. Bischoff, *Elias Canetti, Stationen zum Werk* (Bern: Peter Lang, 1973), 57. See the proverbs "Eile mit Weile" and "Kommt Zeit, kommt Rat" as well as numerous proverbial expressions in *Die Blendung* (Vienna: Herbert Reichner, 1935), 158–64.

[27] For numerous examples of aphorisms based on actual proverbs, see Wolfgang Mieder, ed., *Antisprichwörter,* 3 vols. (Wiesbaden: Gesellschaft für deutsche Sprache, 1982, 1985, and 1989); and W. Mieder, ed., *Verdrehte Weisheiten: Antisprichwörter aus Literatur und Medien* (Wiesbaden: Quelle & Meyer, 1998). For aphorisms built on proverbial expressions, see W. Mieder, ed., *Phrasen verdreschen: Antiredensarten aus Literatur und Medien* (Wiesbaden: Quelle & Meyer, 1999).

[28] See Karl Friedrich Wilhelm Wander, *Deutsches Sprichwörter-Lexikon,* 5 vols. (Leipzig: F. A. Brockhaus, 1867–1880; rpt. Darmstadt: Wissenschaftliche Buchgesellschaft, 1964), vol. 4, col. 1285 (no. 20). See also August Otto, *Die Sprichwörter und sprichwörtlichen Redensarten der Römer* (Leipzig: Teubner, 1890; rpt. Hildesheim: Georg Olms, 1971), 360; and Ida von Düringsfeld and Otto von Reinsberg-Düringsfeld, *Sprichwörter der germanischen und romanischen Sprachen,* 2 vols. (Leipzig: Hermann Fries, 1872–1875; rpt. Hildesheim: Georg Olms, 1973), vol. 1, 189–90 (no. 378).

[29] Harald Fricke, "Elias Canetti: Die Tradition der Innovation," in H. Fricke, *Aphorismus* (Stuttgart: Metzler, 1984), 132–39. Here: 137.

[30] Lappe, *Elias Canettis "Aufzeichnungen 1942–1985,"* 108.

[31] Jürgen Söring, "Die Literatur als 'Provinz des Menschen': Zu Elias Canettis Aufzeichnungen," *Deutsche Vierteljahrsschrift für Literaturwissenschaft und Geistesgeschichte,* 60 (1986): 645–66. Here: 665.

[32] Uwe Schweikert, "'Schöne Nester ausgeflogener Wahrheiten': Elias Canetti und die aphoristische Tradition," in *Canetti lesen: Erfahrungen mit seinen Büchern,* ed. Herbert G. Göpfert (Munich: Hanser, 1975), 77–86. Here: 84.

[33] Lappe, *Elias Canettis "Aufzeichnungen 1942–1985,"* 60.

Canetti's *Aufzeichnungen*

Sigurd Paul Scheichl

E LIAS CANETTI'S *AUFZEICHNUNGEN*, or notebooks, accompany his work over more than fifty years and provide a comprehensive overview of his thought about the masses, the isolation of the individual, power, the fear of global destruction, survival and death, the traditions of literature and philosophy, myths and mythology, language,[1] and the problems of satire, as well as comments on his own writings. Whatever Canetti tried in his other books reappears in the *Aufzeichnungen*.[2]

The wide intellectual range of the *Aufzeichnungen* is surely one of the reasons why they have been neglected in Canetti scholarship. Although they are often cited as interesting self-interpretations on the part of the author or as providing parallels to his systematic studies of major problems, there are few studies focusing on the *Aufzeichnungen* as such. Even valuable introductions into the work and thought of Canetti, such as Dagmar Barnouw's,[3] pay much more attention to the novel, the plays, the autobiography, and to *Masse und Macht* than to the *Aufzeichnungen*. The task at hand, then, is an account of the writing contained in the notebooks, a study of their structure (or lack of it), and, finally, observations on some of their formal and stylistic particularities, rather than an analysis of Canetti's thought.

I shall begin with two general remarks. The first is an exclusion: Eric Leroy DuCardonnay[4] advances strong arguments for an inclusion of *Die Stimmen von Marrakesch* (1967) in a study of Canetti's notes, among them the subtitle *Aufzeichnungen nach einer Reise*. The predominantly narrative character of the chapters in this book, however, provides an equally strong argument for its exclusion from such a study. *Die Stimmen von Marrakesch* is closer to the autobiographical books, which it precedes by nearly ten years, than to the *Aufzeichnungen*. Canetti's publisher seems to have been of the same opinion. The Hanser edition of Canetti's complete works prints *Die Stimmen von Marrakesch* as well as *Der Ohrenzeuge* (1974) separately from the *Aufzeichnungen*. Second, I shall avoid discussing the problem of genre. Thomas Lappe, taking as a point of departure a study of Canetti's notes, has tried to establish a particular genre, the *Aufzeichnung*, in twentieth-century literature, particularly German literature.[5] I am skeptical that this is a useful expansion of the categories used in genre discussion, all the more so because any definition of genre tends to become normative and is therefore rarely helpful.

Of course, diary, sketch, essay, and aphorism are genres to which Canetti's *Aufzeichnungen* can be compared. Some of the notes are, indeed, aphorisms in the narrowest sense of the term, and Harald Fricke had good reason to include them in his study of the German aphorism,[6] though he did so without discussing the problem that these notes are not only *Aphorismenketten* (chains of aphorisms) but chains of texts that do not correspond to his own definition of the aphorism. In the *Aufzeichnungen,* Canetti often presents himself as taking part in the aphoristic tradition by, for example, mentioning great aphorists of the past or by obliquely referring to them. Fricke has shown that an allusion to Lichtenberg stands at the very beginning of the published *Aufzeichnungen* (*PM,* 9),[7] and we also find more than once the names of, for example, La Rochefoucault and Joubert. But Canetti also quotes from diaries, including those of Friedrich Hebbel, Jules Renard, and Cesare Pavese, among others.

If the statement "Hitler müßte jetzt als Jude weiterleben" (*PM* [1945], 93) is in its pointed structure indeed a classical aphorism, if this radical thought cannot be expressed but in this aphoristic form,[8] other texts in the *Aufzeichnungen* seem closer to the form of the essay, such as a remark on Mark Twain only a half of a page in length (*Aufz. 1973–84,* 23–24), or the fairly long reminiscence about the Oxford anthropologist Franz Baermann Steiner (*Aufz. 1992–93,* 17–19); many notes are reflections on personal experiences or on the author's other works, and completely lack the generalizing aspect considered typical of the aphorism. Fricke includes the *Aufzeichnungen* in his study of the German aphorism without differentiating between the notes according to the genre they might belong to, but, on the other hand, he quotes only notes that correspond to the classical type of the aphorism; this is perhaps a trick, but a useful one. The last thing we should do is, of course, split up the evident unity of these books by classifying the notes by genre and then analyzing them according to the principle of genre rather than the order in which the author published them. If Canetti had wanted to do so, he could have published separate volumes of aphorisms, short essays, and so forth. In fact, one of his aphorisms of 1978 reads:

> Jetzt heißen seine Gedanken Aphorismen, ein Name wie von Prokrustes. (*Aufz. 1973–84,* 42)

Due to the particular characteristics of Canetti's work, a discussion of genre would not do justice to these rich collections of thoughts and ideas.

I shall use the word "notes" as an equivalent for *Aufzeichnungen.* Although Lawson's term "jottings"[9] has something of the casual sound of Canetti's word *Aufzeichnungen,* it does not seem appropriate for the description of a group of texts with a definite literary structure. A fundamental problem regarding the assessment of the *Aufzeichnungen* is raised by Canetti's own account of the process and intention of their writing, in his preface to the first collection of notes. Originally, he alleges, these notebooks had an entirely private character; Canetti claims that they were a by-product of *Masse und Macht*, written mainly to make the task of finishing this *opus magnum* more bearable. In other words, they served the function of a "Ventil," a safety valve (*PM*, 7). The connection between the notes and Canetti's great theoretical work are evident even in notes written long after the publication of *Masse und Macht*. By that time, as the author himself says, the *Aufzeichnungen* had become works in their own right (*PM*, 8).

Of course, after their publication the *Aufzeichnungen* became public texts — but did they undergo changes in this process of becoming available to the public? Before the Canetti estate is accessible, we do not know much about the author's selection, about changes, about the stylization and literarization these texts may or may not have undergone between their first, private versions and the form in which we read them now. In her editorial note to the posthumously published *Aufzeichnungen 1992–1993* (99), Johanna Canetti hints at the relation between the original and the final versions of the *Aufzeichnungen*. She informs us that Elias Canetti chose these texts from the handwritten originals, dictated them and again corrected the typescripts. This is the only reliable information available about the process of transformation from private note to literary text, and indeed, it may not be valid for the earlier *Aufzeichnungen*.

Some *Aufzeichnungen* previously published in reviews apparently underwent changes before their publication in a book; Lappe and Barnouw give lists of these.[10] *Die Provinz des Menschen* (1973) includes the preceding volumes of *Aufzeichnungen* published in 1965 and 1970, but omits some notes contained in the earlier books. Other notes were changed; these changes seem to be slight and are no philological sensations.[11] Finally, *Nachträge aus Hampstead* (1994), containing additional texts from the years covered in *Die Provinz des Menschen*, proves beyond a doubt that Canetti's selection from his notes was a very deliberate one.

These preliminary observations on the textual history of the *Aufzeichnungen* suggest that the form and perhaps even the order of the notes in the various collections are not quite as spontaneous as the author wants us to believe. This is not to deny the spontaneity of the original versions of the notes. However, the accessible versions are not in all aspects identical with the drafts, which in many cases have been refined. The author himself always insisted that he excluded a certain number of notes, perhaps even a large number, from publication (cf. *Aufz. 1942–72*, 7).

Canetti's own presentation of his *Aufzeichnungen* as texts casually jotted down while he was preoccupied with a major book may be another reason for the relatively low esteem in which they are held by literary scholars and perhaps also by readers. The writer's account of their genesis, which concerns only the *Aufzeichnungen* prior to 1960, has prompted readers to classify them as minor works — which they certainly are not. Canetti's first volume of *Aufzeichnungen* appeared in 1965, comprising notes written between 1942 and 1948; *Alle vergeudete Verehrung* (1970) the second volume, contains notes from 1949 to 1960. *Die Provinz des Menschen* combines these first two volumes with only minor changes and adds notes from 1960 to 1972, that is, from the period after *Masse und Macht*. Fourteen years later Canetti published *Das Geheimherz der Uhr: Aufzeichnungen 1973–1985* (1987), followed by *Die Fliegenpein: Aufzeichnungen* (1992), which is the only one of these books that does not provide any dates for the notes included. *Nachträge aus Hampstead: Aus den Aufzeichnungen 1954–1971* appeared after the writer's death, but the selection is still his own.[12] The notes contained in this volume are taken from the years previously covered in *Alle vergeudete Verehrung* and *Die Provinz des Menschen,* and correspond chronologically to *Das Geheimherz der Uhr;* again, the selection seems to be Canetti's own. Future research on the *Aufzeichnungen* will have to take into account that notes from the same year can be found in different volumes. *Aufzeichnungen 1992–1993* collects notes from the writer's last years; his daughter maintains that the edition is based on a manuscript approved by her father. The few notes published in various reviews or anthologies since 1956 will not be taken into consideration in this essay.[13]

There are two approaches to arrive at a description of the form of Canetti's notebooks. Obviously, the form of the books requires as much attention as the form of the individual notes. When Canetti first began to write the notes, he was occupied with *Masse und Macht,* which is something approaching a coherent study of an anthropological problem: a systematic study by an author who tended to reject all systems. If the early notes were, as the author stated, a safety valve during the writing of the great book, they also functioned as a defense of Canetti's freedom against the necessities of a system.

One early note on Aristotle explains both Canetti's personal — narrative rather than abstract, perhaps even phenomenological — approach to the problem of masses or crowds in his treatise and his apparent need to write ostentatiously spontaneous, decidedly unsystematic *Aufzeichnungen* while he conducted his studies on power and the masses.[14]

> Beklemmendes Gefühl der Fremdheit beim Lesen des *Aristoteles.* [. . .] Die Abhängigkeit der Wissenschaft von den Ordnungen des Aristoteles, bis auf unsere Tage, wird einem zum Alpdruck [. . .]
>
> Sein Denken ist in allererster Linie ein Abteilen. Er hat ein entwickeltes Gefühl für Stände, Plätze und Verwandtschaftsbeziehungen, und etwas wie ein System der Stände trägt er in alles hinein, was er untersucht. Bei

seinen Abteilungen ist es ihm um Gleichmäßigkeit und Sauberkeit zu tun und nicht so sehr darum, daß sie stimmen. [. . .] Heute noch gibt es Menschen, die sich einem Gegenstand nicht nähern können, ohne seine Abteilungen daran zu applizieren; und manch einer denkt, daß in den Schachteln und Schubladen des Aristoteles die Dinge ein klareres Aussehen haben, da sie in Wirklichkeit darin nur toter sind. (*PM* [1943], 38–39)

Without naming the Greek philosopher, the same attack is repeated more concisely, as an abstract of a grotesque story not told, in *Die Fliegenpein:*

Er hat sich an den Einteilungen seines Lieblingsphilosophen erhängt. (*F*, 38)

The structure of the *Aufzeichnungen* books is entirely anti-systematic and thus anti-Aristotelian, due both to the genesis of the early notes and the author's later selection from and arrangements of them. The books represent inventories, or one great inventory, of the manifold thoughts of a twentieth-century intellectual who observes his surroundings, conscious of his own literary work and that of others, and has strong personal preoccupations. He thinks of all of these aspects of Western civilization at once and, in the sense of *Verwandlung* (transformation), from many different points of view.

Harald Fricke considers "kontextuelle Isolation," contextual isolation, one of the dominant qualities of aphorisms.[15] Although under normal circumstances every sentence is integrated into a text that is itself embedded in a situation of communication, the aphorism stands for itself, even if it is found within a chain of other aphorisms. Only in a graphic or spatial sense does it continue the preceding aphorism or precede the one that follows it. Take the following sequence of notes from *Nachträge aus Hampstead* (*NH*, 39), written in 1960, as an example:

Einer, der dem Tod entkommt, weil er nie etwas von ihm gehört hat.

Nachteil der Religionen: daß sie immer von denselben Dingen sprechen. — Vielleicht ist das einer der Gründe, warum so lebendige Geister wie Stendhal von Religionen nichts hören wollen.

Ein Mann, der nicht mehr spricht, nichts außer *bleibenden Sätzen.*

Die Frau, die alle großen Männer gekannt und überlebt hat. Einer von ihnen will nicht sterben. Ihre Verzweiflung.

The first note takes up a central topic of Canetti's thought, death. It constructs a utopian situation, the situation of a man who has never heard anyone speaking about death and therefore is able to escape the fate of all living beings. From that point Canetti leaps to a particular quality of religion and, still in the same note, shifts the focus to one of his masters in world literature, Stendhal. Only one word in the description of this writer, "leben-dig," could be, but need not be, understood as referring by contrast to the preceding *Aufzeichnung*. The third note in this chain resembles the first by virtue of its form: but *Einer* and *Ein Mann*, like *Die Frau* in the fourth note, are frequent beginnings in notes that present utopian situations. Notes that begin this way are experiments of thought. They show what happens in real life by exaggerating and isolating particular trends of individual or social life. But the parallel between the first and the third note does not go beyond this initial similarity. The third note does not touch upon the fundamental problem of death but is rather an ultra-concise satire of the use of language by people imbued with their own importance. Similarly, the fourth note has a satirical tinge, turning against an attitude that men like to attribute to certain women.

My short remarks on this group of arbitrarily selected notes should not be taken as interpretations, but as a hint at the wide range of Canetti's thought in the *Aufzeichnungen*. Primarily, this sequence of notes is an ex-ample of contextual isolation. In the following, I shall show the presence of enormous *Sprünge* (*PM*, 8) between these notes, *Sprünge* denoting gaps and leaps. The author leaps from one invented situation to another, from one exaggerated character — the man who only talks in sentences valid for eter-nity — to the next, the lady who despairs because one of the great men she has known is not ready to die in time for her to survive him. These succinct and overdrawn stories are juxtaposed in the book with general reflections on death, religion, and literary remarks with which they seem to have nothing in common except their place on one page in one volume of *Aufzeichnun-gen*. The consequence of such leaps are gaps in the book, *Sprünge* in its texture that cannot and must not be filled. Between the invention of the man who escapes death because he has never heard it talked about and the observation that Stendhal had no interest in religion there is hardly any connection, and we should not try to establish one. We cannot be farther from a system than in a structure like the one described above, a structure that seems purely additive, the unity of which appears guaranteed only by the person of the writer.

The leaps and gaps and the intended discontinuity of the notes are of course not only a question of form, but also a major topic of these books: the rejection of any Aristotelian or post-Aristotelian system. As another of Canetti's notes runs, "Der Verlust einer vordergründigen Einheitlichkeit [. . .] ist kaum zu bedauern, denn die eigentliche Einheit eines Lebens ist eine geheime, und sie ist dort am wirksamsten, wo sie sich unabsichtlich verbirgt" (*PM*, 8). Any unity in such a work would have to be superficial and in manifest contradiction to the diversity of reality as conceived by the author. Another quotation from Canetti, from the introduction to his book of essays *Das Gewissen der Worte*, is perhaps even more instructive. Again the author wants to justify the diversity of subjects addressed in the collection: "Aber um eben dieses Nebeneinander war es mir zu tun, denn nur scheinbar handelt es sich um Unvereinbares. Das Öffentliche und das Private lassen sich nicht mehr voneinander trennen, sie durchdringen einander auf früher unerhörte Weise."[16] And when in one of these essays, "Dialog mit dem grausamen Partner" of 1965, Canetti discusses his work on *Masse und Macht* and the necessity of the concomitant writing of *Aufzeichnungen,* he states laconically: "Wie kann etwas gut sein, das so vieles bewußt ausschließt."[17]

This wish for an all-inclusive vision of the world is the formal principle of the notebooks. It cannot be fulfilled by a systematic presentation of the writer's observations and experiences. If there is any continuity in these books, it is based on leitmotifs, both of form and of thought. The frequent parallel beginnings with *Er* . . . (He . . .) represent one means of creating formal unity. And of course, Canetti often returns to his major themes: death, language, animals, authors he admires the most, the power of names, and so forth. The recurrence of certain notions is both an indication of their importance to the writer and a technique of tying the books together.

Nevertheless, the diversity is enormous. The notes written in 1961 in *Die Provinz des Menschen* (215–19), which I quite arbitrarily take as an example, touch on the following subjects in only five pages: the brevity of truly important sentences; knowledge; old age; drama and masks; the language of angels; brutal force (*Gewalt*) as a means of ending brutal force; originality of thought; reading; the nature of secrets; death; adjectives; description; change of perspective; Delphi in Greece (and here is a rare case of two consecutive notes with the same motif); the ear as the dwelling place of the intellect; Heraclitus and Aristotle; and history. The list is incomplete because some *Aufzeichnungen* resist being reduced to one notion.[18]

The books of *Aufzeichnungen,* then, turn a sum of fragments into a whole, but they become a cohesive entity only because they allow so much room for tensions and contradictions. A manifold world is reflected in a complex writer's manifold book. Hard as it is, we do justice to Canetti's books of notes only if we try to read them as a whole; paradoxically, while they were not conceived for this mode of reading, the *Aufzeichnungen* nevertheless demand it. A systematic study of literature naturally has problems with books the wealth and diversity of which is conceived as a disavowal of any system. We have good reasons to believe that this structure of the *Aufzeichnungen* and the difficulty of systematically describing them are additional reasons for the comparative lack of attention literary research pays them.

After these observations on the formal aspects of the notebooks, it is important to remark on the form of the individual notes as typified in selected *Aufzeichnungen.*

One important feature is Canetti's use of pronouns. Although it is a well-known grammatical rule that a personal pronoun can be employed only if it refers to a preceding noun, Canetti has a preference for beginning notes with personal pronouns, such as *er* and *sie,* for which no referent has been established. In *Nachträge aus Hampstead* one finds twenty-four notes with this feature on thirty-five pages. This unconventional use of personal pronouns and of the definite article also contributes to the effect of contextual isolation.

In many of these notes beginning with the pronoun "er," the pronoun seems to stand for the author, who also figures as *ich, du,* and *man* (one). "Er wartet auf ein Wort das ihm alle Worte rehabilitiert und rechtfertigt" (*PM* [1952], 150) obviously refers to Canetti himself, who is very much present in these notebooks, which are in principle subjective. The *Er* of "Er sagt nichts, aber wie er es erklärt!" (*PM* [1967], 253) is certainly not the author but rather his opposite, an alter ego perhaps. The note can be read as the nucleus of a not yet written novel or play, as one of the author's extremely reduced stories.[19] Of course, the story is not told by Canetti but has to be invented by the reader, who is only given a hint at its central character, a man, *Er,* who has nothing substantial to say but whose rhetoric is brilliant enough to cover his lack of ideas. What is fascinating about an *Aufzeichnung* like this is its potential for generalization. It is even possible that Canetti permits his readers to relate this sentence to his own work. But one is more ready to take it as the rudimentary stage of a satire on politicians, philosophers, or literary historians. One can almost hear *him* (ihn) talk and talk and talk, without saying anything; but this depends on our imagination. We also hear his public either laughing at him or, more likely, bursting out in enthusiasm about his rhetoric. We can even give *him* an actual name, we know *him.*

If Canetti had written *Aufzeichnungen* in the late twenties, he might well have jotted down something like *Er liebte Bücher und zündete seine Bibliothek an* or *Einer, der Bücher liebt und Feuer an seine Bibliothek legt* or *Dort zündet man Bibliotheken an, weil man Bücher liebt.*

We are close to Canetti's *phantastische Aphorismen,* his fantastic aphorisms, texts between horror and laughter, which Peter von Matt has analyzed.[20] Many of them begin in the same way, with the phrase *Dort* or *Ein Land, in dem* [. . .]. Formulae like these are among the leitmotifs in the *Aufzeichnungen* that I have mentioned; their repetition indicates the transition from statements that reflect reality more or less exactly to another mode of thinking.

In *Das Geheimherz der Uhr,* such *Dort-Aufzeichnungen* are frequent, and the following presents a series of them:

Dort gehen die Leute in Reihen aus, es gilt als unverschämt, sich allein zu zeigen.

Dort muß jeder, der stottert, auch hinken.

Dort werden die Hausnummern täglich gewechselt, damit keiner nach
Hause findet.

[. . .]

Dort knüpft ein Satz an den andern an. Dazwischen sind hundert Jahre. (*GU*, 163–64)

Canetti sketches imaginary ways of life: a life far from the isolation of the
individuals in our society; a form of life in which the handicaps of people are
brutally doubled, or in which society does not want to distinguish between
psychic and physical handicaps; a grotesque form of complete disorder,
which corresponds exactly to Canetti's dislike of systems; a fantastic form of
communication, which respects the rules for forming texts but does not at
all respect the unity of time necessary for effective communication. These
fantastic aphorisms are perhaps less comical than those quoted by Peter von
Matt from *Die Provinz des Menschen,* but they follow the same principle.
Canetti, in a Swiftian way, exposes the invalidity of the normal conditions of
life in a utopia or dystopia, and thus poses the question of their validity in
our reality.[21] These *Dort* or *Ein Land, in dem* formulae, then, are not only
a formal sign for the transition between two worlds but a stylistic device for
repeatedly contrasting reality and possibilities — both positive and negative — a signal that Canetti is here arranging an experiment of the mind.

Many of the *Aufzeichnungen* use the infinitive; many others have no
verb at all, at least not in the principal clause. A few examples from *Aufzeichnungen 1973–1984:*

Charaktere tauschen.

Eigene Zusammenhänge für das Geschehen finden. Spätere?

Ein Amazonas aus Bedenken.

Idioten zu scheinbaren Ratgebern einsetzen.

Der angenehme Augenblick, in dem ein Haß nicht mehr besteht.

Eine Szene aus berstenden Säulen. (*Aufz. 1973–84,* 41, 43, 52, 59, 60)

Ideas expressed in this form, without a defined tense, without an acting
person, claim to be valid independent of time and of development. These
sentences are completely static; their content is not a real or possible event,
but what is said by the writer is true at any time. *Eine Szene aus berstenden
Säulen* may be the destruction of the Philistines by Samson, the result of the
bombing of Nazi buildings, or the destruction of an age-old masterpiece of
architecture by an earthquake. The important thing is the everlasting impression of destruction.

"Der angenehme Augenblick, in dem ein Haß nicht mehr besteht" (*Aufz. 1973–84*, 59) is a happy moment that has come and, as we may hope, will come very often, in the history of humanity as in the life of individuals. By relegating the verb into the secondary clause, Canetti accentuates the character of the happy moment rather than the event of the ending of hatred. The frequent use of the infinitives such as in "Charaktere tauschen" (*Aufz. 1973–84*, 41) should not be misunderstood as a form replacing the imperative, though this function of the German infinitive — *Den Rasen nicht betreten!* (Keep off the lawn) — may have prompted Canetti's preference for it. But the main function is one of generalizing, of rendering the content of such sentences independent of persons and, again, independent of time. "Charaktere tauschen" can be read as a rule for an interesting life, it may be understood as a counsel by or a wish by the author for others or for himself, or, again, as the implied principle of a mind experiment. The infinitive is a simple and effective way of avoiding an unambiguous meaning and opening many perspectives for the imagination. Among the notes without a verb, many consist of hardly more than one noun with the corresponding article, and perhaps an attribute. Some examples of such reductions that are full of ambiguities from *Das Geheimherz der Uhr* are "Lesefrüchte eines Analphabeten" (*GU*, 91) or "Rache der Lesefrüchte" (*GU*, 116). "Bruderkuß zwischen Tintenfischen" (*GU*, 92) is in a funny way grotesque if we read it literally and imagine squids kissing; a figurative reading presents a satirical impression of contacts between writers. The independence of the image from a sentence or a short text, in which it could, of course, be integrated, its total contextual isolation — going far beyond the contextual isolation normal for aphorisms — makes the image even more effective.

A device typical of Canetti is his employment of new words such as *Gottverzehrer* — "Der Gottverzehrer und sein Hunger" (*GU*, 86), "Der Ehren-Schneider" (*GU*, 102) — in a kind of isolated and isolating note. "Der Altexperimentenhändler" (*PM* [1968], 268) is an earlier example of Canetti's sensitive use of the possibilities of German word formation; "Gewissens-Erträge" and "Hintergründlichkeit" (*Aufz. 1992–93*, 43, 93) show that Canetti continued to make use of this kind of pun in his latest notes. His use of the available patterns of German morphology for the invention of such words and their total isolation gives an impression of a grotesque world in which conscience and interest on money change places, in which used experiments are sold like used television sets.

A quite different but still characteristic feature of the *Aufzeichnungen* is Canetti's prodigal use of intertextuality. The notes are not only rich in names of other writers, who are often praised, but frequently attacked; they not only *allude* to other literary texts, but many of them *consist* of sentences taken from a wide range of books. Normally Canetti provides the sources. It is not only Shakespeare, Lichtenberg, Goethe, Büchner, Stendhal, and

Kafka who are quoted, more often than not without a word of commentary, but also texts from ancient and exotic civilizations and ethnographic books. In his introduction to *Alle vergeudete Verehrung*, Canetti speaks of the revelations such ethnographic sources have been for him; he wants his readers to partake in these adventures of the mind.

Apparently, Canetti identifies with many of the sentences he quotes. Numerous elements from other works integrated into the *Aufzeichnungen* color the notes in their entirety. Many of the references to other, earlier texts are to predominantly satirical writers — Cervantes, Quevedo, Kraus. This suggests the tradition in which Canetti wishes to be placed. These particular "pre-texts" correspond to some of the stylistic features mentioned earlier, namely, features characteristic of satire.

If Canetti thus presents himself as a writer impregnated by tradition, the texts taken from ethnographic studies and reports show his interest in truths of human life far beyond Western culture. Many *Aufzeichnungen* pertain to the field of anthropology and revolve around the problems of *Masse und Macht*, crowds and power. Clearly, both faces of Canetti — that of the satirist and that of the anthropologist — are present in his notebooks.

These remarks on the *Aufzeichnungen* only address some of the most surprising stylistic devices Canetti uses in these short prose texts. Many other aspects of these inexhaustible books, for example, the formal parallels between notes, have not yet been touched on. The evolution of Canetti's style from the early to the late *Aufzeichnungen,* his use of the first person and of the second person pronoun, the variations in length of the notes, and the use of metaphor and pun deserve closer attention in a comprehensive study.

I place particular importance on Canetti's artistic achievement in these *Aufzeichnungen*, which has been noted by most Canetti scholars, but tends to be forgotten when readers are overpowered by their scope and wealth. The notebooks are just as rich in brilliant sentences as they are in new thoughts and insights; even if many notes have been jotted down spontaneously without further correction, the *Aufzeichnungen* must be considered a major work of art. In his letters Canetti insisted on the important place of the *Aufzeichnungen* in his work: "Die Aufzeichnungen werden mir immer wichtiger und es scheint mir ein fruchtbarer Ansatz, sie zum Mittelpunkt einer Betrachtung meines Werkes zu machen," he wrote to Ingo Seidler; and to William Stewart, "Mehr als die Hälfte meiner Bücher, darunter eine so zentrales wie die 'Provinz des Menschen,' sind in England gar nicht erschienen."[22] Finally, one of Canetti's last notes sums up what readers should think of this part of his work:

Welche Huldigung ans Tier- und Menschsein, diese Aufzeichnungen!
Bis zur letzten Minute: halte an ihnen fest! (*Aufz. 1992–93*, 50)

A debt of gratitude is due to this magnificent writer for adhering to the discipline he imposed on himself, for continuing to jot down his notes until the last minute.

Notes

[1] Compare Susanna Engelmann, *Babel — Bibel — Bibliothek: Canettis Aphorismen zur Sprache* (Würzburg: Königshausen & Neumann 1997).

[2] The following of Canetti's notebooks will be dealt with here, *Aufzeichnungen 1942–1948* (Munich: Hanser 1965) cited as *Aufz. 1942–48; Alle vergeudete Verehrung: Aufzeichnungen 1949–1960* (Munich: Hanser, 1970), cited as *Aufz. 1949–60; Die Provinz des Menschen: Aufzeichnungen 1942–1972* (Frankfurt: Fischer, 1976), cited as *PM; Das Geheimherz der Uhr: Aufzeichnungen 1973–1985* (Munich: Hanser 1987), cited as *GU; Die Fliegenpein: Aufzeichnungen* (Munich: Hanser, 1992), cited as *F; Nachträge aus Hampstead: Aus den Aufzeichnungen 1954–1971* (Munich: Hanser, 1994), cited as *NH; Aufzeichnungen 1992–1993* (Munich: Hanser, 1996), cited as *Aufz. 1992–93; Aufzeichnungen 1973–1984* (Munich: Hanser, 1999), cited as *Aufz. 1973–84.*

[3] Dagmar Barnouw, *Elias Canetti* (Stuttgart: Metzler, 1979).

[4] Eric Leroy DuCardonnay, *Les "réflexions" d'Elias Canetti une esthétique de la discontinuité* (Bern: Lang, 1997).

[5] Thomas Lappe, *Elias Canettis "Aufzeichnungen 1942–1985": Modell und Dialog als Konstituenten einer programmatischen Utopie* (Aachen: Alano/Rader, 1988). See also Lappe, *Die Aufzeichnung: Typologie einer literarischen Kurzform im 20. Jahrhundert* (Aachen: Alano/Rader, 1991).

[6] Harald Fricke, *Aphorismus* (Stuttgart: Metzler, 1984), 132–39.

[7] Fricke, *Aphorismus,* 138.

[8] Fricke, *Aphorismus,* 136.

[9] Richard H. Lawson, *Understanding Elias Canetti* (Columbia, SC: U of South Carolina P, 1991), 77. Lawson seems to classify the *Aufzeichnungen* among the essays.

[10] Lappe, *Elias Canettis "Aufzeichnungen 1942–1985,"* 243–44; Barnouw, *Elias Canetti,* 116.

[11] Fricke, 33.

[12] Engelmann, 7. The volume itself does not contain any editorial information.

[13] See Lappe, *Elias Canettis "Aufzeichnungen 1942–1985,"* 243–44.

[14] Compare Stefan Baldauf, "Die transzendentale Phänomenologie Edmund Husserls als Methode in Elias Canettis *Masse und Macht.*" Diplomarbeit, University of Innsbruck, ms. 1997.

[15] Fricke, 10–14.

[16] Elias Canetti, "Vorbemerkung," in *Das Gewissen der Worte: Essays* (Munich: Hanser, 1976), 7–8. Here: 7. Cited hereafter as *GW.*

[17] Elias Canetti, "Dialog mit dem grausamen Partner," in *Das Gewissen der Worte*, 50–65. Here: 52.

[18] Penka Angelova at Veliki Trnovo University prepared an index of the names and beginnings of Canetti's *Aufzeichnungen,* which to date has not been published. An index of central notions, which she also plans to undertake, will be a very difficult task.

[19] Compare Peter von Matt, "Der phantastische Aphorismus bei Elias Canetti," in *Elias Canetti: Londoner Symposium,* ed. Adrian Stevens and Fred Wagner (Stuttgart: Heinz 1991), 9–19. Here: 16.

[20] von Matt, "Der phantastische Aphorismus bei Elias Canetti," 16.

[21] von Matt, "Der phantastische Aphorismus bei Elias Canetti," 16.

[22] Letters quoted by Lappe, viii.

Staging a Critique of Modernism: Elias Canetti's Plays

Helga Kraft

The Making and Reception of the Plays

THE RECEPTION OF CANETTI'S DRAMATIC WORK, which includes three plays, has been uneven. Due to an initial hesitation by the author to publish his dramas, a lack of interest from theaters, and the banning of his writings in Germany and Austria during the Nazi period, the plays did not reach the stage until long after completion. For years after writing the plays, only a small circle of people could enjoy them, through the readings that Canetti held either for friends or small audiences. The initial theatrical performances of his first two plays took place in 1965, more than thirty years after their creation in 1932 and 1934 respectively: *Hochzeit* (published 1964) and *Komödie der Eitelkeit* (published 1934). His last play, *Die Befristeten*, written in 1952 (published 1964), premiered in 1967 in Germany. However, Canetti's plays had little impact on the theater, and their productions were short-lived.[1] The theater director Hans Hollmann calls Canetti's plays "Wortdramen," word-plays. In his opinion they could only work with naturalist scenery or in a space implying irony and denunciation. Each unnecessary item on stage would diminish the text and prevent the effect of the cascade of words.[2]

On stage the plays were rarely a success.[3] Also as texts Canetti scholars found them less satisfying than the rest of his works. The critic Dagmar Barnouw even considers the plays outdated. She argues that they do not focus on the inner complexities of their time. Despite intriguing *Grundeinfälle* and occasional brilliant articulations, the plays only seem to touch on important issues. From Barnouw's present point of view at the end of the turn of the millenium the texts appear curiously innocent of the dynamics of the period in which they were written.[4] Richard Lawson finds fault in the cerebral quality of the plays.[5] Such criticism seems narrow, since the plays are of a special intricacy and are actually more responsive to the complexity of their time than other more frequently performed plays. Instead of focusing on issues that are passé, as Barnouw claims, they uncannily foreshadow future attitudes, injustices, and violence in late twentieth-century and early twenty-first century society. For that and other reasons it is possible to consider Canetti's plays as being ahead of their time and hence underrated or even misunderstood. Approaching them as representations of "evil" and "soul" on the philosophical level, or in terms of their proximity to expressionism and the absurd, limits the significance of Canetti's cultural contribution.[6] Since contemporary cultural theory has traced the breakdown of modernism, we are able to recognize in Canetti's plays a postmodern structure in which discussion based on terms such as totality, sin, and the like has become misleading. It is not enough to consider his dramatic work — as Iring Fetscher does — as satire in the traditional sense.[7] Fetscher admits in his analysis of the plays that it has become hard to write satire, and he points to the dissolution of satire at certain times.[8] It must be concluded that such genre classification no longer fits Canetti's dramatic work. The author expresses through his drama a new form of criticism directed against modernity that other works, such as the novel and the essay, could not demonstrate in a similarly succinct and expressive fashion as his mimetic representations do.

It must be noted that traditional dramatic forms are of no interest to Canetti. He learned first from Karl Kraus how to direct scathing tirades against society, and then he moved on to Gogol's works, which taught him critical realism and linguistic playfulness. Most important, from Büchner (especially from *Woyzeck*, famously a play ahead of its time), he gleaned the technique of innovative dramatic experimentation. With such models Canetti embarked on analyzing the hidden ills of society, leaving behind the notion of progress characteristic of modernity. Choosing a futuristic setting and a burlesque structure that borders on slapstick, his drama goes beyond the expressionist and impressionist stage productions of the first half of the twentieth century. As a playwright Canetti never had any interest in a new realism in the manner of Brecht. His style is closer to Fritz Lang's *Metropolis* than to that of his contemporary playwrights. In addition there are Asian influences. Canetti's drama emulates the Kabuki theater with its masks and stylizations. In a conversation with Manfred Durzak, the writer emphatically insisted: ". . . ich bin gegen die Entwicklung im Drama. Für mich spielt das Drama überhaupt jenseits der Zeit. Alles, was einen zeitlichen Ablauf im Sinne von Entwicklung ins Drama hineinbringt, ist für mich undramatisch."[9]

Aristotelian structures were especially suspect to Canetti. He writes in *Die Provinz des Menschen* that reading Aristotle gave him an uneasy feeling. The dependency of Aristotle on classifications he considered a nightmare. For Canetti Aristotle had an underdeveloped understanding of societal rankings which he carried into anything he examined. Canetti objects to Aristotle's use of categories to achieve exactness and clean divisions and to what he perceived as an indifference to whether they were correct or not.[10]

To counteract this kind of social bias Canetti writes non-Aristotelian drama with little or no plot, but replete with ciphers and images, stylized language, acoustic masks, strong social criticism, caricature, and stereotypes. A similar approach has been adopted in postmodern theater, and similar structures can be found in the plays of late twentieth-century writers such as the postmodern Austrian playwrights Marlene Streeruwitz, Elfriede Jelinek, and Peter Turrini. Therefore it is not surprising that Canetti's plays have been revived in the last decades of the twentieth century and the beginning of the twenty-first century, primarily in acting schools and high schools. In the new stagings, postmodern elements are emphasized, for instance the use of dolls rather than actors for many of the roles in Canetti's play *Hochzeit*.[11]

Experiments for the Stage

In Canetti's experiments for the theater, he scrutinizes the project of modernity in its claim to construct and realize improvements in society. His plays conclude that European culture offers merely an illusion of progress. Existing societal belief systems or structures that might have functioned more or less well for a while do not allow for any forward movement. Yet inadequate orientational systems, value systems — be they of religious or secular origin — continue to dominate the popular imagination and persist for lack of other points of reference. When Canetti started writing his plays in the 1930s, traditional value systems had become thoroughly corrupted in the countries where he lived, Germany, Switzerland, and Austria.[12]

It seems logical that Canetti would write for the stage at the beginning of his career, when he shared with many other writers a distrust of what language can express. In the theater he could reach people not only through the written word but have an acoustic and visual impact as well. He wanted to transmit to his audiences a vivid sensual experience beyond conventional, rational understanding, forcing them to think through his experimental models of society and to draw their own conclusions: ". . . ich möchte, daß der Zuschauer selbst operiert mit diesem Einfall [the Grundeinfall of the play], daß er die Abwandlungen des Themas mitvollzieht, so als ob er sie sich auch selbst hätte denken können."[13] Canetti hoped that people would participate creatively in working out their own variations of possible solutions to the dilemma presented on stage. It is not surprising that at that time Canetti thought of himself primarily as a dramatist. Indeed, a close reading of his fiction reveals his tendency to employ dramatic strategy in other genres as well.

In all of Canetti's fiction, human figures are often constructed with comic exaggeration. They do not necessarily fit traditional stereotypes but embody individual adaptations of objectionable societal practices that Canetti reifies. At the beginning of his career the writer drafted the first of a proposed series of eight books that delineated many such fictional characters. He called this series "Comédie Humaine an Irren" (Comédie Humaine of Madmen). In this draft Canetti created various figures embodying exaggerated representations of strange obsessions. Some characters in the novel *Die Blendung* are taken from this abandoned project.[14] For instance, the scholar Kien is not merely a stereotype of the unworldly scholar he first appears to be, but he also embodies the danger posed by people one-sidedly immersed in science, a pitfall that Canetti presents with ridicule and sympathy at the same time. Canetti's strategy of characterization developed in the "Comédie Humaine" is especially evident in his two early plays, but his approach to constructing such bizarre figures continued throughout his career. It has been shown that the collection of monologues, *Der Ohrenzeuge: Fünfzig Charaktere* (1964), which is significantly included in the major edition of his plays, is suitable for performance as well. Starting in the 1990s, one-man performances of the brief and hilarious characterizations from this volume have been staged in Germany.[15] The difference is that the characters in the plays represent themselves, while in *Der Ohrenzeuge* they are only described. Canetti establishes a connection between his characters and those delineated by the Greek philosopher Theophrastus, whose characterizations made up the basis of Greek comedy.[16] Wendelin Schmidt-Dengler considers the major difference between these characters and those in Canetti's *Ohrenzeuge*, and finds in Theophrastus the creation of phenotypes in the ideal sense. He points out that for Canetti it is not important to portray the individual singularity that is opposed to the sameness which the masses require. Rather, the text shows how differentiated the masses can be.[17] Rather than copying what he finds in society, Canetti designs his characters through language in a specific way. Instead of generalizations, the figures are intended to exhibit an individuality that is a reflection of their personal and private specificities. Schmidt-Dengler insists that through these personal characteristics, Canetti nonetheless is not interested in saving individuality against the organization of the masses and thus preserving the individual against the general sameness. Rather he shows how differentiated the masses can be in his contemporary society.[18] Behind this kind of display lurks the struggle for power. All the characters represent different ways of gaining and exercising personal power. As Canetti argued in his major work, *Masse und Macht*, everyone is obsessed with the desire to control other people.

In creating his farcical characters and plays critical of society, Canetti continues a long Austrian tradition that started in the nineteenth century with the dramatists Nestroy and Raimund. His experiments on stage reflect innovation and a clear perception of a twentieth-century crisis to be explored by new artistic means.

Canetti's Plays and the Critique of Modernism

A major problem regarding the reception of Canetti's plays might be found in his choice of science fiction topics for two of his plays, *Komödie der Eitel-keiten* and *Die Befristeten*. Roger Elwood notes in his preface to a collection of science fiction plays, "There are not a great many science fiction plays available. The two forms do not meld easily. It is difficult to translate the imaginative leap characteristic of science fiction writing into the hard reality of dialogue between articulate characters. Writing a science fiction play is a bit like trying to picture infinity in a cigar box."[19] It is not certain if Elwood's considerations partially account for the relative minor stage success of Canetti's plays. In any case, as a playwright he was not so much interested in capturing infinity through science fiction but in the alienation effect made possible by this choice for his criticism of the so-called "natural" givens in the culture of which he was part. he moves beyond *Hochzeit,* which is still anchored in contemporary society. Here he uses a slapstick structure to reveal the breakdown of traditional values based on essentialist ideas, while the two science fiction plays that follow make it clear that Canetti did not believe in salvation through modernist individuality. W. G. Sebald notes that Canetti's strongest critique of twentieth-century culture focuses on the understanding that the violence festering in society is falsely regarded as inevitable. The plays reflect this opinion. Sebald admired Canetti's insistence on deviating from the conception of professional historians who consider the principle of power as normative and natural. Canetti, says Sebald, takes the opposite stance and is concerned with a pathography of power and violence.

Sebald recognizes that Canetti demonstrates the way that closed societal systems continually demand the sacrifice of outsiders for its power processes. He sees power not as an objective reality but a concept that develops randomly from a subjective imagination. Only by using violence does such power create an imaginary world that stands tautologically for reality.[20] A closer look at the plays below will reveal the accuracy of this observation.

While historiography tends to neutralize the insanity created by violence, this kind of thought process — drawing from anthropology, history and psychology — has not only gone into the writing of *Masse und Macht* but also into the making of Canetti's dramatic work. Although Canetti consistently disavowed Freud's findings in psychoanalysis and never motivated his characters accordingly, he was interested in sociopsychology, a mass motivation that is the basis of any culture. When Peter Laemmle regards Canetti's dramas as "a piece of concrete psychoanalysis; that is, they make visible the reaction to drives that are unconscious, displaced, or sublimated under external moral pressure,"[21] he moves Canetti closer to Freud than is warranted. It can be said, however, that Canetti's dramas demonstrate how a society manipulates such drives, perceived or real, through fear-instilling measures.

Some critics want to recognize in Canetti the search for a genuine, pre-cultural human nature. Robert Elbaz and Leah Hadomi believe that in his plays Canetti obsessively attempts to recover the unique reality different from reality accessible through language, a pre-word, a harmonious and synthetic reality, where all subjects or objects interpenetrate and amalgamate with one another."[22] They see such tendencies in Canetti's exploration of language, which would lead to the recovery of some Utopian dimension to cleanse the historical process from the destructive effects of alienation.[23] I do not agree with their view. The expressionist endeavor of finding the "wahre Mensch," the genuine human being, is mistaken in the case of Canetti. Like Kafka, he realizes that such a basic quality of human life — if it ever existed — cannot be recovered. Instead, in his dramas he experiments with different models of cultural development. Ralph Willingham recognizes Canetti's ideas as dystopian visions. Yet, when Willingham says that the writer reaffirms the virtues of the old order by holding up alternatives to ridicule, he, too, misunderstands Canetti, since the writer makes it clear that human culture has not produced any worthy order in the past to yearn for or to bring back.[24]

In his study of Canetti's *Die Blendung* William C. Donahue focuses on the novel's analytical and comical staging of the end of modernism and draws parallels to Canetti's dramatic work written at the time of the novel. Canetti's plays — the best of which is *Hochzeit,* which was written during the time he was working on *Die Blendung* — share the novel's fundamental critique of a radically diminished social sphere.[25] Donahue believes that the answers to the questions posed in Canetti's early work — including two of the dramas, *Hochzeit* and *Komödie der Eitelkeit* — were further explored in the non-fiction study *Masse und Macht.*

Donahue finds *Masse und Macht* to provide an incomplete answer based on an expansive survey of world mythology, folklore, and anthropological reports. Here as well as in his plays Canetti shows that mankind is social by nature. This is for him a fundamental characteristic and not a sign of drive-sublimation, as Freud understood it. Donahue recognizes in Canetti the belief that we have the inherent ability to evolve toward higher forms.[26]

Yet, none of the historically examined social structures necessarily form a straight trajectory toward higher forms. After all, is a higher form a better form? This would be a value judgment, which Canetti refrains from making in his plays. Although Canetti may have believed in the transformative power of mankind's social nature, in his drama he explores the problems of cultural evolution that do not necessarily include progress or betterment. In *Hochzeit* we witness the failings of Western society that has evolved to its logical end: a dystopia. The title of the play is ironic, as the German word for wedding, "Hochzeit," also means "high time," or culmination. A wedding, an event in which two people are joined in the most intense contract existing in most cultures, is being celebrated. However, both bride and bridegroom betray the union and each other while the celebration is still going on, and all the guests participate in turning the event into a Sodom and Gomorrah. It is all a sham, and Canetti presents the "Hochzeit," the high point of Western culture, as a harbinger of its end. In an aphorism he remarked "There is no doubt: the study of man is just beginning, at the same time that his end is in sight."[27]

As it turns out, this play is just as topical today as it was when it was written in 1931, but for different reasons. In *Hochzeit*, as in his other plays, extreme individualism is void of any enlightened element. The characters coexist in one house, yet each one waits for the current owners, who are old and sick, to die, in order to take possession of the property. They pursue this task ruthlessly and without any consideration for each other; no one lifts a finger to help the other, be they parents, business people, lovers, or doctors. The intellectual aesthete, Dr. Schön — probably a reference to Viennese writers whom Canetti disliked[28] — treats life as an impersonal game for his own amusement and profit, and sees no need to lend a helping hand. The building must be understood as an allegory of the human community, and as its structure crumbles, it becomes evident that modernity, to a large extent because of its emphasis on individuality, is a bankrupt concept. Nothing but empty words remain from the old ideals, values, and morality. All that is left is the fulfillment of animal needs and the craving to take everything. Thus, the community is deprived of the glue that provides cohesion. It has become an unsafe place for all inhabitants. For Canetti, the necessary basis, human interrelation, is lost, and the crash is inevitable. Although Canetti was always skeptical of easy answers to problems, he strongly believed in sharing as an expression of an intersubjectivity that could correct the usurpation of power. In *Masse und Macht* he states his views with unmistakable clarity:

> Die Frage der Gerechtigkeit ist so alt wie die der Verteilung. [. . .] Mit der Anerkennung dieser Teilung beginnt die Gerechtigkeit. Ihre Regelung ist das erste Gesetz. Es ist bis zum heutigen Tage das wichtigste Gesetz und als solches das eigentliche Anliegen aller Bewegungen geblieben, denen es um das Gemeinsame menschlicher Aktivität und menschlichen Daseins überhaupt zu tun ist.[29]

In his dramas Canetti shows that there is no basis for a successful culture. By means of a group of extreme caricatures, *Hochzeit* grotesquely exaggerates the obsession of ownership and power and the illusions needed for a pathological self-gratification that have become, in Canetti's view, the foundation of Western society. So-called human values are shown to be a means to attain these ends. Love and loyalty break down as they are revealed to be mere illusions, and the underlying interest in sexual indulgence is revealed along with the buildup of power over others through possession. Thus, the central cipher of the play, the house that everyone wants to own, is destroyed along with its inhabitants.

At the time Canetti wrote this play, Hitler's shadow and his manipulative invocation of traditional values such as love for country and family was falling ominously on "the house of Europe." At the beginning of the new millennium Canetti's warnings implicit in *Die Hochzeit* are still not outdated, since these values continue to be invoked to justify exploitation of "our" house or habitat, the earth, for profit. Canetti by no means pleaded to go back to pure values nor did he accept the illusions of past ideologies as absolutes. These would serve only to reconstruct a culture that has run its course. In *Hochzeit* he sketched the breakdown of human relations, the inability to communicate, as all of the inhabitants merely articulate their desires and use language to fulfill them.

The Structure of the Plays, Language, and the Acoustic Mask

Canetti received his impetus for his writings through Karl Kraus, from whom he learned that individual speech patterns are the key to the innermost character of a speaker. As Laemmle notes, "Karl Kraus's idea that language is 'the great betrayer' of human character, that in language the 'depravity of the soul' finds expression, is the linguistic-critical satirical starting point of Canetti's early plays."[30] Eventually distancing himself from Kraus, Canetti expressed pride in a stylistic invention that he claimed to be his very own contribution to literature, the "acoustic mask," which each character in Canetti's fiction possesses. Not only the words and sentences a character is in the habit of speaking constitute the acoustic mask, but the sound and modulation of the voice as well as the gestures accompanying the utterances. For his characters Canetti had specific voices, ways of speaking, dialect, volume, timbre, hesitation, accompanying gestures, and so forth in mind. This is why he was so fond of reading his own plays aloud in front of small or large audiences, which he did innumerable times, as described in detail by Klaus Völker.[31]

As far as his dramatic works are concerned, the acoustic mask poses a number of problems that Canetti must have realized. Once a play is out of the writer's hands, only the written word remains, and everything else is up to the actor, director, or the reader to interpret or reinvent the writer's concept of the acoustic mask. Often, the language part of the mask is as stylized as in Greek drama and reflects types that are fixed because of cultural tradition, yet with the difference that Canetti fashions a truly individual masks, not phenotypes. They have special capabilities. For instance, they can reveal trends. Gitta Honegger suggests that "Canetti's plays foreshadowed the collapse of a culture and exposed the fascist mentality trapped behind acoustic masks."[32] Through the acoustic mask Canetti also attempts to reveal troublesome social phenomena that cannot be articulated as a narrative. It gives dramatic expression to certain cultural practices that have not yet reached general awareness or crystallized into known stereotypes. Unfortunately in respect to the mask, critics used the mask of traditional drama as a measuring stick for Canetti's drama without recognizing his postmodern invention. In a rather one-sided interpretation Richard Lawson complains that the mask "amounts to a weakness in drama — fish out of water, or rather an intellectualized fish in a dramatic sea, where it lacks the strength to sustain drama and move it forward."[33] Canetti does not want to move the drama forward. With the help of the masks, he lifts it out of the temporal sequence. It is important to him that the changes that the characters undergo be sudden. Canetti calls this sudden change "mask-switching" (Maskensprung).[34] He explained in his interview with Manfred Durzak that it is "nur ein Mittel. Es ist ein Mittel dort, wo es z.B. in einem der üblichen schlechten Dramen um wesentliche Entwicklung geht. Um zu zeigen, ob ein Mensch ein anderer geworden ist, da würde ich den Maskensprung einsetzen."[35] Similar identity changes occur, for instance, in *Hochzeit*, where Canetti makes a point of having his characters reverse their behavior without establishing a developmental cause. He is playing with the concept of identity in a postmodern fashion, indicating that identity is not something fixed or homogeneous, nor does it develop in a straight line. In Canetti's thought, subjectivity and individuality are not based on the enlightenment idea of individual traits endowed by nature and only in need of the proper nurture to unfold. Instead, he shows that one identity is just as possible as the other, and that they can be switched.

Canetti's deviation from traditional drama places his plays outside both the genres of comedy and tragedy. He does not use acts but parts, which he calls *Bilder* (pictures), or locations. They constitute a new blend of tragedy and comedy, the grotesque, and even slapstick. Canetti would protest against any traditional characterization applied to his works. What Salman Rushdie has said about *Die Blendung* applies to Canetti's dramatic work as well; Rushdie notices a negative, ironical, and in his view specifically German inflection.[36] Canetti toys with horror, and the greater the horror becomes, the louder and more piercingly he forces the audience to laugh. No comedy has ever ended as *Hochzeit* does, in the seeming destruction of all the characters. *Komödie der Eitelkeit* culminates in a frightening ending in which the communal experiment fails and all the citizens, who at first were compelled to shout "we, we, we" at the beginning of the play after being forced into an idealized Orwellian society supposedly free of vanity, scream "I, I, I," starting the problem all over again. Yet the excesses to which people go to circumvent new taboos in this play are presented as highly comical, if not grotesque. As the stuttering teacher is transformed into a smooth-speaking, screaming orator, we are reminded of Charlie Chaplin in *The Great Dictator.* It is laughable when people furtively try to glimpse a reflection of themselves in water puddles, in shiny metal, even in the eyes of people, or at the end pay to go to a bordello-like establishment in order just to look at themselves in a mirror. *Die Befristeten,* a bleak work written much later than the other two plays, after the Second World War, has fewer comedic elements but is not entirely without them.

Sources of meaning and the basis of life stories from which the people in *Die Befristeten* draw are not based alone on governmental guidelines of their utopian state. Brief moments of yearning that reach beyond the reality of their society are expressed by the characters in each of the plays. Such yearning, which relates to particular myths or belief systems no longer recognized in society, does not imply that these represent universal truths. Canetti takes a postmodern stance, as he recognizes the power of fictitious sources of meaning, especially in difficult and oppressive times. In *Hochzeit* a dying old lady, the wife of the building's caretaker, who throughout the play (and throughout her life) was never allowed to speak up, and whose personal feelings were drowned out by her husband's biblical litany, reminisces at the very end, "Und da hat er mich auf den Altar zogen und hat mich küsst und so lieb war er" (70). This kind of romantic yearning, or sentimentality, this potential for a life she never experienced, is an important element in Canetti's writings. It includes the value of all other elements ruling people's lives, from actual experience to myth. In this case the altar can be compared to the altar in the "Minnegrotte," or cave of love, as described in a story well-known in Germany, that of Tristan and Isolde, the ancient romantic allegory of absolute love, recorded most famously in versions by Gottfried von Strassburg and Richard Wagner.[37] In *Hochzeit* sentimentality and yearning is as important as cynicism and criticism. In Canetti's world, none of the various approaches to creating meaning in life — intellectual, instinctual, metaphysical — possesses a higher truth or produces a preferable cultural environment.

In his interview with Durzak, Canetti discussed the circular structure of his plays. At the end of *Hochzeit,* after periodic reversals, we are back at the beginning. Canetti theorizes, "so ist dann zum Schluß wieder diese Ursituation da. Man soll also eigentlich mit dieser Ursituation wieder entlassen werden. Das habe ich mir so gedacht, daß damit das Denken überhaupt erst wieder beginnt."[38] This thought is illustrated by the circularity of Hochzeit. The owner, the old woman ("the alte Gilz"), who metaphorically has become one with her house, has the last word in the play, saying, "I am still alive," while the parakeet repeatedly voices the word "Haus . . ." as the bird did at the beginning of the play (12, 70). Since the old woman still lives, one could argue against the common interpretation that the house is totally destroyed in the end. The circle is closed, the problem of a bankrupt place has been highlighted and critically dissected, but it has not been solved. The house is still there, and the owner lives on.

The parakeet's screeches are typical of the repetitious language that is employed in all of Canetti's plays. Such an automatic repetition by someone who cannot comprehend what is being said affects all the characters. They repeat themselves over and over. By means of this strategy Canetti underscores the cultural performativity of what our language — and with it social reality — has become. Although the individual "masked" speaker might have a unique way of reflecting his culture through speech, communication suffers because of this. Yet, they do not only babble in stereotypes. As they speak to each other, Canetti makes evident the hundreds of subtle and hidden ways that personal power is pursued through language. Contrary to charges by some critics that this hinders the dramatic effectiveness of the plays a good performance will draw the viewers' attention to the underlying drama of deception and yearning.

Class and Gender

Just as Büchner's *Woyzeck*, Canetti's plays are concerned with class. They are populated with the little people of society, and Canetti sets them off against powerful and exploitative elements, as did Büchner. At the same time, he connects gender and class. Canetti has been criticized for his portrayal of women.[39] Other critics reject such criticism, for instance Donahue, who does not agree with the argument that in Canetti's works there is a negative view of women. He argues that on the contrary the writer engages in a critique of misogyny. "Canetti's specific contribution, [. . .] is not only to draw our attention to the gendered status of the subject, but more specifically to indict the canonical high German (and European) construction of culture for enshrining misogyny as both normal and normative."[40] In the three plays, no representative of either gender is spared ridicule because of his or her absurd stereotypical gender-based behavior, and the gendered roles they are forced to play in society for their self-preservation are exposed as destructive and often grotesque. Because Canetti is interested in the influence of basic instincts on culture, gender and sex are closely related in his works. In *Hochzeit*, for instance, all of the male characters sexually exploit the retarded daughter of the building's caretaker. The ancient physician, stereotyped already by his name (Dr. Bock) — uses his practice to initiate sex with all of his female patients. He is proud of his prowess at the age of eighty. No intersubjective link between him and the women seems to exists except basic gratification through sexuality. As Canetti not quite convincingly intimates, all the women — the underaged girls as well as the older women — enjoy Dr. Bock's lovemaking and want more. Here a male fantasy is played out.

Quite obviously the play is not written from a modern, feminist point of view, and it is obvious that in Canetti's other works as well, the male voice is dominating. Yet, Canetti cannot be accused of androcentrism. Jenna Ferrara's indictment goes a little too far when she implicates Canetti for "submerging" women's voices, and encoding his own deep-seated hatred of women.[41]

In *Komödie der Eitelkeit* Canetti uses another example to criticize the class-gender combination. He draws caricatures of two human beings, one male, one female: Franzl Nada and Franzi Nada. They are a brother and a sister of advanced age, and — as their names attest — two nobodies in society. They are being used as beasts of burden. Franzl has spent his life carrying heavy loads for rich people, making him a cripple. The sister, in a stereotypical, self-sacrificing female manner has taken the blame for a crime her brother was accused of and spent years in jail for him. They manifest the effects of a system built on exploitation, misogyny, and the oppression of low-status males. They are captured and incarcerated for ridiculous "crimes," as they are performing a service that everyone needs: providing mirrors and flattery for money to maintain the individual's self-image. This duo of doom is only a part of the whole; the master who burdens and torments these two servants bears a version of the same first name: François. He is the first one who obeys the societal dictates and leaves at the end the virtual prison the community has become, where master and slave are identical.

In Canetti's third play, *Die Befristeten,* in which he tried out a new premise for the culture it portrays, basic structures have not changed. A class system has evolved from different privileges. The variations in life expectations recreate inequities and a class system, but one that is different from those with which we are familiar. The people who received the highest numbers at birth and live the longest are clearly the lords. Those with low numbers are the pariahs, and do not even receive an education. Gender inequity results as well. Men with privileged numbers and an assured high life expectancy take wives with a low number, allowing them to remarry many times during their long lives, thus being guaranteed young and beautiful spouses until the end.

Identity and Intersubjectivity

Canetti's gloomy models of future societies are not much better than the model twentieth-century society inherited from preceding centuries. In his second play, *Komödie der Eitelkeit,* Canetti experiments with the future of individual identity in a mass culture as it emerges at the height of modernity. Having traced the failure of the existing cultural model in his first play, *Hochzeit,* the second play envisions Western society only a little further in the future. As in all his plays, he uses a "Grundeinfall," a basic premise or basic idea, in all of its repercussions and causal effects in a certain cultural environment.

Although *Komödie der Eitelkeit* was written in the first half of the twentieth century, the odd *Grundeinfall* still reflects an unresolved cultural reality at the beginning of the twenty-first century, as will be exemplified below. In Canetti's play, the basic premise is a society in which all images of people are banned, for instance photographs, mirrors, and movies. This is not a totally new invention. In the past ideas of prohibiting visual representation were focused on a monotheistic god. The protestant reformation of the sixteenth century forbade the display and production of any images of God. Iconoclasts in their fanatic fervor destroyed all pictures and sculptures in churches and elsewhere, in addition to annihilating all pleasurable sights of art and beauty that distracted from the splendor of the supposed afterlife. Vanity is one of the seven deadly sins in Christian religion, and is connected to pride. While vanity is mostly concerned with appearance, pride is based in a desire to be God, at least in one's own circle or environment. At times mimesis, such as the theater provided, was prohibited as well because it was felt to encourage the breaking of taboos. The same prohibition of realistic images — although not abstract decorations — has existed for centuries in Islamic countries and has recently caused political difficulties on a global basis.

Canetti's *Grundeinfall* is based on a potential direction in which society could go and has partially gone in some countries. Considerations regarding the bankruptcy of societal belief systems have received increased attention at the turn of the millennium as religious fundamentalism, with its restriction of personal freedom, has succeeded in capturing the imagination of many people both in the East and the West. Fundamentalism has forced large groups of people in some Islamic countries where politics and religion are linked into an extremely restricted mode of existence and expression, and permitted harsh and unusual punishment for those deviating from the prescribed life. The prohibition against representations of God's image was expanded to almost all images — including television programs, theater, photographs, non-decorative art, and even the faces of women — by the Taliban regime in Afghanistan, just as in Canetti's play. Lip service is paid to the old religious belief system to produce a morality convenient to those in power, allowing them to reap profits by exploiting the masses and ignoring their own inhuman behavior. In Canetti's *Komödie der Eitelkeit* — written in 1934 when Hitler's henchmen were burning books — all public and private photographs and mirrors are collected and publicly burned and smashed. The smashing of the mirrors in this play and the banning of theater uncannily reminds the audience of the *Kristallnacht,* or Night of Broken Glass, in 1938 as well as the prohibition of movies and television by the Taliban in the year 2000. In *Komödie der Eitelkeit* people must not see their own faces. In Afghanistan in the year 2000, women were beaten and arrested when part of their face or hair showed from under their burka, and people received severe jail sentences for teaching girls or possessing photographs.

In testing the *Grundeinfall* in his play, the prohibition of all images, Canetti shows that the obliteration of all individuality is clearly no solution to vanity. People yearn to look at themselves, to find out for themselves who they are. They must break taboos that prevent them from embarking on this endeavor. Their aberrant behavior in the face of the new law, their sneaky ways of hiding their disobedience, suggests a fundamental need for self-knowledge, for a formation of a conscious, personal subjectivity and individuality through self-perception. Jacques Lacan conjectures this in his mirror-stage theory, which postulates that human beings are becoming human beings through a process of self-recognition via reflection.[42] By understanding oneself as an objective other, as a reflection in the mirror, one becomes an intersubjective cultural being and is at the same time able to interact meaningfully with human beings within a culture and language.

The determination by governmental officials in Canetti's play that such individuality breeds immorality or selfishness and needs to be banned is a dangerous perversion of a basic need within our culture that will entail major repercussions in all fields of human interaction. In the play the opposite of the desired communal sharing is achieved. Banning the implements of vanity causes people to shrink into isolation. Governmental social engineering that runs counter to basic needs cannot be tolerated indeterminably without destroying people's humanity, and will eventually be rejected — as the people did in Canetti's play and as the women in Afghanistan began to do in response to measures that obliterate their individuality after the end of the Taliban rule in 2001. Social critics and politicians were inspired by Canetti's analysis of the modern condition because it shows that society is doomed when rules and regulations take over. One of these critics, Daniel Cohn-Bendit, a publicist and politician, feels a deep kinship with Canetti's work. He is inspired by Canetti's conclusion that civil society constitutes the opposite of mass society. For Cohn-Bendit, a society that wants to survive cannot be based on the docile consensus of a mass society but on confrontation of the issues and the differentiation of sub-cultures as well as the affirmation of difference. Yet Canetti nowhere in his plays gives evidence that such confrontation and differentiation can be successful.[43]

Although Canetti does not offer prescriptions or solutions, he demonstrates the consequences of overuse of norms and rules. Some of Canetti's critics have taken the notion of vanity as an ethical defect too literally. Seeing oneself is but one aspect of subjectivity, without which there cannot be a functioning human community. Rather, to know oneself is the precondition of knowing and communicating with others. Canetti plays with the extremes of fulfilling such a basic need by exaggerating the length to which people will go to fulfill it: in his play, many attempt to capture their own reflection in other peoples eyes; they go fishing to be near the water; they look into puddles in the street; and they purchase small pieces of mirror for enormous sums of money. The established rules appear more and more ridiculous as a result. Here Canetti's quirky humor sets in: for instance, fishing is only allowed when people sit with their backs to the water, and people go around flattering others for a fee.

In *Die Befristeten* Canetti goes one step further than in the previous play. It is a model of an alternative society that moved away from the present subject-centered Western world ages ago. Yet it becomes just as repressive, despite its high moral and ethical ambitions. This utopian society — as most of the ones imagined by thinkers in the past — is built on a shared belief. In this last play, Canetti not only criticizes society but tackles the basic trauma of human beings: they know that they will die, and fear death throughout life.

The alternative system Canetti concocts to produce meaning in the face of death is based on a constructed ideology, on a lie. On such a lie — or if you will, supposition about human nature — any belief system and consequently any society is based. Even Kafka, whom Canetti greatly admired, realized that an illusion could hold together an endangered community, as poignantly demonstrated in his 1924 fable "Josephine die Sängerin oder das Volk der Mäuse." In the utopian society of *Die Befristeten,* a divine law has been introduced long ago to stamp out the ills rampant in primitive society, when human beings lived in terror because of the uncertainty about the moment of their death. For Canetti death is the archenemy, and underlying each social system are strategies to conquer people's fear of death. Canetti, as Barnouw notes, was not so much concerned with "eternal life but rather a longer and better one, taking seriously . . . the social and political implications of the experience of death, the arch-anxiety of time passing, the arch-desire for permanence."[44]

In *Die Befristeten,* Canetti's *Grundeinfall* is the basis of a new belief system that has become second nature and is considered a given. The stability of society is assured by an allocation of different ranges of individual life spans for its citizen. By a simple change of law, individual striving is supposedly removed. All people are told when they will die, and therefore lose fear of the unknown, and make do with the time they have at their disposal. There is no reason to fear violent crime. Through punishment for aberrant behavior in this social engineering project, murder and the fear of death are seemingly removed from the human experience.

The readers and viewers of the play have to suspend their disbelief to accept the premise because people usually fear death no less if they know that they will die at a certain time (as do condemned criminals, old people, or terminally ill people). But in the context of the play, it makes sense that instead of parents choosing a name, each person receives a number from the government at birth that indicates the years available until the preordained moment of death. This number remains sealed within a capsule. The guardian of the capsules — a most powerful, revered, and trusted high priest in the state, the "Kapselan" — opens each capsule at death and confirms the exactness of the date. This act is to convey a sense of certainty in human life.

However, the center of this belief system is empty because the capsules everyone carries around their necks from birth actually do not contain anything at all. Consequently, the high priest of both the legal and the divine truth is a liar, and the center of the community's ethical code is meaningless. Yet those who question the belief system, as does the protagonist, Fifty, are persecuted and condemned to death. This is a paradox and a test, if in fact the truth sets a person free. In the play, as the fabric of societal construction is scrutinized, it becomes evident that lies about the moment of death also conceal the fact that people are not actually at peace within this system. As the drama unfolds, Canetti makes it clear that the strength of people's beliefs — even though based on nothing — is demonstrated by the fact that they indeed seem to die at the preordained time. Perhaps they lose a sense of time; perhaps they lose the will to live, causing the shutdown of their own body's vital functions.

The continuity of cultural meaning is eroded from the moment its basis is questioned or its emptiness is revealed. Canetti here, too, is ambivalent about the value of a belief system. He seems to intimate that it is irrelevant what the center of a belief system is as long as it promotes survival. Yet, once Fifty has discovered the social lie, the system breaks down. With this new knowledge, the people in the play lose all orientation. The friend of Fifty imagines his sister dead at the age of twelve — as he was conditioned to think — rather than to search for her as an old woman who had just gone away and who might still be alive. He cannot give up his old beliefs. His imagination is linked to the cultural consensus of the system that provides him with mental stability and calmness of mind.

In all of his plays Canetti poses the question how to break through a system in which everyone is enmeshed, the people in power and the victims of their abuse. No answers are given in his dramatic work. In fact, he gave up writing fiction altogether, including drama, because of its inherent limitations in dealing with societal conflict. In *Hochzeit,* Canetti brings his audience back to the question of property and lack of human interaction at the end of the play. In *Komödie der Eitelkeit* he confronts the viewers at the end with the unresolved dichotomy of the individual person and community interests. In *Die Befristeten,* when the curtain falls, the play returns to its beginning by posing the question of how human beings can live a meaningful life in society despite the fact that they know they must die. Can social engineering as shown by Canetti — whether undertaken for good or bad reasons — produce anything but violence?

Notes

[1] Elias Canetti, *Komödie der Eitelkeit* (Munich: Weismann, 1950); Canetti, *Hochzeit, Komödie der Eitelkeit, Die Befristeten: Dramen* (Munich: Hanser, 1964), cited hereafter as *HEB*. Canetti, *Der Ohrenzeuge, Fünfzig Charaktere* (Munich: Hanser, 1964).

[2] Hans Hollmann, "Arbeit an den Dramen," in *Hüter der Verwandlung: Beiträge zum Werk von Elias Canetti,* ed. Werner Hofmann (Munich: Hanser, 1985), 234.

[3] The premiere of *Hochzeit* in Braunschweig in 1965 caused a scandal and resulted in a complaint being lodged with the police for its lewd scenes. No less a public a figure than Theodor Adorno came to Canetti's defense, stating that the play's intentions were honorable. The *Komödie der Eitelkeit* also premiered in Braunschweig in 1965. *Die Befristeten* had its world premiere in Oxford, England in 1954 and had to wait until 1967 to be performed in Vienna. In the late 1970s, Canetti's plays were more successful on stage, as for instance *Komödie der Eitelkeit* in Basel in 1978.

[4] Dagmar Barnouw, "Utopian Dissent: Canetti's Dramatic Fictions," in *Critical Essays on Elias Canetti,* ed. David Darby (New York: G. K. Hall & Co., 2000), 132.

[5] Richard H. Lawson, *Understanding Elias Canetti* (Columbia, SC: U of South Carolina P, 1991), 46.

[6] See Krum Gergicov, "The szenische Interpretation des totalen apokalyptischen Bösen in zwei Aufführungen des Dramas 'Die Hochzeit' von Elias Canetti auf der bulgarischen Bühne," in *Autobiographie zwischen Fiktion und Wirklichkeit,* ed. Penka Angelova and Emilia Staitscheva (St. Ingbert: Röhrig Universitätsverlag, 1997), 277–96.

[7] Iring Fetscher, "Elias Canetti als Satiriker," in *Hüter der Verwandlung,* 217–31.

[8] Fetscher, 229.

[9] Elias Canetti/Manfred Durzak, "Akustische Maske und Maskensprung. Materialien zu einer Theorie des Dramas. Ein Gespräch," *Neue Deutsche Hefte,* vol. 22:3 (1975): 515. This conversation has been translated into English by David Darby as "The Acoustic Mask: Toward a Theory of Drama," in *Critical Essays on Elias Canetti,* 106.

[10] Elias Canetti, *Aufzeichnungen 1942–1985: Die Provinz des Menschen; Das Geheimherz der Uhr* (Munich: Hanser, 1993), 48–49.

[11] *Komödie der Eitelkeit* was staged at the Petrinum Gymnasium, Linz in March 2002, Theater-AG des Scheffel-Gymnasiums in June 1999, the Jungmannschule Eckernförde in 1999; the Theater-AG der Edertalschule in 1998. *Hochzeit* was produced at the Theater-AG der Edertalschule, Lahr in 1992; *Die Befristeten* by Anstifter, Freies Theater Heidelsberg in July 1999 and the Theater-AG des Bischöflischen Gymnasiums St. Ursula in March 2002.

[12] Hermann Broch, a writer whom Canetti admired and with whose theories on decline of values — "Wertzerfall" — Canetti was familiar, had influenced the younger Canetti in this aspect of his work.

[13] Durzak/Canetti, "Akustische Maske und Maskensprung. Materialien zu einer Theorie des Dramas. Ein Gespräch," *Neue Deutsche Hefte,* vol. 22:3 (1975): 507.

[14] Elias Canetti, *Die Blendung* (Munich: Hanser, 1963).

[15] The actor Michael Pundt from Junges Bremer Theater has presented on stage almost a third of the fifty characters during various tours through Germany, starting in 1991. The actor is still performing the Canetti program, predominantly in Germany, but also in Switzerland and Austria. Personal email from Mr. Pundt to the author, 24 January 2004.

[16] Theophrastus, *Characters* (Cambridge: Harvard UP; 2003).

[17] Wendelin Schmidt-Dengler, "Ganz nah und dicht beisammen. Zum 'Ohrenzeugen,'" in *Blendung als Lebensform: Elias Canetti,* ed. Friedbert Aspetsberger and Gerald Stieg (Königsstein: Athenäum, 1985), 85.

[18] Schmidt-Dengler, 85.

[19] Roger Elwood, *Six Science Fiction Plays* (New York: Pocket Books), vii.

[20] W. G. Sebald, "Kurzer Versuch über System und Systemkritik bei Elias Canetti," *Etudes Germaniques,* 39/3 (1984): 268–75. Here: 268.

[21] Peter Laemmle, "The Power and Powerlessness of the Earwitness: The Dramatic in Canetti's Early Plays," in *Critical Essays on Elias Canetti,* 109–20. Here: 111.

[22] Robert Elbaz and Leah Hadomi, "The Temptation of Utopia and the Problematics of Language in Canetti's *Auto da fé,*" *Orbis Litterarum* 49 (1994): 253–71. Here: 266.

[23] Elbaz and Hadomi, 267.

[24] Ralph Willingham, "Dystopian Visions in the Plays of Elias Canetti," *Science-Fiction-Studies* 19 (1992): 69–74. Here: 70.

[25] William Donahue, *The End of Modernism: Elias Canetti's Auto-da-Fé* (Chapel Hill: U of North Carolina P, 2001), 204.

[26] Donahue, 205.

[27] From: WEB: www.intelligentsianetwork.com/canetti/canetti.htm.

[28] Canetti indeed incorporated real persons into his dramas, as he related to Manfred Durzak for instance in the case of Francois Fant in *Komödie der Eitelkeit,* about whom he remarked "that enormously arrogant and spoilt person. . . . was a very bad Viennese writer by the name of Paul Frischauer." Durzak/Canetti, "Akustische Maske und Maskensprung. Materialien zu einer Theorie des Dramas. Ein Gespräch," *Neue Deutsche Hefte,* vol. 22:3 (1975), 96.

[29] Elias Canetti, *Masse und Macht* (Hamburg: Claassen, 1960), 216.

[30] Laemmle, "The Power and Powerlessness of the Earwitness: The Dramatic in Canetti's Early Plays," 113.

[31] Klaus Völker, *Die Dramen. Text + Kritik: Zeitschrift für Literatur* 28 (1970): 34–43. Here: 39.

[32] Gitta Honegger, "Acoustic Masks — Strategies of Language in the Theater of Canetti, Bernhard, and Handke," *Modern Austrian Literature,* 18/2 (1985): 57–60. Here: 59.

[33] Richard H. Lawson, *Understanding Elias Canetti* (Columbia: U of South Carolina P, 1991), 43.

[34] Durzak/Canetti, "Akustische Maske und Maskensprung. Materialien zu einer Theorie des Dramas. Ein Gespräch," *Neue Deutsche Hefte,* vol. 22:3 (1975): 515.

[35] Durzak/Canetti, 515.

[36] Salman Rushdie, "Die Schlange der Gelehrsamkeit windet sich, verschlingt ihren Schwanz und beisst sich selbst entzwei," in *Hüter der Verwandlung: Beiträge zum Werk von Elias Canetti,* ed. Werner Hofmann (Munich: Hanser, 1985), 89.

[37] The minnegrotto in Gottfried von Strassburg's "Tristan": The allegory of minne (love) stems from church symbolism; the grotto is described like a cathedral and alludes to a house of love. In Canetti's *Hochzeit* the bed takes the place of the altar. Gottfried von Strassburg, *Tristan,* vol. 2. Based on the text by Friedrich Ranke, re-edited and translated into New High German. (Stuttgart: Philipp Reclam Jun, 1980), verses 16716–16723, 411.

[38] Durzak/Canetti, 509.

[39] See for instance Kristie Foell, *Blind Reflections: Gender in Elias Canetti's Die Blendung* (Riverside: Ariadne Press 1994), and Richard H. Lawson, *Understanding Elias Canetti* (Columbia: U of South Carolina P, 1991).

[40] Donahue, *The End of Modernism: Elias Canetti's Auto-da-Fé* 47.

[41] Jenna Ferrara, "Grotesque and Voiceless; Women Characters in Elias Canetti's Die Blendung," in *Proceedings and Commentary: German Graduate Students Association Conference at New York University,* ed. Patricia Doykos Duquette, Mathew Griffin, and Inike Lode (New York: n.p. 1994), 86–94. Here: 86, 93.

[42] See Jacques Lacan, "The Mirror Stage as Formative of the Function of the I," in *Écrits: A Selection* (New York: Norton, 1977), 1–7.

[43] Daniel Cohn-Bendit, "Die Macht der Massen und das Gewissen der Individuen," in *Der Stachel des Befehls: IC Canetti Symposium,* ed. John Pattillo-Hess (Vienna: Löcker, 1992), 114.

[44] Barnouw, 129.

"Gute Reisende sind herzlos":[1] Canetti in Marrakesh

Harriet Murphy

ALTHOUGH WRITTEN IN 1954, Canetti's notes on his trip to Morocco were not published until 1967. Herbert Göpfert, his Munich editor, maintains that this was because Canetti did not think them significant.[2] In spite of this, reviewers of *Die Stimmen von Marrakesch* have complimented Canetti on his superbly classical prose and his passion for detail and immediacy, on an ability to transform apparently insignificant scenes into parables or epiphanies, on his unusual combination of sarcasm and mysticism, on his deeply felt sense of death, on his attraction to the intensity of life he was able to find in the dejected, and those children, beggars, storytellers, and blind people he comes across on his trip.[3] Even his arch-critic Marcel Reich-Ranicki made a generous exception to this particular work, and cordially pronounced it magical, and a work of "Dichtung."[4]

Die Stimmen von Marrakesch certainly implies that in ordinary life there is much hidden gravity, complexity, and mysteriousness. I shall be arguing that the work also implies that receptivity — particularly the play of the eyes and the ears — is an aesthetic ritual without ethical implications.[5] The strict separation of the aesthetic from the ethical is a questionable underlying truth that is kept obscured in Canetti's travelogue because it is concealed behind a veil of multicultural richness, in particular, evidence of the exotic Jewish and Muslim influences in Marrakesh. These doubtlessly seem doubly alluring and mysterious to readers experiencing Morocco vicariously outside Africa, as mediated textually in literary German. Individuals Canetti meets who are either Muslim or Jewish are, however, not primarily seen as representative of their Muslim or Jewish cultures. Rather, any serious discussion of the doctrines underpinning Jewish or Muslim life is dismissed or erased in favor of an aesthetic-ethical absolute, which will appeal to Canetti's Western audience. This is the secular, humanist view that life is a transient pose or performance *for the eyes and for the ears* of a spectator subject, in this case the writer/flâneur Elias Canetti, on holiday in Morocco from London, a cosmopolitan Jew who speaks French with the people he meets, most of whom can only manage broken French, which limits the scope for serious exchanges. Canetti, the writing subject, thus emerges as the principle protagonist of the work even though he appears so self-effacing, and the primary subjects in the stories seem to be Others different from himself. Canetti also continually stresses his receptivity to the sounds and sights of the human and other subjects around him. Yet, there are virtually no attempts to object to the rituals of injustice, cruelty, manipulation, oppression, and suffering. Instead of mediating an informed account of the constituent elements of the Jewish and Muslim cultures unlikely to be known to his readership, the individuals Canetti dwells upon are shrouded in superficially beguiling mystique. Proceeding in this manner implies the understated worldview that life is perpetual warfare, the extent of which is hidden because the rituals of exchange are so emphatic. The cumulative effect of all the narrative devices of exposition and dialogue make the banal and everyday seem mysterious, a "real presence" of the kind discussed by George Steiner in *Real Presences* (1989). Yet the latter goes beyond the appearance of the ordinary in the sense meant by Steiner. As the eternal present and the ahistorical combine, the readers are simply a momentary part of a drama of an immediate experience, a domestic, commercial, sexual, or religious ritual that begins and ends quite inauspiciously, as if it were a brittle fragment of life requiring no real meditation. One could go even further than Steiner, and talk about a *questionable* cult of the metaphysics of presence in *Die Stimmen von Marrakesch*.[6]

We shall conclude that critics should link the apparently inconsequential phenomena of everyday life in *Die Stimmen von Marrakesch* to an ancient heresy known as Gnosticism.[7] According to Hans Jonas, Gnosticism is a Jewish phenomenon; a pre-Christian idea that all the world is only matter; that embattled spirits are trapped and imprisoned in matter; that matter remains unredeemed; and that man has not the power or the will to resist the pull of the flesh. Historically this anti-Christian heresy is revived in the West to subvert and undermine the promise of spiritual redemption from sin made by the "Word made flesh and dwelt amongst us" given by the very Messiah whom the Muslims and Jews reject. The standard polemical work written in the second century against the threat posed by Gnosticism, by St. Irenaeus of Lyons, titled *Against the Heresies,* argues from a Christian point of view that the Gnostics who rejected the Son of God were fiercely dualistic, at war with the possibility that the soul could heal the body.[8] The Gnostics posited instead a kind of *Urmensch,* a primeval human being who was unable to transcend himself because of a sustained resentment to the doctrine of the Incarnation. As it is the doctrine of the Incarnation that Christians, not Muslims and Jews, believe has redeemed the flesh in perpetuity from slavery to sin, we will be looking closely at how *Die Stimmen von Marrakesch* negotiates representation of the flesh.

The view that some of Canetti's writing revives Gnosticism helps provide a coherent interpretation that explains why the work seems to sponsor the categories of the primitive and atavistic that we have associated with

Canetti since *Masse und Macht.*[9] *Die Stimmen von Marrakesch* provides a sharper focus on the "benefit" of the disciplining of non intellectual matter provided by commercial, religious, domestic, or sexual rituals only in that it tells stories involving identifiable human beings, unlike *Masse und Macht,* which largely comprises summaries of sociological and cultural history, the wealth of which material submerges the individual. As Gnosticism always goes hand in hand with a "gnosis," secret knowledge mediated sub-textually to readers, we will show that the secret hidden in *Die Stimmen von Marrakesch* is that the rituals of cruelty, violence, manipulation, opportunism, or barbarism are integral parts of the human condition such that we can do nothing about them. Readers are expected to collaborate with these hidden first principles, which do not recognize the power of the will, of the spirit, or of the desire to resist compulsion. That Canetti's Gnosticism is also a vote of confidence in the primitive and the atavistic, or the non-intellectual and the anti-intellectual, can be read in two ways.[10] He is indifferent to self-conscious human subjects and human intellectuals who are able to transcend themselves, others, or mere matter. There are no examples of such people in the Muslim or Jewish cultures in Marrakesh, they all remain in chains. Important for the thesis that *Die Stimmen von Marrakesch* is Gnostic is that Canetti the traveler is the possible exception to this rule. He is at least free to benefit from the endemic slavery of the flesh around him on the stage of life, in the form of an exalted aesthetic experience, which provides him with so much sensual stimulation. Does this constitute a counterargument to Gnosticism? No. Because Canetti's independence from matter only provides him with a temporary illusion, one that he can only validate by transcribing it in the written word. It does not lead to any human development and merely provides a pretext for literary life. Second, *Die Stimmen von Marrakesch* is set in a city where haggling, bargaining, and personal contacts seem to define all aspects of private and public life, where what one might call exploitation has been raised to the dignity of a ritual that does not need to be questioned. The city, and the principle in this organized form, is alien to Western readers on this count alone. Its dynamics cannot be covered by the descriptive terms "feudal" or "capitalist" or by the polemical Marxist terms "feudal/capitalist." The work is also solitary and anti-intellectual in that Canetti avoids negotiating the modern conception of urban life in the West with which his readers are more likely to be familiar. Authors such as Tönnies, Simmel, and Benjamin all take an interest in cities in the industrialized West like Paris and Berlin.[11] *Die Stimmen von Marrakesch* focuses, by contrast, on the facets of a North African city. In this environment standards of trade are still personal, with the result that Marrakesh life seems to be resistant to the Marxist inspired accounts of Western-style consumerism, commodification, and alienation. In other words, Canetti avoids dealing with the influence of the aesthetics, economics, and politics of the intellectual Left on theory, literature, and criticism that relates to the city and the largely materialist interpretations of human life in German philosophy and cultural thought since Hegel and Marx. According to this tradition, the material influences acting on human subjects conspire to produce a negative monolith called "society." This kind of thinking can be radically simplistic, usually a mix of rhetorical ideas about the impossibility of change, rather than practical strategies for change.[12] But Canetti's travelogue is not in favor of intellectual thinking and does not even offer counter-arguments to these dialectics and simplistic notions of cause and effect, preferring to ignore them by substituting the cult of immediacy. This helps to explain why we have no vision, just anecdotal fragments, and certainly none of the apocalyptically flavored cause-effect determinism that appeals to those who prefer the intellectual Left's positions and who are often predisposed to defeatism and despair. When *Die Stimmen von Marrakesch* does appear to call into question the nature of the link between the material and the spiritual, it does so only to insist on the tactical necessity of survival as a human instinct, which is why the world of Marrakesh appears atavistic.[13] Canetti's characters have already capitulated to the demands of atavism: they buy, sell, eat, drink, and socialize without any concern for the world beyond the immediate. This principle, the Gnostic one of compulsion, is fully endorsed to the extent that it resists being synthesized into a rhetorical argument about the wider context of exploitation, misery, injustice, or cruelty, upon which, as we have already indicated, Canetti is himself parasitically dependent for his own momentary experiences.

The first vignette in *Die Stimmen von Marrakesch,* "Begegnungen mit Kamelen" (*Marrakesch,* 7–15), for instance, knows about cruelty to animals. Canetti does not really glamorize the cruelty in the sense of making what is actually primitive an example of the élan vital, like the intellectual Right tends to do in Schiller, Kleist, Nietzsche, in Surrealism and Futurism, or in French theater of cruelty. Neither does he convert the episode into a piece of agitprop to suit the designs of the intellectual Left, as does Brecht. The predictable liberal response to the slaughterhouse — likely to involve a condemnation of cruelty as universally awful, as if there were a necessary causal link between sending animals to the slaughterhouse and sadism — does not emerge (so Canetti will not be co-opted by the animal rights movement). Canetti simply makes the ritual the logical climax to a story involving action and drama, with a limited prehistory and limited aftereffects. Those who are involved in sending camels to the slaughter house participate in a relatively impersonal economic and social ritual in Marrakesh, one that both literally concentrates the minds of the community and allows it to earn its living. The animals are slaughtered as efficiently as possible; no one involved is deranged, indulging his instincts for murder. That said, one might reasonably ask what is the interest of such a cold-blooded story. If in the immediate sense the story is just a chronicle of how camels are literally deprived of their freedom, the deprivation is grotesque because they are tortured by their keepers and a rope is sewn through the nostrils; the background is a struggle accompanied by piercing cries of pain. But this immediacy elicits the most introductory observations from Canetti, the commentator, about the meaning of the ritual. The story is "tragisch"; the struggles of the camels "unerwartet," "unheimlich," and "verzweifelt." As the camel traders try to subjugate the camels, the ritual is repeated in other ways in the human world. Beggars pester the travelers hoping to subjugate them and compel them to part with money. Other camels grazing on the sidelines give the impression of being part of a different world. But their comparative security and peace is just an interlude before they too become part of the ritual and will be sent to be slaughtered. Canetti then extends his thesis, which levels the differences between the human and animal world, by introducing an analogy, stating that camels majestically chewing their fodder are similar to "alte englische Damen, die würdevoll und scheinbar gelangweilt den Tee zusammen einnehmen, aber die Bosheit, mit der sie alles um sich herum betrachten, nicht ganz verbergen können." This is a vague and strange identification that reflects on Canetti's conviction that humans are as at war with one another as greedy animals who have no control over their appetites. The level of generality is partly responsible for the disturbing "mystery." For instance, as the story progresses, the collective of camels merges with the collective of old, tea-drinking women, which then merges with "die blauen Männer," the "blue men, from the Atlas mountains." This collectivization of the flesh reaches its logical climax with the clear indication that the camels are on the way to the slaughterhouse, and to the related expectation that the dead flesh can then be sold after it has been purified of blood in accordance with Islamic law. At this point Canetti begins a serious conversation with one of the camel traders who fought in the First World War. The subject matter reinforces the already oppressive atmosphere. The camel trader regrets the decline in standards of warfare. Modern warfare is all about machines; formerly men at least were significant, he says. He is proud of the wounds he sustained. Yet he abruptly leaves Canetti because he spots an opportunity to ingratiate himself with other lurking foreigners, but only after he has related the horror story of how camels with rabies can be a menace to the human world. The smell of blood on those who work in slaughterhouses triggers an impulsive response over which the rabid camel has no control. He often terrorizes his executioners, even taking revenge by asphyxiating men in bed asleep at night. Neither glamorization of violence nor protest, this kind of storytelling is certainly morally detached and indifferent, but it is also a meditation on the near-universal reality of war, aggression, subjugation, opportunism, and suspicion from which there is no relief. Canetti allows his eyes to record the events. He allows his ears to record the sounds of pain and suffering. But his mind does nothing more than cover the primitive and atavistic with a superficial veneer of superiority or detachment. "Während der übrigen Zeit unseres Aufenthaltes in der roten Stadt sprachen wir nie mehr von Kamelen," he concludes of his friend's and his own decision to avoid confrontation (16).

Likewise, "Die Suks" is a highly sensual evocation of another economic and social ritual, haggling in the market place (16–20). While the liberal Left might here indulge its aesthetic and moral disgust for money, and reach out for the magic words "commodity" and "commodification," Canetti observes the human instincts for survival and self-respect with a combination of morally neutral detachment and awe, and reverence. This vignette develops into an appreciation of the moral skills and pride at stake for both parties in any exchange. But it could be said to begin where "Begegnungen mit Kamelen" left off: "Es ist würzig in den Suks, es ist kühl und farbig. Der Geruch, der immer angenehm ist, ändert sich allmählich, je nach der Natur der Waren. Es gibt keine Namen und Schilder, es gibt kein Glas. Alles was zu verkaufen ist, ist ausgestellt. Man weiß nie, was die Gegenstände kosten werden, weder sind sie an ihren Preisen aufgespießt, noch sind die Preise fest." The hidden theme is the near-universal presence of undifferentiated matter, which can only be relieved by changes in the air Canetti breathes in through his nostrils, those organs that had been so attacked by the camel traders. Apart from this single pointer, everything is an open question; the prices are not fixed but will be arrived at after a period of haggling. The repetition is visible. "Da hockt ein Mann inmitten seiner Waren . . . Aber der Mann im Gelaß neben ihm, der ganz anders aussieht, sitzt inmitten derselben Waren" (17). The men at the bazaar are *the same,* all selling the same wares — leather handbags — in exactly the same way. It is only because Canetti indulges his own fantasy in the narrative that the reader is momentarily afforded relief from the monotony: "Man wäre gar nicht verwundert, wenn sie plötzlich in rhythmische Bewegung gerieten, alle Taschen zusammen, und in einem bunten orgiastischen Tanz alle Verlockung zeigten, deren sie fähig sind" (17), he suggests. Just as in the first sketch, where Canetti's own imagination directed us away from the camels and to the idea of old, tea-drinking ladies as animals, he now allows his imagination to extemporize, and in a quasi-surrealist way, would have us reflect on an impossible thrill, that of the leather hand bags combining in a Dionysian dance. He imagines the material and immobile momentarily animated by some primeval life-spirit, the only link being desire — the desire of the traders and their handbags to attract their passing audiences and the desire of dancers to command the attention of their spectators. Just as the camel trader had made a value judgment about the comparatively poor standards of warfare in his day because of the advent of the machine, Canetti regrets that machines have taken over in the handbag world, which are now mechanically produced, whereas they were once the handiwork of individuals. He then regrets the passing away of artisan life in the West, the absent home, which is now a point of reference in a comparison that favors the East from Canetti's own perspective: "Denn zur Verödung unseres modernen Lebens gehört es, daß wir alles fix und fertig ins Haus und zum Gebrauch bekommen, wie aus häßlichen Zauberapparaten" (18). Following this Canetti presents a less personalized statement of his moral detachment from the West in a serious cultural comment on the way Muslim culture casts a veil over, or deprives, women of their ability to see. But it is the fact that all aspects of the work process involved in the manual production of handbags are visible that is important in this acknowledgement of the reality of the invisibility of women: "In einer Gesellschaft, die so viel Verborgenes hat, die das Innere ihrer Häuser, Gestalt und Gesicht ihrer Frauen und selbst ihre Gotteshäuser vor Fremden eifersüchtig verbirgt, ist diese gesteigerte Offenheit dessen, was erzeugt und verkauft wird, doppelt anziehend." The acknowledgement that women are hidden is not a sign that this story is going to open up Muslim culture to critical scrutiny (18). Why? Because Canetti is absorbed by his own deprivation, which is only temporary and is amply compensated for, unlike the permanent deprivation experienced by the Muslim women. What is visible — the handbags — becomes doubly thrilling for those who like feasting their eyes and ears on displays, ergo maintaining the status quo of the permanent deprivation of women is in order. This personal reality supercedes objective reality and points to the reality of Canetti's ego, the demand for instant gratification in particular.

Canetti also relishes the thrill of bargaining and is dismissive of those who do not have the requisite skills ("jeder Dummkopf," 20); he is jealous of the intimacy between the salesman and his product: "Eine Intimität, die verführerisch ist, besteht zwischen ihm und seinen Gegenständen" (19). The art of bartering is the subject of the meditation here: "Manche entwaffnen einen durch Hochmut, andere durch Charme. Jeder Zauber ist erlaubt, ein Nachlassen der Aufmerksamkeit ist unvorstellbar" (21). So saying, Canetti's thesis is related to the brief interlude of the Dionysian dance. There is uniformity at the material level in the bazaar. But in the human world it is possible to elevate the relatively banal task of buying and selling into a ritual in which men collaborate with men in a thrilling exchange before one party parts with money and acquires his purchase, as if he has displayed some real genius, or participated in a magical event. "Die Brotwahl" (83–84) recapitulates most of this love of bargaining and admiration for the agonistic possibilities of exchanges in which superiority and one-upmanship can be manifested in word or deed as part of a challenge on mutually gratifying terms, a feature, I argued, which was central to *Die Blendung*.[14]

For a work in which Canetti shows off his own delight at the power of his own eyes, it is interesting how frequently we come across those who have been completely deprived of their sight. "Die Rufe der Blinden" (21–24) extends the idea clarified in the preceding story of the importance of relying on one's wits to earn a living. It admires the skills blind beggars have to acquire for survival. It concludes with something approaching awe as Canetti marvels at the commitment the blind men have made to praising Allah, a word repeated again and again: "Ich habe begriffen, was diese blinden Bettler wirklich sind: die Heiligen der Wiederholung" (25). But it begins with Canetti's admission, following a vague gesture towards the mysterious process of literary writing, that he had no intention of learning any of the Berber languages. Why? In order to protect his ears, to preserve his ears for the magical ritual of listening to strange noises without understanding them or desiring to understand them: "Ich wollte von den Lauten so betroffen werden, wie es an ihnen selber liegt, und nichts durch unzulängliches und künstliches Wissen abschwächen" (22). He not only intends to preserve his aural purity, he has no intention of exploring intellectually the meaning of the aural and visual signs of the Arab world that is so foreign to him. So, although Canetti becomes fascinated by the blind men invoking Allah, the fact they are doing so only to attract donations does not provoke any negative commentary. Why? The scene is simply a performance, the sounds just "akustische Arabesken um Gott, aber wieviel eindrucksvoller als optische." Rather than penetrate through to the meaning of the words, rather than reflect on the obvious contradiction between appearing to be holy while attempting to earn a living from one's public performance, Canetti is simply content to see the intensity of the sounds as evidence of the Gnostic principle of spirit trapped in matter in an unredeemed, unregenerated form, animated only by undifferentiated energy: "Es ist eine besondere Energie des Forderns darin" (24). Having acknowledged that the Muslims believe that the poor collectively enter paradise ahead of another collective, the rich, indicating another level of conformity that attracts no critical comments, Canetti then admits he made a failed attempt over a period of time, once in England, to sit at home and mimic the blind beggar, invoking Allah repetitively, as if he too wished to merge with an amorphous collective of undifferentiated sound. In spite of this, the vignette concludes with a hymn to monotony, as if it were something superior.

"Der Speichel des Marabu" (25–30) looks at another blind beggar in a way that also awakens our physical and moral disgust, since in the story the blind man uses his spit and his tongue to find out precisely how generous people have been with their money. Questions of hygiene figure quite prominently in *Die Stimmen von Marrakesch,* and Canetti is at first both attracted and disgusted by the way the beggar slobbers over his donations. He has no sympathy for him, but he does admit to having a certain amount of reverence for the physical pleasure the beggar derives from the rather grotesque act, perhaps even jealousy. Once again Canetti allows his fantasy free reign. In the first instance he assumes that the man is blessing his donors, believing, like the beggar, and in keeping with Islamic law, that it is possible to buy one's way into paradise. Only later is Canetti disabused of this assumption by another character: "Das ist ein Marabu. Er ist blind. Er steckt die Münze in den Mund, um zu spüren, wieviel Sie ihm gegeben haben" (28). At this point Canetti does not adjust his illusion that the beggar was thinking about the afterlife, when in fact he was only counting his current assets. He assumes that the momentary has merely outlived its transient value, and therefore turns to another distraction, substituting himself as the central issue and claiming that he has become the beneficiary of a true blessing from a blind beggar, whose morality is at least open to question in the eyes of a skeptical readership: "Er wandte sich mir zu und sein Antlitz strahlte. Er sagte einen Segensspruch für mich her, den er sechsmal wiederholte. Die Freundlichkeit und Wärme, die während seiner Worte auf mich überging, war so, wie ich sie noch nie von einem Menschen empfangen habe" (30).[15] Without having entered into any relationship, Canetti's passivity, reflected by his moral/intellectual indifference in meditation after the event, leaves behind a strange impression, a man who is capable of denying material reality and the reality of materialism altogether. The idea of a professional beggar whose holiness is part of a well rehearsed performance is morally repugnant to the Christian or humanist audience digesting the story in the West. Yet the story overlooks the materialist culture of Islam in favor of Canetti's own needs. He is so adept at surrendering himself to momentary gratification, and he has no idea what the holy man "says" because he cannot speak his language. Nonetheless, he is prepared to assume that his warmth is genuine.

This ability to divorce the serious from the transitory is often presented to the reader as a sign of Canetti's own moral purity. He is, for instance, shocked in "Die Verleumdung" (84–90) to discover that the children who are beggars are already aware of their attractiveness to older men and can already be bought at a price. Canetti becomes friendly with the man who runs the restaurant and who reports faithfully a grubby story about a visit to a prostitute in which he relishes the fact that he got away without having to pay for services rendered. *Die Stimmen von Marrakesch* began with a meditation on trade in camel flesh and the stories return repeatedly to trade, even trade in human flesh. At what level is there any real difference? None. This is the Gnostic secret — that life is trade — in either money or flesh. Often the two come together in prostitution, quite logically it would seem, given the Gnostic proposition. Why? Because unredeemed matter has no alternative but to surrender to impulse or compulsion. And as there is no higher level than this reality, it makes sense to expect some kind of material reward from the momentary pleasures of the flesh. The spirit that might desire something more permanent or more meaningful is thus partly trapped because of the absence of faith in a higher spiritual reality. Therefore that selfsame spirit is compelled to be frustrated; it has no external sources of consolation or support, no way of escaping to freedom. The universal slavery of the flesh is not a choice but a burden; it makes objective orientation outside of momentary illusions impossible, and it makes anything resembling objective morality and objective truth redundant. In place of such deep-seated desires for a higher spiritual reality, we have the iron hand of tyranni-cal law, ritual, and social convention, from which there is only transitory relief for a transitory presence in Marrakesh, the spectator and purveyor of illusions, Canetti.

In "Stille im Haus und Leere der Dächer" (30–33), "Die Frau am Git-ter," and "Scheherezade" (33–39 and 93–103), for instance, we dwell in some detail on the inflexible laws governing the conduct of women under Islamic law. We see how the Gnostic proposition of the undifferentiated nature of all matter effectively underpins Islamic law. Women under Islamic law are expected to be the same. They are all wearing veils and cannot be identified individually. But Canetti does not mind. He is not interested in individual women. "Die Frau am Gitter," who is exceptionally not wearing a veil, is no more free because she is without the symbol of her sameness. To Canetti, she is just a source of oracular noise anyway, undifferentiated, not only because Canetti has no way of understanding what her Arabic words mean, but because he is quite happy to superimpose a level of purely private meaning on the raw materials he has in front of him by assuming that the language he cannot understand is full of "Koseworte" — terms of endear-ment, and "Zärtlichkeit" — tenderness: "Ihre Worte kamen wie aus einem Brunnen und flossen ineinander über" (33). As it happens, this analogy just keeps present in the reader's mind, for all its attempts to be imaginative, the idea of undifferentiated mass. So in spite of the fact that she is exceptional both within Marrakesh and in Canetti's eyes because she is a source of mys-tery that he has fabricated for his own consumption, she never succeeds in transcending the reality of her enslaved state as undifferentiated mass. The human world is continuous with the material world, and vice versa, as Ca-netti's ability to merge the two continues: "Die Häuser sind wie Mauern, man hat oft lange das Gefühl, zwischen Mauern zu gehen, obschon man weiss, dass es Häuser sind: Man sieht die Türen und spärliche, unbenützte Fenster. Mit den Frauen ist es ähnlich, als unförmige Säcke bewegen sie sich auf den Gassen weiter" (35). The vignette "Stille im Haus und Leere der Dächer" merely affirms the cultural truism already identified about Islamic women, and is no more than a recapitulation. They are expected to wear a veil. It is not permitted for men to speak to them or to observe them when they are alone.

In "Scheherezade" the theme of the trade in flesh continues, but not before the principle of undifferentiated mass has been reaffirmed. This time we are told the bar receives three kinds of types, French, American, and

English guests; and they all pay the same 120 francs for a glass of cognac. The generalities disappear once we are introduced to Monsieur and Madame Mignon. The move from the general to the particular does not bring relief because the former spends most of his time at the brothel across the road. The lonely and desolate individual Ginette then appears center stage and seems to represent the possibility of hope as the single most fully developed person in *Die Stimmen von Marrakesch*. She is looking for someone to relieve her of her unhappiness, as her parents have abandoned her for undisclosed reasons, and her husband is a man she does not really love. She is a woman waiting for a knight in shining armor, one who has hope, even if of rather an unhappy kind. She may be looking for a permanent, higher, spiritual reality, the very reality capable of transcending the transient, material world of *Die Stimmen von Marrakesch*. But no. Slavery is a fact of life, even when the principle appears to be contradicted. For instance, both Ginette and her husband have actually rebelled against Islamic law and convention. Her husband was disinherited because he married a foreigner. She was disinherited because she married an Arab. Are they any more free for exercising a purely personal choice? No. Why? Because Ginette's husband has turned out to be a lousy husband. Why? Because he sleeps with young men, and forces her to sleep with rich Arabs. Why? Because he has not renounced the rights of Arab men under Islamic law, even though he may have been prepared to forego an inheritance to get the woman he originally wanted, Ginette. Where does this leave us? We are obliged to return to the Gnostic proposition, the theme of the universal anarchy associated with the compulsive desires of the flesh, and to the realization that the story is a bitter insight into the institutionalized anarchy associated with marriage under Islamic law. This permits the practice of polygamy for men, as it also permits men to have sexual relations with men and women outside marriage in any form, all of which rights are not given to women. It also permits trade in human flesh in the literal sense, and for money, as if it were normal. In addition, because the wife/prostitute Ginette is not allowed to keep the money she makes, we are forced to remember that in Islam women are not really human beings, but instruments of gratification enchained to men, their owners. This is not really what Western humanism calls patriarchy, nor is it what the West knows to be prostitution, but something much more insidious. The double life and the double standards are formally and universally approved and sanctioned by Islamic law and social convention. From a Western perspective, this endemic enslavement of the flesh under the law is tempered by traditions that reject the Gnostic proposition. In the Catholic tradition, marriage is a sacrament and the bonds of marriage indissoluble because monogamy is upheld as an ideal by the sixth commandment, which condemns adultery. In the Protestant tradition, divorce is permitted, and a second marriage in church is allowed. In the humanist tradition, there is even greater variety. In civil society prostitution is generally legal and tolerated, but in general only as a lesser evil. The fact that relatively small numbers of men may be leading a double life or that it is possible to run prostitution rackets involving large sums of money does not affect the mainstream view that marriage, continuous with monogamy and family life, is still the norm. Neither do the widespread trafficking of refugees or economic migrants as sex workers or the recent promotion of same-sex unions alter traditional bourgeois views on sexuality. None of the information concerning the poor Ginette, which Canetti receives from secondhand conversation, leads him to draw any conclusions or ask any questions about the doctrinal and cultural differences between the West and the East. The story ends with vague generalizations about the English and Americans, and not generalizations that acknowledge the superiority of Western views of marriage or question the culture of slavery and polygamy in Islam. For Canetti cultural comparisons do not serve any analytical purposes, they simply serve one private purpose, his personal gratification. Yet Canetti knows that Ginette is not happy; she is not satisfied with the status quo; she has a yearning for something better and more beautiful. To all of which his story has no reply, at any level.

Two stories affirm the Jewish presence in Marrakesh, "Besuch in der Mellah" and "Die Familie Dahan" (39–53 and 53–79). In the first the Jewish quarter is the scene of much buying and selling. But Canetti interweaves this material reality with another kind of material reality, his own devotion to human types, stereotypes, and archetypes: "Ich ging so langsam wie möglich vorüber und betrachtete die Gesichter. Ihre Verschiedenartigkeit war erstaunlich. Es gab Gesichter, die ich in anderer Kleidung für Araber gehalten hätte. Es gab leuchtende alte Juden von Rembrandt. Es gab katholische Priester von listiger Stille und Demut. Es gab Ewige Juden, denen die Unruhe über die ganze Gestalt geschrieben war. Es gab Franzosen. Es gab Spanier. Es gab rötliche Russen. Einen hätten man als den Patriarchen Abraham begrüssen mögen, er sprach herablassend zu Napoleon und ein hitziger Besserwisser, der wie Goebbels aussah, mischte sich ein" (40). This surrender to the drive of his own imagination and affirmation of the belief that the world is only full of undifferentiated representatives of Arab, Jewish, Catholic, French, Spanish, and Russian countries produces a logical fruit. Having superimposed a fantasy world of his own involving the prophet Abraham and the historical figures Napoleon and Goebbels, Canetti begins to think of the Eastern doctrine of the transmigration of souls, linking the story once again to Gnosticism. It is a Gnostic truth that there are no boundaries between people and things because all is matter and what spirit there is in matter is only trapped therein. So, the doctrine of the transmigration of souls is its perfect expression, promising that one can return as a dog or a camel after the moment of one's own death, and vice versa ad infinitum. The progressive erosion of boundaries is the work of Canetti's own imagination, and it is the only story that "Besuch in der Mellah" really tells. This idea that there is no such thing as objective reality, that everything is in flux, and that men and women are obliged to improvise their way through life is recapitulated in its most mundane form in the very business of haggling. The law that operates in trade is the law of suspicion and fear. It is the belief that the external world, especially the human world, is a hostile threat, all of which imposes on the aggressive individual the burden or duty of devotion to absolute vigilance in bartering in order always to have the upper hand and the illusion of gain, victory, and domination. Life is a permanent competition, and there is no respite. The activities before Canetti's eyes and ears do not compel him to enter into anything more than a utilitarian relationship with the individual human figures in front of him. In addition, they provoke the realization that there is no time, no past, no present, no future; there is no place, either Marrakesh or London; there are no boundaries between people or which can keep people in productive, dynamic, stable relations with one another. Time and place, self and other have to be negated by the ego, which demands the right to reign supreme over time, place, and others: "Ich mochte nicht mehr weg von hier, vor Hunderten von Jahren war ich hier gewesen, aber ich hatte es vergessen und nun kam mir alles wieder. Ich fand jene Dichte und Wärme des Lebens ausgestellt, die ich in mir selber fühle. Ich *war* dieser Platz, als ich dort stand. Ich glaube, ich bin immer dieser Platz" (40). Is this a triumph, a victory? Or is this a deceptive triumph and victory, nothing more than an illusion? And could this possibly be tyranny masquerading as self-fulfillment and self-transcendence? The real point here is that an ahistorical, real presence in the imagination is achieved at the cost of the denial of objective reality. As if admitting that he is the victim of illusions, he records his debt to "die glückliche Verzauberung."

Having acknowledged his debt to alchemy and magic, Canetti takes us closer to the heart of his occult project. Magic has an instrumental role in denying objective reality in another way, he says. It helps to hide a profoundly unpalatable truth about the human condition — human mortality. Canetti visits the Jewish cemetery. Here he realizes that all his own temporary illusions are just palliatives against death, which has no meaning, and which represents only the bitter end of natural life. "Auf diesem wüsten Friedhof der Juden aber ist nichts. Er ist die Wahrheit selbst, eine Mondlandschaft des Todes. Es ist dem Betrachter herzlich gleichgültig, wer wo liegt. Es ist die Wüste aus Toten, auf der nichts mehr wächst, die letzte, die allerletzte Wüste" (49). Put positively, we could argue that the reality of human mortality is the cause for the flight into the inner world of the imagination and the temporary relief afforded there by merely momentary illusions. Death triggers off this chain reaction; writing deflects attention from the inevitable progress and process of death; writing is thus not free from this burden, but an expression of the fact that there is no escape; writing is itself absolutely dependent on human mortality as the ultimate origin and ultimate end. The conclusion is this: there is no transcending death because there is nothing after death. This is the Gnostic secret of the perpetual present of war and warfare.

Having penetrated through to this "heart of darkness" — and Canetti has already stated in passing that "gute Reisende sind herzlos" — Canetti takes refuge in what appears to be a safe haven, the Jewish domestic world, where he meets well-to-do, educated, cosmopolitan Jews for the first time in "Die Familie Dahan." This verges on comedy. Canetti is set up. It is assumed that he as a Jew has contacts even with the Lord Samuels of this world and can use his network to find employment for the whole family. In spite of the combination of amused amazement at their tactics and surprise at their insistence, manipulation, and naïveté, Canetti cooperates passively and does not put up a fight, even though he regrets having entered their house, and regards the son Elie as stupid. The single reason for this capitulation is vanity. Canetti is delighted that they take an interest in his own Sephardic origins. Elie has his same name, Elias; Elie's father repeats his name when he hears it for the first time, which causes Canetti to begin to fall for him. The capitulation is complete when Elie mentions that his father is a great scholar who reads all through the night. This vague information is enough to trigger a response of complete subjugation. On the strength of it he yields to all of Elie's demands, despite his moral repugnance. Attraction is capable of exercising a tyrannical hold over him, and it is in large part about affirming his own identity at the most superficial level, his love of his own name, his origins, his love of his own profession, writing and reading, in other words, his vanity. The external world merely provides stimuli that gratify the given vanity of this human subject, and the commitment to gratification is absolute, such that gratification is capable of negating all counter-demands, including the original moral reluctance to cooperate with the endemic assumption among his Jewish host's family that people are really to be used for the purposes of self-advancement. Canetti appears to be satisfied that mutual exploitation is just part of the human condition. In Canetti's travelogue the sense of the gates of perception of the imagination seems, then, to be limited, even though Canetti rejoices in the "depth" of his ears and the "length" of his sight. While his own power over himself and his literal and figurative subjects is seemingly limitless, the relative powerlessness of the masses never amounts to more than a purely rhetorical flourish, never a rhetorical question about the quality of life. This lack of concern raises a serious question about Canetti's humanity and humanism, since the one feeling missing in his survey of the formlessness of mass and matter in human beings is that of compassion or empathy. This paralysis of feeling, together with the proliferation of senseless power relations and injustice, links all the stories to one archetypal theme only, to the idea of circularity, to eternal repetition, rather than to organic growth and development over time. Why? Because the Gnostic thesis denies the true uniqueness of individuals. Put another way, one could argue that *Die Stimmen von Marrakesch* depicts a truly soulless world; instead of souls we have strong egos or weak egos. The demands of Elias Canetti's ego are those of a cultural capitalist, and they take precedence over objective reality again and again; meanwhile, with the exception of Ginette, characters encountered in Marrakesh are never individually differentiated and remain compelled to exercise their false freedom by merging together periodically in classic economic, sexual, or social rituals, all of which Canetti chronicles for us in detached terms. In many ways, then, *Die Stimmen von Marrakesch* is a classic clash between East and West, a serious example of a clash of civilizations.

The recently invented disciplines of cultural studies and multicultural studies tend, however, to avoid the polemical and controversial, which is why *Die Stimmen von Marrakesch* and Canetti in general — even though both are heavily indebted to Jewish, Muslim, and "primitive culture" — have not been taken seriously on their curricula. Equally the ideology and speculative theories of Edward Said's *Orientalism* (1978), a work that has given rise to colonial studies and postcolonial studies and has produced an undifferentiated call for global human rights, has done little to advance a scholarly understanding of the history, law, and theology of Islam.[16] Until some of these tendencies have been corrected, and until the liberal arts combine with the political sciences and take Samuel P. Huntington's *The Clash of Civilisations* (1996) seriously as a critical tool with which to open up the East;[17] until the liberal arts negotiate the documentary accounts of real life under Islam made available to the West by the German journalist Peter Scholl-Latour or the polemical essay *Die Verachtung der Massen* (1999–2000) of a dissident like Peter Sloterdijk, students and teachers of humanities subjects will continue to remain ignorant of the dominant historical and doctrinal trends that separate the West from the East.[18] Put another way, cultural and multicultural studies should be sufficiently catholic to embrace the ongoing war between a theological and an anti-theological account of human life, by couching their explorations in the framework of what is an ancient, not a modern, polemic between Christianity and Gnosticism. Cultural studies, however, on account of the devotion to its founding fathers — Hegel, Marx, Matthew Arnold, Horkheimer and Adorno, F. R. Leavis, R. Williams, and Roy Pascal — are far too insulated, and far too parasitically dependent on materialist interpretations of history. To embrace theology it would also be difficult to attempt a revaluation of culture in the light of the epic conflict between the doctrines and theology of the Christian West and the non-Christian East. Yet this discussion is particularly pertinent in the light of the high-profile campaigns for tolerance toward all religions in the media, politics, and academia.[19] Only when we open up the debate about the doctrinal

differences between the West and the East will we be able to draw a preliminary conclusion as to whether the predominantly Jewish interest in the
psychology of the masses in a Western or Eastern context, from Freud
through Broch to Canetti and Erich Fromm, is anything more than purely
descriptive or phenomenological. *Die Stimmen von Marrakesch* could be a
valuable key in such a discussion. This essay meanwhile invites us to ask a
simple question first: what contribution does *Die Stimmen von Marrakesch*
really make to the crisis of culture and language, if life in Marrakesh is so
atavistic and primitive, if its culture is hostile to the sanctity of life, and if the
German language is just a relatively powerless instrument that encodes the
instinctual in documentary form for consumption by readers in the West,
who themselves are likely to have little or no influence or authority over the
power of inequality, injustice, violence, oppression, cruelty and mutual
exploitation in the East? Can it really be right to treat a writer who so faithfully chronicles the mass powerlessness of the weak as a kind of aesthetic sociology or aesthetic phenomenology, and who derives such a private, sensory,
or aural thrill from his detached/indifferent encounters, as a *critic* of the masses?

Notes

[1] Elias Canetti, "Die Rufe der Blinden," *Die Stimmen von Marrakesch* (Munich:
Hanser, 1967).

[2] Herbert Göpfert, "Zu den Stimmen von Marrakesch," in *Elias Canettis Anthropologie und Poetik,* ed. Stefan H. Kaszyński (Munich: Hanser, 1984), 135–50. Here:
135–36.

[3] Rudolf Hartung, "Glück in Marrakesch," *Süddeutsche Zeitung,* October 5/6, 1968;
Manfred Durzak, "Canetti war in Marrakesch," *Die Welt,* November 7, 1968;
Werner Helwig, "Tod in Marrakesch," *Rheinische Merkur,* December 6, 1968;
Wolfgang Hädecke, "Der Mensch soll ein Geheimnis sein," *Christ und Welt,* No-
vember 22, 1968.

[4] Marcel Reich-Ranicki, "Marrakesch ist überall," *Entgegnung: Zur deutschen Literatur der siebziger Jahre* (Stuttgart: Deutsche Verlags-Anstalt, 1979), 47–54. Here: 54.

[5] See Edward Rothstein, "The Secret Life of Elias Canetti: Dreams of Disappearance," *The New Republic,* January 8–15, 1990, for the opposite claim that there is a
kind of inhuman perversity to this fascination.

[6] Caren Jane Caplan, "The Poetics of Displacement: Exile, Immigration and Travel
in Contemporary Autobiographical Writing" (Ph.D. diss., University of California,
Santa Cruz, 1987).

[7] The standard, modern work on Gnosticism is by Hans Jonas, *The Gnostic Religion:
The Message of the Alien God and the Beginning of Christianity* (Boston: Beacon Press,
1958).

[8] Hans Urs von Balthasar, ed., *The Scandal of the Incarnation: Irenaeus against the
Heresies,* trans. by John Saward (San Francisco: Ignatius, 1990).

[9] Elias Canetti, *Masse und Macht* (Hamburg: Claassen, 1960).

[10] The extent of the material on this debate is such that it would be pointless to try and provide a survey. Names like Foucault, Fredric Jameson, Christopher Norris, and Alex Callinicois represent the disappointment of the liberal Left with the success and/or substance of the liberal offensive of the 1960s and thereafter. Kurt Sonnheimer's review of his own sympathy for and then rejection of the liberal offensive in Sonnheimer, *Das Elend unserer Intellektuellen: Linke Theorie in der Bundesrepublik Deutschland* (Hamburg: Hoffmann & Campe, 1976), is interesting for the claim, which is crucial to this essay, that the importance ascribed to totalizing theory by the humanities is questionable, not least because this facilitates a problematic detachment from reality. Raymond Tallis approaches the issue of this theory's dominance from the other side of the political/intellectual spectrum.

[11] For a more recent, largely negative reading of the status and value of sociology, see *Die Zeit* (June 14, 1996, and June 21, 1996).

[12] See Ronald Taylor, *Aesthetics and Politics: Ernst Bloch, Georg Lukács, Bertolt Brecht, Walter Benjamin, Theodor Adorno*, afterword by Fredric Jameson (London: NLB, 1980).

[13] See Ernst Bloch, *Das Prinzip Hoffnung* (Frankfurt: Suhrkamp, 1959). Bloch is a good example of the limitations of the idealism of the intellectual Left. Bloch's definition of idealism is reduced to the state of living out unfulfilled desire as a way of life, which is why he focuses on classic case studies of the problem in literature, such as Hamlet, Faust, and Don Quixote. The work is full of pious confidence that creating utopias in the mind is a sign of the existence of the moral life.

[14] Elias Canetti, *Die Blendung* (Munich: Hanser, 1963).

[15] See Edgar Piel, *Elias Canetti* (Munich: Beck, 1984), 140–46; Friederike Eigler, *Das autobiographische Werk von Elias Canetti: Identität. Verwandlung. Machtausübung* (Tübingen: Stauffenberg, 1988), 142–51; and Axel Gunther Steussloff, *Autorschaft und Werk Elias Canettis: Subjekt — Sprache — Identität* (Würzburg: Königshausen und Neumann, 1994), 173–207, for more on the poetics of Canetti's Marrakesh piece.

[16] Edward Said, *Orientalism: Western Conceptions of the Orient* (London: RKP, 1978).

[17] Samuel P. Huntington, *The Clash of Civilizations and the Remaking of World Order* (New York: Simon & Schuster, 1996).

[18] Peter Scholl-Latour, *Allah ist mit den Standhaften: Begegnungen mit der islamischen Revolution* (Stuttgart: Deutsche Verlags-Anstalt, 1983) and *Aufruhr in der Kasbah: Krisenherd Algerien* (Stuttgart: Deutsche Verlags-Anstalt, 1992); Peter Sloterdijk, *Die Verachtung der Massen: Versuch über Kulturkämpfe in der modernen Gesellschaft* (Frankfurt: Suhrkamp, 2000).

[19] See Hans-Peter Raddatz, *Von Gott zu Allah? Christentum und Islam in der liberalen Fortschrittsgesellschaft* (Munich: Herbig, 2001).

Space in Elias Canetti's Autobiographical Trilogy

Irene Stocksieker Di Maio

I N *DIE GERETTETE ZUNGE: GESCHICHTE EINER JUGEND*, the first volume
of his autobiographical trilogy,[1] Elias Canetti recounts a game his father
played with his younger brother Georg in the nursery of their house in
Manchester, England. Father and son would alternately state the house
number, street, district, city, and country of their residence, and Elias always
concluded their game by chiming in "Europe" (*GZ*, 61). This geographical
game burns in Canetti's memory because it was the last exchange he shared
with his father. Young Elias's exclamation "Europe" is multivalent. Completing the address gave him a sense of wholeness (*GZ*, 61). The exclamation
evinces the boy's delight in learning and showing off his knowledge. It is
linked to his extended family's notion that the Danube port city of Roustchouk was not Europe but rather part of the Orient. It may be interpreted
as a sign of Canetti's nascent cosmopolitanism. Canetti's recollection of this
game certainly demonstrates the centrality of geographic space in his life
from an early age. The significance of geographic space is palpable in other
boyhood interests — Elias's collection of stamps from various countries and
his jigsaw puzzle map of Europe, which he could put together while blind-
folded, identifying the countries by feeling their shape.

Critics have often noted that Canetti's teleological organizing principle
for the stuff of his autobiography is the selection of those experiences of the
world, especially of places, events, people, conversations, and readings, that
shaped the autobiographical subject into the author of the earlier works: the
novel *Die Blendung*,[2] the drama *Hochzeit*,[3] and, above all, the massive anthropological study *Masse und Macht*.[4] Although scholars clearly understand
that Canetti experiences the world concretely, rather than theoretically or
systematically,[5] it has been only briefly noted that he frames these experiences of the world in terms of spatial relations. Gerald Stieg, for example, in
his early study of the autobiography based on the first two volumes published, maintains that space plays an extraordinary role and that the relationship between the terms *Weite* and *Enge* in Canetti's work deserves a study
in itself,[6] and Gerhard Melzer incisively treats the central importance of
orders of intellectual magnitude in the trilogy.[7] This essay focuses on the

predominant types of space Canetti deploys to narrate the story of his psychic and intellectual formation. We will see that the most significant spaces in the autobiographical trilogy comprise not only the geographical spaces noted above — countries, cities, streets — but also nature, interiors and the furniture and pictures within them, as well as the space of the body. Canetti's descriptive diction and metaphors with respect to these spaces reveal much about his relationships to people central to his life and about his evaluation of ideas, historical events, and literary and artistic works. Indeed, the spatial imagery that permeates the trilogy is key to understanding Canetti's worldview.

Countries and Cities

Whereas the main titles of the autobiographical trilogy underscore the senses — *Die gerettete Zunge, Die Fackel im Ohr, Das Augenspiel* — the subsections, especially of the first book, focus on places, that is, on space: Roustchouk, Manchester, Vienna, Zurich-Scheuchzerstrasse, Zurich-Tiefbrunnen, Frankfurt, Berlin, and Grinzing. Canetti writes of his exposure to the powerful and contrasting impressions he absorbed from the changing locations of his earlier life (*FO*, 9). That Canetti lived in a number of countries and experienced diverse, multilingual populations early on is the most commonly known and remarked-upon aspect of his life. Critics agree that this experience, coupled with his Jewish heritage, shaped Canetti into a cosmopolitan citizen of the world.[8] Here I will summarily review the qualities, values, and concepts Canetti associates with the countries and cities where he resided before taking a closer look at types of space that have not enjoyed as much critical attention.

For Canetti geographical locations — countries and cities — entail concepts, but these concepts are always grounded in experience. He equates Roustchouk with multi-ethnicity and linguistic diversity, England with orderliness and freedom, Switzerland with democracy, Vienna with culture, Frankfurt with the turmoil of early Weimar inflation, and Berlin with intense and palpable creativity. Each city and country bears complex and varying emotional charges. In Roustchouk, young Elias came to know fierce extremes of emotion: fear, love, and hatred. His parents linked Roustchouk with stifling oppression and tyranny. Elias's mother, nevertheless, also associated Roustchouk with the pleasurable sight and smell of the abundant fruits and flowers in her family's orchard. Elias's father experienced happiness in Manchester, but his wife still felt stifled by the extended family. Zurich was an intellectual paradise, a place where young Canetti could take in vast amounts of knowledge. The cities of Canetti's late adolescence and early manhood continued to contribute to his emotional and intellectual growth in diverse ways. Frankfurt introduced him to social, economic, and political turbulence; Vienna was his entry into an engaged literary world; and Berlin was a stunning and confusing locale in which he moved through the vast chaos of the new (*F*, 289).

In writing of the "extraordinary role" of delayed encounters in his life, Canetti puts cities on par with people, pictures, and books in terms of emotional intensity of his relationship to them. He transgresses Western categories of animate and inanimate by claiming there are cities he yearns for (he does not specify which ones) as if he had been predestined to spend his whole life in them. That he deliberately avoids visiting them only increases the intensity of his longing (*A*, 13). Canetti grants cities the capacity to feel emotions by underscoring the reciprocity of love and desire, claiming that he learned early on from one of his mother's suitors that a city can love a human being (*GZ*, 93) just as a person can love or yearn for a city. For each individual, different cities — and by extension countries — are a more or less suitable temperamental and intellectual fit.

Canetti frequently uses spatial metaphors when describing the emotional and intellectual impact of the various places he resided. "Vastness" and "diversity" are words that crop up often in the description of his development in Zurich, where he experienced learning physically and spatially (*GZ*, 236). During this period Elias felt indebted to his mother's magnanimity, a capacity to fearlessly acknowledge the validity of the contradictory and the irreconcilable. This capacity, which he describes in terms of generous space, evoked both his admiration and astonishment (*GZ*, 198).

When his mother orchestrated his sudden expulsion from the Swiss paradise, convinced he knew nothing of the real world, she announced she was taking him "in die Inflation nach Deutschland" (*GZ*, 327). The formulation "*into* the inflation" is odd because of its spatial dimension. Bernd Widdig points out that the rampant inflation that convulsed German politics, society, and culture at the time is a theme of *Die Blendung* and *Masse und Macht* as well as of Canetti's autobiography.[9] In his chapter on inflation and the crowd in *Masse und Macht*, Canetti proposes that money is a crowd symbol and that in modern times inflation is a crowd phenomenon. He notes the ambiguity of the word *million*, saying it can refer to money or people. Thus, he asserts, the negativity of inflationary growth leads to people, to the crowd feeling depreciated, that is, diminished. Canetti continues the spatial metaphor in contemplating the role the Weimar inflation played in the scapegoating of the Jews — itself an inflationary process (in that it increased exponentially) — under National Socialism (*MM*, 207–12).

The intense, integral connections between geographic space and the emotional and intellectual landscapes is encapsulated in Canetti's description of his profound admiration for Isaac Babel, with whom he kept company in Berlin in 1928, and for the locus of Babel's *Geschichten aus Odessa* (1926, Odessa Tales)[10] published by the Malik house. The similarities between the atmosphere and people of Roustchouk and the characters who populate

Babel's tales struck a chord with Canetti. Ironically, Canetti's recognition of this connection between two cities frequently considered to be backward and provincial transpired in, of all cities, Berlin, where innovation and the celebrity of the week was all that had value. Canetti, who learned early from his parents — and through the historical fate of the Jews in the Diaspora — to be a cosmopolitan European, comes to understand through Babel that to be open to the world is more a state of mind than a matter of geography. Since he learns from Babel not to avert his eyes from the provinces, but to gaze mentally eastward to Odessa as well as westward to Vienna, his world expands. In his imagination Canetti relocates Odessa on the map, placing it at the mouth of the Danube, so that his mind can flow freely from Vienna, through Roustchouk, to Odessa and back. The redrawn mental map accurately reflects his psychic state (*FO*, 268–69).

Underlying the East-West dichotomy[11] manifest in the passage concerning Isaac Babel and the locale of his stories is the problematic notion of the "Oriental." Canetti had negative received notions of the "Oriental" that he learned to question but which still linger in the text. Oriental signifies a slow pace, indolence, and backwardness. This negative concept of the Oriental was prevalent in his immediate and extended family. Young Canetti easily assimilated his family's mindset that opposed backward Oriental Roustchouk to modern, enlightened Europe. However, on his final Danube voyage in 1924, the young university student began to question his inherited prejudices about the barbaric Balkans through his encounter with Dr. Menachemoff, the physician who had delivered and attended him. Because the physician's interests and knowledge concerning the progress of the sciences astonished Canetti (*FO*, 83), his account suggests that in the future he would be less ready to automatically designate the East as superstitious and the West as enlightened.

Despite his early learning of stereotypes about the Oriental, Canetti did feel an affinity with what was Turkish because his grandfather had grown up in Turkey, his father had been born there, and in his native city there were many Turks (*GZ*, 26).[12] So when he read Johann Peter Hebel's story "Denkwürdigkeiten aus dem Morgenland" (Memorabilia from the Orient) from *Das Schatzkästlein* (1811; The Treasure Chest),[13] which begins with the lines "In der Türkei, wo es bisweilen etwas ungerade hergehen soll" (*GZ*, 284), the exotic felt like a familiar homeland. A further positive reference to the Oriental is his description of his wife-to-be, Veza. Of their first encounter Canetti writes that she was a rare, exotic creature one would have expected to see on a Persian miniature (*FO*, 72). Yet Hebel's story and Veza's appearance remain in the realm of aestheticized exoticism. Indeed, the moral of justice and compassion in Hebel's tales, where the narrator concludes, "Es ist doch nicht alles so uneben, was die Morgenländer sagen und tun,"[14] must also have struck a chord, but Canetti does not remark on this.

Canetti draws a distinction between his Sephardic heritage, which he calls Spanish or "spaniolisch" (the German equivalent for Ladino), implicitly making it Western, and his roots in the Balkans and Turkey, which he calls Oriental. When he was a Gymnasium student, his relationship to his family and its Sephardic heritage was fraught with conflict, and he contrasted his "commercial" Jewish ancestors, who had led an Oriental life in the Balkans, with their "intellectual, creative" Jewish ancestors in medieval Spain (*GZ,* 251). But he did not occupy himself with his Spanish heritage until the outbreak of the Spanish Civil War, when he felt an urgent need to become acquainted with Spain (*A,* 274). Prior to this, the baseless caste pride and arrogance of some Sephardic Jews had deterred him from laying claim to that heritage (*A,* 274). Under the tutelage of Dr. Sonne, an Ashkenazic Jew, Canetti was finally introduced to medieval Sephardic poets, whom he still refers to as Spanish (*A,* 274). Canetti learned to respect the poems that Dr. Sonne translated orally from the Hebrew because Sonne also translated Moorish poems from the Arabic, showing him a balanced overall picture (*A,* 275). Canetti resists fanatic identification with just one strand and is able to identify with people of many times and places, as expressed in an aphorism of 1944 written in response to the Holocaust, in which he resists the temptation to identify solely with the recently murdered Jews and to be altogether and only a Jew:[15]

> Die größte geistige Versuchung in meinem Leben, die einzige, gegen die ich schwer anzukämpfen habe, ist die: ganz Jude zu sein. . . . Die neuen Toten, die lange vor ihrer Zeit Toten, bitten einen sehr, und wer hat das Herz, ihnen nein zu sagen. Aber sind die neuen Toten nicht überall, auf allen Seiten, von jedem Volk? . . . Kann ich nicht weiterhin allen gehören, wie bisher, und doch Jude sein?

The Sephardic literary tradition, to which he came rather late — in contrast to the spoken Ladino (the medieval form of Spanish used by the Sephardic Jews in exile) of his childhood — is a hybrid tradition: a mixture of Spanish, Hebrew, and Arabic. Canetti does not use the term "hybrid," nor does he appear to consider the Sephardic tradition Oriental, despite its partial origination in the Near East. He is, however, well aware of the irony of being taught about the Sephardic literary tradition by an Ashkenazic Jew, from that German branch of Jews that his Sephardic family looked down upon (*A,* 274–75).

It took a concrete, indeed threatening political situation — fascism in Spain — to finally motivate Canetti to examine his literary heritage. Yet even though one political situation aroused Canetti's interest in Spain, the most threatening political situation of all, German fascism and the oppression of the Jews, never caused him to take any particular interest in Palestine. Certainly Canetti must have reflected on whether Palestine had meaning for him because, when he visited Bulgaria for the last time as a student, he saw his eloquent cousin Bernhard Arditti, a convert to Zionism, recruit emigrants to Palestine. Further, his friend Sonne was one of the founders of modern Hebrew poetry, and emigrated to Jerusalem at the same time Canetti emigrated to England in 1937. But Canetti was interested in his cousin's recruitment efforts solely as a crowd phenomenon and because he was amazed that the Ladino of his childhood, which he had regarded as a stunted language for children and the kitchen (*FO*, 90), could be used to speak about universal matters. He marveled that his cousin's Ladino oratory filled people with such passion that they earnestly considered turning their back on a country where they had been settled for generations and where they were well off and respected, to move to an unknown land that had been promised to them thousands of years ago, but didn't even belong to them (*FO*, 90). In his description of the Zionist groundswell, Canetti makes it clear that the emigrants are persuaded by an idea rather than material or territorial concerns. Canetti has a strong sense of place, but for him place is a matter of choice predicated upon an affinity with culture and language. His own cosmopolitan experiences, enabled by education, class, and family fortune, were at the root of this intellectual mobility. Thus it seems natural to him that he chose Vienna and German, his brother Georg Paris and French (*FO*, 210), and his cousin Bernhard Palestine and Hebrew (*FO*, 89). Nevertheless, when Canetti was finally forced into exile, he began to identify more strongly with his Sephardic ancestors. Citing a conversation Canetti had with the novelist Horst Bienek, Martin Bollacher points out that Canetti characterized himself as a Spanish poet in the German language, who perhaps was the only literary person in whom the languages of the two great expulsions lay so close together.[16] He was referring, however, to the expulsions of Jews from Spain and Germany, not to the first expulsion in Biblical times.

Tracing Canetti's intellectual development and sense of place in the world, then, his trilogy reveals the complex process by which he shifted from simplistic notions of the Oriental; to an examination of these notions prompted by exchanges with figures such as Menachemoff, Babel, and Sonne; to a more nuanced understanding and appreciation of the Sephardic tradition with its hybrid Spanish, Hebrew, and Arabic origins. In terms of Canetti's gradual development of interest in his Sephardic heritage, however, we note that he stopped at Spain and did not pursue Hebrew or Arabic strands, although he was an avid student of two other cultures denoted as Oriental: China and Japan. Based on history and concrete experience, Canetti's identifications are as fluid as his imaginary map of the Danube and its ports, which is charted according to temperament and cultural and intellectual affinities.

Nature and the Outdoors

Although the urban center is the predominant locus of experience for the modern European author and intellectual, nature — both in its original and manmade states — is a significant space in this trilogy because it is intertwined with personal relationships and intellectual work.

Canetti's grandfather Arditti's wonderful orchard and rose garden were the solace and compensation his mother offered young Elias as an antidote to the hated weekly visits with the paternal grandfather. There stood the mulberry tree where his mother had perched and read books during her own girlhood and the Bulgarian roses whose scent afforded her so much sensual pleasure. In Canetti's relationship with his mother, the scent of roses from Roustchouk forms an arch between the time of her childhood and the time of her death. Further, that his mother clandestinely picked fruit in violation of the Sabbath for the boy's sake underscores the Edenic nature of the garden and the early intimacy between mother and son (*GZ*, 28). Yet Canetti believes his father had a greater appreciation of nature than his mother, apart from her pleasure in the orchard. This love of nature is one of the firm links between father and son. He remembers strolling with his father through a meadow full of flowers and high grass along the Mersey; his father found the English word "meadow" to be especially beautiful. Most important was their last stroll through this meadow, when his father tenderly assured him: "Du wirst werden, was du gern willst" (*GZ*, 55). Thus Canetti associates the beauty of the stroll in nature alongside his father with an early promise of fulfillment in life that ran counter to customary Canetti family expectations.

Canetti describes the grounds at Villa Yalta on Lake Zurich, where he boarded while attending school in Zurich, as idyllic. There was a yew tree to climb, and apples fell to his feet with no prohibitions (*GZ*, 221). At Villa Yalta and environs, the boy was free to roam and explore — away from the possessiveness, the meddling, the tensions, and the dictates of his nuclear and extended family.

In contrast, Canetti's account of his extended hiking trip in the Karwendel mountains while he was a university student reverberates with recent relational tensions and inner turmoil. A tremendous blow-up with his mother had preceded this trip, for she suddenly and arbitrarily wanted to quash the long-planned outing. Thus, the sight of the bare, rugged, chalk mountains marked for Canetti a new beginning; he felt as if he were leaving everything behind and starting out with nothing but naked stone (*FO*, 136). Canetti sees an affinity between the characteristics of the rock in this mountain range and the monumental project he was about to embark on. The bare rock, from which nothing was to be mined and carried away, becomes the metaphor for the preparatory work for his study on crowds and power, an arduous intellectual journey that would often seem unyielding and for which he could take no shortcuts (*FO,* 138). He would not publish his insights in fragments; rather he needed to first understand the phenomenon in its entirety.

The Sellrain valley, where he spent the final week of the hiking trip, and the surrounding Karwendel mountains met young Canetti's intellectual and emotional needs as he initiated his study of crowds and power. In the valley he spent mornings reading and taking notes on Freud's *Massenpsychologie und Ich-Analyse* (Group Psychology and the Analysis of the Ego).[17] The weather's wonderful crispness and clarity when Canetti began reading (*FO,* 141) sharpened his ability to focus, to be an intellectually and critically independent reader (*FO,* 143–44). Moreover, the ability to attain his immediate goals — reaching mountain peaks during afternoon hikes — provided Canetti assurance that he would achieve his long-term, more remote intellectual goals (*FO,* 144). Further, the very air around him, in which there was so much space, as well as clarity and direction of the wind ("in der so viel Platz war, aber auch Klarheit und Richtung des Windes") became the vent for the chaos of hatred, resentment, and confinement that had built up during the preceding year in the family quarters (*FO,* 144). He could freely articulate his negative emotions, and the wind swept his words away.

Memories of his experience of nature during early youth are idyllic, comprising intimate moments with his mother in lush gardens and abundant orchards in Roustchouk, reassuring strolls in English meadows with a father he lost all too soon, and independence on the grounds of Villa Yalta in Zurich. As Canetti matured, nature represented the arduous emotional and intellectual terrain he had to negotiate. Yet its contours and forces also gave him direction, and its spaciousness intellectual freedom.

Streets

Streets are the public space where Canetti bore witness to historical events that shaped his worldview and his life projects. During the First World War, on the *Limmatquai* in Zurich, Canetti and his mother witnessed opposing groups of French and German soldiers greet each other in the solidarity of their wounds. The mother's barely concealed weeping at this sight displayed her compassion and fierce opposition to war (*GZ,* 203–4), her enduring legacy to Canetti, the foe of death and destruction. On a Frankfurt street, the Gymnasium student absorbed another profound lesson about the misery humans cause each other when he saw a starving woman collapse, which onlookers blamed on the inflation (*FO,* 46). In Frankfurt he also was deeply agitated by the vehement political discussions on the street where the most diverse sorts of people incessantly voiced their convictions at each other (*FO,* 79).

Two central themes of Canetti's writing — the crowd and conflagration — are foreshadowed by his earliest experience in Roustchouk when he ran into the street to follow a crowd racing to a fire. The first crowd he consciously witnessed as an adult was the workers' demonstration protesting the murder of Walter Rathenau, the Jewish-German foreign minister, on a street in Frankfurt. He felt a strong gravitational pull to join the march (*FO*, 80), although he did not. These early experiences of crowds and conflagration culminated in the revolutionary event that had the deepest influence on his subsequent life: the spontaneous protest of the Viennese workers on July 15, 1927, in which they set fire to the Palace of Justice. This time Canetti became part of the crowd and fully dissolved into it (*FO*, 230–31).

Definitive for Canetti's life's work on crowds was the "illumination" — "die Erleuchtung" — the special light that suddenly came upon him as a violent feeling of expansion on the Alserstrasse during his first winter in Vienna (1924–25) (*FO*, 118). Fifty years later the autobiographer still views this illumination as something *"unexhausted"* (*FO*, 118). Dashing along the street, tripping and stumbling, but an integral part of the energy, the force that moved him, Canetti realized that there is such a thing as a crowd instinct, which is always in conflict with the individual's instinct, and that the struggle between the two of them can explain the course of human history (*FO*, 119). The conflagrations Canetti witnessed in the streets of Roustchouk and Vienna anticipate the monstrous conflagration of Kien's library that concludes *Die Blendung,* and his experiences of the gravitational pull of crowds and the illumination that propelled him was the impetus and continuing motivation for *Masse und Macht* (*FO*, 236–37).

Underlying Canetti's narration of these crowd experiences in the street is his dispute with Freud. Because Freud's life, according to Canetti, unrolled in his medical office and in his study of individuals, he failed to recognize the elementary nature of the crowd instinct (*FO*, 142). Surely during the decades Canetti worked on *Masse und Macht,* he spent many hours in his own study reading numerous sources. And certainly the individual is a component of his own thesis, for it is precisely the tension between the individual and the crowd that Canetti seeks to understand. By focusing on the defining moments on the street, Canetti claims greater authenticity for his thesis compared with Freud's because of the immediacy and visceral concreteness of his experiences.

While Canetti discusses city streets primarily as sites of public events formative for his literary and intellectual development, streets have psychic parameters as well. Realizing that the proximity of his student room to Veza's family's apartment fed into his own insecurities and jealousy, Canetti understood that there needed to be more distance between them, preferably a distance equal to the expanse of the entire city of Vienna (*FO*, 210). The physical distance he established through his move to the outskirts of Vienna to achieve an emotionally healthier space between himself and Veza also benefited his writing. After he left Veza late at night, he would walk up and down the dark streets and visit the taverns to hear and absorb the voices of those who were not given the power of articulate speech (*FO,* 336). He subsequently recorded these diverse manners of speech, which he calls acoustic masks (*FO,* 208), in *Die Blendung* and his drama *Hochzeit.*

Canetti was not a casual flâneur who merely let impressions come upon him. Rather, when he was writing he raced through the streets as if driven, or he obsessively pursued the object that caught his attention. He vested these encounters with the full force and intensity of his own intellectual pursuits. The oddest example is his stalking of the young girl who radiated tempestuous life as she raced up the Himmelstrasse during the noon hour. Because the girl had something he saw as Oriental in her features, Canetti associated the girl's "impetuousness" and "fascinating breathlessness" with the Kabuki theater (*A,* 207). At the time of writing *Das Augenspiel* in the seventies, he understands how he had deluded himself about the obsessive nature of his pursuit, when he found himself almost daily on the Himmel-strasse at noon, but did not admit to himself that it was for the girl's sake, telling himself he was merely going his own way (*A,* 207). The deliberate-ness of his pursuit and the degree of his self-deception is underscored by the precision with which he describes his stealth and the direction of his steps as he left his second-floor study to go out on the street (*A,* 208).

Canetti also describes his more leisurely, habitual ride on the No. 38 streetcar with a geometric precision similar to his account of the compulsive pursuit of the girl. He notes both the randomness and the predictability with which certain passengers got on and off the streetcar, as well as how they filled the volume of space and their distribution within that space. His dis-tance from and angle of vision toward these passengers allowed him to observe them and provide thumbnail sketches of Viennese artists and others associated with the arts in Vienna. The route of the streetcar also has a personal dimension, because the passing of the Chemical Institute became a historical reenactment of Canetti's own career course, and he breathed a sigh of relief each time the streetcar drove by and he escaped the institute (*A,* 263).

Finally, Canetti characterizes his walk through the streets of Paris during his mother's funeral procession as a journey of almost mythic magnitude. It seemed to him as if the procession followed the coffin through the entire city en route to Père Lachaise (*A,* 302). A brother at either side, Canetti forged ahead, proudly and defiantly as though interceding for his mother against the whole world (*A,* 302). Based on the principle that the more ground covered, the greater the funeral (*A,* 303), and, by implication, the greater the guarantee of his mother's immortality, Canetti wanted the procession to stretch through the entire city. Yet ultimately Canetti did not immortalize his mother through this procession extended in his imagination. Rather, believing that human beings live on through the work they leave behind or in the memory of the survivors, Canetti immortalizes his mother through his autobiography.[18]

Interiors

Perhaps it was the imprint of the childhood geography game that prompts the autobiographer to almost obsessively record street names and house numbers as he narrates his transitions from place to place. Canetti's precise notation of these addresses underscores that the domestic spaces in which he dwelled are as intimately connected with his emotional and intellectual development as are the cities where he resided.

If, as he claims, everything that Canetti experienced in mature life had already happened in Roustchouk, then the primary locus of these early experiences is the extended family compound. In its autonomy and self-sufficiency, with a configuration facing inward, this compound may be considered a quasi-interior space. Noting his lack of talent at topographical drawing, a skill he admired in Stendhal, Canetti resorts to verbal description of the layout of the residential buildings around the courtyard garden (*GZ*, 18–19). The compound comprised three houses facing a central courtyard. When one entered the large gate of the compound, Grandfather Canetti's house was immediately to the right. It was statelier, larger, and brighter than the two houses on the opposite side of the central courtyard, which were adjacent to each other and joined by a common porch, and which his father and uncle and their families occupied. This configuration clearly demonstrates the family's tight bonds as well as the patriarch's reign.

Canetti states that the earliest childhood prohibition he recalls had to do with space, for he was not permitted to leave the courtyard and garden (*GZ*, 264). But the compound was large and varied enough for young Elias not to feel restricted. Further, the dimensions of his parents' home were etched into his sensual memory (*GZ*, 21) as on the eve of each Sabbath Elias would race in alternating fear and fascination from the front of the house to the kitchen and back, loudly announcing the arrival of the gypsies.

In its permanent and temporary residents this compound mirrored Roustchouk's multiethnic and multilingual population: the Romanian wet nurse, the Bulgarian servant girls, the Armenian woodchopper, his mother's Russian friend. His grandfather Canetti sang Turkish and Ladino songs; his parents' language of intimacy was German. Multiethnicity and multilingualism were Canetti's first foundational experiences in the family compound; the full range of human emotions was his second. Within the compound Elias experienced jealousy, murderous rage, revenge, longing, and devotion, to a degree that was *hautnah* when he raised the woodchopper's heavy axe determined to kill his cousin Laurica, and she avenged herself by pushing Elias into a vat of scalding Danube water, causing his skin to peel off. Canetti can not recollect the physical pain but remembers the yearning for his father, who had recently departed for Manchester. Both wounds were healed only by his father's hasty return. Thus in addition to murderous hatred, Canetti knew early on the restorative powers of profound devotion.

Some of Canetti's later residences were as capacious as the family compound in Roustchouk, the two-story house in Manchester, and the lovely quarters he and Veza shared in the villa at Himmelstrasse 8 in Grinzing after they married. Others were as small as the single room in Vienna's Hagenberggasse. In his experience, whether smaller dwellings were perceived to be intimate or cramped spaces had more to do with the relationship among its inhabitants than with their actual area. Thus Canetti perceives the apartment in the Scheuchzerstrasse in Zurich, where he, his mother, and two brothers lived simply without any servants, to be an idyllic place. But this paradise could not be recreated five years later in the cramped apartment in Vienna's Radetzskystrasse which Canetti describes in two chapters, one titled "Enge" (*FO*, 96–103). In part his sense of emotional confinement had to do with the presence of people outside of the nuclear family — the landlady's son residing with them, the pregnant maid — who provoked revulsion or strife.[19] The larger issue, however, was the five-year span of time between the residences in the Scheuchzerstrasse and the Radetzkystrasse. Canetti was now a young man who had enjoyed freedom of movement in the intervening years. In these crowded conditions he could not evade his mother's relentless interrogations and dogmatic assertions about his intellectual interests, since he had to pass through the common living room to reach his bedroom study. The year on Radetzkystrasse was the most oppressive year Canetti remembers (*FO*, 103), but the narrow confines also gave him the strength to resist and push out again (*FO*, 106).

In the course of his formation, Canetti's world expanded through rooms shared with people outside of his extended family. As a young boy Canetti sought out the familiar in new spaces. The open windows and doors leading into the garden of Miss Lancashire's one-story school in Manchester made the boy from Roustchouk feel at home in the classroom. His attachment to certain classmates was linked to geography. He unconsciously associated little Mary Handsome's red cheeks with the red of apples from Istanbul sung of in a Ladino children's song he had heard in Bulgaria. He befriended a boy named Donald on the strength of his ability to identify the countries where various stamps originated and with a gift of stamps from Bulgaria (*GZ*, 58). Later, however, he shared space with people as diverse as the four Herder sisters in Villa Yalta, who were occupied with the arts and provided Elias a calm, stable environment for reading and writing, and the boarders at the Pension Charlotte in Frankfurt, where, to use Bernd Widdig's apt description, the sixteen-year-old experienced a modern, homeless society, a "panopticon of German society" during the inflation of the early Weimar period.[20]

Canetti's descriptions of rooms that extended beyond the confines of his immediate family also reflect his attitude toward their inhabitants. The autobiographer carefully draws the location and the layout of Veza's apartment in the Ferdinandstrasse before recounting the fierce struggle between Veza and her tyrannical stepfather that had taken place on this site prior to Canetti's appearance on the scene (FO, 124–25). Because she had trained the demanding old man not to cross her threshold, Canetti's own welcome into her room was all the sweeter. Especially after the break with his mother, he found asylum amidst the pictures and books in what he calls the "blossoming room" ("das blühende Zimmer": FO, 125), once again transgressing established categories such as living and inanimate to capture his feelings when he entered the space imbued with his beloved's qualities.

In contrast to Veza's room, Alma Mahler's "private museum" of trophies in her house on the Hohe Warte repelled Canetti. He found the heavy, slightly tipsy, celebrated beauty's memorialization of herself through the accomplishments of former husbands and lovers repugnant (A, 52).[21] However, a room connected with figures celebrated for their artistic creativity could also inspire awe. Canetti accepted the conductor Hermann Scherchen's invitation to participate in a modern music festival in Strasbourg partly because of his strong feelings for the Storm and Stress movement in German literature and Strasbourg's association with Herder, Goethe, Lenz, and the later Büchner (A, 56–60).[22] In the imposing house — formerly the Auberge du Louvre — in the Salzmanngasse, his assigned host led him to a large, comfortable room, furnished in the style of the eighteenth century (A, 57) and presented him with a *Musenalmanach* from the 1770s, containing a poem by Lenz. Even before his host had informed him of the tradition that Herder had received Goethe here daily, Canetti was overtaken by an intense feeling that it was unseemly for him to sleep in this room (A, 57). Unlike Alma Mahler, who laid claim to reflected glory, Canetti did not feel worthy of the honor of sleeping in a room that Herder had once occupied, and believed he was being punished by insomnia for profaning the space (A, 59). Here Canetti captures his own precarious position and aspirations at that time. As the author of a novel that had not yet found a publisher, Canetti was much closer to Lenz, who had never been really admitted to the sanctum sanctorum where he belonged (A, 58), than to Herder and Goethe. But by stating that his host treated him as he might have deserved later on (A, 58), Canetti reveals his own desire to gain critical recognition and, despite his account of how humbled and undeserving he felt at the time, implies that he now has gained that recognition: by the time the third volume of his trilogy was published, Canetti had been awarded — among many literary honors — the Nobel Prize.

Some of the rooms where Canetti lived are just as noteworthy for their vistas as for their interior configuration. From the window of the second-floor room in the Hagenberggasse Canetti looked out over many trees toward the asylum Steinhof, "the town of madmen," where six thousand people resided (*FO*, 219). No other view could have been more conducive to creating *Die Blendung*, that manifestation of paranoia and delusion. But would Canetti even have moved into the lovely Himmelsstrasse 8 villa when he and Veza married had he known that the owner of a nearby house was the publisher Ernst Benedikt? For four months following this discovery Canetti banished the Benedikt house from existence by not looking at it. This maneuver was similar to Kien's ignoring Theresa in *Die Blendung*, as Frau Benedikt astutely noted when she and Canetti were introduced in a café (*A*, 220). Canetti was initially alarmed by Frau Benedikt's assertion that the characters of *Die Blendung* practically lived in her house because her daughter, Friedl, so avidly admired the novel (*A*, 220). Friedl, an aspiring author who wished to become Canetti's pupil, began to pursue him on the street as obsessively as he had pursued the Kabuki girl, who turned out to be Friedl's younger sister. Finally, curiosity about how the Benedikt household could accommodate such a wide range of figures, from his own mad characters to Thomas Mann, prompted Canetti to accept a dinner invitation to this long-shunned place.

From his early, sensuous, instinctual perception of the family compound in Roustchouk to the rather convoluted, cerebral — yet not untouched by prejudice — understanding of the Benedikt house, Canetti's treatment of interior spaces is defined by the human dynamics within. Interior spaces can denote intimacy and security, but more often they are the site of life and death struggles to establish individual identity and maintain psychic boundaries.

Furniture

Readers of Canetti will recall the battle for power and control between Kien and Theresa in *Die Blendung* that is waged through furniture. They remember the enormous chandelier suspended over the heads of the guests in the drama *Hochzeit* that ultimately comes crashing down on the avaricious, decadent, hypocritical denizens of Vienna. In the autobiographical trilogy, too, furnishings often play a symbolic role, functioning as do interior spaces to convey the emotional tenor of human relationships and aspirations.

A table, be it at home or in a public establishment, is the site of a community where family, friends, acquaintances, boarders, or those of like interests assemble. At the table that stretched from end to end in his parents' generously-proportioned living room at the Roustchouk compound, the family gathered tribe-like to observe its rituals during the feast accompanying his brother Nissim's circumcision and Passover Seders. Such occasions provided family members ample opportunity to comment on each other's actions and behaviors. Canetti emphasizes the table's length to capture the size of his extended family, and to underscore the diverse opinions the family members would voice about each other while at table. In contrast, the small card table in the house in Manchester's Burton Road where Elias and his recently widowed mother quietly and solemnly shared a supper, she reassuring them both with the utterance "Du bist mein großer Sohn" (GZ, 50) stresses the uncommon intimacy between the two and characterizes the boy's new role following his father's death. That the mother and her three sons ate together at the table in the small apartment in Zurich's Scheuchzerstrasse suggests a particularly harmonious interlude for what remained of the nuclear family. But the configuration at this table also raised class issues. Mother and children were without benefit of a house daughter's (Haustochter's) services because Frau Canetti could not become accustomed to the Swiss democratic practice of eating together with a servant (GZ, 174). Social and class issues were magnified at the boarding-house table in Frankfurt, where Canetti observed his mother's discomfort as cynical witticisms about the social and political events of the day flew back and forth. In the Berlin of the twenties, Canetti himself would feel ill at ease at tables in expensive restaurants such as Schwanecke. People were there merely to be seen, lest in their mind they should cease to exist. On the night he met Isaac Babel, young Canetti, who could not yet claim any authorial success, joined a large group at a long table and demonstrated his insecurity by hovering on a chair at the far end, near the door (FO, 270). Babel, arriving late, displayed his characteristic sensitivity and kindness by leaving the restaurant rather than depriving the young man of his chair. But on subsequent evenings both men stood together at a counter in the more humble Aschinger's to eat pea soup and observe people (FO, 272).

Tables, when serving as desks, are also the site where intellectual work takes place. Following the evening meal in the Scheuchzerstrasse apartment, young Elias reverently carried the yellow-bound volumes of Strindberg to the table for his mother to pore over. This act of reading was both communal and solitary. Because literature was Canetti's bond with his mother, and he was reading Dickens with a flashlight under the covers while she read at the table, there was some commonality in their endeavors. But the mother clearly indicated that she wanted him out of the way so that she could commence reading, and she prohibited him from reading Strindberg. The boy respected both boundaries. Reading Strindberg further denoted the mother's autonomy and her participation in communities of which Canetti had as yet no knowledge because only decades later did she disclose that during her first stay in a sanatorium in Reichenhall, her doctor, who had introduced her to Strindberg, implored her to leave her husband and marry him.

In Zurich's Villa Yalta, Elias and the schoolgirl boarders gathered around the large hall table to do their lessons and write letters. This was a comfortable and comforting community for Elias. As the sole male in residence he also had privileged access to a desk in the back schoolroom for his "serious writing." But even though he sat by himself, he did not write *Junius Brutus* in isolation, because he was working out his own family's drama of a father's curse on his son and intended his creation to be a gift for his mother.

Later, having returned to Vienna to begin his university studies, Canetti took particular pleasure in mentoring his younger brother George because — as he tells the reader with self-irony — George asked him questions about everything he knew. The brothers sat with their books and notebooks at the large, square table by the window. Canetti repeats his description of the size, shape, and position of this table, emphasizing the importance of the brothers' reciprocal relationship during those "Lernabende" (*FO*, 59).

In Wieland Herzfelde's garret apartment in Berlin, Canetti was pleased with "the lovely round table" the Malik house publisher put at his disposal (*FO*, 251). Away from the hubbub of the streets and the cramped and noisy publishing house, Canetti — who felt bombarded by all the new ideas and impressions avant-garde Berlin hailed — could work undisturbed, assisting with Herzfelde's biography of Upton Sinclair. The table's pleasant roundness suggests Herzfelde's approbation of his assistant's abilities.

The most modest work table, the folding table the farmer and his wife set up for Canetti outdoors in the Sellrain valley, may have been the most important (*FO*, 141). Far from Vienna, where Freudian slips and the Oedipus complex were high fashion (*FO*, 116–17), he began reading and taking notes on Freud's study of crowds. The simple folding table suggests a humble, perhaps somewhat provisional or uncertain beginning to Canetti's life project. Yet at it Canetti commenced to engage in a dialogue with one of the most influential thinkers of the twentieth century.

People often chose furniture to project their self image and to express their fantasies. When the sculptor Fritz Wotruba invited Canetti to the home he and his wife Mariana shared with his mother in a working-class section of Vienna, the glass-topped coffee table, along with the tubular steel chairs — representing "eine etwas programmatische Modernität," as Canetti wrote (*A*, 100) — in their room stood in sharp contrast to the rest of the simple house, juxtaposing Wotruba's working-class origins to Mariana's artistic aspirations for her husband. And the absence of a table — of any furniture at all — nevertheless made a pronounced statement. In Berlin, Canetti's best friend, the poet Ibby Gordon displayed her anti-bourgeois modernity by disdaining convention and throwing a housewarming party in her empty apartment. She invited the guests, artists, writers, and their patrons, whom she expected to be inventive, to *say* the furniture (*FO*, 284).

In contrast, beds, the second item of furniture to appear in crucial sections of the autobiography, are the locus of the most primal and intimate human relations: birth, sex, and death. Canetti's first and last mentions of a bed in the trilogy are connected with his mother — the bed where she gave birth and her deathbed. During his brother Nissim's birth, the four-year-old Elias heard his mother wailing from the bedroom, and when he finally was allowed into the room to view the newborn brother, his mother lay in bed white and motionless. The sound and sight of childbirth and its aftermath left the boy feeling alienated from his mother (*GZ*, 24). However, Canetti remembers with pleasure the Sunday mornings in the house on Burton Road when he and his brothers romped in his parents' bed, and his father was especially playful (*GZ*, 69). From this same bed young Elias later kept nightly vigil, afraid his widowed mother would leap out the window (*GZ*, 49). Because Canetti begins the narration of the family's time in Manchester with the vigil scene, out of chronological order, he emphasizes the intensity and significance of fearing his mother's death, of being made the guardian of her life (*GZ*, 49), and of beginning to assume his father's role.

Canetti's early memories of beds involve the pain of birth and the intimacy of family. Beds where sexual intercourse takes place remain unseen and are mentioned only to convey Canetti's unusual innocence in sexual matters during adolescence, although he discreetly notes that the taboo against sexual love soon crumbled in a natural way (*GZ*, 269). This taboo was both self-imposed and cultivated by his mother. Why did Fräulein Rahm's gentleman caller plead and whimper in the adjacent room of the Pension Charlotte (*FO*, 41–42)? What about the whistling, teasing, giggling, and grunting in the adjacent room of the guesthouse at St. Agatha, which was occupied by a stage director and his much-younger girlfriend (*FO*, 196)? And just in case Elias was wondering what was going on in Johnny Ring's tiny room in the apartment they shared in the Radetzkystrasse — which the adolescent was not — Canetti's anxious mother reinforced his innocence in sexual matters by suggesting that Johnny Ring's male visitor must be sleeping under the bed while the dog was sleeping on the bed with Johnny (*FO*, 100–101).

The most important bed scene, framed entirely in terms of spatial relations, ends the trilogy with the chapter "Tod der Mutter." It takes place in Paris at the bedside of Canetti's estranged, angry mother, who did not want to see him because he had deceived her and concealed his marriage to Veza. Canetti gained access to his mother through a final deception, bringing her "roses from the garden in Roustchouk." The room filled with the fragrance, and Canetti was included in the fragrant cloud (*A*, 297). But this acceptance was only momentary, for after a while she began commanding him to sit farther and farther away until he had moved into the corner of the small room (*A*, 298). When Canetti's younger brother, the physician George, entered the room and suggested that Canetti sit closer, his mother replied,

"Dort ist es besser" (*A*, 298). In contrast, she kept George close to her and expected his ministrations. Canetti's ritual with his mother was rehearsed daily: "Sie sah mich an, bis sie mich haßte. Dann sagte sie: 'Geh!'" (*A*, 300). Canetti interprets his mother's behavior toward him as punishment not only for abandoning her for another woman but also for his youthful possessiveness: "Um sich von mir zu lösen, hatte sie sich krank gefühlt, war zu Ärzten gegangen und an ferne Orte gefahren, in die Berge, ans Meer, es konnte überall sein, wenn ich nicht dort war" (*A*, 301). At the opening of the deathbed scene, the reader learns she had suffered from asthma for many years. However, the mother's chronic illness may also have been a psychic malaise. David Denby wonders whether "Canetti's mother was mad, and did he not notice her madness because it was entirely devoted to *him*?"[23] Even though Canetti's self-accusation reveals a continuing egocentrism, in that he sees himself as the sole cause for his mother's need to get away — after all, she first went to a sanatorium while her husband was still alive — Canetti understands more fundamentally than does Denby what ailed his mother. Canetti comes to recognize that his mother, an educated woman of keen intelligence, did have a life of her own — apart from husband, children, and extended family — and needed even greater autonomy, a room of her own, or, in the current vernacular, her own space.

Pictures

There are a variety of paintings, for which Canetti uses the term *Bilder*, that played an important role in shaping his perception of the world. These pictures include Rubens's *The Blinding of Samson*, Brueghel's *Six Blind Men* and *Death's Triumph*, Michelangelo's Sistine Chapel ceiling, and Grünewald's *Isenheimer Altar*. Recounting how moved he was while watching dancing peasants in Prague because he recognized them from Breughel, he reflects on the reciprocal relationship between a picture and its viewer. He believes that paintings mold our experience. The pictures that we incorporate determine the path we will take in life (*A*, 292). Maintaining that there is no better route to reality than paintings (*FO*, 110), Canetti develops a kind of viewer response theory, for reality does not exist independently of the viewer, who brings his own experience to make the picture come to life (*FO*, 110). Canetti does not speak of paintings in abstract aesthetic terms but very concretely. Pictures can become as much a part of our psyche as the native soil, the homeland, the geographical space in which we are grounded.

Canetti's framed reproductions of Michaelangelo's prophets and sibyls from the ceiling of the Sistine chapel that he received as a Christmas present in Zurich taught him his single most fundamental lesson about life and art: how creative defiance can be if it is tied to patience (*GZ*, 316). The prophets did not speak to him through the Bible, nor as Jews, but were mediated by

Michelangelo's creative struggle. Canetti imagined the words from the old prophet Isaiah's half-open mouth (*GZ*, 318) — an elaboration on his childhood conversations with imaginary people in the pattern of wallpaper in the nursery of the Burton Road house (*GZ*, 51). Michelangelo's pictures were later replaced by reproductions of the Isenheim Altar. From a dual post-First World War and post-Holocaust perspective, Canetti reflects on the entire day he stood before that medieval altar in Kolmar in 1927. Grünewald's dying Christ conveyed to him a truth about art — that it could capture a memory of the dreadful things that people do to one another (*FO*, 217). Canetti claims it is the task of art to hold the truth before our eyes — not to provide us solace or catharsis (*FO*, 217). When Canetti finally acquired the reproductions with details of the Isenheim Altar, he hung them in his room, which overlooked the insane asylum Steinhof, and began writing *Die Blendung*, the novel with main characters who are brutally and grotesquely mad. The reality of the pictures Canetti chose to incorporate into his life and which inspired his literary production is profoundly moral, providing valuable lessons about human nature, the heights of its creativity and the depths of its depravity.

Body

Reflecting on his love for Veza and his fascination with her mystery, Canetti writes that nothing is more irresistible than the temptation to enter another person's inner space (*FO*, 154–55). Canetti appreciated Veza as one of those persons who knows how to place her words, and so, during her silences, when she closed her eyes when smiling and seemed to be contemplating herself from the inside (*FO*, 154), Canetti sought those words. Because her smile reached from her to the observer (*FO*, 154), Canetti did not feel excluded by Veza's closed eyes; thus his desire to enter her thoughts, to seek her words does not seem transgressive to him. What Canetti particularly admired in Veza was that she had found characters in great literature and internalized them "for her own multiplicity." She had implanted them in herself, and they thrived in her, each sharply delimited (*FO*, 154). Veza's great capacity to take in literary characters (*FO*, 154) demonstrates not only a rich interior life but also her intellectual independence, specifically from Karl Kraus, who still held Canetti in fetters (*FO*, 154). In addition to Veza's intellectual abilities and imaginative powers, Canetti notes her great empathy for the pain and vulnerability of others, a further sign of her emotional expansiveness.

In contrast to Veza, Anna Mahler — the woman Canetti loved with the kind of passion that gnaws away because it is unrequited, and who inspired the third volume's title — *Das Augenspiel* — was, as Canetti put it, nothing but eyes. All the rest was illusion. Even though Canetti sensed this right away, it was difficult for him to acknowledge that Anna's eyes were more spacious than her person (*A*, 70). Canetti reiterates the infinite depth and spaciousness of the eyes to which he so precipitously fell prey, repeating that he happily gave them everything he had. Whereas he wished to plumb Veza's inner space to fathom her thoughts and words, it seemed to him that Anna's eyes were a bottomless lake into which he plunged everything he could think and say: verbally, in his manuscript, and in letters sent three times a day. Anna, whose own medium was clay, not words, was merely the reflective mirror for the narcissism of a young man seeking to make his mark in the world.

Eyes are also prominent in Canetti's encounter with his mother on her deathbed. Canetti's account of the deathbed scene begins with a topographical description of the mother's face. What the author had admired about his mother and describes in spatial terms — the vast, spacious forehead, suggesting her keen intellect, and her magnificent wide nostrils, indicative of her capacity for sensual pleasure — was now shrunken and diminished. The eyes barred him psychic access (*A*, 296). In the brief moment in which she accepts the "roses from Roustchouk" and her son, the mother's eyes and nostrils enlarged and her forehead seemed to widen. Canetti had the impression that her features grew larger and stronger (*A*, 297).

Whereas the words Canetti chooses to characterize his relationships to the three most important women in his life reveal the desire to enter, to fathom, to gain acceptance, to fill the void, or to simply drown in the deep,[24] that is, to penetrate surfaces that might ultimately yield, the words he uses to describe his friendship with the two men he most valued — Fritz Wotruba and Dr. Sonne — are quite different in the context of space. Canetti likens his conversations with Wotruba, who, he believes, was interested in nothing but the power of words and the power of stone, to a wrestling match, stating "Beide Leiber waren immer da, sie verschwanden nicht, sie blieben *undurchdringlich*" (*A*, 95–96, my italics). Canetti's image of the stony hardness, "the impenetrability" of the two men's bodies to characterize their conversations indicates that he considers Wotruba to have been a worthy and equal interlocutor when he and the sculptor tested their ideas on each other. Given the disparity in their physiques, the image of the powerful sculptor and the diminutive author wrestling verbally might evoke a smile. But this image is effective in underscoring the materiality of words, which both men took extremely seriously.

Words are the common denominator of Canetti's relationships to both Fritz Wotruba and Dr. Sonne. What Canetti appreciated in Sonne, a far less corporeal figure than Wotruba, was that at a time when impending political catastrophe caused the coffeehouses to be flooded with self-important or self-pitying chatter, Sonne spoke in the third person, in order to distance himself from his surroundings in the café he frequented daily (*A*, 127). In

Sonne's case, distance does not signify estrangement between himself and his interlocutor but rather a sovereign objectivity, knowledge, and wisdom.

In sum, the spatial dimension of Canetti's descriptions of Veza, Anna, and his mother — the women to whom he was most intimately bound, of his friend Wotruba, and of his mentor Sonne reveals differing dynamics. In the case of the women, the balances of power were ever shifting. But Canetti's desire that women might yield, or that he could penetrate, do imply a wish to conquer, to be, in the final analysis, superior. In contrast, the impenetrable fastness of both Wotruba and Canetti in their encounters underscores the egalitarian nature of their friendship, whereas to his mentor Sonne Canetti readily grants a position superior to himself.

Conclusion

Canetti's intellectual and psychic journey takes him through great geographic and mental distances, both in the present and in the past. Throughout the autobiographical trilogy Canetti views movement — from country to country, city to city, within an urban space, or in nature — as positive, for it exposes us to powerful experiences, provides definitive insights, and releases creative energies. Canetti plots out the geometry of interior spaces and their furnishings to reveal the dynamics of the relationships of those who inhabit and occupy them, be these relationships hierarchical, egalitarian, stifling, oppressive, or communal and lovingly intimate. Canetti believes that human beings have the imaginative power to invest space with the qualities we need and desire, tempered by our emotional and intellectual affinities as well as our historical circumstances.

The nouns that characterize Canetti's autobiography are vastness, amplitude, expansion, and magnanimity. Canetti requires — and reveres — ample space to fearlessly absorb, process, understand, grow, learn, develop, create, and blossom without fear. He seeks no illusory harmonies, fully acknowledging the discomfort, the turbulence, and even the chaos that exists in the world. But he rejects and pushes out against anything provincial, confining, restricting, cramped, narrow, or closed. He demands for himself and for humanity space that is physically, mentally, and emotionally capacious enough to accommodate diversity, powerful and contrasting impressions, conflicting ideas, incompatibilities, clashing opinions, and the full range of human emotions and experience.[25]

Notes

[1] Elias Canetti, *Die gerettete Zunge: Geschichte einer Jugend* (1977; rpt. Munich: Hanser, 1994). Cited as *GZ*. *Die Fackel im Ohr: Lebensgeschichte 1921–1931* (1980; rpt. Munich: Hanser, 1993). Cited as *FO*. *Das Augenspiel: Lebensgeschichte 1931–1937* (1985; rpt. Munich: Hanser, 1994). Cited as *A*.

[2] Elias Canetti, *Die Blendung* (1935; rpt. Munich: Hanser, 1963).

[3] Elias Canetti, *Hochzeit* (written 1932; Munich: Hanser, 1964).

[4] Elias Canetti, *Masse und Macht* (Hamburg: Claassen, 1960). Cited as *MM*. See, for example, Gerald Stieg, "Betrachtungen zu Elias Canettis Autobiographie," in *Zu Elias Canetti*, ed. Manfred Durzak (Stuttgart: Ernst Klett, 1983), 158–70. Here: 162; Sigurd Paul Scheichl, "Hörenlernen. Zur teleologischen Struktur der autobiographischen Bücher Canettis," in *Elias Canetti: Blendung als Lebensform*, ed. Friedbert Aspetsberger and Gerald Stieg (Königstein/Ts.: Athenäum, 1985), 73–79; Richard H. Lawson, *Understanding Elias Canetti* (Columbia: U of South Carolina P, 1991), 11; Dagmar Barnouw, *Elias Canetti zur Einführung* (Hamburg: Junius, 1996), 40; Penka Angelova, "Canettis autobiographische Trilogie als Bildungsroman," in *Autobiographie zwischen Fiktion und Wirklichkeit*, ed. Penka Angelova and Emilia Staitscheva (St. Ingbert: Röhrig, 1997), 47–62; Friederike Eigler, "'Fissures in the Monument': Reassessing Elias Canetti's Autobiographical Works," in *Critical Essays on Elias Canetti*, ed. David Darby (New York: K. Hall, 2000), 261–75. Here: 265.

[5] For example Zsuzsa Széll, "Ist 'Wahrheit ein Meer von Grashalmen'?: Zu Canettis Denkhaltung" in Joseph P. Strelka and Zsuzsa Széll, *Ist Wahrheit ein Meer von Grashalmen?* (New York: Peter Lang, 1993), 11–16.

[6] Stieg, "Betrachtungen zu Elias Canettis Autobiographie," 162.

[7] Gerhard Melzer, "The Only Sentence and Its Sole Possessor: The Symbolic Power of Elias Canetti," in *Critical Essays on Elias Canetti*, ed. David Darby, 215–26. Here: 219.

[8] See Irene Stocksieker Di Maio, "'Heimat,' 'Örtlichkeiten,' and Mother-Tongue: The Cases of Jean Améry and Elias Canetti," in *Der Begriff "Heimat" in der deutschen Gegenwartsliteratur/The Concept of "Heimat" in Contemporary German Culture*, ed. Helfried W. Seliger (Munich: iudicium, 1987), 211–24.

[9] See Bernd Widdig, "Tägliche Sprengungen: Elias Canetti und die Inflation," in *Einladung zur Verwandlung: Essays zu Elias Canettis "Masse und Macht,"* ed. Michael Krüger (Munich: Hanser, 1995), 128–50.

[10] Isaak Emmanuilovich Babel, *Geschichten aus Odessa* (Berlin: Malik, 1926).

[11] In a slightly different context, Ritchie Robertson stresses that Canetti "evaded familiar categories of 'Western' and 'Eastern'" with respect to his Jewish identity, in *The "Jewish Question" in German Literature, 1749–1939: Emancipation and its Discontents* (London: Oxford, 1999), 342.

[12] Kristie A. Foell notes that Canetti's "earliest identity spans not only Eastern and Western Europe . . . but also the great Muslim empire." "July 15, 1927: The Vienna Palace of Justice is Burned in a Mass Uprising of Viennese Workers, Central Experience in the Life and Work of Elias Canetti," in *Yale Companion to Jewish Writing*

and Thought in German Culture 1096–1996, ed. Sander L. Gilman and Jack Zipes (New Haven: Yale UP, 1997), 464–70. Here: 468.

[13] Johann Peter Hebel, *Schatzkästlein des rheinischen Hausfreundes* (Tübingen: Cotta, 1811).

[14] Johann Peter Hebel, *Gesammelte Werke,* vol. I (Berlin: Aufbau, 1958), 246.

[15] Elias Canetti, *Die Provinz des Menschen: Aufzeichnungen 1942–1972* (Frankfurt a.M.: Fischer, 1976), 61.

[16] Martin Bollacher, "Mundus liber: Zum Verhältnis von Sprache und Judentum bei Elias Canetti," in *Elias Canettis Anthropologie und Poetik,* ed. Stefan H. Kaszyński (Munich: Hanser, 1984), 60–61.

[17] Sigmund Freud, *Massenpsychologie und Ich-Analyse: Gesammelte Werke: chronologisch geordnet,* vol. 13, ed. Anna Freud (Frankfurt: Fischer, 1968–1978).

[18] For further elaboration on the theme of death in Canetti's works see, for example, Franz Schuh, "Schreiben gegen den Tod," in *Der Stachel des Befehls,* ed. John Patillo-Hess (Vienna: Löcker, 1992) 44–56, and Thomas H. Macho, "Triumph des Überlebens," in *Der Stachel des Befehls,* 57–64.

[19] Compare Stieg "Betrachtungen zu Elias Canettis Autobiographie," 162.

[20] Widdig, "Tägliche Sprengungen: Elias Canetti und die Inflation," 131, my translation.

[21] Friederike Eigler contends that Canetti's derogatory portrayal of Alma Mahler as an exaggerated inspirational muse is based on a stereotype common at the turn of the last century. Canetti fails to take into account that she sacrificed the possibility of a musical career at her much older husband's request. Eigler, *Das autobiographische Werk von Elias Canetti: Verwandlung, Identität, Machtausübung* (Tübingen: Stauffenburg, 1988), 180–82.

[22] In his speech accepting the Büchner prize, Canetti treats in more detail the importance of Strasbourg for Büchner's life. Elias Canetti, "Georg Büchner," in *Das Gewissen der Worte* (Munich: Hanser, 1983), 213–15.

[23] David Denby, "Learning to Love Canetti: The Autobiography of a Difficult Man," *The New Yorker* (May 31, 1999): 106–13. Here: 108.

[24] For a more detailed analysis of Canetti's relationship to these three women, see Hannelore Scholz, "'Keine Angst geht verloren, aber ihre Verstecke sind rätselhaft': Frauen im autobiographischen Wahrnehmungsspektrum von Elias Canetti," in *Autobiographie zwischen Fiktion und Wirklichkeit* (St. Ingbert: Röhrig Universitätsverlag, 1997), 248–68.

[25] I wish to thank Katherine A. Jensen, Michelle Massé, and Anna Nardo for reading portions of this paper, and for their many helpful suggestions and support.

Philosophy and Social Thought

Canetti and Nietzsche:
An Introduction to *Masse und Macht*

Ritchie Robertson

*M*ASSE UND MACHT IS A STUDY OF human nature and human society
in the tradition of Darwinian naturalism that runs, by way of
Nietzsche and Freud, down to the sociobiological literature of our own day.[1]
"Naturalism" here is not a literary but a philosophical term. It implies the
attempt to study human life as part of nature, with the help of the natural
sciences, and without reference to any non-natural or supernatural concepts
such as divine revelation, a God-given order, or Platonic forms. Darwinian
naturalism is a grandiose attempt, in Nietzsche's words, to translate man
back into nature, to remove the idealistic scribblings that had disfigured the
original text "homo natura."[2]

Darwin's name provides a convenient label, or emblem, for this project,
but he did not initiate it. In the seventeenth century, Thomas Hobbes constructed an anthropology, or an account of humanity, based ultimately on
scientific materialism, in which nature usurped the place of God. The Enlightenment tried to devise a more optimistic anthropology, in which man's
natural desires and drives were declared good.[3] The theory of evolution set
out in *The Origin of Species* (1859) and explicitly applied to humanity in *The
Descent of Man* (1871), though contested in its time, eventually pulled
together many previous explorations of man's place within the natural world
and confirmed that man was to be understood not as divinely created but as
a special kind of animal.[4] "We no longer derive man from 'spirit,' from
'divinity,' we have put him back among the animals," wrote Nietzsche.[5]
Once convinced that man had evolved from animals, subsequent thinkers
could speculate about how modern social institutions and moral standards
had developed from equivalents in human prehistory, and these in turn from
analogues to be observed in the social life of animals. Among such speculations, Nietzsche's *Zur Genealogie der Moral* (1888, *The Genealogy of Morals*)
is a particularly radical attempt to explain how man became an animal that
could make and keep promises, distinguish the morally "evil" from the
merely "bad," and develop the ascetic ideals that were the foundation of
culture;[6] while Freud in *Totem und Tabu* (1913, *Totem and Taboo*, 1919)
undertook to derive the institutions of society, art, and religion from the

Oedipus complex as supposedly embodied in the social life of early man. Both are indebted to evolutionary thought, though neither Nietzsche nor Freud accepted Darwin's particular version of evolution.[7] Canetti, though explicitly hostile to both Freud and Nietzsche, admitted that he needed Freud as an adversary, and the same seems to be true of his relationship to Nietzsche. Certainly *Masse und Macht*, with its constant reference to the practices of "primitive" societies and to the behavior of animals, belongs in this intellectual company.[8] These speculations continue in present-day socio-biology and in the often fascinating writings of successful biological popularizers such as Richard Dawkins, Daniel Dennett, and Matt Ridley.

Part of the fascination of Darwinian naturalism comes from its deep ambivalence, and my aim in this essay is to show how *Masse und Macht* shares this ambivalence. To acknowledge our biological and in some respects psychological kinship with animals corresponds to our self-knowledge, and can make us feel more at home in the world. On the other hand, some animal behavior is profoundly unedifying. Many animals eat their young: eaglets kill their siblings; if a lioness with cubs takes a new mate, the lion will kill the cubs before siring his own.[9] With our closest relatives, the chimpanzees, we share a disposition to inter-tribal violence. *Masse und Macht* documents the varieties of violence in great detail. Of course there is also ample evidence for altruism and cooperation among animals.[10] But these examples show that, despite the hopes of the Enlightenment, "nature" cannot provide a standard for human behavior. Many different behaviors are natural. If we prefer some to others, our preference follows a standard that cannot itself be derived from nature. Here Darwinian naturalism reaches its limit. Without acknowledging the limit, naturalists generally search among primitive and animal behaviors for those that seem desirable and may be propagated and strengthened among ourselves.

Against the background of this ambivalent fascination with our evolutionary heritage and its possible implications, I want especially to link Canetti with Nietzsche. Anyone publishing a book called *Masse und Macht* challenges comparison with the author of *Der Wille zur Macht*.[11] Canetti presumably did not know what textual scholars have now established: that the latter book, though much read, is not an authentic work by Nietzsche, but a scissors-and-paste job done by his sister on his late notebooks, designed to present a more systematic account of his thought than any he himself published. Nietzsche's concept of the will to power underlies his authentic works of the 1880s, including *Zur Genealogie der Moral*. Power, for him, has two aspects. It means the power to dominate: the power of the master over the slave, of the ascetic over his body, of the thinker over his subject. It also means the sensation of pleasure arising from such domination, from the overcoming of resistance and the incorporation of other organisms. He was inspired by the arguments of the biologist Wilhelm Roux that the constituent cells within every organism, far from forming a harmonious whole, are constantly contending for dominance.[12] "A living being wants above all to *release* its strength; life itself is the will to power."[13] Such enjoyment of strength extends all the way up to human beings and human society. A relatively crude enjoyment comes from the physical domination of other people; a subtler pleasure comes from controlling one's own body, as a fasting ascetic does, and a yet subtler from controlling one's own mind, as is done, in Nietzsche's view, by the religious believer who persuades himself of the truth of irrational and illogical dogmas. In all these instances, Nietzsche conceives of power as solitary and unshareable. An isolated individual exercises power over other people, over himself, or over an object. This individual is descended from Hobbes's asocial man who reluctantly enters into a contract with others in order to enjoy the benefits of social life.[14] For an account of the distribution of power within institutions, where it eludes the complete control of any individual, we have to go to Nietzsche's modern disciple Michel Foucault.[15]

Canetti's conception of power is similarly asocial, as his most searching critic, Axel Honneth, has pointed out.[16] That is why his book has two foci, crowds and power, the one acting as complement and corrective to the other. How this works will become clearer if we reverse the order of Canetti's exposition and deal first with power. Power, for Canetti, is located first and foremost in the individual's body, in the physical nature that we share with animals. The basic gesture of power is killing one's prey. The basic instruments of power are the organs of the body. The hand that seizes, grips, and squeezes its victim, the mouth that begins its incorporation, and the teeth that grind it down so that it can be digested are primeval sources of terror and ultramodern symbols of power. Ancient terrors can be reawakened by the grip of the policeman's hand on one's shoulder, by the mouth-like opening of the prison door, and by the order of military formations as smooth, regular, and inexorable as a row of teeth.

Despite this emphasis on the body, Canetti firmly dissociates power from mere brute force. He illustrates it with the example of the power of a cat over a mouse, which is psychological even more than physical. He finds it in various social practices, especially those surrounding the act of eating. Incorporating one's food, grinding it down, converting some into nutrition and expelling the rest as waste matter is the elemental exercise of power. Although shared meals might be interpreted as a basic social activity, Canetti understands them rather as an armed truce among potentially hostile individuals who implicitly declare that they will not eat one another. A latent threat survives in the sight of other people's teeth and in the presence of those rudimentary weapons, the knife and the fork. Laughter, in which we bare our teeth, is associated with food. Originally it expressed pleasure at the prospect of food; now it expresses our sense of power over a helpless being whom we could eat. Here Canetti mentions Hobbes's attribution of laughter to "sudden glory" caused "by the apprehension of some deformed thing in another, by comparison of which they suddenly applaud themselves" (*MM*, 255).[17] But he adds that Hobbes was only half right. Hobbes did not know that laughter was originally an animal reaction, a substitute for eating; hyenas laugh when food is snatched away from them.

These examples already illustrate some of the strengths and weaknesses of Canetti's account of power. Its main strength is its reliance on vivid interpretive accounts of familiar experiences. From the phenomenology of power, his descriptions of grasping and eating, Canetti moves rapidly to its psychology. Because his descriptions are so arresting, he entices us into accepting the Hobbesian account of human nature that accompanies them. Humans are intrinsically solitary, engaged in a war of all against all. Social life is a temporary cessation of hostilities. According to Canetti's account, indeed, we ought all to be cannibals, because to incorporate another person by eating him should be such a satisfying exercise of power. But we are not, and perhaps never were. Cannibalism, if it exists, is a rare and poorly attested practice.[18] That in itself should make one question Canetti's account of power. Solidarity among humans, it seems, is a stronger force than among lions or eagles; we tend not to devour one another.

The form of psychological power that Canetti describes most persuasively is the power of the survivor. He evokes the satisfaction of an old man in surviving all his acquaintances, the triumph of a person who has luckily survived a plague or other catastrophe, and the contentment of a ruler who has eliminated his rivals or massacred large numbers of his subjects. His account of power leads up to two case studies in paranoia. One is the Indian despot Muhammad Tughlak, who, being annoyed by the inhabitants of Delhi, expelled them all and subsequently took pleasure in contemplating a vast city in which only he and his household were left. The other is the judge Daniel Schreber, whose autobiography recounts his paranoid fantasies of being the last surviving human being and being summoned by God to generate a new race.[19] Canetti's exploration of these cases is not only fascinating in itself but provides an indirect way of talking about Hitler, the paranoid despot who is scarcely ever named in *Masse und Macht* but makes his presence felt throughout.

Nevertheless, Canetti's claims need qualification. He ignores the fact that survivors of a disaster often feel trauma rather than triumph. The sole survivor of an air crash may well feel guilty at surviving when others have undeservedly perished. Such a person asks, "Why was I spared?" and finds no answer. Moreover, if Canetti's claims about the satisfaction of surviving were entirely true, they should apply pre-eminently to survivors of the Holocaust, who have escaped the deaths that overtook six million others. Yet their testimony shows that Holocaust survivors are most likely to be deeply traumatized.

For our purposes, the most interesting survivor described by Canetti is the Roman historian Josephus. Josephus helped to lead Jewish resistance to the Romans in the campaign that ended with the fall of Jerusalem in A.D. 70. Afterwards Josephus hid in a cave with forty followers who were all resolved to commit suicide. Unable to dissuade them, Josephus proposed that they should draw lots; that the first man to draw a lot should be killed by the second, the second by the third, and so on until only one was left, who, out of solidarity with his defeated nation, would undoubtedly kill himself. This was done. The soldiers killed each other, reassured by the certainty that their commander would die with them. But Josephus, who contrived to draw the last lot, did not kill himself. Left with one other man, he escaped from the cave, as he had always intended to do, and surrendered to the Romans, among whom he later rose to fame and fortune.

This narrative of betrayal illustrates the "prisoner's dilemma," a situation often used in recent sociobiological discussions about the relative merits of solidarity and self-interest.[20] Put twenty people in separate booths, unable to communicate with one another. Tell each that if he refrains from pressing the buzzer, he and all the others will receive a thousand dollars, but if anyone does press the buzzer, he will receive a hundred dollars and the rest will get nothing. If all the participants trust the others, all will become rich. But if I do not trust the others, it makes sense for me to press the buzzer and at least get a hundred dollars. For if somebody else presses the buzzer, I shall get nothing at all. Which is more rational: mutual trust, with the risk of being deceived, or self-interest by practicing deceit? Josephus chose the latter. His followers died in the belief that he would loyally die with them; he deceived them and profited at their expense. The modern reader may think that he was obviously right to save his own life; but he did so by violating the shared readiness for heroic death, a value he professed to share with his followers, and so betrayed them just as surely as the cheat in the "prisoner's dilemma" betrays the others by depriving them of money. Such situations have often been used to advocate selfish individualism. Canetti is not commending Josephus' behavior, but describing it as an example of how survivors and leaders enjoy power. Along with physical survival and material benefits, Josephus gained "das erhöhte Gefühl seines eigenen Lebens, durch den Untergang seiner Leute genährt" (*MM*, 276). Just as, in eating, one gains renewed vitality by incorporating food, so the Nietzschean will to power strengthens one's sense of life when one can overcome and incorporate others, and it seems that the best way of doing so is to kill others or at least bring about their deaths for one's own benefit. Thus, Canetti presents Josephus as a witness for a Hobbesian war of all against all, sustained by a Nietzschean will to power.

Skeptically, though, we may wonder how much Canetti's chief survivors — Muhammad Tughlak, Schreber, and Josephus — tell us about ordinary human nature. The first two were aberrant individuals. It might be argued that their mental aberrations revealed with exceptional clarity the urge to survive that is part of everybody's nature. But that would be a circular argument. If Canetti were not already convinced that the urge to survive is fundamental to humanity, such oddities as Tughlak and Schreber could not serve as illustrations. As for Josephus, his betrayals took place in exceptional circumstances. The people he betrayed were already dead and therefore did not know that he was untrustworthy. But even though deceit may permit escape from an extraordinary situation like his, it cannot provide the basis for normal social relations. Social institutions depend on mutual trust. I need to assume that my spouse, my colleagues, my lawyer, my accountant, and so forth are normally going to deal honestly with me. That is the point of the "prisoner's dilemma": to show that although self-interest may seem most expedient in the short term, in any longer perspective it is most practical to trust people, even at the risk of occasional deception. The unusual circumstances in which Josephus found himself give no guidance to the normal functioning of social institutions.

When Canetti discusses how institutions work, he presents an even bleaker picture than Hobbes. As a fundamental relation between people, he posits the situation where one gives another an order. He traces this situation to animal life, in which one species takes flight for fear of another, predatory species. Hence the command is always backed up by a threat, ultimately the threat of death. The command has two parts: the momentum that forces the recipient to obey, and the sting that stays behind in him. By this metaphor Canetti means that a command, once obeyed, is not over and done with; rather, it leaves its recipient in a state of resentful subordination. The only way to free oneself from this subordination is to establish a situation in which one exercises power by issuing the same command to someone else. This happens most regularly in the sequence of generations. Parents discipline their children; the children, resenting their subordination, grow up and discharge their resentment by disciplining their children in turn. Philip Larkin sums up the process in the well-known lines:

> Man hands on misery to man.
> It deepens like a coastal shelf.[21]

Having shown how the command structures family life as the transmission of power, Canetti makes a yet more radical move by linking this transmission with one of the most agonizing problems thrown up by twentieth-century history: the problem of how ordinary people can commit atrocities. The only person who can receive a command without feeling its sting, Canetti says, is the executioner. The command he receives is to kill someone else. Hence the threat of death that underlies the command does not apply to him, for he can instantly divert it onto the person whom he kills. Hence, he kills with the good conscience of someone who is doing his duty. "Der Henker ist der zufriedenste, der stachelloseste der Menschen" (*MM*, 379).

Whatever the merits of this explanation, Canetti has at least confronted the problem of explaining how mass murderers have an easy conscience. He is implicitly addressing the responsibility of ordinary people for the Holocaust. That issue has been forcefully raised by Christopher Browning's study of a reserve police battalion from Hamburg whose members were drafted to exterminate Jews in the village of Józefów in occupied Poland. Only twelve out of five hundred men accepted the chance to avoid participation. The rest obediently shot Jews in the back of the neck, a few with sadistic pleasure, but most in an unenthusiastic but conscientious manner.[22] More recently, Daniel Goldhagen has argued that Germans, because of ingrained anti-Semitism, positively enjoyed killing Jews.[23] His argument fails, but only because there is ample evidence that Poles, Latvians, and Ukrainians enjoyed it, too.[24] The controversy aroused by Goldhagen may have resulted not only from the flaws in his thesis but from reluctance to accept the facts he documents. Canetti's account of the executioner places these data in a still more disturbing light. If one follows his thinking, the problem is not why 488 Hamburg policemen agreed to kill Jews; the puzzle is why twelve refused.

Looking more broadly at Canetti's account of the command and its sting, we can see that his description closely corresponds to Nietzsche's account of primitive social relations in *Zur Genealogie der Moral*. Nietzsche's treatise is divided into three parts, of which the second should really be taken first because it considers the transition from animal to humanity. Nietzsche asks how animals, which live from moment to moment, turned into human beings, who can remember the past, plan the future, make and keep promises, and, in historical times, cultivate a conscience. All these capacities, Nietzsche argues, must have been instilled in primeval man by the practice of cruelty. We can infer this prehistory from ancient accounts of debt and credit. Ancient codes of law such as the Roman Twelve Tables gave the creditor the right to punish a defaulting debtor by cutting bits off his body (another example would be Shakespeare's *The Merchant of Venice*). Thus the relation between creditor and debtor was originally a relation between bodies — an active and a passive body — and governed by cruelty. In Nietzsche's account, this was the fundamental social relation. The relation between the individual and the community was conceived analogously. Whoever damaged the community was expelled and made into an outlaw whom anyone could kill. Thus in Nietzsche's narrative, the relation between creditor and debtor corresponds to the relation Canetti assumes between the person who commands and the person who obeys. Both are inscribed in the body and supported by the threat of death. Both are antagonistic and unequal relationships. Here as elsewhere, Canetti depicts power as a zero-sum game: my gain is your loss. These unequal pairs form the cells of which society is composed. Canetti illustrates the larger societies from the examples of an army, governed by commands, and the Muslim practice whereby huge crowds of pilgrims stand on the plain of Arafat outside Mecca, enduring extreme discomfort while awaiting the commands of Allah.

We have now traversed the most forbidding part of Canetti's moral world. Its landscape is bleak, rugged, and alarming, but also vivid and colorful. Canetti is sharply aware of how power resides in the body, in its organs and gestures, and of the symbolism based on the body. The basic relation between bodies is that between predator and prey. Social life is at best a suspension of hostilities. Canetti supports his view by detailed reference to ethnography, ethology, and history. His enormous reading frees him from a conventional European perspective. He keeps close to his primary sources, paraphrasing and quoting them, often at more length than is necessary to his argument. The despotism of Muhammad Tughlak as reported by Ibn Batuta, the Mongol troops as described by William of Rubruck, are made vividly present to us. This technique also attacks the chronological arrogance or present-mindedness that often makes us think that only the recent past is relevant and that earlier ages belong to a backward or primitive past that we can ignore. *Masse und Macht* undoes myths of progress. By disclosing the operation of power in many different cultures, it produces a kind of simultaneity. Canetti professes to be showing us the stubborn substance of human nature.

Is there any relief from the remorseless operation of power? This is where the other half of Canetti's title, "crowds," *Masse*, becomes important. For in the crowd Canetti sees a counterweight to the exercise of power and hence a curious kind of hope. His other source of hope is in transformation (*Verwandlung*), an elusive but crucial concept that emerges late in his treatise. For the moment, however, let us look at crowds.

Theorists of society in the century preceding Canetti's work paid close attention to crowds.[25] They had noticed the role played by crowds in modern revolutions, especially in such events as the storming of the Bastille or the invasion of the Tuileries in the French Revolution. Their best-known representative, Gustave Le Bon, argued that the crowd embodied a regression from rationality to a pre-civilized, collective mind. Le Bon maintains that the crowd mind resembles that of a hypnotized subject; that crowds are violent, fickle, incapable of reason, prone to collective hallucinations. In short, they display the qualities that are almost always observed in beings belonging to inferior forms of evolution, such as women, savages, and children. The prominence of crowds in modernity indicates the degeneration of society.[26] Freud used Le Bon's work in his essay *Massenpsychologie und Ich-Analyse* (1921, *Group Psychology and the Analysis of the Ego*, 1959). Freud transfers his emphasis from the psychology of the crowd to the psychology of leadership. He argues that each member of the crowd is attached to the leader by libidinal bonds, regarding him as an unattainable object of love. The leader exercises a kind of hypnotic influence over the crowd, and this collective hypnosis enables members of the crowd to identify with one another. The crowd therefore represents a regression to the emotional structure of the supposed primal horde, in which a band of brothers were united by their ambivalent attachment to their father. In developing the topic in this way, Freud was implicitly acknowledging that Le Bon's treatise can be read not only as a study of the crowd but as a manual of crowd manipulation. This was why Mussolini and Goebbels avidly read Le Bon's work, and why Hitler absorbed it, albeit at second hand.[27]

Canetti places himself in a different tradition of crowd psychology.[28] It includes Nietzsche, who repeatedly affirms that modern man is a herd animal and that the conventional morality of modern Europeans is simply an expression of the herd instinct. Nietzsche was drawing on the argument by Francis Galton, based on knowledge of cattle and their owners in East Africa, that "the slavish aptitudes in man are a direct consequence of his gregarious nature," which in modern society encouraged conformism too much at the expense of self-reliance.[29] In *Zur Genealogie der Moral* Nietzsche develops this image of the herd animal in his cynical account, parodying the Christian imagery of how the priest tends his obedient flock. The herd exemplifies the "slave morality," which decries individuality and praises humility, and which, in Nietzsche's view, has come to dominate modern democratic Europe. Its antithesis is the "master morality" of proud, exuberant aristocrats, rejoicing in their strength, chivalrous to one another but casually murderous toward their inferiors. These aristocrats band together in small groups for hunting or raiding parties. Their archetype is the "blonde beast," the lion seeking its prey, or the eagle descending on lambs. Thus, alongside the herd, Nietzsche also introduces its antithesis, the pack, and explicitly identifies both with analogues in the animal kingdom.

These analogues are taken further in a book inspired by Nietzsche that Canetti lists in the bibliography to *Masse und Macht:* Wilfred Trotter's *Instincts of the Herd in Peace and War* (1919).[30] Trotter was the brother-in-law and close friend of Ernest Jones; from 1905 to 1908, Jones and Trotter were partners in a medical practice on Harley Street, and it was from Trotter that Jones first heard of Freud. However, Trotter's intellectual allegiance was to Nietzsche, under whose influence he became, according to Jones, "the most extreme, and even blood-thirsty, revolutionary in thought and phantasy that one could imagine, though there was never any likelihood of this being expressed openly."[31] Trotter agrees with Nietzsche in denouncing conventional morality as an expression of the herd instinct. Individuals sensitive enough to resist it are condemned to isolation and mental instability. It is, however, dangerously anachronistic for this simple mental type to be in charge of complex modern society, and Trotter thinks it necessary for man to progress toward a gregarious unit informed by conscious direction, in which man's social instincts can be developed toward altruism and social cohesion.[32] He leaves the reader in no doubt that he is applying biological principles to human society, and criticizes Freud for accepting the human point of view instead of founding psychology on biology.[33] In the part of the book written during the First World War, Trotter equates English society with the socialized gregariousness of the beehive and German society with the aggressive gregariousness of the wolf pack. "When I compare German society with the wolf pack, and the feelings, desires, and impulses of the individual German with those of the wolf or dog," he tells us, "I am not intending to use a vague analogy, but to call attention to a real and gross identity."[34]

Like Nietzsche and Trotter, Canetti sees the crowd in an evolutionary perspective. The crowd originated from the pack, a small group of about a dozen animals or men, joined for a common purpose. The purpose was often hunting, in accordance with man's predatory nature. But the pack could also join together for warfare, for lamentation, and for ceremonies intended to promote the increase of game, crops, or the human population. Canetti follows Freud in scrutinizing the reports of totemism among Australian aborigines, but he interprets them differently. Freud thought the totem animal symbolized the father killed and eaten by the primal band of brothers. Canetti knows that totems are not always edible animals: they may be insects, such as lice or mosquitoes, or natural objects, such as clouds, rain, grass, wind, or the sea. All these, in his view, are natural symbols of increase, and in making them into totems, the aborigines are expressing a desire to have equally numerous descendants. In the pack, Canetti sees a basic social formation. Instead of the Nietzschean dyad of creditor and debtor, or Canetti's dyad of commander and subordinate, we have here a formation in which all are equal. Even if different members of the pack have different functions, each one is indispensable, and they operate jointly, not under the direction of a leader.

The crowd is a larger and looser formation, but it shares with the pack a focus outside itself and a pleasurable feeling of density. Only in the crowd can modern man overcome the Hobbesian individualism and isolation to which he is otherwise condemned. At the outset of his book, Canetti draws attention to a widely shared feeling, the fear of being touched, which compels us to maintain our personal space and only allow our intimates to penetrate it. In the crowd, we gladly surrender our personal space and merge into the mass. Crowds may come into being for many different purposes: to watch a spectacle, to attack or destroy, or to flee from a danger in collective panic. But whatever the purpose, every member of the crowd is equal. Here Canetti differs sharply from Le Bon and Freud, who thought that the crowd had to be kept in being by a leader. He writes:

Innerhalb der Masse herrscht Gleichheit. Sie ist absolut und indiskutabel und wird von der Masse selbst nie in Frage gestellt. Sie ist von so fundamentaler Wichtigkeit, daß man den Zustand der Masse geradezu als einen Zustand absoluter Gleichheit definieren könnte. Ein Kopf ist ein Kopf, ein Arm ist ein Arm, auf Unterschiede zwischen ihnen kommt es ihnen nicht an. Um dieser Gleichheit willen wird man zur Masse. Was immer davon ablenken könnte, wird übersehen. Alle Forderungen nach Gerechtigkeit, alle Gleichheitstheorien beziehen ihre Energie letzten Endes aus diesem Gleichheitserlebnis, das jeder auf seine Weise von der Masse her kennt. (*MM*, 28)

In contrast to the conservative tradition of crowd psychology, Canetti sees in the crowd a constant potential for renewal. The crowd can free the individual both from his gloomy isolation and from the zero-sum relations of power and subordination that otherwise form the structure of social life. Against the concentration of power that reaches its extreme in the paranoid dictator, there is always hope of a revolutionary eruption of equality in the crowd. The crowd is of course ambivalent. It can bring renewal, and it can also bring destruction. From the perspective of power, the two are the same thing. And for this reason many institutions try to tame the crowd: this has been the goal of all the great religions of the world. Canetti falls into Nietzschean satire in describing how the religions seek to dam the energies of the crowd and turn it into "eine folgsame *Herde*" (*MM*, 23) in which the faithful are regarded as sheep and praised for their submissiveness. Some of his most memorable and persuasive passages, however, are phenomenological accounts of religious ceremonies: the mourning for Hussein at Karbala, which is central to Shi'a Islam, the "standing on Arafat" undertaken by pilgrims to Mecca, the descent of the Holy Fire in the Greek Chapel of the Sepulchre at Jerusalem, and the ritual of the Roman Catholic mass.

In finding a potential for renewal in the crowd, Canetti unwittingly agrees with a group of left-wing historians working at the same time. They sought to defend the historical crowd against standard conservative charges that it was merely a lawless mob or, as an eighteenth-century English clergyman called it, a "lawless and furious rabble."[35] Their defense emphasizes two aspects of the crowd that Canetti ignores. First, the crowd consists of people who already have beliefs and values and who may have combined in order to assert their belief in, for example, fair food prices against extortion by traders.[36] Thus we hear of an orderly crowd in Ireland that seized corn from businessmen who were hoarding it for export and sold the corn in the market at what was considered a fair price.[37] Second, the crowd is not always an undifferentiated mass, but often has leaders who not only whip up its fury but direct it toward ends that can be constructive as well as destructive, such as the redistribution of food or the assault on the Bastille.[38] These features of the crowd are screened out by Canetti's timeless, anthropological approach. Unlike historians who attempt complex portrayals of actual crowds, Canetti retains (but revaluates) an earlier conception of the crowd as a shapeless mass.[39]

Canetti's other source of hope is the concept of transformation. The chapter dealing with this concept is opaque in its argument. By contrasting its beginning with its end, however, we can see the core of Canetti's social theory. Transformation is illustrated by the South African bushman. A bushman can sense the approach of another person, or of an animal such as a springbok or ostrich, by a presentiment that is not an intellectual experience but is registered in his body. Thus if a woman leaves the hut, carrying her child by a leather thong over her shoulder, her return is anticipated by her husband who feels the sensation of her thong pressing against his own shoulder. Or the bushmen may sense the distant presence of springbok by feeling in their own feet a sensation that they identify as the feet of the springbok rustling in the bushes. In these transformations, the bushman becomes the other being, and feels the other's sensations in his own body. But he does not become the other so entirely as to surrender his own identity. He remains himself, and the transformations he experiences are "saubere Verwandlungen" (*MM*, 390).

Thus transformation is the antithesis of the confinement in one's personal space with which Canetti began his book, and it offers an alternative to absorption into a crowd. Canetti discovers traces of transformation in many myths and ceremonies: in legends where beings like Proteus metamorphose themselves in order to escape their captors; and in the belief that shamans transform themselves into other beings in order to enlist their aid. But just as the great religions seek to domesticate the crowd, so political institutions seek to control, limit, or even prohibit transformation. They may do so by setting up figures or masks as symbols of power. Figures, like the animal figures that represented the Egyptian gods, represent the endpoint of transformation, while the mask, by its rigidity, represents the antithesis to the natural mobility of the face. The despot wears a mask, either literally or by assuming an inscrutable expression, while the subjects of despotism are obliged to look impassive. (One is reminded of Czeslaw Milosz's account of *ketman*, his name for the habitual dissimulation practiced by subjects of the Soviet Union and its satellites.[40] Milosz took the term from Count Arthur de Gobineau's account of Persian religion,[41] a book that Canetti also used, especially for its account of the mourning ceremonies of Shi'a Islam.) The despot retains the power of undoing his subjects' transformation by unmasking and thus destroying them. Despotism itself is founded, according to Canetti, on a perverted transformation, namely slavery, that turns human beings into animals:

Sobald es Menschen gelungen war, so viel Sklaven beisammen zu haben wie Tiere in Herden, war der Grund zum Staat und zur Macht-haberei gelegt; und es kann gar keinem Zweifel unterliegen, daß der Wunsch, das ganze Volk zu Sklaven oder Tieren zu haben, im Herrscher um so stärker wird, je mehr Leute das Volk ausmachen. (*MM*, 442)

This description does not apply only to tyrannies like that of the Soviet Union. For, in Canetti's view, we transform a person into a slave as soon as we limit him to a single kind of work and oblige him to do as much as possible in the least possible time: in other words, when we oblige him to be "productive." Canetti's polemical allusion here is to the division of labor in modern industrial society, which, as Marx charged, reduces workers from whole human beings to mere "hands," valued only for their productivity. The political thrust of *Masse und Macht* is directed against capitalism as well as communism, liberalism as well as fascism.

Masse und Macht thus contains two not quite parallel narratives. Both form part of Canetti's theory of human nature in that they concern the ultimately biological drives, based in man's animal nature, in which Canetti finds the motive forces of social development. The larger narrative concerns the development of social life from the unequal dyad of command and obedience to the despotism illustrated not only by Muhammad Tughlak and his twentieth-century analogues, but by the reduction of industrial workers to a condition that Canetti equates with slavery. The essential solitude of the individual reaches its extreme in the paranoid dictator. An uncertain hope lies in the periodical outbursts of the crowd, which, though anarchic and often destructive, liberates its members from solitude into coherence in a single mass, and from subjection to power into a state of equality.

The smaller narrative begins with the hunter-gatherers of the Kalahari and their capacity for transformation, a physical empathy with another being that does not threaten one's own integrity. People with this capacity are not confined to the prison of the self and are not obliged to escape from it into the crowd. Transformation implies a mobility and fluidity that are anathema to power. The despot, concealed behind his rigid mask, wishes all his subjects to share the same rigidity.

This narrative seems to lack even the doubtful hope that lay in the conflict of crowds with power. Canetti does not say how transformation can escape from control. But one can imagine an answer. In modern culture we have many opportunities for empathy in reading literature about other people and other cultures. The imaginative response of the reader in recreating the novelist's characters may be seen as an attenuated version of transformation. Canetti relies on our capacity for empathy when presenting us with anecdotes from many different cultures. To read *Masse und Macht* is to practice an empathy across cultural boundaries. And since Canetti insists so much on bodily experiences of the crowd and of power, to read his book sympathetically is to gain an increased awareness of one's body, and to be brought back to the bedrock of human nature and evolutionary continuity with other natural beings, that are among the presuppositions of Canetti's Darwinian naturalism.

Notes

[1] Elias Canetti, *Masse und Macht* (Hamburg: Claassen, 1960). Cited as *MM* and page number.

[2] Friedrich Nietzsche, *Jenseits von Gut und Böse*, in *Werke*, 3 vols., ed. Karl Schlechta (Munich: Hanser, 1966), vol. 2, 696.

[3] Matthew Bell, *Goethe's Naturalistic Anthropology: Man and Other Plants* (Oxford: Clarendon Press, 1994), 1–67.

[4] See Charles Darwin, *The Origin of Species by Means of Natural Selection, or the Preservation of Favoured Races in the Struggle for Life,* ed. J. W. Burrow (London: Penguin, 1968); *The Descent of Man, and Selection in Relation to Sex* (Princeton: Princeton UP, 1981).

[5] Friedrich Nietzsche, *Der Antichrist,* in *Werke,* vol. 2, 1174.

[6] Friedrich Nietzsche, *Zur Genealogie der Moral,* in *Werke,* vol. 2, 761–900.

[7] See Sigmund Freud, *Totem und Tabu,* in *Studienausgabe,* ed. Alexander Mitscherlich et al., 10 vols. (Frankfurt a.M.: Fischer, 1970), vol. 10, 287–444; Lucille B. Ritvo, *Darwin's Influence on Freud* (New Haven and London: Yale UP, 1990); and Jean Gayon, "Nietzsche and Darwin," in *Biology and the Foundation of Ethics,* ed. Jane Maienschein and Michael Ruse (Cambridge: Cambridge UP, 1999), 154–97.

[8] Elias Canetti, *Die Fackel im Ohr: Lebensgeschichte 1921–1931* (Munich: Hanser, 1980), 137–38. See Heide Helwig, "Canetti und Nietzsche," in *"Ein Dichter braucht Ahnen": Elias Canetti und die europäische Tradition,* ed. Gerald Stieg and Jean-Marie Valentin (Bern, Berlin, Frankfurt a.M.: Lang, 1997), 145–62. Here: 145.

[9] Daniel C. Dennett, *Darwin's Dangerous Idea: Evolution and the Meanings of Life* (London: Penguin, 1995), 478.

[10] Matt Ridley, *The Origins of Virtue* (London: Penguin, 1997).

[11] Friedrich Nietzsche, *Der Wille zur Macht: Versuch einer Umwertung aller Werte* (Stuttgart: Kröner, 1930). This edition is not based on the original edition of 1901 but rather on the enlarged edition of 1906. On its composition, see Ernst Behler, "Nietzsche in the Twentieth Century," in *The Cambridge Companion to Nietzsche,* ed. Bernd Magnus and Kathleen M. Higgins (Cambridge: Cambridge UP, 1996), especially 287–89.

[12] Wolfgang Müller-Lauter, "Der Organismus als innerer Kampf. Der Einfluß von Wilhelm Roux auf Friedrich Nietzsche," *Nietzsche-Studien* 7 (1978): 189–223.

[13] Müller-Lauter, 189–223.

[14] Thomas Hobbes, *Leviathan, or the Matter, Forme and Power of a Commonwealth Ecclesiasticall and Civill,* ed. Michael Oakeshott (Oxford: Blackwell, 1957), 81.

[15] See Keith Ansell-Pearson, "The Significance of Michel Foucault's Reading of Nietzsche: Power, the Subject, and Political Theory," in *Nietzsche: A Critical Reader,* ed. Peter R. Sedgwick (Oxford: Blackwell, 1995), 13–30; and Thomas Gutmann, "Nietzsches 'Wille zur Macht' im Werk Michel Foucaults," *Nietzsche-Studien* 27 (1998): 377–419.

[16] Axel Honneth, "Die unendliche Perpetuierung des Naturzustandes. Zum theoretischen Erkenntnisgehalt von Canettis *Masse und Macht,*" in *Einladung zur Verwandlung: Essays zu Elias Canettis "Masse und Macht,"* ed. Michael Krüger (Munich: Hanser, 1995), 105–27.

[17] Hobbes, 36.

[18] W. Arens, *The Man-Eating Myth* (New York: Oxford UP, 1979).

[19] Daniel Paul Schreber, *Denkwürdigkeiten eines Nervenkranken* (Leipzig: Oswald Mutze, 1903); trans. Ida MacAlpine and Richard A. Hunter as *Memoirs of my Nervous Illness* (London: Dawson, 1955).

[20] See Ridley, *The Origins of Virtue* (London: Penguin, 1997).

[21] Philip Larkin, *High Windows* (London: Faber, 1974), 30.

[22] Christopher R. Browning, *Ordinary Men: Reserve Police Battalion 101 and the Final Solution in Poland* (New York: Harper Collins, 1992).

[23] Daniel Jonah Goldhagen, *Hitler's Willing Executioners: Ordinary Germans and the Holocaust* (New York: Knopf, 1996).

[24] Steven E. Aschheim, *In Times of Crisis: Essays on European Culture, Germans, and Jews* (Madison, WI: U of Wisconsin P, 2001).

[25] John S. McClelland, *The Crowd and the Mob: From Plato to Canetti* (London: Unwin Hyman, 1989).

[26] Gustave Le Bon, *The Crowd* (London: T. Fisher Unwin, 1896), 17.

[27] Denis Mack Smith, *Mussolini* (London: Weidenfeld & Nicolson, 1981), 127; Ralf Georg Reuth, *The Life of Joseph Goebbels,* trans. Krishna Winston (London: Constable, 1993), 81; and Ian Kershaw, *Hitler 1889–1936: Hubris* (London: Allen Lane, 1998), 156.

[28] Ritchie Robertson, "Between Freud and Nietzsche: Canetti's *Crowds and Power,*" *Austrian Studies* 3 (1992): 109–24.

[29] Francis Galton, *Inquiries into Human Faculty and its Development* (London: Dent, 1907), 47. First published 1883.

[30] Wilfred Trotter, *Instincts of the Herd in Peace and War* (London: Oxford UP, 1953).

[31] Ernest Jones, *Free Associations: Memories of a Psycho-Analyst* (London: Hogarth Press, 1959), 101.

[32] Trotter, 129.

[33] Trotter, 57.

[34] Trotter, 154.

[35] Edward P. Thompson, *The Making of the English Working Class* (London: Gollancz, 1963), 62.

[36] Edward P. Thompson, "The Moral Economy of the English Crowd in the Eighteenth Century," *Past and Present* 50 (1970), 76–136.

[37] Thompson, *The Making of the English Working Class,* 64.

[38] George Rudé, *The Crowd in the French Revolution* (Oxford: Clarendon Press, 1959).

[39] Mark Harrison, *Crowds and History: Mass Phenomena in English Towns, 1790–1835* (Cambridge: Cambridge UP, 1988), 36.

[40] Czeslaw Milosz, *The Captive Mind* (London: Secker & Warburg, 1953).

[41] Arthur de Gobineau, *Les Religions et les philosophies dans l'Asie Centrale,* in *Oeuvres,* ed. Jean Gaulmier, 3 vols. (Paris: Gallimard, 1983), 415. First published 1865.

Images of Male and Female in Canetti's Fictional, Autobiographical, and Theoretical Work

Johannes G. Pankau

D EALING WITH IMAGES OF MALE AND FEMALE, and gender relationships in general in Canetti's works is a tricky task. Differing from many of the prominent representatives of Viennese modernism, Canetti avoids theories that claim to reveal the secrets of gender identity and sexuality. In one of the volumes of his autobiography, *Das Augenspiel,* he describes the predominance of psychoanalytic discourses in the intellectual circles of postwar Vienna:

> Im allgemeinen war es [. . .] so, daß zu jener Zeit in Gesprächen nichts gesagt werden konnte, ohne daß es durch die Motive, die dafür sofort bei der Hand waren, entkräftet wurde. Daß für alles dieselben Motive gefunden wurde, die unsägliche Langeweile, die sich von ihnen ver- breitete, die Sterilität, die daraus resultierte, schien wenige zu stören.[1]

The "motives" Canetti mentions are sexual ones, and the patterns of expla- nation are derived from Freud's libido theory; Canetti criticizes the psycho- analytic "obsession" that took hold of writers such as Hermann Broch. He objects to all theories and literary works that regard the sexual forces as gods or quasi natural laws. In particular, he objects to the Freudian approach based on libido and *thanatos.*[2]

Canetti carefully observed the profound social, cultural, and political changes and contradictions after the fall of the Danube monarchy, and he looked for new ways to comprehend them: "Was immer geschah — es geschah ungeheuer viel und es stürzte rapid noch viel mehr zu —, es war durch keine gängige Theorie zu begreifen" (*A,* 267). Statements like this imply the negation of all "master theories" and at the same time show the birth of a new one.

Early on Canetti used different modes of writing and investigation: while working on the fictional representations in the novel *Die Blendung* and in his dramas he began his study of crowds and power, which eventually led to the publication of *Masse und Macht.*[3] He developed his own forms of expression in constant communication with other writers and intellectuals, as his autobiographies clearly demonstrate, but at the same time he insisted on the complete independence of his own writing and thinking. This self-imposed isolation has motivated most interpreters of Canetti's writings to focus on the inherent structures of his work, the connections between the different genres the author used and the intentions he pursued. Though Canetti's relationship to earlier theories of the crowd — Le Bon and especially Freud — and his position within literary modernism have been investigated numerous times, there is still a tendency to view his work as a more or less closed entity.[4]

Any study dealing with Canetti must also take into account the critical assumptions at work at key points of the analysis: Canetti appears both in his self-definition and in the eyes of many of his interpreters as an enemy of power. Yet there are critics who identify "ein keinesfalls ungebrochenes Verhältnis zu Macht und Besitzergreifung"[5] on the part of the author, especially in regard to his relationship to women. In order to understand Canetti, it is necessary to thoroughly examine the structures of his work on the one hand and the interdependencies of the other forms of discourse present in his writings on the other, even in those cases where the author denies the existence of such linkages altogether.

Canetti's approach to his central themes — crowds and power, death and change (*Verwandlung*) — is phenomenological and in a certain sense hermetic, consciously separated from the philosophical, sociological, and psychological systems developed since approximately 1900.[6] Canetti's distrust of scientific terminology and "system-thinking" can easily be extrapolated from all of his writings and has often been emphasized by researchers. Rather than theoretical terms he seeks concrete, "bodily" forms of description that favor primary, direct experience.[7] Thus Canetti's concept of crowds and power is the result not of a strict scientific methodology but of a, as Peter Friedrich calls it, "literarische Gegenwissenschaft" (literary anti-science).[8] In scientific terms it can be regarded as an empiric rather than a philosophical anthropology.[9] At the same time, Canetti is strictly opposed to any form of historicism. The modern type of individual appears to be only another shape or mask (*Maske*) of archaic patterns, hence the notion of evolution seems to be rejected. Canetti's thinking, though not completely separate from modernist discourse, nevertheless traces back to ahistoric concepts of social development.[10] This connection should not be overstated: after all, the establishment of ahistoric entities (*Wesenheiten*) has been a trait of mainstream thinking since the last part of the nineteenth century, for instance in the attempts to construct the "Wesen" of the sexes from mythical origins. These premises have grave consequences for Canetti's view of sexuality, gender relations, and his images of the body. The author develops a kind of "Triebkonzept" not primarily related to sexuality or gender specific qualities but based on tendencies and desires relating to crowd formation. Canetti explains this emergence as a sudden "enlightenment" (*Erleuchtung*) during his time in Vienna, when he discovered a "Massentrieb" that stood in contradiction to another force, the "Persönlichkeitstrieb" — an assumption that could be used to explain human history in general.[11]

The result of this approach is a distinct anti-individualism. The individual does not represent specific qualities determined by race, gender, and so on, but rather functions as a mere carrier of power relations. Contrary to Viennese psychological realism or psychoanalytic concepts, the inner development of the individual in relation to his/her environment does not shape reality. Instead, actual behavior is the result of super-individual laws. This has consequences for Canetti's genre-specific modes of writing: in his fictional works he is not interested in psychological insights. As a storyteller he presents his characters without individualized profiles. In this sense it is true that personality remains "empty" in Canetti's writings.[12] As a theorist, he favors the analysis of outward appearances, the surface (*Oberfläche*) of things and persons, and the respective mass and power relations. Canetti's concept — however complex the character or the analysis — is finally one-dimensional. His anthropology is ultimately based on order and obedience, the desire to rule over others, to attain power and to survive.[13]

This does not mean that questions of gender and body politics are not present in Canetti's writings. It can be said that bodies and their reactions and interactions are the central elements of his mass theory. Canetti finds a peculiar tension of pure physicality at the core of all human relations and at the same time a distancing from bodily expressions caused by fear. Physical closeness, though longed for as a means of delimitation by the masses, is never a source of pleasure or fulfillment, but a dynamic element in the formation process of crowds. In *Die Blendung,* Kien, who with all his might tries to keep his distance, perishes in the crowds. Therese, the metropolis, and the fire must be read as symbols of the masses. In this sense one can consider Canetti's procedure an archeology of the body, with the body seen not as a carrier of symbolic meaning but of dynamic action.[14] Body movements are not primarily expressions of emotional states but rather the results of biologically founded patterns or instincts. The fear of physical contact (*Berührungsfurcht*) as the basis of crowd formation is not explained by means of intrapsychic events — in fact it is not explained at all, but functions as a premise for Canetti's theory. The title of the first chapter of *Masse und Macht,* "Umschlagen der Berührungsfurcht," is indicative of this approach: Canetti is not preoccupied with the reasons for this fear, but with its effects. The first paragraph is characteristic of the whole procedure:

> Nichts fürchtet der Mensch mehr als die Berührung durch Unbekanntes. Man will sehen, was nach einem greift, man will es erkennen oder zumindest einreihen können. Überall weicht der Mensch der Berührung durch Fremdes aus. Nachts oder im Dunkel überhaupt kann der Schrecken über eine unerwartete Berührung sich ins Panische steigern. (*MM,* 11)

"Fear" is from an anthropological point of view a non-specific term that can be applied to animals as well. The term gains its specific validity only in connection with another phenomenon that appears soon thereafter and forms the core of the whole book: the possibility of overcoming this fear in the crowds, which Canetti calls "redemption," "Erlösung" (*MM*, 12). This view is radically anti-metaphysical: the body does not mirror intrapsychic mechanisms and drives (the "soul"), but in a very direct sense functions as an agent initiating processes of crowd formation. Furthermore, redemption is not connected with a positive utopian perspective — spiritual or secular — but is instead the product of fear. Any idea of progress as a result of positive human association, or enlightenment as a program, is rejected. As Peter Sloterdijk puts it in a recent publication:

> Canettis Intuition hebt böse und deutlich den Umstand hervor, daß schon in der ersten Konstitution des Massensubjekts die opaken Motive überwiegen. Denn in der Masse versammeln sich die erregten Einzelnen nicht zu dem, was die Diskursmythologie ein Publikum nennt — vielmehr verdichten sie sich zu einem Fleck, sie bilden Menschen-Kleckse, sie strömen zu dem Ort, wo es am schwärzesten ist von ihnen selbst.[15]

Canetti and the Misogynist Discourse

Canetti is a moralist, and in his view the writer has a responsibility of preserving human qualities in a modern world characterized by exterior achievements and specialization. In a reality he sees as the "verblendetste aller Welten," he is the "Hüter der Verwandlungen."[16] This translates into the rejection of all forms of repressive power — resisting the "Machthaber" in all his manifestations. Power relationships appear universal, but most rulers in Canetti's writings are male. Hitler, as the prototype of the ruler, is afflicted by the paranoid mania to outdo all others, to continue growing without boundaries, that is, to go on living forever and thus overcome death.[17] Nevertheless an important question has been posed recently in particular by female researchers: does the enemy of power himself have an inclination to that which he condemns? What does it mean when an expert like Dagmar Barnouw thinks that Canetti had to fight a "harten Kampf um Subliminierung der eigenen Machtgelüste"?[18] Does she attribute this struggle to the author or to the person, or perhaps even both? As is often the case with Canetti, different levels of possible interpretation tend to be mingled. If one moves away from Canetti's postulates to his actual behavior and attitudes based on critical accounts, one easily arrives at forms of biographical explanation, which are problematic for textual analysis. Barnouw correctly identifies a hate for certain female figures in Canetti's work that grows into contempt. As evidence she names one fictional character, Therese in *Die*

Blendung; one personal acquaintance who appears in his autobiography, Alma Mahler-Werfel; and one from literary history, Felice Bauer, as depicted in his essay on her relationship to Kafka.[19] All three evoke the author's contempt (*Verachtung*) to a certain extent because he thinks they tried to exploit their male partners' creativity and power and succeeded in surviving them.[20] If the "misogynist" explanation seems plausible at first glance, it is only because no attempt has been made to differentiate between the different types of the characterization of women in Canetti's writings. One cannot deny that Canetti's picture of Alma Mahler-Werfel is primarily negative: "Dieser war es um Macht zu tun, in jeder Form, um Ruhm besonders, um Geld und um die Macht, die Lust verleiht" (*A, 172*). Yet to trace remarks like that back to the presumption that she rejected Canetti as a lover is not only banal but also analytically problematic because it denies the aesthetic character of the autobiography as a narrative.[21] There are of course numerous questions that might be pursued in an effort to link any writer's — and in specific Canetti's — personal gender experience to his or her textual production. Is it adequate to leave out certain biographical contradictions regarding a writer who always insisted not only on aesthetic values, but also on the personal integrity of a poet, a *Dichter*? And, specifically, does the realization, as Barnouw puts it, of the "Symbiose von Mimesis und Analyse, Ausübung und Denunzierung der Macht" lead to a new evaluation of Canetti as a male writer?[22] Rather than trying to solve the problems implied by the critique of Canetti as a writer and as a person, I shall try to show certain aspects of the male and the female as they are presented in some of his works and to explore connections to other lines of discourse. Canetti hates, but he also loves and adores. In his autobiographies he depicts both, also with respect to the important women in his life. Both the complicated relationship with his mother and the marriage to Veza Taubner-Calderon (which appears to have been harmonious) seem to be characterized by a deep, mutual love. A different image of Canetti, focusing on his time in London, is offered by John Bayley in his book *Iris: A Memoir of Iris Murdoch*. Bayley refers to Canetti as a "sage" or as the "Dichter" or — as he ironically puts it — as the "monster of Hampstead." It is as the latter that Canetti is presented as a kind of guru or magician who bewitches the intellectual women around him. His victims include Bayley's later wife, Iris Murdoch, who was deeply impressed by the writer in exile, that is, she fell "under his sway."[23] However, Bayley's report about Canetti sleeping with Iris, "possessing her as if he were a god,"[24] while Veza was in the same flat may contribute to scandalizing the author. Some of the book's German reviewers indeed concentrated on the contradiction between the self-acclaimed moralist and the exploiting individual. Nevertheless, Bayley himself — who had earlier published a serious essay on *Die Blendung* and *Masse und Macht* — is careful to avoid mixing up real life, literary characters, and literary work. Feminist critics have hinted at the way Canetti denied Veza's existence as a writer in her own right numerous times.[25] The thesis of a hidden misogynist tendency in Canetti's writings is not only based on such biographical references, but is also part of more serious literary criticism. Susan Sontag claims that Canetti's early novel *Die Blendung* was inspired by an extraordinary hatred for women.[26]

This calls to mind Weininger's infamous *Geschlecht und Charakter,* Karl Kraus, maybe Freud, and possibly many other intellectual and literary men around 1900, who were involved in the "Frauenwissenschaft" — Women's Studies — of the time. Canetti quotes Veza in *Die Fackel im Ohr* as calling him an "eingefleischter Frauenfeind" (*FO,* 205) during their literary conversations.[27] It is difficult to say how seriously this was meant, but it is clear that in her article, Sontag is not just speaking of the fictional framework of *Die Blendung,* but also of its creator; Kien's misogynist attitude seems to be identified with the position of the author.[28]

Sontag is writing about Canetti the man, but — and this is important — through references she takes from the fictional text. Hannelore Scholz, another voice in this chorus, thinks Canetti's image of women was indeed deeply shaped by Otto Weininger's influential misogynist book, the traces of which can be found in the writings of a whole generation of Austrian authors. Canetti, Scholz maintains, "teilte wohl auch [. . .] Weiningers Ansicht, daß die Verweiblichung der Gesellschaft, die überall zu entdecken sei, die männlichen Werte unterhöhle."[29] Again convincing proof is lacking, showing the necessity of further research to investigate the intertextual references and traditions that were of significance for Canetti's theoretical and literary approach. The opinions summarized here tend to generalize partial aspects of Canetti's work without integrating them into the general concept of his writing. The antinomy of spirit and body, incorporated in the opposition of femininity and masculinity, idealism and sensualism, for example, that is so obvious in *Die Blendung* seems rooted in the predominant tradition of male *Frauenwissenschaft,* which reaches from psychiatric theory in the late nineteenth century (Krafft-Ebing, Mantegazza) to Freud's at least partially biased view of women, from the idolization of women to their marginalization in literature. On the other hand one cannot stop here but must keep in mind the important developments of the time, especially after the First World War, such as the social and economic crises. Crises including the rise of political extremism and mass movements, and the inflation are the ruptures that form the basis of Canetti's writing. The short account of some opinions expressed in late twentieth-century Canetti research is useful to this discussion because I think that generalizing Canetti's views on women — and men — is principally questionable and unproductive. However coherent and consistent Canetti's writing, including his autobiography, may seem, and the author has contributed greatly to this impression, we find many partly contradictory elements in his writings. Contradictions occur even though from the start his thinking is characterized by a clear, basic line that can be illustrated by terms such as mass, power, change (*Verwandlung*), the usage of recurrent literary devices such as the acoustic mask (*akustische Maske*), and a strong resistance against the predominant figures of thought of his time such as individual psychologism and sociological analysis in the Marxist sense. In the following I shall therefore develop certain elements that can be found in different writing modes, elements that appear in Canetti's work over time, but change with the phases of the author's life.

Canetti and Freud: "Doppelmasse"

Dealing with Canetti's views on women and femininity, it seems inevitable to take into account the author's mostly implicit inner dialogue with Sigmund Freud.[30] Both intellectuals were interested in exploring the development of culture, the phenomenon of masses, and the role of the sexes. The assumption that women only marginally participated in the process of building civilization unites numerous thinkers since the late nineteenth century. It is one of the central topoi, especially in Vienna modernism, as exemplified by the writings of Karl Kraus and his disciples. Comparing the sexes, Freud thought that the male subject had always functioned as the driving force in the cultural process because men had developed a stronger capability of sublimation.[31] This construction has its basis in the identification of femininity and nature, which can also be found in the works of representative male authors of the same period, Frank Wedekind, Arthur Schnitzler, and Peter Altenberg.

It is obvious that Freud and Canetti start from different premises. Suffice it to refer to one basic difference, the antithesis of unification (symbiosis) and separation. In Freud's psychoanalytic view, the original philogenetic as well as ontogenetic movement is one of coming together in which sexual energy (libido) urges toward the temporary unification of different entities, the sexes. Only the hindering effect of civilization with its necessity for the individual to control his originally amorphous sexual strivings leads — especially in the context of the Oedipus complex — to the development of individual and collective differences, the construction of moral instances (*Über-Ich*) and a firm sexual identity. Contrary to this genetic approach, Canetti's primal scene (*Urszene*) is completely different. It is one of separation, of distance from one body to the next. In Canetti's opinion the phenomenon of mass formation gains a significance that can be compared to Freudian urges (*Triebe*). In *Die Fackel im Ohr* he refers directly to these theoretical assumptions: "Es [das Phänomen der Masse, J. G. P.] schien mir nicht weniger elementar als Libido und Hunger. [. . .] Es ging [. . .] darum, es voll ins Auge zu fassen, als etwas, das immer bestanden hatte, aber jetzt mehr als je bestand [. . .]" (*FO*, 143).

This, in Canetti's reductionist view, constitutes a universal anthropological fact. His basic assumption of a drive towards separation, the fear of entering into a symbiosis with other humans according to Freud and as implied in Norbert Elias's theory of civilization,[32] is only the result of a long process of development, which means it is of secondary nature. In terms of ontogenetic development Freud sees an analogous movement: by nature the baby strives to keep the intimate union with his mother as long as possible. Only outward influences provoke separation, and this process is marked by grave conflicts. Canetti on the other hand is not interested in such developmental processes. He insists on a universal, unchangeable nature of humanity, whose historical manifestations differ only to a certain degree. His construction shows a principally lonely individual, characterized by a so-to-speak hereditary dislike of physical closeness similar to that described by Hobbes. It is only driven by the fear of death — another central motive in Canetti — and therefore represents a kind of society structured by a brutal hierarchy, the Leviathanian state.[33]

Canetti's phenomenological approach, which claims to be without epistemological predecessors, has a central pillar in the basic opposition of male and female, but not in a psychological sense. Discussing the formation of the "Doppelmasse," the dual mass or crowd, Canetti names three basic anthropological divergences: the one between men and women, between the living and the dead, and between friends and enemies (*MM*, 67–68). For him the gender difference is a universal fact, again in sharp contrast to Freud's as well as Weininger's concepts, which both start from the assumption of a biologically determined bisexual structure in both male and female, which only through the individual and collective development is changed to a more or less distinct sexual identity. The difference in view goes back to divergent paradigms: Canetti's view is not psychological, but rather explicitly antipsychological. He is not interested in inner processes but in the visual and auditory perception of physical traits, behaviors, and forms of expression. The chapter "Die Doppelmasse" in *Masse und Macht* shows this procedure in an exemplary way (*MM*, 67–72). Dealing with the relationship of the sexes, Canetti first comments on a possible objection to his assumptions — the fact that men and women share a communal life in marriage and the family. To prove his point that this fact is only superficial, Canetti has to go back to "ursprünglichere Lebensverhältnisse" (*MM*, 68), an approach he uses in most of *Masse und Macht*. He refers to the report of a French traveler, Jean de Léry, from 1557, about a celebration of a primitive tribe in Brazil, the Tupinambus (*MM*, 69). Women and men first appear as independent mass formations that enter into a functional contact with each other, which works either in a supporting or in a hindering way, as Canetti shows with reference to the legends of the amazons. There is a dialectic between utilization by contact and separating resistance, which — as I will show — can also be observed in some of Canetti's literary works. He places the emphasis on the separation of the two masses that come into contact by means of sheer necessity, not because there is any affectionate bond between them.

This anti-individualism in particular marks the decisive separating line between Freud and Canetti. In Freud's *Massenpsychologie und Ich-Analyse,* the individual functions as the starting point for the analysis of collective processes. And more than that, individual psychology comprehends the social psychology of the crowds: "Im Seelenleben des Einzelnen kommt ganz regelmäßig der andere als Vorbild, als Objekt, als Helfer und als Gegner in Betracht, und die Individualpsychologie ist daher von Anfang an auch gleichzeitig Sozialpsychologie [. . .]."[34] Canetti's criticism of Freud — the adoption of psychological terms for the analysis of collective phenomena — is combined with another critique, Freud's therapeutic distance, which — contrary to Canetti — can only perceive masses from the outside. As "abstinenter Analytiker," he was never himself affected by their fascinating power.[35] Canetti declines this method because he does not regard it as adequate for the analysis of the collective development of his era, which he considers merely as a new shape of an archaic structure.[36] This also has consequences regarding the opposition of male and female. Unlike Freud and Adler, Canetti does not operate with the individualistic model traditionally used for the explanation of collective structures. Instead there is a transformation of collective mass structures into individualist literary figuration in the subtext of his writings. Canetti's reductionist method, which has been criticized for its unhistorical premise, is not principally anti-modernist. It can be regarded as a progressive form insofar as it attempts to overcome the biological and pure psychological approach predominant in earlier gender discourse. The construct of male and female as independent mass formations surpasses Weininger's biologism as well as Freud's psychologism. Canetti's method is located somewhere in between concrete sociological analysis and the reduction to archaic structures, the assumption of invariable entities (*Ursprungsdenken*). This procedure, however, establishes Canetti's position as an outsider in the analysis of crowds and gender images because he does not share one of the central premises of modern thinking in these fields; he denies "jedwelche Gültigkeit der widersprüchlichen und komplexen Evolution der Moderne."[37]

Die Blendung

Some of the difficulties in trying to grasp specific forms of the gender and body problem lie in the different writing personae as well as the variety of modes and genres Canetti uses — a novel, plays, literary essays, aphorisms, his theoretical opus magnum, *Masse und Macht,* and his autobiographies. Some researchers make a fundamental distinction between the fictional works and the theory of crowds formulated in *Masse und Macht.* For the topic of gender relationships this is of particular importance. Bernd Widdig for example thinks that — contrary to the novel — there are no traces of the contemporary gender discourse in *Masse und Macht*.[38]

This is true only in one sense: the clash of genders, here personified in the main characters of Kien and Therese, that structures much of the plot of *Die Blendung* is not the center of *Masse und Macht*. It is actually only one manifestation of a — in Canetti's understanding — more comprehensive area of conflict, that of crowds and power. In the essay, "Das erste Buch: Die Blendung," Canetti identifies the experience of a fire at the Viennese judicial palace, the *Justizpalast,* as the starting point of the project, which was planned as a further series titled "Comédie Humaine an Irren." This event shaped the perspective of Canetti the author: "Ich wurde zu einem Teil der Masse, ich ging vollkommen in ihr auf, ich spürte nicht den leistesten Widerstand gegen das, was sie unternahm."[39] Another element that Canetti shares with other modernist novelists of the time, such as Broch, Musil, and Döblin, is also described in the essay: the attempt to renew the novel as a genre able to mirror the present state of reality as one of disintegration. For Canetti this attempt does not result in the disintegration of the narrative structure but rather in the construction of extreme characters whose interactions show the essence of this reality (*GW,* 229). To this end Canetti uses — among other elements — gender specific stereotypes in a reversed sense to reveal the character deformation that takes place under the auspices of the universal power struggle. Kien can be seen as the "blinded" male individual in his hopeless struggle against the crowds. Indeed, the figure is equipped with nearly all the attributes that had been associated with masculinity in gender discourse since the late nineteenth century: he is antisocial, thus lonely, spiritual, rational, intellectually creative, unsensual, in short, almost the ideal M-type in Weininger's sense, but exaggerated to an illusionary, absurd extent. Of course, the corresponding extreme is found in the formal characteristics of the Therese figure: she is marked by her strong physical appearance (symbolized, for example, by the skirt), by her desires for sex and possessions, by her lack of intellectual capacity and interest, and by her vanity. As much as metaphorically possible, her radical form represents the brute force of the crowd. This mode of stereotyping has a long tradition. It reaches from Weininger and Le Bon to Hitler's *Mein Kampf,* in which the crowds are configured as female. There is, however, a significant difference between these patterns and the ones Canetti applies: neither one of the antagonistic parts in *Die Blendung* is shown as victorious or in the least superior in the sense of cultural or moral value. Instead, there is only ruthless narrative objectivity: all of the characters are prone to illusion and self-deception; all of them are egotistical to an absurd degree. There is not one allusion to suggest the possibility of understanding or compromise. Not only does Canetti work with gender clichés, he expands and extends them, approaching Strindberg's concept of an eternal war of the sexes that resembles Hobbes's idea of an unrestricted civil war of all against all without a Leviathan. In this sense *Die Blendung* cannot be exclusively read as a representation of the gender conflict (although many of its figurative elements are taken from this repertoire), but as a vast metaphor of the clash of physical entities under the laws of crowd formation. It may be justifiable to say that Canetti's treatment of masculinity and femininity has only a limited functional meaning within this greater context, that it is a variable in his "system."

Gender clichés in Canetti's novel are not to be taken literally. Nor can the character of Therese be taken at face value. Even though she seems more realistic than Kien in her desire for power and her ability to achieve her immediate aims, she too is utterly deluded. In the final analysis Kien and Therese are not antagonistic but complementary characters. In the context of the novel the misogynist cliché is reversed in two directions: the image of the sensuous woman who absorbs "vital" and creative energy from the man has been reduced to a female figure whose sensuality manifests itself only in an overwhelming, plump bodily form and an illusionary belief in her own attractiveness. The male character on the other hand is creative only in a restricted, self-centered sense of esoteric scholarship. In other words, they are nothing more than literary devices, those of the grotesque and the caricature, both of which are central structural elements of the novel and fitting forms with which to express gender reversals. In addition, the ideological construction of an irreconcilable struggle of the sexes in *Die Blendung* is extended into the political realm: in taking the protofascist blend of anti-capitalism and misogyny of the 1920s to its logical extreme, Canetti is offering an implicit criticism.[40]

The Model of Masses and Its Transference in Fictionalized Figures

The fictitious individuals in some of Canetti's literary works — primarily *Die Blendung* — can be defined as "solo-masses" that develop an instrumental relationship to each other. Their connection, which does not have its basis in any emotional qualities such as love or affection, is inevitably fragile and threatened by a movement of the underlying power structures. This, as is shown in the development of the relationship of Kien and Therese, provokes a power struggle that on one level appears as an expression of the principal antinomy of men and women based on gender, but on a deeper level is the result of their functioning as individualized masses. The development of the contact between the sexes in *Die Blendung* derives from the attempt of mutual usage, or even exploitation. Kien approaches Therese and finally marries her to save his material property, which is worthless to him as such, but which is ultimately the expression of his fixation on immaterial, spiritual values: his huge collection of books. Thus he is forced to take into account Therese's needs and desires although they stand in sharp contrast to his own ideals. He has to satisfy Therese's wishes to a certain degree, which also has comical effects as shown by the grotesque depiction of sex as an essential element of married life (*Blendung*, 57–59). He is under pressure to transcend his way of life and thinking to a partial denouncement of his own monadic existence. Such an effort, which does not correspond to his personality, is doomed to failure from the beginning, and so the fatal mechanism of destruction begins. In some ways Kien is similar to Canetti's traveler from *Masse und Macht*, who in the women's house is forced to establish a connection to the female part of the tribe, but as an alien, a "Fremdkörper," that does not really belong to their specific mass. The result is danger, distinctly felt by Léry:

> Er fühlt die Erregung der Frauen mit, doch kann er nicht wirklich zu ihrer Masse gehören. Er ist ein Fremder, und er ist ein Mann. Mitten unter ihnen, und doch von ihnen getrennt, muß er fürchten, zum Opfer dieser Massen zu werden. (*MM*, 70)

What happens to the Frenchman involuntarily as a result of more or less accidental circumstances happens in the novel as the result of a self-inflicted strategy involving a great blindness — "Verblendung" — or even as the result of madness. Kien's attempt to keep a distance while coming closer on the level of outward behavior leads to a loss of control, for his behavior, the external overcoming of distance, is dictated by calculation and has no correspondence to an inner attitude. The principle of "Doppelmasse," dual mass, and its purpose "sich zu *erhalten*" (*MM*, 67), does not apply here because it needs, according to Canetti, to be in a balance that is not stable but has to be established again and again. For a lasting "Zwei-Massen-System" (*MM*, 68), it is necessary that there be "auf beiden Seiten das Gefühl von ungefähr gleicher Stärke" (*MM*, 68). In the narrative structure of *Die Blendung*, especially regarding the Kien-Therese relationship, the lack of balance is shown. According to Canetti's epic principle this theme is not developed in a subtle psychological mode but rather satirically with hyperbolic constructions that reveal the purpose of the narrative: to show a pattern of mass collusion represented by two antagonistic forces, male and female, flesh and spirit, materialism and idealism. The extreme reduction and the various forms of hyperbolic devices are principles that Canetti already observed in his early stages as a writer and are realized in most of his later works, including the extremist view of people, whether they be fictional as in his dramas, or as they occur in his aphorisms and notes and in the autobiographies. The tendency to character reduction has, unlike in Brecht's writings, no basis in the intention of the author to develop model situations for a didactic purpose — *Aufklärung*. On the contrary, it originates in the same way as the analysis of crowds or masses inspired by the author's personal emotional involvement. As Canetti told Mechthild Curtius during a conversation in 1974: "Ich schreibe aus Haß."[41] The extreme depiction of the female character Therese is not necessarily an expression of misogyny or *Frauenhaß*, even though the more general traits of this character function in analogy to contemporary antifeminist clichés. The conscious renunciation of psychological empathy is expressed by Erich Fried, who commented on the reflection of personalities in Canetti's autobiographies. Fried knew Canetti, and he points out that Canetti was more interested in the depiction of typical traits that often appear in a rather grotesque manner than in the precise exploration of single personalities.[42]

Der andere Prozeß

The transference of the model of the Doppelmasse in gender relationships can also be seen in another genre, literary criticism, namely Canetti's Kafka study *Der andere Prozeß*. Here, contrary to *Masse und Macht*, he deals with an erotic constellation.[43] Again Canetti sees the relationship in question, that of Franz Kafka and Felice Bauer, from the point of the preservation of masses and the balancing of power. Bernd Witte describes Canetti's representation of Kafka's position by emphasizing that Kafka tried "Felice als distanzierende Macht gegen die eigene Familie zu benutzen, die ihm als die ursprünglichere Gefährdung seines Schreibens erscheint."[44] Here again, the plan fails: the reality of the long-distance relationship proves to be stronger than Kafka's intention to initiate a situation that protects his writing self without threatening this dedication to writing with new demands. Indeed, a tendency to perceive the man-woman relationship from a purely functional point of view is obvious in the Kafka essay. This, however, is too generalized a statement, since the subject is not a normal love relationship but the connection of a singular individual — a literary author like Canetti himself — to a woman who does not belong to this class — again a constellation similar to the one in the *Blendung*. It is the case of a woman who loves the writer and most of all wants to be together with him as a lover or wife. Characteristically, in Canetti's subjective view Felice is characterized mainly by her simplicity and naturalness: "Felice war eine einfache Natur, die Sätze aus ihren Briefen, die er zitiert [. . .], beweisen es hinlänglich" (*Prozeß*, 81). Canetti stresses two qualities in Felice in particular, her concreteness and her activity:

> Das Wichtige an Felice war, daß es sie gab, daß sie nicht erfunden war und daß sie so, wie sie war, nicht von Kafka zu erfinden gewesen wäre. Sie war so verschieden, so tätig, so kompakt. Solange er sie aus der Ferne umkreiste, vergötterte und quälte er sie. (*GW,* 93)

This remark is interesting in more than one respect. Felice appears as the antithesis to Kafka's literary inventions; she represents un-fictionality, physical presence. It is the distinctiveness from his literary cosmos that, as Canetti believes, fascinates him, leads him to idolization, but also to hurting her. Her personality is reduced to functioning as a muse, and indeed, in the entire text Felice only appears in her relationship to the singular existence of the writer. The emphasis on the concrete physical shape corresponds with the problematic physical existence of the man, the writer: "Die besondere Empfindlichkeit für alles, was mit seinem Körper zusammenhing, hat Kafka nie verlassen" (*GW*, 89). Kien in *Die Blendung* has a similar sensitivity that is shown in his asceticism and his dislike of eating, which is reminiscent of Kafka. The male writer and scholar remains absent from physical actions; he tries to escape from the bodily world because the body is only the medium of brutal violence, not of lust. And this is exactly the point of origin in *Masse und Macht:* all the actions of the masses and collectives can be traced back to the archaic impulses of the human body.[45] This is where the literary medium comes into play as the means of overcoming physicality. Comparing Canetti's Schreber and Kafka analyses, Gerhard Neumann stresses the significance of both texts as documents of a transformation of the human body into text.[46]

Kafka regards the connection to Felice Bauer as productive and fertile as long as it is not so close as to threaten his physical integrity as a writer. The cipher for this threat is marriage (combined with children); in Canetti's essay it is called "Schafott" (*GW,* 96). In other words it implies the extinction of his personality as a writer, hence death. Again, there are elements that can be found in Weininger and other misogynist authors since the turn of the century, for example, Canetti's early idol Karl Kraus. The happiness and fulfillment that the female part can find in the intimacy of marriage and partnership, the singular male individual has to search for in the textual effort, in the "Einsamkeit des Schreibens" (*GW,* 97). Kafka's desperate struggle and his final defeat result from the necessary surpassing of a state that from the beginning has been precarious. The "masses" of the male and female that — to go back to the imagery of the quoted passage in Canetti's essay — rotate as circulating planets in distance and dependency at the same time approach each other so closely that they almost touch each other, a closeness that has dangerous consequences for the male part since the physical masses always prove to be the stronger ones.

Whenever there are emotional bonds between the sexes, forms of love, they result from a shared textual experience, the transformation of the female bodily existence into the spiritual and intellectual realm of the man. In this sense Canetti thinks, "daß Liebe bei Kafka [. . .] durch sein geschriebenes Wort entstand. [. . .] Bei jeder der drei [für ihn wichtigen Frauen] entstanden seine Gefühle durch Briefe" (*GW,* 111). Canetti speaks of love and feelings in the context of a textually inspired and structured relationship. But this is not a form of romanticized eroticism. The underlying element is power, a power struggle that finally leads to a break. Again, Canetti argues not from an individualistic standpoint — it is not Kafka's personal relationship to his father that seems to be the decisive moment in his struggle — it is a powerful institution that affects the fate of its members: the family. The father merely functions as the central part of this system.[47]

And in the final analysis, the love relationship also functions according to the frightful laws of the family system; and again a fight becomes necessary to save one's own identity, the fight against the loved person: "[. . .] als die Gefahr einer eigenen Familie drohte, hatte der Kampf gegen Felice dasselbe Motiv und denselben Charakter" (*GW*, 132).

The Mother and Veza — Female Figures in the Autobiographies

The autobiographies clearly show the connection of love, literature, and power, particularly in the mother-son relationship, as the basis of all future relationships to women. It has often been argued that the close bond between mother and son, as developed in *Die gerettete Zunge*, is inspired by language, conversation, and literature, and it can be maintained that the ego in the autobiographies becomes a writer out of love to his mother.[48] But as the autobiographies show, there is another element that leads to constant quarrels and tensions, and finally to the turning away from his mother: she had established the *Zwangssystem*, the dictatorial system, which the son fears and finally begins to hate. At this point Canetti's later wife Veza comes into play. Veza represents all of the love of the world of literature the mother had conveyed to him, but she also represents a different female type, one capable of keeping a distance. Veza is the non-possessive woman who supports the process of breaking away from the mother. Yet, the constellation of the male-female relationship sketched in *Der andere Prozeß* can be found in rudimentary form here as well. In his preface to the first edition of *Die gelbe Straße* (1989), Canetti emphasizes "das überwältigende Maß an Dankbarkeit [. . .], das ich ihr schulde."[49] Veza appears as the savior from the fight within the family, the struggle with his mother. And as in the case of Kafka, the woman appears in a form of concreteness that tends to de-individualize the subject.

Additionally, Veza stands antagonistic to his mother in yet another respect: just like Kafka's Felice in Canetti's view is important because of her mere existence and the fact that she was not invented, also Veza's role as the savior has its roots in her sheer natural being.[50] Whereas the mother's relationship to her own sex is marked by contempt, rivalry, and resistance against the erotic aspects of womanhood, Canetti sees a deep "Parteilichkeit für Frauen" as one of the predominant features of Veza, which expresses itself especially in "Bewunderung für Schönheit, Verführung und Hingabe," qualities that traditionally are attributed to women ("Veza" 7). Yet an additional element already present in the Kafka essay can be seen here, too. It is true that Veza never urged Canetti into the family system, but there is another danger: she is a literary woman, a writer in her own right who could occupy male property. It has been remarked that Canetti, in spite of his enthusiastic descriptions of Veza, never really perceived her as the writer she was, at least not in his public statements. There are numerous empty spaces in the picture we get of Veza through Canetti's eyes. "Die Beschreibung [. . .] gleicht einem Bild mit unscharfen Konturen und weißen Flecken" ("Veza" 7). Canetti's treatment of Veza in the context of literature seems symptomatic. She becomes an icon, a Madonna, but only in reference to his own literary works. In his foreword Canetti emphasizes that all his writings that appeared after her death in 1963, except for one, are dedicated to her as a gesture of thankfulness. Yet Canetti ignored and one can say in a way suppressed her own independent voice.

Gender Relations and Power in the Dramatic Work

Another facet of the images of male and female in Canetti's work is the constellation of a collision within the restricted space of a house, as represented in the drama *Hochzeit*. There is a close connection between this play and the novel, and there are countless intertextual references to Büchner's *Woyzeck,* the Austrian "Volksstück," Sternheim's satirical drama, and the critical depiction of prefascist, petty bourgeois life in Horvàth's plays, even to the circular structure of Schnitzler's *Reigen*. In this context I shall only elaborate on the aspect of gender relationships and the role of sexuality in the context of the institutional framework. Adorno may serve as an expert witness to the Braunschweig performance of the play, which ended in a scandal. He wrote that the author showed a "Pandämonium blinder Triebhaftigkeit."[51] Canetti, however, is no successor of Wedekind or Strindberg. Also in *Hochzeit,* the issue at hand is the problem of power and its unmasking (*Entlarvung*) through the technique of a figure's self-denouncement (*Selbstanprangerung*), a device Canetti found impressive in Büchner's *Woyzeck*. What is revealed in the play is actually the greed of nearly all characters, and the house functions as a leitmotif throughout the drama. All gender relations, the legitimate and the extramarital ones, are infected by greed. According to Foucault the family functions as the place of exchange between sexuality and alliance.[52] As is clear in the picture of the family Thut, the law enters the sexual order since the thematic framework of the play is the institutionalization of love — wedding and family. In satirical exaggeration Canetti displays the concern for family and children as mere phrases. The love for the baby that is initially expressed in the conversations between the teacher and his wife is shown to be founded in the demand for property. Here again Canetti shows the constellation of a couple that has a connection not based on emotional considerations but on a mutual functionalization. The same applies to other characters in the play whose relationships are rooted either in commercial interests or in sheer sexual greed. The self-centered attitude is critically shown in a female figure, Gretchen, who can be understood as a variation of the "new woman" present in the works of the "Neue Sachlichkeit." The egotistic male desire appears in the type of the old libertine Dr. Bock, who openly confesses to his abuse of young girls and to the abortions women had who became pregnant by him. "Er macht den Frauen Kinder, dann kommen sie zu ihm, er kratzt sie aus, er kratzt seine eigenen Kinder aus den Weibern heraus und läßt sich dafür bezahlen."[53]

In these satirically exaggerated scenes, Canetti reflects upon sexuality and sensuality as he had experienced them during his first stay in Berlin, a lifestyle that scared and disgusted as well as fascinated him. The "young Puritan," as he calls himself, is confronted with a concrete form of sexuality that has nothing to do with the liberalized form of gender discourse he had encountered in Vienna. It is a "härtere Sexualität," and Canetti uses a strong word to characterize his immediate reaction: "Ich sah vieles, das ich immer verabscheut hatte. Es wurde einem unaufhörlich vorgeführt, es gehörte zum Charakter des damaligen Berliner Lebens. Alles war möglich, alles *geschah* [. . .]" (*GW*, 228). He also discovered the expressions of direct sexuality in the *Ecce Homo* portfolio of George Grosz, and even though the images it contained were artistic artifacts, the directness of representation resulted in Canetti's taking them for reality:

> Ich wurde jetzt durch diese unerhört harten und erbarmungslosen Darstellungen in sie [sexual matters, J. G. P.] hineingeworfen und hielt sie für wahr, es wäre mir nicht eingefallen, sie zu bezweifeln, und so wie man manche Landschaften nur noch mit den Augen bestimmter Maler sieht, so sah ich Berlin mit den Augen von George Grosz. (*FO*, 266)

It is the world of metropolis, libertinage, and decadence that Canetti faced in Berlin, and just as in *Die Blendung* or in *Hochzeit,* these phenomena are not perceived in a psychological sense but appear as madness. "[. . .] diese Welt, die ich in drei Monaten nicht bewältigen konnte, schien mir eine Welt von Irren" (*GW,* 228).

In this text the sexualized sphere is again revealed as one that is ruled by violence below the surface. Despite the interest young Canetti shows for the heterogeneity in the artistic and intellectual circles of Berlin, there is an underlying threat of being hurt and even destroyed. In *Die Fackel im Ohr* Canetti expresses this fear through the image of the beaten meat: "Als mürbes Stück Fleisch, so ging man in Berlin herum und fühlte sich noch immer nicht mürbe genug und wartete auf neue Schläge" (*FO*, 281). Similarly, the central subject of *Hochzeit* is not sexuality, but the union of sexuality and violence, the egotistic motives of men and women, their greed for power and property, their basic loneliness, and their inability to find a means of communication. From this viewpoint, coming together as individuals is impossible. The communication the protagonists develop is purely instrumental and ego-related, which is seen in the structures of the dialogues. Especially the central scene of the wedding party uses the technique of "Aneinandervorbeireden" — talking at cross purposes. It is this technique that also structures the verbal interactions of *Die Blendung*.

In *Komödie der Eitelkeit*, Canetti expands this perspective into the sphere of political totalitarianism by presenting the model of a society based on reversed rules: namely the ban of visual representation of the self in mirrors and photography. Based on this essential idea (*Grundeinfall*) — which is, according to Canetti, decisive for the writing of a drama — the context of crowd formation and of change or transformation is worked out. In the process the play makes use of grotesque effects that qualify the *Komödie der Eitelkeit* as an early example of the drama of the absurd. Again, the author is not interested in the psychological development of his figures but in their power-driven interactions in the face of an extreme situation that leads to changing power relations and attempts to cope with a paradoxical world. In this respect the early dramas and the novel *Die Blendung* have obvious structural affinities.[54] Even though the comedy appears to be rather abstract, it does display an almost panoramic view of a society shaped by the rise of totalitarian ideology.[55] Canetti himself, as he points out in *Das Augenspiel*, regarded his comedy as a political play, a warning against the dangers of fascism: he hoped for immediate effects on the public — the political situation did not yet seem irreversible (*A*, 127).

As in his other works, Canetti plays with gender stereotypes and certain elements from psychoanalytical discourse taken from the context of Viennese modernism. Along with the dichotomy of male and female qualities, the lack of communication between the sexes, and the circular forms of their encounters, he portrays the problem of a mutual narcissism rooted in the dialectic of subjective desires and a collective will to gain power over others. Even though the personal need to be reflected (symbolized through the instruments of mirrors and photography) is obvious in the different reactions of men and women, the theme of "Spiegelverbot" is not dealt with on an individualized level, but is expressed as a direct political tendency toward mass development under the conditions of dictatorship.[56]

Conclusion

Canetti's images of the female are ambivalent. We find harsh resistance, hate, and disgust, but also a longing for adoration, attitudes that can be traced back to stereotypical male views. Women, as they appear in *Die Blendung,* in the dramas, and in the autobiographies and the theoretical statements, seem potentially dangerous as long as their predominant trait is a demanding dependency on traditional expressions of femininity: physical sexual attraction, isolation from the world of the spirit, demand for marriage, family, and children. In these demands they threaten the destination of the male individual that in its positive form is always directed to spiritual, intellectual, and artistic values. From this point of view, Canetti's propensity for "intellectual" women can be easily explained, as can the counterimage that appears in his fictional works: the disdain of the purely physical, sexual woman. These attitudes may be viewed as an echo of Weininger's credo, that woman as woman is always hostile to man as long as she is not able and willing to turn away from her specific femininity. In this context spiritualization and de-sexualization appear as the only form of a projected harmonization. Canetti's view, however, cannot be reduced to these stereotypes. On the one hand, difference appears as threat, but on the other hand, starting from the model of the dual masses, it is the basis for the encounter of the sexes, and thus possesses a positive potential, however fragile and changeable it may be. Canetti offers no solutions. But his scope of thinking may suggest one hope for the dilemma of the sexes: the principle of permanent change is also applicable to human relations. It is this dynamic, perhaps more than any other, that prevents the author from the slipping into the realm of stereotypes and clichés.

Notes

[1] Elias Canetti, *Das Augenspiel: Lebensgeschichte 1931–1937* (Munich: Hanser, 1985), 158. Cited hereafter as *A.*

[2] Cf. Irmgard Fuchs, "Elias Canetti, ein Aristokrat der Verwandlung," in *Österreichische Literatur und Psychoanalyse,* ed. Josef Rattner and Gerhard Danzer (Würzburg: Königshausen & Neumann, 1997), 295–324. Here: 305; Dagmar Barnouw, *Elias Canetti zur Einführung* (Hamburg: Junius, 1996), 133.

[3] Elias Canetti, *Die Blendung* (Munich: Hanser, 1963) cited hereafter as *Blendung; Masse und Macht* (Hamburg: Claassen, 1960). Cited hereafter as *MM.*

[4] See Barnouw 133, 182; Axel Honneth, "Die unendliche Perpetuierung des Naturzustandes. Zum theoretischen Erkenntnisgehalt von Canettis *Masse und Macht,*" in *Einladung zur Verwandlung: Essays zu Elias Canettis "Macht und Macht,"* ed. Michael Krüger (Munich: Hanser, 1995), 105–27. Here: 116; Fuchs, 306.

[5] Barnouw, 241–42.

[6] See Heike Knoll, *Das System Canetti: Zur Rekonstruktion eines Wirklichkeitsentwurfes* (Stuttgart: M & P, 1993), 3.

[7] See Knoll, 8; Honneth, 105–27. Here: 106; Theo Stammen, "Lektüre des Anderen — Elias Canettis anthropologischer Blick," in *Canetti als Leser,* ed. Gerhard Neumann (Freiburg: Rombach, 1996), 161–76. Here: 173; Hildegard Hogen, *Die Modernisierung des Ich: Individualisierungskonzepte bei Siegfried Kracauer, Robert Musil und Elias Canetti* (Würzburg: Königshausen & Neumann, 2000), 124.

[8] Peter Friedrich, *Die Rebellion der Masse im Textsystem: Die Sprache der Gegenwissenschaft in Elias Canettis "Masse und Macht"* (Munich: Fink, 1999), 11.

[9] See Stammen, 168.

[10] See Friedrich, 260. Regarding Canetti's "ahistoric" approach see Susan Sontag, "Geist als Leidenschaft," in *Hüter der Verwandlung: Beiträge zum Werk von Elias Canetti* (Munich: Hanser, 1985), 90–110. Here: 105. Hansjakob Werlen, "Ohnmächtige Hoffnung. Die Stimme des Individuums in *Masse und Macht,*" in *Einladung zur Verwandlung,* 151–62. Here: 158.

[11] Cf. Elias Canetti, *Die Fackel im Ohr: Lebensgeschichte 1921–1931* (Munich: Hanser, 1980) 119. Cited hereafter as *FO.*

[12] See Friedrich, 262.

[13] See Barbara Bauer, "'Unter dem Eindruck der Ereignisse in Deutschland.' Ideologiekritik und Sprachkritik in Elias Canettis *Komödie der Eitelkeit,*" in *Canetti als Leser,* ed. Gerhard Neumann (Freiburg: Rombach, 1996), 77–111. Here: 81.

[14] Lothar Henninghaus, *Tod und Verwandlung: Elias Canettis poetische Anthropologie aus der Kritik der Psychoanalyse* (Frankfurt: Peter Lang, 1984), 39.

[15] Peter Sloterdijk, *Die Verachtung der Massen: Versuch über Kulturkämpfe in der modernen Gesellschaft* (Frankfurt: Suhrkamp, 2000), 13.

[16] Elias Canetti, "Der Beruf des Dichters," in *Das Gewissen der Worte: Essays* (Munich: Hanser, 1978), 257–67. Here: 263. Cited hereafter as *GW.*

[17] Elias Canetti, "Hitler, nach Speer," in *Das Gewissen der Worte,* 163–70.

[18] Dagmar Barnouw, "Blick, Rückblick, Verwandlung," in *Tod und Verwandlung,* ed. John Pattillo-Hess (Vienna: Kunstverein Wien, 1990), 132–42. Here: 137.

[19] Elias Canetti, *Der andere Prozeß* (Munich: Hanser, 1965); "Der andere Prozeß. Kafkas Briefe an Felice," in *Das Gewissen der Worte,* 72–157. Cited hereafter as "Prozeß."

[20] See Barnouw, "Blick, Rückblick, Verwandlung," 140.

[21] See Hannelore Scholz, "'Keine Angst geht verloren, aber ihre Verstecke sind rätselhaft.' Frauen im autobiographischen Wahrnehmungsspektrum von Elias Canetti," in *Autobiographie zwischen Fiktion und Wirklichkeit,* ed. Penka Angelova and Emilia Staitscheva (St. Ingbert: Röhrig Universitätsverlag, 1997), 249–68. Here: 266.

[22] Barnouw, "Blick, Rückblick, Verwandlung." 140.

[23] John Bayley, *Iris: A Memoir of Iris Murdoch* (London: Duckworth, 1999), 54.

[24] Bayley, *Iris: A Memoir of Iris Murdoch,* 54.

[25] See John Bayley, "Canetti und Macht," *Hüter der Verwandlung: Beiträge zum Werk von Elias Canetti* (Munich: Hanser, 1985), 133–47, and Sibylle Mulot, "Befreun-

det mit der Geliebten," *Der Spiegel*, December 27, 2001. Also: Angelika Schedel, *Sozialismus und Psychoanalyse: Quellen von Veza Canettis literarischen Utopien*. (Würzburg: Königshausen & Neumann, 2002).

[26] Cf. Sontag, 94.

[27] Otto Weininger, *Geschlecht und Charakter* (Vienna: Braumüller, 1903; 1906).

[28] Cf. Sontag, 94.

[29] Scholz, 266. See Gisela Brude-Firnau, "Wissenschaft von der Frau? Zum Einfluß von Otto Weininger, 'Geschlecht und Charakter' auf den deutschen Roman," in *Die Frau als Heldin und Autorin*, ed. Wolfgang Paulsen (Bern: A. Francke, 1979), 136–49; Johannes G. Pankau, "Körper und Geist. Das Geschlechterverhältnis in Elias Canettis Roman *Die Blendung*," *Colloquia Germanica* 23/2 (1990): 146–70; Elfriede Pöder, "Spurensicherung. Otto Weininger in der *Blendung*," in *Blendung als Lebensform*, ed. Friedbert Aspetsberger and Gerald Stieg (Königstein/Ts.: Athenäum, 1985), 57–72.

[30] Cf. Michael Rohrwasser, "Schreibstrategien. Canettis Beschreibungen von Freud," in *Psychoanalyse in der modernen Literatur: Kooperation und Konkurrenz*, ed. Thomas Anz (Würzburg: Königshausen & Neumann 1999), 145–66; Michael Rohrwasser, "Elias Canettis literarische Auseinandersetzung mit der Psychoanalyse in seinem Roman *Die Blendung*. Anmerkungen zum Verhältnis von Literatur und Psychoanalyse," in *Convivium: Germanistisches Jahrbuch Polen 2000* (Bonn: Deutscher Akademischer Austauschdienst, 2000), 43–64.

[31] Cf. Sigmund Freud, "Das Unbehagen in der Kultur," in *Studienausgabe*, vol. 9 (Frankfurt: Suhrkamp, 1974), 191–270. Here: 233.

[32] Norbert Elias, *The Civilizing Process* (New York: Urizen Books, 1978).

[33] On the influence of Hobbes on Canetti, see Honneth, "Die unendliche Perpetuierung des Naturzustandes. Zum theoretischen Erkenntnisgehalt von Canettis *Masse und Macht*," in *Einladung zur Verwandlung: Essays zu Elias Canettis "Masse und Macht*,*"* ed. Michael Krüger (Munich: Hanser, 1995), 105–27. Here: 107; Gerald Stieg, "Canetti und die Psychoanalyse: *Das Unbehagen in der Kultur* und *Die Blendung*," in *Elias Canetti: Londoner Symposium*, ed. Adrian Stevens and Fred Wagner (Stuttgart: H.-D. Heinz, 1991) 59–73. Here: 62.

[34] Sigmund Freud, "Massenpsychologie und Ich-Analyse," in *Studienausgabe*, vol. 9 (Frankfurt: Suhrkamp, 1974), 61–134. Here: 65.

[35] Whereas Canetti regards himself as a part of the crowd, Freud transfers his therapeutic model of a fundamental distance between psychoanalyst and patient to social phenomena. See for example Sigmund Freud, "Bemerkungen über die Übertragungsliebe," in *Studienausgabe*, Ergänzungsband (Frankfurt: Suhrkamp, 1975) 217–30. Here: 223.

[36] See Endre Kiss, "Elias Canettis 'Masse und Macht' in methodischer Sicht," in *Autobiographie zwischen Fiktion und Wirklichkeit*, ed. Penka Angelova and Emilia Staitscheva (St. Ingbert: Röhrig Universitätsverlag, 1997), 223–32. Here: 228.

[37] Werlen, 158.

[38] See Bernd Widdig, *Männerbünde und Massen: Zur Krise männlicher Identität in der Literatur der Moderne* (Opladen: Westdeutscher Verlag, 1992), 205.

[39] Elias Canetti, "Das erste Buch: Die Blendung," in *Das Gewissen Der Worte*, 222–33. Here: 224–25.

[40] Cf. Bernd Widdig, "'Tägliche Sprengungen': Elias Canetti und die Inflation," *Einladung zur Verwandlung: Essays zu Elias Canettis "Masse und Macht,"* ed. Michael Krüger (Munich: Hanser, 1995), 128–50. Here: 144.

[41] See Mechthild Curtius, "Blendungen. Autobiographie in der Wirklichkeit," in *Autobiographie zwischen Fiktion und Wirklichkeit*, 91–99. Here: 92.

[42] Cf. Mechthild Curtius, ed., *Autorengespräche: Verwandlung der Wirklichkeit: Gespräche mit 13 Autoren* (Frankfurt: Fischer, 1991), 66.

[43] Gerhard Neumann, "'Yo lo vi.' Wahrnehmung der Gewalt: *Canettis Masse und Macht*," in *Einladung zur Verwandlung*, 68–104. Here: 87–88.

[44] Bernd Witte, "Elias Canetti," in *Kritisches Lexikon zur deutschsprachigen Gegenwartsliteratur (KLG)*, ed. Heinz Ludwig Arnold (Munich: Edition Text + Kritik, 1978), 11.

[45] See Honneth, 105.

[46] Cf. Gerhard Neumann, "Lektüren der Macht. Elias Canetti als Leser Daniel Paul Schrebers und Franz Kafkas," in *Canetti als Leser*, 137–59. Here: 153.

[47] See Canetti, *Das Gewissen der Worte*, 132.

[48] See among numerous others, Dagmar Barnouw, *Elias Canetti* (Stuttgart: Metzler, 1979), 5.

[49] Elias Canetti, "Veza," in Veza Canetti, *Die Gelbe Straße: Roman,* ed. Elias Canetti (Munich: Hanser, 1989), 5–9. Here: 5. Cited hereafter as "Veza."

[50] See Canetti, "Veza," 5.

[51] See Harry Timmermann, "Tierisches in der Anthropologie und Poetik Elias Canettis. Mit Beispielen aus dem Gesamtwerk," in *Elias Canetti zu Ehren: Sprache im technischen Zeitalter* 94, ed. Walter Höllerer and Norbert Miller (Stuttgart: Kohlhammer, 1985), 99–126. Here: 117.

[52] See Hubert Orlowski, "Auf vielen Hochzeiten tanzen. Zu den Stücken von Wyspianskis *Hochzeit*, Canettis *Hochzeit* und Gombrowicz' *Die Trauung*," in *Canettis Aufstand gegen Macht und Tod*, ed. John Pattillo-Hess and Mario L. Smole (Vienna: Löcker, 1996), 80–88. Here: 86. See Michel Foucault, *Sexualität und Wahrheit: Der Wille zum Wissen* (Frankfurt: Suhrkamp, 1987), 131. See also Michel Foucault, *The History of Sexuality*, trans. Robert Hurley (New York: Vintage Books, 1990).

[53] Elias Canetti, *Hochzeit. Komödie der Eitelkeit. Die Befristeten.* (Munich: Hanser, 1964), and also "Hochzeit," in *Dramen* (Frankfurt: Fisher, 1976), 45.

[54] See Barnouw, *Elias Canetti zur Einführung* (Hamburg: Junius, 1996), 37.

[55] See Bauer, "'Unter dem Eindruck der Ereignisse in Deutschland.' Ideologiekritik und Sprachkritik in Elias Canettis *Komödie der Eitelkeit*," in *Canetti als Leser*, ed. Gerhard Neumann (Freiburg: Rombach, 1996), 86.

[56] Possible similarities to Lacan's concept of a "stade de miroir" remain speculative. See Barnouw, *Elias Canetti*, 33.

Canetti's Final Frontier: The Animal

Dagmar C. G. Lorenz

> *Der Morgen, so lustig, als wäre*
> *er für immer angebrochen.*
> *Tiere auf allen Seiten*[1]

THE STATEMENTS ABOUT ANIMALS in Elias Canetti's works reveal the
scope and direction of the author's thought as few other topics do. In
her anthology *Elias Canetti über Tiere* (2002), Brigitte Kronauer writes that
Canetti's relationship to animals is indicative of the much-debated fascination with and concern about power that permeated all phases of his career
as a writer and critic. Rather than considering Canetti the "ruthless tyrant
who paradoxically criticizes the exertion of power" as some critics have
characterized him,[2] Kronauer emphasizes his desire for equality among all
living beings:

> Etwa unter der empörten Zurückweisung einer absoluten Sonderstellung
> des Menschen gegenüber dem Tier den generellen Ekel des Autors vor
> Machtanmaßung; sein Interesse für die Dynamik von Mengen und
> Massen bei der Darstellung großer Tierherden; seine Weigerung, sich
> trotz des unwiderleglichen Augenscheins mit dem Faktum des Todes
> abzufinden, also im Schlachthaus das Schlachten nicht zu akzeptieren,
> nicht zu glauben, daß etwas (hier die erschlagenen Schlangen im Sack)
> "ganz tot sein könnte."[3]

Scattered throughout Canetti's work, observations about animals and
the relationship between humans and animals seem strangely at odds with
the human-centeredness of the dominant philosophies and ideological programs of his era such as Marxism, fascism, existentialism, and humanism. In
fact, there is a development in Canetti's thoughts on animals that leads from
his earlier, mostly abstract configuration of the concepts "man and animal"
as myth or metaphor to a more literal understanding of animals and to a real
concern for their well-being in a world increasingly dominated and devastated by humans. "Die Laute der Wale. Im Grunde empfinde ich Scham,
diese friedlichen Laute von Geschöpfen zu hören, die sich gegen uns nicht
zur Wehr setzen können," he wrote in 1992 (*Tiere*, 98). Such statements
transcend the anthropocentric patterns of the post-Enlightenment and place

Canetti into the context of post-humanist, postmodern movements concerned with ecological issues and animal rights.[4] For example, in a statement made in 1985, Canetti expressed his refusal to take part in the domestication of nonhuman animals, which would result in making them subservient to him: "Kein Tier hat ihn erkannt. Er war keinem Tier geheuer. Er weigerte sich, ein Tier zum Diener zu nehmen" (*Aufz. 1942–85*, 530). Canetti's attitude calls to mind basic tenets of twenty-first century animal rights activism as expressed in an article on *The Animal Rights FAQ* Web site: "In a perfect world, all of our efforts would go toward protecting the habitats of other species on the planet and we would be able to maintain a 'hands off' approach in which we did not take other species into our family units, but allowed them to develop on their own in the wild."[5] Canetti's reservations against his own privileged position as a human being, which was sanctioned by his society, calls to mind views expressed by radical animal advocates.

Even Canetti's earlier thought experiments involving the process of transformation (Verwandlung) and his half playful, half-serious notion that animals might be contained within the human form and vice versa reveal the remarkable extent to which his views were already at variance with the Judeo-Christian Great Chain of Being and the Cartesian hierarchy. He made pertinent statements as early as 1943, for example: "Man möchte jeden Menschen in seine Tiere auseinandernehmen und sich mit diesen dann gründlich und begütigend ins Einvernehmen setzten," and "Immer wenn man ein Tier genau betrachtet, hat man das Gefühl, ein Mensch, der drin sitzt, macht sich über einen lustig" (*Tiere*, 13; 10).

Canetti seems torn between his desire to communicate with animals and his reluctance to transcend the traditional boundaries that prevent him from establishing a physically and emotionally close relationship with an animal. Nonetheless he writes about relationships with other species in a unique mixture of prophecy and playfulness, both of which underlie his eclectic anthropological and cultural analysis. Over time, the trajectory of his statements about animals shifts. Sometimes the individual, the person or the animal, and at other times the objective, quasi scientific observer of species is stressed. In the latter case, in keeping with the scientific and philosophical discourse of the Occident, Canetti juxtaposes the categories of homo sapiens and animal in a conventional binary manner.

In his pathbreaking study *Animal Liberation*, Peter Singer points out that the accepted anthropocentric method of categorizing animal species "lumps together beings as different as oysters and chimpanzees, while placing a gulf between chimpanzees and humans, although our relationship to those apes is much closer than the oyster's" and reflects "the prejudices of its users."[6] Although Canetti does not dispense with the categories human and animal altogether, they are frequently undermined and questioned in such a way as to direct the reader's attention to the impossibility of defining or even imagining representatives of different species in isolation from one another. Canetti's repeated synthesizing of human and animal traits suggests a sliding scale that precludes both the divine creator and the abhorrent beast. Were it not for his frequently expressed love of his own species, his often profoundly pessimistic statements could be taken for outright misanthropy, for example:

> Die Kernfrage aller Ethik: soll man den Menschen sagen, wie schlecht sie sind? Oder sollte man sie in ihrer Unschuld schlecht sein lassen? Um diese Frage zu beantworten, müßte man erst entscheiden können, ob die Kenntnis ihrer Schlechtigkeit den Menschen eine Möglichkeit beläßt, besser zu werden, oder ob es eben diese Kenntnis ist, die ihre Schlechtigkeit unausrottbar macht. Es könnte ja sein, daß das Schlechte schlecht bleiben muß, sobald es einmal als solches ausgesondert und bezeichnet worden ist; es vermöchte sich dann zwar wohl zu verbergen, aber es wäre immer da. (*Aufz. 1942–85*, 136)

Critics have discussed Canetti's preoccupation with issues such as death and survival, anthropology, mass psychology, nation and nationhood, gender and ethnicity, and the concept of transformation (*Verwandlung*).[7] Canetti's works have been the subject of literary interpretations that explore his choice and use of genre, narrative strategy, literary devices, and his relationship to authors such as Nietzsche, Broch, and Kraus.[8] Considering the scope of Canetti criticism at the beginning of the twenty-first century, it seems surprising that his life-long probing into the categories of human and animal have rarely been carefully examined even though they reveal basic assumptions of his anthropology, his cultural criticism, and his self-assessment as a human being. Brigitte Kronauer's *Elias Canetti über Tiere*, which lists most of Canetti's statements on animals, reveals the centrality of this issue, but other scholars and critics have steered clear of Canetti's unorthodox utterances or interpreted them in abstract or psychological terms. The latter approach stands in contrast to Canetti's concrete lament over the loss of animal life and his yearning for love and intimacy between humans and non-humans: "Kein Tier habe ich umarmt. Ein ganzes Leben habe ich mit qualvollem Erbarmen an Tiere gedacht, aber kein Tier habe ich umarmt," he wrote in his notes of 1982 (*Aufz. 1942–85*, 480). The term "friend" and the concept of friendship applied to animals, who in Western civilization have been traditionally considered objects for domestication, taming, hunting, extermination, or slaughter, is particularly surprising because it presupposes equality between the partners as well as affection and trust.

Canetti's disagreement with Cartesian notions of human superiority has several possible sources. For one, it must be read in the context of Western philosophical debates such as Descartes versus La Mettrie. The latter considered human and non-human animals machines thus challenging Descartes' claims according to which human beings were superior because of their linguistic behavior and the supposed possession of an immortal soul.[9] Jewish notions such as the transmigration of souls, transformation, and the synthesis of human and animal characteristics also contributed to Canetti's view on animals. The work of Franz Kafka, by whose writings and personal life Canetti was fascinated, were replete with animal imagery, instances of transformation, and the blurring of species boundaries.[10] Canetti's outlook on animals furthermore calls to mind Buddhist attitudes with which he had become familiar through his friendship with the Buddhist Fred Waldinger and his own study of Buddhist texts. Buddhist thought does not allow for a qualitative difference between human and non-human life, and all life is conceptualized as one. Injury to humans and animals as well as other conceivable living beings is considered harmful to the victim but, even more so, to the perpetrators.[11]

Canetti was aware of the way Nazi propaganda manipulated the categories "human," "animal," and "subhuman" to make the exclusion and persecution of Jews and other "undesirables" palatable to the German public. The construct "animal," envisioned as life without conscious awareness, soul, or self-determination was invoked to rationalize the murder of the disabled, euphemistically referred to as euthanasia — mercy-killing. In the Nazi propaganda film *Der ewige Jude,* Jews in the Lodz ghetto are visually equated with rats, and the narrator explains: "Just as the rat is the lowest of animals, the Jew is the lowest of human beings."[12] In *Animals in the Third Reich,* Boria Sax writes that "'human' status has often been in practice a matter of race, nationality, gender, class, and many other factors."[13] Whether he comments on actual persons and animals or examines animal mythology and imagery, Canetti avoids constructing polarities, be it the polarity of human and animal, be it that of noble and ignoble animals.[14]

Finally, Canetti's regret about his failure to establish a personal relationship with an animal seems a further attempt to distance himself from the kind of *Tierliebe* (love of animals) practiced in Nazi Germany. Examining the Nazi topos of the "love of the German people for animals," Sax points out that "the Nazis did not recognize or respect the nearly unconditional love that often characterizes not only close friendship and marriage but also relations between people and their pets. Their government tried to direct the attention of its citizens away from personal relationships to more abstract ideals such as the race or the state. The laws on animal protection show this odd reluctance to individualize animals, which can indeed make the reader wonder how far the vaunted love of other creatures extended beyond providing painless death."[15]

In 1993, in his last volume of *Aufzeichnungen,* Canetti makes the following startling admission, that includes also Jewish tradition in the attitudinal patterns of which he is critical:

In allem, was ich über Tiere gesagt habe, komme ich mir wie ein Schwindler vor, weil ich so wenig mit ihnen *erfahren* habe. Ich habe die Mythen über sie verschlungen, und manchmal habe ich die Tiere *ange-sehen*, nie mehr, aber ergriffen, als wäre ich in einem der alten Verwandlungsmythen. Sonst war es nichts. Ich habe mich nie über Jahre einem Tier angeschlossen. Meine Scheu davor war zu groß. Wenn es etwas Göttliches in meinem Leben gegeben hat, so war es diese scheue Verehrung für Tiere. Was hätte Moses mit all meinen goldenen Kälbern getan? Hätte er mich wie einen Ägypter erschlagen? Mich verdammt und verbrannt? Meine Tiere vor mir geschlachtet und sie Opfer genannt? (*Aufz. 1992–93,* 75)

Alongside this implied criticism of the position accorded animals in Judaism, which, like all Western cultures, emerged from a prehistory of killing and sacrifice, Canetti acknowledges his own ignorance regarding the creatures termed animals — the ultimate other — in distinction to "us," *homo sapiens*. The admission of ignorance is all the more astonishing because Canetti is anything but shy about claiming knowledge about remote civilizations, tribal cultures, and women's psychology, all of which were designated as the other by twentieth-century Western men.

From a feminist point of view Lynda Birke comments on the dominant anthropocentric point of view in Western civilization as follows: "The term animal can mean many different things . . . Opposed to humans, it tends to mean everything we think we are not, or whatever we wish to transcend — the beast within for example,"[16] and she continues to write: "Separating ourselves from less worthy 'others' is . . . a common trait. Feminists have been critical of this separation, not least because women have so often been other to men. 'Othering' is a trait that links to concepts of global domination, in its reliance on defining what is human against those who are conquered."[17] In contrast, in the case of Canetti, even in the early writings, the term animal is also applied to everything that "we" are also. Rather than being configured as the opposite of "us," animal behavior and character are viewed as an integral part of the human psyche, the human condition. Anne Fuchs points out that in *Die Stimmen von Marrakesch*, Canetti recognizes the "vitality and desire for life" also in those "barely existing on the borders of life," and she points out that at first he almost mistakes the one-legged beggar for an animal.[18] By doing so, he establishes a parallel between the human and non-human animals: the camels, the donkey, and ultimately, the narrator.

Even though in his critical terminology Canetti adheres to the traditional categories *Mensch* and *Tier,* he is cognizant of the function of these terms within the larger ideological system, namely to justify the supremacy of humans over other species. In his notes of 1945, the following sarcastic entry is found: "Welche erstaunliche Hierarchie unter den Tieren! Der Mensch sieht sie so, wie er sich ihre Eigenschaften gestohlen hat!" (*Aufz.*

1942–85, 111). Adverse to clannishness and group thinking, including nationalism, Canetti likewise rejects the attitude defined by Richard Ryder as "speciesm."[19] In his aphorisms he challenges the established binary model, asserting that the very term "animal" proves the limitation of man, and in *Nachträge aus Hampstead* (1994), he leads it ad absurdum by asserting that man *is* all the animals he knows (*NH,* 135). In his general thought structure, Canetti transcends traditional boundaries. Similar to ecofeminists such as Carol Adams and Joan Dunayer, he "collapses male/female and masculine/feminine dualities" and works, as they do, "toward a challenging new definition of human nature."[20] Similarly, in his analysis of power he incorporates hierarchical rankings into a comprehensive, nontraditional worldview, and he illustrates in his works, as Fox states about ecofeminism, "that the domination, oppression, and exploitation of women and nature, or women and animals, form 'interlocking systems.'"[21]

Despite his analysis of animal traits within the human psyche and his emphasis on diversity of species, despite his abhorrence of eating, particularly meat eating, and his plea for animal protection, Canetti seems to have felt that he was not able to overcome speciesm, the least recognized form of intellectual prejudice of his time. His failure consists, he suggests, in not having established a proper relationship with animals. Again, the term friendship emerges as an implied partnership based on mutual cooperation, and respect. "Du hast unter Tieren nicht einen einzigen Freund. Nennst du das Leben?" (*Aufz. 1942–85,* 516) In the writings of Lawrence and Susan Finsen, who describe the Animal Rights Movement as a progression from "compassion to respect," notions occur that are not at all alien to Canetti's thought: "a deep ecologists' holistic vision," and "genuine egalitarianism," and an "ethics of caring."[22]

A careful reading of Canetti's statements shows an increasing personal engagement with animal issues. In his cerebral, abstract, and occasionally apodictic remarks of the 1940s, which are interspersed with an occasional emotional outcry motivated by the horrific events in Europe and the Nazis' use of the category "animal" to defame the Jews as "Other," animals are addressed rather infrequently, particularly in the aphorisms of the late 1940s and 1950s. However, there are exceptions: "O Tiere, geliebte, grausame, sterbende Tiere; zappelnd, geschluckt, verdaut und angeeignet; raubend und blutig verfault; geflohen vereinigt, einsam, gesehen, gehetzt, zerbrochen; unerschaffen, von Gott geraubt, in eine täuschendes Leben ausgesetzt wie Findelkinder!" (*Aufz. 1942–85,* 54). At the same time, one must keep in mind that *Die Stimmen von Marrakesch,* an account of a journey to Morocco in 1954, reveals a genuine fascination with animals, including individuals of two species: a camel and a donkey. In the mid-1960s, Canetti took up the topic with renewed interest, issuing strong indictments against homo sapiens and the murderous ramifications of cultural accomplishments both ancient and modern. From the 1980s until his death, Canetti articulated his increasing longing to understand animals on their own terms and frustration over his inability to do so.

Canetti's increasing alienation from monotheism goes hand in hand with his fascination with Buddhism and Hinduism, both of which emphasize the fundamental unity of all living beings. His eclectic approach to religion is linked to his attitude toward animals as suggested by statements such as the following in *Die Fliegenpein:* "Der *Ton* der Ägypter ist dein eigener, wie sonst kein Ton. *Tiere* so heilig wie die Schrift" (*F,* 119). In other places he expresses profound compassion, a sense of communality, and the desire to overcome the limitations of his own species, for example when he writes that he would like to experience the death of an animal as an animal (*Aufz. 1942–85,* 410). Despite his frustration about the limited possibilities of communication with animals because of the lack of a common language, Canetti assumes a basic emotional similarity between the species, a connectedness interrupted only by the striving for power and control by human beings. "Es gibt nichts, was Mensch und Tier mehr gemeinsam haben als die Liebe. Der Tod ist beim Menschen etwas anderes geworden. Er hat sich des Todes so sehr bemächtigt, daß er ihn nun auch für alle trägt. Die Verbindung von Tod und Liebe aber ist eine ästhetische. Daß sie auch zur Höherbewertung des Todes geführt hat, ist ihre Sünde, eine der schwersten, sie ist durch nichts zu sühnen" (*Aufz. 1942–85,* 318). Thus he considers love to be a capacity shared by man and other species — and possibly the medium to overcome their separation — and considers man's awareness of and efforts to master death to be that which causes him to be estranged from other species. At the same time, Canetti suggests that if man gained the ability to understand the language of non-human species it would have detrimental effects on them. A revealing aphorism reads: "Beim Nachtmahl fragte ich sie, ob sie gern die Sprache der Tiere verstehen möchte. Nein, das möchte sie nicht. Auf meine Frage: Warum nicht? Zögerte sie ein wenig und sagte dann: Damit sie sich nicht fürchten" (*Aufz. 1942–85,* 416). As much as Canetti refuted the reality of death, he refuted the necessity of killing, the notion that, as Fox writes, "Humans have to kill in order to survive."[23]

There are parallels between Canetti's call for non-intrusiveness and respect for other species and the point of view of contemporary animal rights proponents, who are often held in contempt in highly industrialized and technologically advanced society. Paul Shepard is an advocate of industrial and technical "progress" whose criticism of the animal rights viewpoint can be considered typical of the majority opinion of Western civilization. He questions the notion common to the animal rights and ecological movements that other species have a "fundamental right to be," regardless if they serve any human purpose or plan, and he accuses those who, like Canetti, speak up for animals, of anti-humanism.[24] Indeed, Canetti frequently insinuates, as do environmentalists, that the overabundance of humans is detrimental to other species, that it diminishes energy, other resources, and the living space of all species. He also deplores the extermination of species, the reduction of natural populations, and the loss of quality of life for living beings who have no choice in the matter. In other words, he shares the "kind of sentimental morality," as Shepard and like-minded conservatives would call it, that is found among alternative groups fundamentally dissatisfied with the course of modern civilization.

However, Canetti's thoughts, even though they presuppose alternative views, also supersede the ideas held by moderate ecologists and adherents of animal protection positions. There is little doubt Canetti aligned himself with the educated urban mind that Shepard takes to task for its hyperliberalism. A critical intellectual, Canetti had a keen notion of the potential as well as the limitations of human pursuits, including his own. Indeed, he was, more so than some social and ecological activists, who refuse to acknowledge language as a valid category to distinguish between human and non-human animals, cognizant of the importance of language. Upon numerous occasions he reflected on the topic of animals and their lack of human speech and speculated about the frightening effect human language might have on other species.[25] Occasionally a tone of derision aimed at his fellow humans enters his observations, for example, in the assertion that animals are more amazing than humans — a speaking animal would be little more than a human being (*Aufz. 1942–85*, 289). Canetti did not share the activists' optimism that it is possible to reverse the destruction of species and habitats caused by humans. At the same time he also acknowledges the dynamics of mutual destruction in the lives of animals in a note of 1992: "Ist alles Beute? Ist alles Fraß? Man hält sich nicht umsonst an den Tieren schadlos. Je ernster man sie nimmt, je unablenkbarer man ihnen zu ihrem Recht verhilft, umso mehr bestätigt sich die Welt in ihrem Netz des Fraßes. Kein Ausweg. Verzweiflung durch Erbarmen" (*F*, 41).

Obviously Canetti stands apart from activists, especially social, political, or animal rights, in his despair about the way the world functions and in his anger about the basic conditions of life and the cruelty of its creatures. All of these are fundamental and without remedy. Precisely because Canetti recognizes the inescapability of suffering, death, killing, and being killed, he does not believe in an omnipotent being or a personal creator one could hold accountable, even though he often uses God as a reference point *ex negativo* as in the following aphorism:

> Ich schäme mich für Menschen, die Gott verfallen. Es sind oft gute Menschen, um gut sein zu können, brauchen sie eine Macht, die Güte nennt und begrenzt. Um ihre angeborenen Schlechtigkeit zu bekämpfen, mit der wir alle es zu tun haben, brauchen sie Gehorsam und de-

kretierte Übungen. Sie hätten recht, wenn es sich nicht gezeigt hätte, daß dieser Gehorsam den Charakter jedes Gehorsams hat, und da sie diesen Charakter nicht kennen, handeln sie blind und erziehen sich mit enormer Selbstüberwindung zu Werkzeugen. (*Aufz. 1942–85*, 109)

Canetti clearly does not accept man's innate superiority. In 1993, for example, he drew a parallel between himself and weaker animals who rebel against the seemingly all-powerful human being, and likened his own aggression resulting from his dissatisfaction with the world to theirs:

> Drohgebärden ganz schwacher Tiere gegen den übermächtigen Menschen. Wie du, aber gegen wen? Wenn ich wenigstens die Witterung meines Übermächtigen hätte! Ich habe nur das Nichts. Aber je deutlicher ich fühle, dass ich nur das Nichts habe, sonst nichts, umso mehr wehre ich mich gegen das Wort dafür: nichts, deutsch fast so unheimlich wie 'néant.'" (*Aufz. 1992–93*, 60)

Contrary to himself, the animals direct their ineffectual threats against a concrete enemy. Canetti, on the other hand, does not know against whom or what to direct his outrage.

In his pervasive pessimism, Canetti rated the outlook for the future of the planet and its inhabitants as grim. Already in 1945, following the bombing of Japan by the United States, he noted that the atomic bomb had rendered all living creatures antediluvian, and in the following decades he observed a progressive environmental decline affecting humans and animals alike. "Alle Geschöpfe sind vorsintflutlich, aus der Zeit vor der Atombombe" (*Aufz. 1942–85*, 97). In *Die Fliegenpein* he writes that it brings him peace of mind to say out loud the names of animals that have not yet been eradicated, but he predicts that in time only a small number of animals of very few species will be left, so rare that they will be fawned upon like gods: "Es beruhigt ihn, daß er die Namen der Tiere nennt. Er ist stolz auf ihre Namen. 'Den gibt es. Den haben wir doch nicht ausgerottet.'" A similar thought also occurred in his earlier aphorisms: "In tausend Jahren: einige gezählte Tiere von ganz wenigen Arten, rar und umschmeichelt wie Götter" (*Aufz. 1942–85*, 455).

Canetti's fascination with animals and the human masses — humans as a species or a collective — go hand in hand. In his discussions of these phenomena, Canetti assumes a position fundamentally different from the dominant discourse by relativizing the individual human being and expanding the concept of one divine entity into the notion of many gods, among them animals, or by dismissing God altogether. Hence his admiration for the Buddha, who has been all beings, and his frequently expressed desire for transspecies experiences:

> In jeder Existenz war Buddha einmal zu Hause. . . . Der Buddha, der
> *Alles* einmal war, hat die umfassendste Existenz, die einem Wesen je
> zugeschrieben wurde. Der Kern dieses Glaubens ist farbig geblieben,
> wie immer er in seiner Ausübung entartet oder verblaßt ist. Er wurde
> zu jedem Tier, das Appetit auf ihn zeigte. (*Aufz. 1942–85,* 189, 379)

The reason why critics have largely neglected these issues is the
anthropocentrism of the dominant culture.[26] Thus the chapter "Ein Irren-
haus" in Canetti's novel *Die Blendung,* devoted to the gorilla-man, the
object of the psychiatrist George Kien's study, has been underinterpreted or
rendered overly abstract.[27] From the narrator's point of view, the creature,
dressed like a man, keeping company with a human woman, and working on
developing his own language, is consistently referred to as "the gorilla."
Represented as an animal with some human characteristics, the being that
was formerly a man and is now in the process of transformation into an
animal, or from an anthropocentric point of view, the man reverting to the
animal state, is positioned at the boundaries between human and animal.
Already this episode contains motifs relevant to Canetti's later position: the
rejection of the theory of evolution as progress because it is utilitarian and
could be used as a justification for genocide.[28] Also present in the gorilla
episode is the theme of transformation, which is central in Canetti's work and
later becomes radicalized by the recurrent notion of role reversals that bring
about poetic justice. For example, animals are envisioned as being superior
to and as holding power over humans. Such thoughts occur in Canetti's
work as early as the 1940s: For example the following statement from 1949:

> Es schmerzt mich, dass es nie zu einer Erhebung der Tiere gegen uns
> kommen wird, der geduldigen Tiere, der Kühe, der Schafe, alles Viehs,
> das in unsre Hand gegeben ist und ihr nicht entgehen kann. Ich stelle
> mir vor, wie die Rebellion in einem Schlachthaus aufbricht und von da
> sich über eine ganze Stadt ergießt; wie Männer, Frauen, Kinder, Greise
> erbarmungslos zu Tode getrampelt werden; wie die Tiere Straßen und
> Fahrzeuge überrennen, Tore und Türen einbrechen, in ihrer Wut sich
> bis in die höchsten Stockwerke der Häuser hinauf ergießen . . . Ich wä-
> re schon erleichtert über einen einzigen Stier, der diese Helden, die
> Stierkämpfer, jämmerlich in die Flucht schlägt und eine ganze blutgie-
> rige Arena dazu. Aber ein Ausbruch der minderen, sanften Opfer, der
> Schafe, der Kühe, wäre mir lieber. Ich mag es nicht wahrhaben, daß das
> nie geschehen kann; daß wir vor ihnen, gerade ihnen allen nie zittern
> werden. (*Aufz. 1942–85,* 155)

Canetti's desire to empower the powerless, to make the abusers experience
the very abuse they inflict, also applies among different animal species. An
early aphorism expresses the desire to watch a mouse kill a cat in the same
manner the cat kills a mouse: not before having played with it to its heart's

content (*Aufz. 1942–85*, 13). It must be noted that in his early writing, Canetti anthropomorphized animals to a far greater extent than he later did. Canetti's criticism of the human species increased over time. Contrary to the Judeo-Christian, Hindu, and Buddhist traditions that accord human beings a privileged position in the universe, he maintained in 1966 that rather than being the most exalted, the "Gottöberste," humans are the lowest life form; they are God's henchmen: "Daß wir hier die Gottuntersten, nämlich Gottes Henker in seiner Welt sind" (*Aufz. 1942–85*, 289). In a similar vein, despite his occasional notes of admiration for Buddhism, he unmasked its self-serving, anthropocentric tendencies:

> Die Schuld als Karma — unsäglicher Hochmut des Menschen: an den Tieren, in denen sie Aufenthalt nehme, bestrafe sich die Niedertracht seiner Seele. Wie wagt er es, Tiere mit seiner Seele zu bestrafen? Haben sie denn etwa eingeladen? Kann es ihnen erwünscht sein, durch sie herabgesetzt zu werden? Sie wollen die Seele des Menschen nicht, sie verabscheuen sie, sie ist ihnen zu gedunsen und zu häßlich. Sie ziehen ihre anmutige Armut vor und weit lieber als von Menschen lassen sie sich von Tieren fressen. (*Aufz. 1942–85*, 358–59)

In another statement Canetti characterized homo sapiens as "the animal that remembers what and whom it murders" — "Der Mensch, das Tier, das sich merkt, was es mordet" (*Aufz. 1942–85*, 293). In 1980, he asserted: "Ich glaube, es wird das letzte, das allerletzte in meinem Leben sein, das mir noch Eindruck macht: Tiere. Ich habe nur über sie gestaunt. Ich habe sie nie erfaßt. Ich habe gewußt: das bin ich, und doch war es jedesmal etwas anderes" (*Aufz. 1942–85*, 448). It seems a logical conclusion, then, to question the value of the human species altogether: "Vielleicht ist kein einziger Mensch es wert, ein Kind zu haben" (*Aufz. 1942–85*, 345). It seems almost a wish when Canetti muses in one of his last aphorisms: "Und wenn die Tiere uns doch noch loswerden sollten?" (*Aufz. 1992–93*, 74).

The process of becoming animal in *Die Blendung* corresponds to the process of opening humanity to the animal being that Akira Lippit terms the "creative solution to the blocked communication between human and animal." According to Deleuze and Guattari this process is central in the work of Kafka.[29] The relationship of humans and non-humans in *Die Verwandlung*, and Canetti's concept of *Verwandlung*, can be used to illustrate the role of literature in reconfiguring the concept of the animal and, in analogy, that of the human being. Kafka's *Verwandlung* and Canetti's gorilla-man episode in *Die Blendung* support the claim that becoming animal is "only a line of escape and retreat — animal being carries its own finitude."[30] Even though becoming animal for Canetti is a willful act, contrary to the metamorphosis that happens seemingly involuntarily to Gregor Samsa, it initiates the subject into a world that follows its own distinct set of rules. In both cases, the mediation of a human being — in Kafka Gregor's sister, in Canetti the lover-secretary — is necessary to establish a semblance of communication between the two spheres.

Canetti's later statements suggest similar views to those of Max Horkheimer and Theodor Adorno, according to which Western humanism depended on the exclusion of animals and a historical progression that culminated in the justification of mass murder. The National Socialist state, Horkheimer and Adorno maintained, "excused the elimination of Jews from the 'German' populace by transforming them first into nonhuman or animal others, 'to the condition of a species.'"[31] In 1943, when the information about the Holocaust was becoming available, Canetti noted: "Es ist nicht auszudenken, wie gefährlich die Welt ohne Tiere sein wird" (*Aufz. 1942–85*, 35). In general terms, Canetti does not consider the slaughter of animals and the killing of humans as categorically different, as a note from 1992 in *Die Fliegenpein* reveals: "Das Töten ist das Schlachten, was den Tieren geschieht, geschieht uns, später, aber nicht viel später; nur nicht spät genug, um ganz vergessen zu sein. Wie ein Gerücht, das lange nachhallt, schlachten, töten, schlachten, töten. O Gott, wenn es dich gäbe, daß du damit ein Ende machst" (*F*, 25). One year later he noted that it is necessary to confront the problem of murder committed against animals and the disabled, suggesting that in both instances the same dynamics are involved. "Morde an Tieren und Morde an Behinderten konfrontieren. Ist es dasselbe?" (*Aufz. 1992–93*, 58).

There are, indeed, countless derogatory statements about humans — as a species and as individuals — throughout Canetti's oeuvre. Yet, these must be read in light of others expressing admiration and love for his kind, for example, in the first part of *Die gerettete Zunge*. Here, the narrator admits that despite the low esteem in which he holds human beings, there is only one thing he truly hates, namely death, mankind's only enemy (*GZ*, 11). Canetti's condemnation of killing, including killing for a cause, was part of his mother's legacy. She had insisted on referring to the First World War as the murdering or slaughtering, "das Morden" (*GZ*, 178). In *Masse und Macht*, he adamantly dismisses the notion that there is a higher meaning, a justifiable purpose to war: "In Kriegen geht es ums Töten . . . Es geht um ein Töten in Haufen. Möglichst viele Feinde werden niedergeschlagen; aus der gefährlichen Masse von lebenden Gegnern soll ein Haufe von Toten werden" (*MM*, 73). When Canetti includes animals in his reflections on killing, he does so disregarding the traditional distinctions between human and non-human beings. Issues traditionally considered, for example, the presence or lack of a soul, the degree of consciousness, language, or the absence or presence of reason, play no part in Canetti's reasoning. In fact, none of the categories on which Western philosophers, theologians, psychologists, and scientists base their hierarchies of species matter to him, most likely because he considers these very hierarchies a rationalization of indefen-

sible acts: war, the death penalty, and euthanasia. Ultimately, the implications of Canetti's thought processes are no less radical than those of the
feminist animal rights advocate Joan Dunayer, who writes that relying on the
definition of mankind based on intellect and brainpower, use of speech, and
symbolic systems exaggerates human uniqueness, and points out that many
nonhuman animals have a highly developed brain. Moreover, many also have
the capacity for abstract reasoning, and some have "the ability to communicate
by means of organized speech." "How would humans fare if expected to learn
another species' method of communication — say that of the bottle-nosed
dolphin?" Dunayer asks.[32]

Aware of the degree to which certain types of killing are validated, Canetti defends his position of radical nonviolence, knowing that there are
people who despise him because he has never killed. At the same time, he
asks himself what will become of the violent human potential of a person
who abstains from using it.

> Alle die ihn verachten, weil er nie getötet hat. D. war der Meinung, daß
> nur einer Mensch ist, der getötet hat. Die Kluft zwischen den "prie-
> sterlichen" Kasten und denen der Krieger und Töter wäre an sich schon
> ungeheuer. Aber dieselben Priester haben noch Tiere getötet, als Op-
> fer. Ob in denen, die unter keinen Umständen töten können, nicht
> schreckliche Kräfte wirksam sind, die die Menschen ihrer nächsten
> Umgebung allmählich umbringen? (*Aufz. 1942–85*, 123)

In short, Canetti regards the proclivity to kill to be ingrained and the ab-
stention from killing a deliberate act of repression. The latter appears to him
absolutely indispensable, as he is concerned about the welfare of animals and
the devastating psychological impact of killing on the surviving humans and
non-humans. Yet, the psychological impact of others' dying seems inescapable.
"Die toten Menschen sind schon zu mächtig in ihm. Was soll aus ihm werden,
wenn die toten Tiere über ihn kommen?" (*F*, 23).

Condemning the subjugation and eradication of the Other under any
circumstances, he frequently ponders how impoverished a world without
animals would be, and whether there are measures to revert the process of
global destruction. For him, re-adjusting intellectual and linguistic habits
takes precedence over concrete measures; thus he recommends that animals
ought to be accorded a more prominent position in human thought to effect
a fundamental change in the discourse on animals, "wie in der Zeit vor ihrer
Unterwerfung" (*F*, 49). Aware that it is impossible to return to a time when
animals occupy a position of sanctity, Canetti recommends as a more modest
measure to pass strict laws to protect them: "Das ist alles, wenig, und doch
das Meiste" (*F*, 49). Since he considers the fate of animals and humans
inextricably linked, he favors interspecies interaction based on equality rather
than patronage. Believing animals to be vulnerable, he suggests for them an

advantageous status to preclude them from being relegated to an inferior position, calling into question the importance of his own species, which he sees as placing the future of all other species in jeopardy. Humanity, according to Canetti, convinced of its pre-eminence, has failed to make the protection of all of life a priority.

Canetti's considerations regarding the long-range consequences of anthropocentrism can in part be understood from his cultural experience. Canetti grew up in an age when Darwin's theory of evolution, anti-vivisectionism, vegetarianism, and the animal protection movement (*Tierschutz*) had changed literature, ethics, and social thought.[33] For example, Emilie Mataja, a feminist novelist and contributor to the publication of the Austrian Humane Society, was one of the many writers involved in the early animal rights movement. She took a passionate stance against the mass killing of birds in upper Italy, and she pleaded for the humane treatment of farm animals. Among Canetti's older and younger contemporaries, there were intellectuals who wrote literary texts featuring animal protagonists. Among those were Marie von Ebner-Eschenbach, the author of the dog novella *Krambambuli* (1887); Franz Kafka, with short stories such as *Die Verwandlung* (1916), *Die Forschungen eines Hundes* (1931) and *Josefine die Sängerin* (1924); Claire Goll, author of *Tagebuch eines Pferdes* (1950), *Die Taubenwitwe* (1952), and *My Sentimental Zoo: Animal Stories* (1942); as well as Gertrud Kolmar, whose poetry and short stories are replete with animal characters, including such works as *Das lyrische Werk* (1955) and *Susanna* (1959; 1997).[34]

In fact, most of those who spoke up for the cause of animal protection and anti-cruelty were involved, as were Ebner-Eschenbach, Goll, and Canetti's wife Veza Canetti, with other progressive movements such as women's emancipation, socialism, pacifism, and initiatives opposing anti-Semitism and slavery, prostitution, and the trafficking of women. Like Canetti they questioned the image of the human species as the crown of creation. Veza Canetti features numerous animal characters in her novel *Die gelbe Straße* (published 1989), which concludes with an episode describing the brutalization of a little girl by a mob of adults and with a sarcastic statement calling into question the superiority of the human species: "Denn der Mensch schreitet aufrecht, die erhabenen Zeichen der Seele ins Gesicht gebrannt."[35] In her last novel *Die Schildkröten*, written immediately after her and her husband's escape to England and published in 1999, sensitivity and concern for the most common animals sets the persecuted Jews apart from the Nazis.[36] She reveals that the fate of the animals and that of Jews follow a parallel course under Nazism.

In Elias Canetti's works all of the pertinent issues concerning the status of animals are addressed, including issues pertaining to food and eating. These latter are central in *Masse und Macht*. Canetti's general aversion to eating calls to mind Kafka's problems with food. In the chapter "Die Einge-weide der Macht," and particularly the subsection "Zur Psychologie des Essens" in *Masse und Macht,* ingesting and digesting are discussed as expressions of power (*MM*, 250–55). Hence Canetti evokes the following utopian vision in his *Aufzeichnungen* in a notation of 1983:

> Er aß zum Schein, um den Gastgeber nicht in Verlegenheit zu bringen. In seinem Lande die Leute hatten sich essen längst abgewöhnt und man hörte nicht das Schreien geschlachteter Tiere. Man lebte von Luft, dort war sie gesunde Nahrung, ihre Aufnahme war nicht an bestimmte Zeiten gebunden, man wußte, nie, dass man aß und Teller wie Gabel und Messer dienten nur als archaischer Schmuck. (*Aufz. 1942–85,* 496)

Equally obvious is Canetti's fascination with actual animals. In "Die Stimmen von Marrakesch" (1967) he terms his encounters with camels "tragisch" — he is deeply saddened, having witnessed their abuse and slaughter. The first sentence of the little volume runs "Dreimal kam ich mit Kamelen in Berührung und es endete jedesmal auf tragische Weise." These experiences render him incapable of speaking about camels for the rest of his journey (*Marrakesch,* 7, 16). On the other hand, he rejoices when he observes the sexual vitality of an abused and neglected donkey, and he concludes the episode titled "Die Lust des Esels" with the words: "Ich wünsche jedem Gepeinigten seines Lust im Elend" (*Marrakesch,* 93). Canetti's work is replete with animal symbolism and mythical animal figures configured as potentialities of the human psyche. Among the many examples cited by Canetti is an Australian myth about humans who transform themselves into different animals — kangaroos, emus, and eagles — to escape a gigantic dog (*MM*, 386–91). Finally, Canetti is concerned with the future of animal species in light of the rapidly progressing devastation of the environment and animal habitats. Foreshadowed in their disappearance, he senses the impending devastation of the world as we know it.

The latter issue ties in with contemporary debates on the environment and animal rights and attests to the far-sightedness of an author whose formative years spanned the era of the First World War. On the one hand, Canetti, who laments that he never embraced an animal, does not and perhaps cannot transcend a more abstract consideration of animals informed by the models according to which his entire work is structured, but which Canetti tries to overcome nonetheless. The duality of human and animal expressed in numerous statements mirrors other polarized concepts such as the "Doppelmassen" of gender, and the living and the dead (*MM*, 67–72). Nineteenth-century thought is for the most part structured according to such polarized models, for example, Bachofen, Nietzsche, Freud, and Weininger, and it proves enormously productive in *Masse und Macht*. At the same time, the polarized categories stand in the way of concrete consideration, preventing a more dynamic approach to the ultimate other, the animal. In the course of his career, Canetti became increasingly aware of the inadequacy of abstractions and metaphors in dealing with other species. The animal rights philosopher Peter Singer questions the term "animal" because it is applied to creatures that bear less resemblance to one another than homo sapiens does to other mammals as well as the usefulness of the standard scientific and philosophical classifications altogether.[37] Even though Canetti does follow the traditional use of the concept "animal," as do most members of his generation, his provocative theses accord him a special place within the debates on humans and animals. Discourses on the environment and power intersect with his analyses, introducing important considerations into the contemporary animal rights debate.

Notes

[1] Elias Canetti, *Aufzeichnungen 1992–1993* (Munich: Hanser, 1996): 93. Cited as *Aufz. 1992–93*. All Canetti quotes follow the Hanser editions. *Aufzeichnungen 1942–1985: Die Provinz des Menschen; Das Geheimherz der Uhr* (1993) cited as *Aufz. 1942–85; Nachträge aus Hampstead: Aus den Aufzeichnungen 1954–1971* (1994) cited as *NH; Die Fliegenpein* (1992), cited as *F; Die Blendung* (rept. Munich: Hanser, 1963), cited as *Blendung; Masse und Macht* (Hamburg: Claassen, 1960), cited as *MM; Die Stimmen von Marrakesch* (1967), cited as *Marrakesch; Die gerettete Zunge* (1977), cited as *GZ*.

[2] Michael Mack, *Anthropology as Memory: Elias Canetti's and Franz Baermann Steiner's Responses to the Shoah* (Tübingen: Niemeyer, 2001), 11.

[3] Brigitte Kronauer, "Nachwort," in *Elias Canetti über Tiere* (Munich: Hanser, 2002), 107–15. Here: 107. Subsequent references to this text will be cited as *Tiere* and the page number.

[4] Animal Rights as opposed to the conventional "Tierschutz." Representatives include philosophers, sociologists and activists such as Peter Singer, Mary Midgley, Carol Adams, Richard Ryder, Marjory Spiegel, Ingrid Newkirk, and Alex Pacheco. The philosophy of "deep vegetarianism," forged by Michael A. Fox in analogy to "deep ecology," attempts to "assess microscopically the macroscopic problems of the human relationship to nature and nonhumans. These issues are receiving considerable attention today because they compel us to reconsider such basic questions as the scope of ethics and the moral significance of someone or something." Michael A. Fox, *Deep Vegetarianism* (Philadelphia: Temple UP, 1999): xix.

[5] LK, "Companion Animals. Question 75." The Animal Rights FAQ. http://www.animal-rights.com/arpage.htm.

[6] Peter Singer, *Animal Liberation* (New York: New York Review, Random House: 1990), vi.

[7] Silke Schmidt-Rinke and Stefan Rinke, "'Das Grundübel alles Bestehenden': Die Todesproblematik in Elias Canettis Roman *Die Blendung*," *Modern Austrian Literature* 31/2 (1998): 81–103; Kristie A. Foell, "July 15, 1927 The Vienna Palace of

Justice Is Burned in a Mass Uprising of Viennese Workers, a Central Experience in the Life and Work of Elias Canetti," in *Yale Companion to Jewish Writing and Thought in German Culture,* ed. Sander L. Gilman and Jack Zipes (New Haven: Yale UP, 1997): 464–70; Peter Glotz, "Der Standort daneben: Elias Canetti und die Gier der Nationen," in *Einladung zur Verwandlung: Essays zu Elias Canettis Masse und Macht,* ed. Michael Kruger (Munich: Hanser, 1995): 578–80; Ritchie Robertson, "Canetti als Anthropologe," in *Einladung zur Verwandlung:* 190–206; Friederike Eigler, "Verwandlung und Machtausübung in der Autobiographie Elias Canettis: Zum Status und zur Funktion autobiographischen Schreibens," Dissertation Abstracts International (DAI), vol. 48/7 (1988), Ann Arbor, MI: 1782A–1783A; Ursula Ruppel, *Der Tod und Elias Canetti* (Hamburg: Europäische Verlagsanstalt, 1995); Kurt Bartsch, Gerhard Melzer, eds., *Elias Canetti, Experte der Macht* (Graz: Droschl, 1985); Dagmar Barnouw, *Elias Canetti* (Stuttgart: Metzler, 1979).

[8] Josef Quack, "Über Elias Canettis Verhältnis zu Karl Kraus: Ein kritischer Vergleich," *Internationales Archiv für Sozialgeschichte der deutschen Literatur* 23/2 (1998): 118–41; Alfred Doppler, "Gestalten und Figuren als Elemente der Zeit- und Lebensgeschichte: Canettis autobiographische Bücher," *Autobiographien in der österreichischen Literatur: Von Franz Grillparzer bis Thomas Bernhard,* ed. Klaus Amann and Karl Wagner (Innsbruck: Studien, 1998): 113–23; Bernhard Greiner, "Akustische Maske und Geborgenheit in der Schrift: Die Sprach-Orientierung der Autobiographie bei Elias Canetti und Walter Benjamin," *Literaturwissenschaftliches Jahrbuch im Auftrage der Görres-Gesellschaft* 34 (1993): 305–25; Lydia Schieth, "Europa-Erinnerung als Rekonstruktion: Autobiographien europäischen Lebens: Elias Canetti und Manès Sperber," in *Suchbild Europa — künstlerische Konzepte der Moderne,* ed. Jürgen Wertheimer (Amsterdam: Rodopi, 1995): 5–17; Harriet Murphy, *Canetti and Nietzsche: Theories of Humor in Die Blendung* (Albany: State U of New York P, 1996); Robert Elbaz and Leah Hadomi, *Elias Canetti, or, the Failing of the Novel* (New York: Peter Lang, 1995); William Collins Donahue, "Elias Canetti's 'Die Blendung' in Literary and Cultural Context," Dissertation Abstracts International (DAI) 56/7, Ann Arbor, MI, 1996; Wolfgang Mieder, "'Die falschesten Redensarten haben den größten Reiz.' Zu Elias Canettis Sprachaphorismen," *Der Sprachdienst* 6/11–12 (1994): 173–80; Anne Fuchs, "Der touristische Blick: Elias Canetti in Marrakesch. Ansatze zu einer Semiotik des Tourismus," in *Reisen im Diskurs: Modelle der literarischen Fremderfahrung von den Pilgerberichten bis zur Postmoderne,* ed. Anne Fuchs, Theo Harden, Eva Juhl (Heidelberg: Winter, 1995): 71–86; David Darby, *Structures of Disintegration: Narrative Strategies in Elias Canetti's Die Blendung* (Riverside: Ariadne, 1992).

[9] Tom Regan, *The Case for Animal Rights* (Berkeley: U of California P, 1983), 9–11. Julien Offray de La Mettrie, *L'homme machine: A Study in the Origins of an Idea* (Princeton: Princeton UP, 1960).

[10] Karl Erich Grözinger, *Kafka und die Kabbala: Das Jüdische in Werk und Denken von Franz Kafka* (Frankfurt a.M.: Eichborn Verlag, 1992), 138, discusses the Cabbalist concept of "Gilgul" denoting beings made up of human and animal characteristics, as well as phases of universal purification which involve animals, plants, minerals, and humans (21). Grözinger comments about Kafka's animal figures: "Der erste Fall ist der Wegfall der Unterscheidungsmerkmale zwischen Mensch und Tier

so dass Menschen zu Tieren, Tiere zu Menschen werden können; der zweite ist der Verlust der allgemein bekannten Gestalt der Lebewesen, der sich in Proportionsverzerrungen oder hybriden Vermischungen verschiedner Tiere bekundet; der dritte ist der Einbruch phatastischer Tiergestalten in eine alltägliche Welt" (137–38). See *Der andere Prozeß: Kafkas Briefe an Felice* (Munich: Hanser, 1965).

[11] See Tony Page, *Buddhism and Animals: A Buddhist Vision of Humanity's Rightful Relationship with the Animal Kingdom* (London: UKAVIS, 1999); Komei Larson, *Buddhism and Respect for Animals* (Mt. Shasta, CA: Shasta Abbey Press, 1980).

[12] Fritz Hippler, dir. *Der ewige Jude* (Tamarelle International Films, 1986).

[13] Boria Sax, *Animals in the Third Reich: Pets, Scapegoats, and the Holocaust* (New York: Continuum, 2000), 159.

[14] Sax, 19–20.

[15] Sax, 120.

[16] Lynda Birke, *Feminism, Animals and Science: The Naming of the Shrew* (Buckingham, Philadelphia: Open UP, 1994): 106.

[17] Birke, 106; 109.

[18] Anne Fuchs, "Elias Canetti's Voices of Marrakesh," *Critical Essays on Elias Canetti,* ed. David Darby (New York: G. K. Hall & Co.), 201–13. Here: 210.

[19] Richard Ryder, *Animal Revolution* (Oxford: B. Blackwell, 1989).

[20] Fox, *Deep Vegetarianism,* 109.

[21] Fox, *Deep Vegetarianism,* 109.

[22] Lawrence Finsen and Susan Finsen, *The Animal Rights Movement in American: From Compassion to Respect* (New York: Twayne: 1994): 254.

[23] Fox, *Deep Vegetarianism,* 155.

[24] Paul Shepard, *The Others: How Animals Made Us Human* (Washington: Island Press, 1996): 316. See also Paul Shepard, *Thinking Animals and the Development of Human Intelligence* (New York: Viking Press, 1978).

[25] Tom Regan (15–16) argues against using language as a criterion, because if the language test held true, "individuals who are unable to use a language lack consciousness. This cannot be true. If all consciousness depended on one's being a language-user, we would be obliged to say that children, before they reach an age when they can speak, cannot be aware of anything. This not only flies in the face of common sense — an appeal that, as noted earlier, Descartes is likely to dismiss as possibly an appeal to prejudice — but, more fundamentally, it makes utterly mysterious, at best, how children could learn to use a language." Regan concludes that "if some humans who lack the potential for language acquisition are conscious, then one cannot deny that animals who lack this potential can be."

[26] Among the exceptions is Edgar Piel's article "Elias Canettis Masse und Macht: Eine phantastische Anthropologie," *Literatur und Kritik* 183–84 (1984): 123–42.

[27] Elias Canetti, *Die Blendung* (1935; rpt. Munich: Hanser, 1963), 436–44.

[28] As is consistently the case in *Die Fliegenpein,* for example page 113.

[29] Akira Mizuta Lippit, *Electric Animal: Toward a Rhetoric of Wildlife* (Minneapolis: U of Minnesota P, 2000), 127.

[30] Lippit, 144.

[31] Lippit, 10.

[32] Joan Dunayer, "Sexist Words, Speciest Roots," *Animals and Women: Feminist Theoretical Explorations,* ed. Carol J. Adams and Josephine Donovan (Duke UP: Durham and London, 1995): 11–31. Here: 21.

[33] Emil Mariott, "Der Vogelmassenmord in Südtirol," *Neues Wiener Tagblatt,* September 22, 1892 and *Erbarm dich deines Viehes* (Innsbruck: Verlag des Thierschutzvereins, 1891).

[34] Marie von Ebner-Eschenbach: *"Die Kapitalistinnen," und zwei andere Novellen* ["Der Muff," "Krambambuli"] (New York, F. S. Crofts, 1928), *Krambambuli und andere Erzählungen* (Stuttgart: Reclam, 1965); Claire Goll: *Die Taubenwitwe* (St. Gallen: Pflugverlag Thal, 1952), *My Sentimental Zoo: Animal Stories* (Mount Vernon, NY: The Peter Pauper Press, 1942) (Original German text: *Ménagerie sentimentale; Tagebuch eines Pferdes* [Thal: Pflugverlag, 1950]), Gertrud Kolmar, "Der Tag der großen Klage," "Gerichtstag totgeplagter Tiere," "Die Kröte," in *Das lyrische Werk* (Munich: Kösel, 1960) 167–68; 159–60.

[35] Veza Canetti, *Die gelbe Straße,* ed. Elias Canetti (Munich: Hanser, 1990).

[36] Veza Canetti, *Die Schildkröten* (Munich: Hanser, 1999).

[37] Singer, *Animal Liberation,* iii.

Historical Contexts

Canetti, Roustchouk, and Bulgaria:
The Impact of Origin on Canetti's Work

Svoboda Alexandra Dimitrova and Penka Angelova

T HE CONNECTION BETWEEN Elias Canetti's perception of places and events
and their representation in his works has prompted us to investigate the
geographical and historical reality beyond the text in Canetti's autobiographical account *Die gerettete Zunge: Geschichte einer Jugend* (1977).[1] We
shall trace the history of Canetti's birthplace, Roustchouk, Bulgaria,[2] where
he spent his childhood years from 1905 until 1911, and explore how the
memory of Roustchouk is represented in his autobiographical, fictional, and
philosophical writings in an effort to outline the way these early experiences
in his native city inspired major themes in his work. We will also examine the
story behind the Canetti's (his father's family's) and the Arditti's (his mother's
family's) arrival in Roustchouk more than half a century before Elias's birth,
and the way the city's history is intertwined with these family histories.
Indeed, the history of Sephardic families like the Canettis is an integral part
of Roustchouk's history, and Canetti's autobiography calls for an assessment
of Bulgarian-Jewish relations as they evolved over time.[3] Of particular importance for Canetti's work is the fate of the Jews in Bulgaria during the
Second World War and the Holocaust. Canetti's thoughts and ideas revolve
around mass movements, mass destruction, the paranoid leader, and power,
and although he did not identify specific events, his worldview was shaped
by the trauma inflicted on Eastern European Jewry by the National Socialists. Even though he had taken exile in England, the fate of his family and
friends in Central and Eastern Europe concerned him deeply. This essay
seeks to shed light on the situation in Bulgaria during these difficult times.

Despite German authors' longstanding fascination with travel and ad-
venture, Bulgaria played only a minor role in German novels and travel
writings. The first known representation of Bulgaria in German literature is
Heinrich von Neustadt's *Apollonius* (1314),[4] a work written prior to the
1364 Turkish invasion of Bulgaria, when Bulgaria was a powerful and influential country. Heinrich describes the courageous and powerful Bulgarian
king, Abacuck, who threatens a northeastern European country named
Armenia.[5] The first mention of Roustchouk occurs in the context of a conflict. *Apollonius* makes reference to different ethnicities in the Balkans: the

Bulgarian king is associated with both Bulgaria and "grosse Romaney," but we also find mention of another king of Romania,[6] and the lines of distinction between Bulgarians and Romanians are thus blurred. Historically, this confusion may arise from the frequent change of rule in this Danube region before the 1364 Turkish occupation, when these territories stood alternately under the control of Bulgarian and Romanian kings — a pattern we will see repeated in the Middle Ages.

To the best of our knowledge, Canetti was the first notable German-language writer who was not only native to Bulgaria, but also claimed it as his homeland. Unlike others born and raised outside Bulgaria, he never considered Bulgaria an exotic country or a foreign territory to be discovered and explored. Rather, in his autobiographical texts Bulgaria is an integral component of his life and character; it is "the divine aspect of his existence," as he confirmed in an unpublished interview with his Bulgarian translator Wenzeslav Konstantinov.[7] The history of Roustchouk, then, inasmuch as it is central to Canetti's own personal history and informs his writing, is of particular interest here. The first settlements in this area occurred during the first century A.D. It was marked on a Roman military map as the castle Pristis (also Sexaginta Pristis).[8] In the Middle Ages Roustchouk was destroyed and rebuilt several times. It was mentioned by name in a pilgrim's travelogue in 1380 as a fort located between two cities, "the Bulgarian Russy and the Romanian Jorgo" (Giurgiu in Romanian).[9] A military map from 1388 records it as one of the twenty-four Bulgarian fortresses on the Danube, and it was the last Bulgarian city to be occupied by the Turks in that year,[10] while the rest of Bulgaria had already been conquered in 1364. In 1445, a Burgundian knight passed the city and described it as a fortress with four towers. During the following centuries, the city was ruled mainly by the Turks, but because of its central location on the Balkan Peninsula it also attracted Wallachians and Russians, who destroyed it several times. The fortress was conquered and destroyed in 1461 by the Wallachian voivode Vladislav Zepesh (ruled 1456–62, known also as Tepes).[11]

In the sixteenth century Roustchouk became a trade center on par with Dubrovnik, Venice, and Genoa; a traveler reported that a huge bazaar took place weekly and that all the townspeople spoke Wallachian, Moldavian, and Bulgarian.[12] The city was mentioned by Dubrovnik merchants as a crossroads of trade as well as in sources describing the victories of the Wallachian voivode Michail Viteazul (1558–1601, also known as Michael the Brave).[13] Viteazul liberated the city from the Turks in 1594 and ruled over it for two years, proclaiming it a part of Wallachia.[14] In the following centuries Russia engaged in numerous wars against the Turks. The Russian army liberated the city once in 1773, again in 1810, and finally in 1878. During the seventeenth and eighteenth centuries the city was re-named several times: it was called Roussig, Roussico, Rotchig, and Ruzchuck;[15] travelers described it as a city with six thousand houses, a fortress, a customs-house, a fountain, baths, two chans (hotels), three hundred stores, and a port.[16]

During the nineteenth century the Balkans became a subject of debate among European politicians. After 1872 Otto von Bismarck attempted to strike an alliance with Austro-Hungary and Russia. Several years later, in 1878, Bulgaria was liberated from Turkish occupation by the Russian Army, and the Bismarck Alliance, represented in the Congress of Berlin, placed a German Prince, Alexander von Battenberg, in power. In general, however, the Balkan region remained Europe's backyard, and a threat and "gunpowder barrel" as Bismarck called it.[17] Though the region had often been envisioned as a strange and dangerous place, the greater powers of France, Germany, and Russia engaged in continuous struggles to gain influence in the Balkans. Partly as a result of these ongoing disputes, the Balkan countries — Bulgaria included — were not particularly enticing as literary subject matter. At least not in the literature of German high culture, for Bulgaria lies outside the boundaries of imagination that otherwise included most of the Central and Southern European countries.

At the turn of the nineteenth to the twentieth century Roustchouk was a small but important port on the Danube, marking the border between Bulgaria and Romania. Elias Canetti was born there on July 25, 1905, and lived there until 1911 with his mother Mathilde Canetti (née Arditti), his father, Jacques Canetti, and his brother Nissim (*GZ*, 44). With the birth of his brother Georg, the family moved to Manchester, England, where his father hoped to succeed in business. Even more important was the couple's desire to escape their despotic father and father-in-law (*GZ* 44–45). At home, the Sephardic family spoke Ladino, a language derived from medieval Spanish and spoken by Sephardic Jews mainly in the Balkans, Turkey, and the Near East, and Canetti learned Bulgarian from the family's housemaids (*GZ* 17, also Canetti in *Gespaltene Zukunft*, 103).

The history of the Canetti family goes back to 1492, when the ancestors of both father and mother were forced to leave Spain under the edict of Isabella the Catholic and Ferdinand of Aragon, which expelled 35,000 families from Spain because of their Jewish origin.[18] Many of these families eventually settled in Turkey. At this point, Bulgaria had been part of the Turkish Empire for a century and a half. For almost four hundred years, the Canetti family had lived in Adrianople (Edirne in Turkish), where Canetti's father Jacques was born, and the family moved to Roustchouk in the 1860s,[19] when it still belonged to the Turkish Empire. The period when the Canettis moved to Bulgaria was one of growth and significant economic development for Roustchouk. According to the city's historian Vassil Doikov, in 1864 Roustchouk had been chosen as the capital of the Danube region and named "Tuna-Vilaet" (Danube Region) by the governor of the Vilaet, Midhad Pasha. This region included thirteen *sandjacks* (districts) with several major cities in the South (Nish, Pirot, and Sofia) and in the East (Varna and Tulcha). Midhad Pasha was one of the leading figures of *Tanzimat* reforms,[20] which affected the double taxation of Bulgarian subjects as well as the educational system in Bulgaria, and had visited Paris, London, Brussels, Vienna, and other European cities in 1858. He was a precursor of the Young Turk movement, which modernized and westernized Turkey, and was keenly aware of the fact that, from a European perspective, Turkey was underdeveloped.[21] Midhad Pasha undertook far-reaching reforms in urban and social development: he eliminated corruption, was instrumental in the construction of new public and municipal buildings such as the railway station, city and consular offices. He included younger men (between forty and fifty) in government affairs, and advocated equality for all subjects of the Turkish Empire.[22]

Midhad Pasha sought to rescue the Turkish monarchy through these reforms and to make it competitive with Central and Western Europe. In the four years of his rule (1864–68), Midhad Pasha transformed Roustchouk into a modern city. His ideas, however, elicited great controversy within the Turkish Empire, and he was deposed after only four years. Some historians compare his importance to that of the Russian Tsar Peter the Great (1672–1725). During Midhad Pasha's rule, the first Bulgarian railroad was constructed connecting Roustchouk with Bulgaria's major city on the Black Sea, Varna; the first hospital, the first post office, and the first nursing home were built, as well as four hotels. Roustchouk became a member of the Danube Ship Society and founded its own local ship association. These dynamic improvements attracted developers, merchants, and businessmen, among them Jewish families from Turkey like the Canettis.

The Jewish community in Bulgaria is said to date back to the time before the destruction of the second Temple (70 B.C.).[23] The first documented Jewish presence is a tombstone found near the town of Nikopol by the Danube River. These Jews were known as *Romagnotes,* and their language as Ladino.[24] Jews had settled on Bulgarian soil as early as during the Middle Ages, but the most significant growth of the Jewish community came after the expulsion of Jews from Spain in 1492.[25] The Turkish Sultan allowed Jews fleeing the Inquisition to settle in the Ottoman Empire, where they were treated with tolerance both by the authorities and by the population of the Balkan Peninsula.[26] These Ladino-speaking immigrants, known as *Sepharades* or *Separdes,* are the ancestors of almost ninety percent of the Jews in Bulgaria today.[27] Jews were mentioned for the first time in Sofia by the Catholic Archbishop Petar Bogdan, who was of Bulgarian descent, and who found, during his visit to Roustchouk in 1640, that most of the customs officers at Danube ports were Jews.[28]

Abraham and Moiss Canetti, the brothers of Elias Canetti's grandfather (also named Elias) were the first members of the Canetti family to move to Roustchouk, in the 1860s. In 1869 they were members of a delegation that met with the Austro-Hungarian Emperor Franz Josef I when he made a stop in Roustchouk on his way to Constantinople.[29] Shortly thereafter, Abraham Canetti was appointed Consul of Austria-Hungary in Roustchouk.[30] Elias Canetti's grandfather and namesake followed his brothers a few years later. Canetti's mother, Mathilde Arditti, was born in Roustchouk. She was the granddaughter of the prominent historian Abraham ben Israel Rosanes, nicknamed Abir, who also founded the first secular Jewish school in the city in 1869.[31] His ancestors seem to have moved to Turkey from the Catalonian city Rosas in 1492, the year of the expulsion of the Jews.[32]

Situated as it is on a crossroads for trade, Roustchouk has been a multi-ethnic site since the Middle Ages. It eventually became a major stop along several important trade routes from Central Europe to the Orient along the Danube River, and was accessible from Vienna by boat, foot, and carriage, and, during Canetti's time, by train. This route continued from Roustchouk to Varna on the Black Sea, and from there by ship to Constantinople. It was common to meet foreign merchants, businessmen, and workers on the streets of this busy city and to hear as many as twelve to fifteen languages: Bulgarian, Turkish, Armenian, Hebrew, Yiddish, Wallachian, Greek, German, English, Spanish, Russian, among others.[33] Roustchouk had four churches, five mosques, and three synagogues. This development fostered a natural multiculturalism and multilingualism as well as tolerance and recognition of the other, acknowledgment and respect between different religions and cultures — all of which would later pose a substantial obstacle to the realization of the Nazi's "Final Solution." After Bulgaria's liberation from Turkish rule in 1878, major improvements continued to be made in the city of Roustchouk.

As mentioned earlier, the twenty-two-year-old German nobleman Alexander von Battenberg (1857–93) was chosen to be king of Bulgaria (1879–93) by the Congress of Berlin. The Congress of Berlin was comprised of several European nations and formed in the attempt to resolve the Balkan conflict between Bulgaria and Turkey, a conflict that arose from Bulgaria's revolt against Turkish rule and in which more than 15,000 Bulgarians were killed. In 1877 Russia declared war on Turkey, and in 1878 Bulgaria was liberated. During the Russian-Turkish war Battenberg fought with the Russian army. He chose Sofia as the capital of Bulgaria because of its central location. However, he spent much more time in Roustchouk, because he considered Sofia just a small dirty village. In 1882, the king initiated the construction of the city hall, the first public building in recently consolidated Bulgaria. This and four other buildings were designed by the Viennese architect Franz Grünanger, and new streets and buildings were constructed in accordance with the city's increasing economic importance. In keeping with the cosmopolitan identity of the citizens of Roustchouk, foreign — mostly Austrian — and eventually Bulgarian architects, construction engineers, and sculptors were invited to create a new, modern European architectural image for the city. Even though Bulgarians were in favor of emancipation, officers rebelled against Battenberg in 1893, and he was deposed.

Another German nobleman, Ferdinand of Saxe-Coburg and Gotha (1861–1948), grandnephew of Ernest I of Saxe-Coburg-Gotha, was chosen — again by the Congress of Berlin, though against Russia's will — to govern Bulgaria, which he did from 1908 to 1918. Canetti wrote that Tsar Ferdinand I was a "friend of the Jews" (*GZ*, 11), probably because many of the Jews were prosperous merchants and the king had maintained good relationships with them. Ferdinand was also aware of recommendations and rules introduced by the Congress of Berlin. The Berlin Treaty included a clause that obligated the Balkan countries "to give equal rights to Jews."[34] Roustchouk's city center was modernized by architects from Austria, Germany, Greece, Armenia, and Italy, among them Nino Rossetti, Georg Lang, Edward Winter, Spiros Valsamaki, Negohos Bedrossian, and Edwin Petricki. They designed projects in various styles: Baroque, Empire, Renaissance, Rococo, Biedermeier: a mixture typical of *fin-de-siècle* Europe;[35] the same amalgam of architectural style found in Vienna's Ringstrasse is characteristic of Roustchouk. The city's forward-looking, completely western European orientation was epitomized by a building named "Chicago," which was constructed in 1900 by a Bulgarian Jew, Solomon Blaustein, who financed the construction with money he had earned from selling Bulgarian postage stamps at the Chicago World's Fair in 1893.[36] This building expanded the imagination of the city's citizens, adding intercontinental visions.

Canetti's grandparents' family home in Roustchouk was designed in 1882 by the architect Spiros Valsamaki (*GZ* 13). Canetti mentions a three-story house, but there were in fact only two floors. Canetti's parents' house was built in the garden courtyard of his grandparents' home, and it was here that Elias spent the first six years of his life. It is now a Canetti museum and houses the head office of the International Canetti Society. The Canettis' merchandise store, built in 1898 and known in Roustchouk as *"la butica,"* the shop, figures prominently in Canetti's childhood memories as the place where, playing with grains, he had a sudden insight into the phenomenon of masses as opposed to the individual. The building ranks among the most attractive architectural sights of the city. Since 2002, the building has served as the Elias Canetti cultural center, which includes a Viennese-style coffee-house. Architecture was not the only element imported and implanted into the city. Fashions, home furnishings, city dance balls, matinees, concerts, and coffeehouses were similarly influenced and defined by Viennese tastes.

Like the coffeehouses in Vienna and Paris, Roustchouk's coffeehouses were characterized by a mix of oriental and European influences. They served as places for social interaction, where guests played cards, dominoes, and billiards, or read the newspapers. The coffeehouse owned by the Armenian Ohanes Enkarlijan served as a club for merchants, and was later transformed into the first Bulgarian chamber of commerce. In another coffeehouse located on Knjajevska Street, the first cinematic screening in Bulgaria took place in 1897.[37] The improvements of the late nineteenth century drastically altered the city's appearance and distinguished it from the southern Bulgarian cities like Plovdiv, which was constructed in the typical southern style called Bulgarian Baroc and built mainly by Bulgarian architects in the tradition of the Bulgarian Renaissance, namely with carved wooden ceilings and ornately decorated niches and walls. Following the model of Paris and Vienna, Roustchouk's citizens also wanted well-constructed streets, and spent the extraordinary sum of 650,000 silver leva to pave some of the main streets with stones from Marseilles.

The economic and financial development also brought forth an educated middle class. This social stratum had its roots in the Bulgarian Renaissance. Roustchouk attracted over twenty foreign bank branches and more than sixty trade representatives. Austro-Hungary, Russia, England, France, and Italy established consulates there; Germany, Belgium, the Netherlands, and Spain opened honorary consulates.[38] The new bourgeoisie made great efforts to integrate European culture into their social life. By the time Canetti was born, close ties had been established between Vienna and Roustchouk, and the city was called "little Vienna" in allusion to its pro-Western orientation and self-identification as a European city. The term also suggests Vienna's interest in expanding its influence further east. Vienna and Viennese culture were the model, the ideal, and the measuring stick for everything good, worthy, and desirable in a city. The new ideas and inspiration coming from Vienna encouraged Roustchouk's citizens to build their city as a European city par excellence. When Canetti writes "und von der Donau war immerwährend die Rede" (GZ, 11), he implies that people's attention was constantly drawn to the river as an important part of their everyday life and their connection with the rest of Europe. The river represented a two-way channel for culture and trade. It was and still is the most international waterway in Europe, connecting ten European countries: Germany, Austria, Hungary, Slovakia, Croatia, Serbia, Rumania, Bulgaria, Moldova and Ukraine. Geographers list more than forty ethnic groups living along the Danube, and four capital cities — Vienna, Bratislava, Budapest, and Belgrade — lie on its banks.[39] Despite the prevailing paradigm of the nation state, the Danube was both a border and a means of communication: it separated, yet formed a link between peoples and cultures. In Nazi-dominated Europe, the Danube was used to transport Jews from all over Europe to concentration camps. In other words, the significance of the river changed, and during the years of 1941 to 1944 it was a route to death, a topic which we will discuss later in this essay.

Cultural life in Roustchouk was yet another aspect of the psychological landscape of the city, and an indication of the integration of European culture into Bulgarian life. The citizens of Roustchouk formed a civil society interested in culture and education, particularly German and Austrian high culture. As early as 1866, following the example of the cultural society *Urania*,[40] the educational and literary society *Zoura* was founded and began its activities with theatrical performances. The idea of the German and Austrian *Urania* was born in the nineteenth century, when scientists and industrialists were searching for ways to impart knowledge to the people in a popular manner. *Urania* societies existed in Vienna, Berlin, Budapest, and other large cities. Between the world wars the most famous presenters and speakers at the Vienna *Urania* included Heinrich Hertz, Max Planck, Albert Einstein, Karl Kraus, Hermann Broch, and Canetti.[41] The example of Canetti's parents reveals that Vienna, home of the Burgtheater and a world famous opera, served not only for Bulgaria but for all of the countries along the Danube as a cultural model. The Bulgarian *Zoura*, in keeping with the ideals of the Vienna *Urania*, aimed at familiarizing the public with contemporary Central and Western European culture and providing a broad-based popular education. *Zoura* was one of the major forces in destabilizing Ottoman rule in Bulgaria, and it represented a major entranceway for cultural imports from Vienna and Bucharest. Musical ensembles, the Bucharest Theater, and the theater troupes of the *Urania* visited the city.

Before long, the need for a theater building in Roustchouk became dire. In one of the new hotels, the Reformatory House, a stage was erected for the performances of traveling theater groups and musicians. The same venue was used for dance lessons, including the waltz, which was fashionable in Vienna. Soon a local drama troupe performed on the stage of the literary society *Zoura*, and theater became one of the city's primary cultural assets. Very soon, in addition to the theatrical life, cinema arrived in Roustchouk: it was one of the first ten cities worldwide where cinematic productions were screened.[42]

Thus theater and, later, cinema played an important role in Roustchouk. On October 10, 1879, one year after its liberation from Ottoman rule, the first Bulgarian theater society was founded. According to its archival documents, its main concern was "to portray heroes of recent and distant history, and thus to serve the national consolidation."[43] In 1897, the year most of the city construction was completed, at the suggestion of the school board, the literary society *Zoura*, and the theater society, the city council decided to build a theater. The plan was to identify a site that would make the building a source of income for the schools, so it was called the "income building" or "money-earning building" (*dohodna sgrada* in Bulgarian). Because it was conceived of as an "income" building, the theater also contained a casino, stores, and a beer tavern, and the *Zoura* Society found its new home there as well. On the second floor, there was a stage for theater performances, balls, matinees, and concerts. In short, it was a center for socializing, education, and culture. The theater was built on the city's edge, the former site of the bazaar. The choice of this location was indicative of the transformation of a small town into a big city: in small oriental cities, the bazaar is the locus of social interaction; in big Western cities it is the theater or the stadium. The new building was completed in 1902, so that it was in existence during Canetti's childhood, and it displaced the city center to where it remains today. Together with the sculpture *Statue of Liberty* (*Statujata na svobodata* in Bulgarian) created by the Florentine architect and sculptor Arnoldo Zocki in 1908, it shaped Roustchouk's central square, now the nexus of sixteen streets, none more important than the others. All other buildings were rearranged around the new center as if in reverence to these two structures. The Viennese architect Raul-Paul Brank designed the theater building, while Georg Lang, also from Vienna, completed the project.[44] Symbolically, the new theater building combined the Bulgarian Renaissance tradition and the Viennese theatrical tradition. The new bourgeoisie wanted to show up in a new robe: the robe of European culture and cosmopolitanism. But it also knew that it was situated on Europe's margins. For Canetti the constellation of "here" *and* "there" was of particular importance: "Die übrige Welt hieß dort Europa, und wenn jemand die Donau hinauf nach Wien fuhr, sagte man, er fährt nach Europa" (*GZ* 11). Though "here" and "there" did not meet, they were connected by the Danube.

1911 marked the end of Elias Canetti's childhood in Bulgaria. The first volume of Canetti's autobiography, *Die gerettete Zunge: Geschichte einer Jugend*, was published in 1977, and serves here as a point of departure for exploring his major themes. The book's opening passages immediately convey the experience of multiculturalism, multilingualism, and sensuality so integral to the author's childhood environment and reflected in his writing throughout his life. In *Die gerettete Zunge* the aging writer describes the city of Roustchouk as follows:

> Rustschuk, an der unteren Donau, wo ich zur Welt kam, war eine wunderbare Stadt für ein Kind, und wenn ich sage, daß sie in Bulgarien liegt, gebe ich eine unzulängliche Vorstellung von ihr, denn es lebten dort Menschen der verschiedensten Herkunft, an einem Tag konnte man sieben oder acht Sprachen hören. Außer den Bulgaren, die oft vom Lande kamen, gab es noch viele Türken, die ein eigenes Viertel bewohnten und an diesen angrenzend war das Viertel der Spaniolen, das unsere. Es gab Griechen, Albanesen, Armenier, Zigeuner. Vom gegenüberliegenden Ufer der Donau kamen Rumäner . . . Es gab vereinzelt auch Russen. (*GZ* 10)[45]

As a young child Canetti was not consciously aware of this diversity and its social and political implications, but he was exposed to it and he felt it. He remembers persons of diverse ethnical background living around him:

there were, among others, the servants, a Cherkessian and an Armenian, and a Russian who was his mother's best friend (*GZ* 10). Roustchouk had neighborhoods of Turks, Sephardic Jews, Bulgarians, and Gypsies, and yet there were no ghettos. The history and geography of the city provided the multiethnicity and multilingualism that created the miraculous image of Roustchouk in Canetti's memoirs.

According to Canetti everything in Roustchouk was in motion. As a boy he experienced fear, safety, and familiarity without demarcation, limitation, or cultural conflict. From the temporal distance of his memoirs he sees Bulgaria neither as an alienated homeland nor as an exotic place. A feeling of the strange and exotic is evoked only in his depictions of older people. There are, for example, the oriental elements in the lives of his grandparents in the chapter entitled "Das Haus des Türken." The title emphasizes the oriental background of his paternal grandfather and creates a distance from which Canetti proceeds to describe his father's ancestral home. There is the grandmother sitting on a Turkish sofa smoking and drinking black coffee, and there is the patriarch as well, who demands his sons' subservience and admiration. Both Canettis come across as exotic and are at the same time part of the author's self and history (*GZ* 28).

In the "miraculous" city of Roustchouk, Canetti perceived events and images of phenomena he would later encounter in other cities: "Alles, was ich später erlebt habe, war in Rustschuk schon einmal geschehen" (*GZ* 10). In this multilingual environment with its religious diversity, the child gradually became aware of his own difference — that between his Jewish home and a predominantly Christian society. These early experiences informed his future writing. In his novel *Die Blendung* (1935) Canetti evokes a chaos that calls to mind the confusing situation of his home environment. In his dramas, he similarly draws on the multilingual experience of his youth. The failure of individual characters or groups to understand one another due to their differences in diction and expression is a key element in Canetti's plays. Dialogues are not used primarily to convey a message or an idea. Rather they enact the confrontation between distinct linguistic patterns that reveal particular mentalities. Canetti's use of language is designed to create distinct dialogue partners, "akustische Masken," as he calls them in "Akustische Maske und Maskensprung. Materialien zu einer Theorie des Dramas," an interview with Manfred Durzak.[46] Canetti compares the acoustic mask to the fingerprint: It not only serves to identify each individual, it also serves as a means to constitute identity and to reproduce a specific mentality:

> Jeder Mensch verfüge über einen bestimmten Wortschatz, Redewendungen und Satzfiguren, die seine sprachliche Präsentation unbewusst strukturieren, so daß man einen Menschen am exaktesten sprachlich

erfasse, wenn man seine akustische Maske reproduziere. ("Akustische Maske und Maskensprung," 19)

Canetti's use of characterization through linguistic patterns places him in close association with late twentieth-century avant-garde authors such as Thomas Bernhard and Elfriede Jelinek. In his interview with Durzak, he also comments that his entire oeuvre bears dramatic characteristics: "Ich glaube, es ist im Kern alles, was ich mache, dramatischer Natur."[47]

Canetti experienced the linguistic diversity of Roustchouk as a fascinating Babylonian confusion. Later in his *Aufzeichnungen 1942–48,* he writes: "Die Tatsache, dass es *verschiedene* Sprachen gibt, ist die unheimlichste Tatsache der Welt. [. . .] Die Geschichte vom Turm zu Babel ist die Geschichte des zweiten Sündenfalls."[48] While Canetti was in Roustchouk, the Babylonian confusion was an integral part of a colorful and diverse life. It lent flavor to everyday life and made it memorable. In his city all languages were admitted. In his home as well as in Bulgarian families in general, at least two different idioms were spoken: a traditional, older one in the family circle, and in public, a modern, urban language that included foreign words and neologisms.[49] Canetti's situation was special insofar as tradition and familiarity were represented by Ladino, an altogether different language, rather than by the Bulgarian vernacular, but it was not enough to create in him a separate consciousness. The Babylonian confusion of his early years continued in his later life, when he chose the German language as his creative medium and continued to write in this language even though he resided in England. He uses the Babylon metaphor to express the convergence of myth and social reality. Babylon remained Canetti's favorite topos of ever-changing reality (*Aufz. 1942–48,* 21).

In *Die Gerettete Zunge* he describes the multilingual environment in Roustchouk: "Es war oft von Sprachen die Rede, sieben oder acht verschiedene wurden allein in unserer Stadt gesprochen, etwas davon verstand jeder . . . Jeder Zählte die Sprachen auf, die er kannte, es war wichtig, viele von ihnen zu beherrschen, man konnte durch ihre Kenntnis sich selbst oder das Leben anderer Menschen retten" (*GZ* 38). The acquisition of foreign languages was not only a precondition for interethnic communication, but communicating in more than one language and changing registers as one spoke were considered desirable skills by the citizens of Roustchouk. The city was the place where Canetti experienced the phenomenon of the crowd for the first time, an experience which in the biblical tradition is closely associated with the Babylonian. This experience was formative for his later work. His early crowd experiences included a crowd of Gypsies, a crowd of relatives waiting for the end of the world, and a crowd of people running toward a burning house, sweeping young Canetti along in its mad rush. Finally, there was a crowd of children following a man who thought he was a chicken (*GZ*

15, 22–24, 33–35, 39–40). Encapsulated in these instances are the different types of crowds that Canetti later examined in *Masse und Macht* as "Festmasse," "stockende Masse," "Hetzmasse," and "Fluchtmasse" (*MM* 13–79).

In *Die gerettete Zunge* Canetti recalls the sensation of running his hand through the sacks of grain in his grandfather's store:

> Ich durfte, wenn meine Hände sauber waren, hineingreifen und die Körner fühlen. Das war ein angenehmes Gefühl, ich fühlte die Hand mit Körnern, hob sie hoch, roch daran und ließ die Körner langsam wieder herunterrinnen; das tat ich oft, [. . .]und war schwer von den Säcken wegzubringen. (*GZ* 14)

Canetti later related this experience to his subsequent definitions of crowd characteristics such as equality and density. He also linked the individual grains to the individual person, and discusses in *Masse und Macht* how the single kernel of grain becomes transformed into a part of the larger whole:

> Die Herkunft des Korns aus Haufen, dem Saatgut, ist so wichtig und bezeichnend wie die Haufen von Körnern, in die es schließlich mündet . . . es hat etwas mit dem zu tun wie das Individuum in der Masse verschwindet und verschmilzt. (*MM* 99)

In Canetti's crowd theory, he uses kernels of grain as well as fire, sea, rain, forest, wind, and sand as metaphors for aspects of the crowd (*MM* 87).[50] Through his experience of witnessing the house fire, Canetti also became aware of the power of the elements, which his experience told him was as overpowering as that of the masses. Again, an original experience, in this case his first experience of fire, assumed universal significance and was later related to other events, such as the burning of the Vienna Palace of Justice. The original network of images and pictures on which Canetti's insights were based was first constructed in Roustchouk:

> [. . .] und da sah ich zum ersten Mal ein brennendes Haus. Es war schon weit heruntergebrannt, Balken stürzten ein und Funken sprühten. Es ging gegen Abend, es wurde allmählich dunkel und das Feuer schien immer heller. Aber was mir weit mehr Eindruck machte als das brennende Haus, waren die Menschen, die sich darum bewegten. Sie sahen klein und schwarz aus dieser Entfernung aus, es waren sehr viele und sie rannten alle durcheinander. (*GZ* 35–36)

As we see later in conjunction with the burning of the Vienna Palace of Justice, Canetti was particularly moved by the social chaos the fire caused. An important element in Canetti's experience of the burning house in Roustchouk is his observation of the way others took advantage of the homeowners' misfortune. The maid, witnessing the "kleine schwarze Figuren," who were "tief gebückt unter der Last eckiger Gegenstände" calls out "Diebe! Das sind Diebe!" (*GZ* 36).

In his interview with Joachim Schickel, Canetti recalled his first confrontation with chaos, or better, disorder, as something colorful, varied, and thus challenging: "Ich kam nach dem Balkan, wo man ein sehr buntes, reiches Leben hatte, in England in ein überaus geordnetes Leben hinein. Ein Haus wie das andere, eine Strasse wie die andere . . ." (*GZ*, 109). The disorder of the south, notably Bulgaria, was the lens through which he was able to recognize the order of the north, in this case England. Only later does chaos come to stand for war: "Das Chaos hat jede Anziehungskraft verloren. [. . .] Das Chaos steht für Krieg. Ich verachte den Krieg noch mehr, als ich ihn hasse" (*Aufz. 1942–48*, 99). Here Canetti constructs a demarcation line between the "colorful" disorder of the Orient and the chaos of war. The early experience of the fire provides a basis for sketching the main characteristics of the crowd in *Masse und Macht*. In *Die gerettete Zunge*, Canetti could not precisely identify what it was that moved him in direction of the fire: the fire itself, or the direction of the crowd's motion:

> Mir wurde ein wenig bang so ganz alleine, auch zog es mich selbst — vielleicht zum Feuer, vielleicht noch mehr in die Richtung, in die ich alle laufen sah. (*GZ* 35)

This perception of movement toward something — of "direction" or *die Richtung* — gained significance later, when he marked it as the third characteristic of crowd in *Masse und Macht:* "Die Masse braucht eine Richtung. Sie ist in Bewegung und bewegt sich auf etwas zu. Die Richtung, die allen Angehörigen gemeinsam ist, stärkt das Gefühl von Gleichheit" (*MM* 30–31). The narrative of the crowd experience occasioned by a fire in *Die Gerettete Zunge* is framed in such a way that it seems to anticipate not only the burning of the Vienna Palace of Justice on June 15, 1927, but also central themes in *Die Blendung* and *Masse und Macht*. Finally, Roustchouk signified to Canetti the place of his origins, his homeland. Such a localized sense of home calls to mind the experience of Austrian authors of the eighteenth and nineteenth centuries, most notably Franz Grillparzer and his affection for Vienna.[51] For the polyglot Canetti, however, every new city where he spent a longer period of time became part of his larger homeland as well. For example, in 1945 he described Vienna as his "real home city" and Zurich as a kind of paradise from which he did not want to be expelled:

> Die einzig vollkommen glücklichen Jahre, das Paradies in Zürich, waren zu Ende. Vielleicht wäre ich glücklich geblieben, hätten sie mich nicht fortgerissen. Es ist aber wahr, daß ich andere Dinge erfuhr als die, die ich im Paradies kannte. Es ist wahr, daß ich, wie der früheste Mensch, durch die Vertreibung aus dem Paradies erst entstand. (*GZ* 330)

Canetti's concept of identity evolved from the Swiss context in conjunction with his acquisition of the German language forced upon him by his mother, and identity plays an important role in his autobiographical writings. Canetti was cognizant of the fact that, in addition to inherited factors, character formation occurs in the context of the many different cultural experiences and coincidences to which an individual is exposed.

Canetti was the only intellectual and literary author of note whose background combined the languages associated with the expulsions of the Jews from Spain in the fifteenth and from Germany in the twentieth century, Ladino and German. Notwithstanding his command of several other languages, Canetti made the decision to write in German. In his interview with Horst Bienek he states that he took the German language along with him exactly the way his ancestors had taken their Ladino when leaving Spain centuries before (*GZ*, 103). In other words, Canetti characterized himself as a writer in German, first as a matter of choice and then as a matter of inner necessity. Linked to his choice is the notion of transformation: a traveler's attitudes and outlooks change when he encounters foreign countries and speaks in new languages. At first he is an outsider who acquires the foreign culture, and then he becomes an insider who discovers a new homeland.[52]

This dynamic view of cultural identity seems to have influenced Canetti's relationship with his father. The father-son conflict, written about so obsessively in German literature, is virtually absent from his work. Rather, in his autobiographical narrative Canetti attaches himself to teachers everywhere, and he enters apprenticeships with both men and women. The father-son relationship is portrayed as one due the highest admiration, and a conflict between Canetti and his father is never mentioned. Having associated his first vivid experiences with Roustchouk, Canetti encounters cities such as Manchester, Vienna, and Frankfurt with an already established framework.

> Es wird mir schwer gelingen, von der Farbigkeit dieser frühen Jahren in Rustschuk, von seinen Passionen und Schrecken, eine Vorstellung zu geben. Alles, was ich später erlebt habe, war in Rustschuk schon einmal geschehen. (*GZ* 11)

With Roustchouk as his point of departure Canetti designed a home country that covers all of Europe. His cosmopolitan homeland calls to mind the geography of Ashkenaz, the homeland conceptualized by European Jews.[53] Nowhere is there an axis or division, nowhere is there an "other." Canetti's supranationalism — "Plurinationalismus" as he calls it in the *Aufzeichnungen 1942–48* (99) is mirrored in the supranational appeal of his work and life. Seven nations supported his nomination for the Nobel Prize: Bulgaria, Germany, England, Austria, Israel, Spain, and Switzerland, countries he had resided in or visited. Canetti's multiple identities include the following: he had British and Swiss dual citizenship; he escaped from Austria with a Turkish passport, and he considered himself part of the Austrian literary tradition, while critics often characterized him as a German-Jewish writer. It is customary for each Nobel-winning author's country of origin to be inscribed on the back of his or her chair in the hall of the Nobel laureates, for example: "Ernest Hemingway, USA"; "Günter Grass, Deutschland." On Canetti's chair, only the name of his native city, "Rousse" appears. Indeed, Canetti was a European thinker par excellence, a cosmopolitan with a special tie to the German language.

Like other Jewish intellectuals of the Shoah generation, Paul Celan, Rose Ausländer, Jean Améry, and Manès Sperber, Canetti had a city of birth, but he did not have a homeland in the sense of a nation state: he belonged to all and to no one: "niemandem gehören, in jedem wachsen; das Beste lieben, das Schlechteste trösten," Canetti wrote in 1946 (*Aufz. 1942–48*, 89). Canetti's homeland was comprised of all the European countries he had lived in or visited. When teaching Canetti's youngest brother Georg the new home address in Manchester, Jacques Canetti inspired Elias to conceptualize the cosmopolitan identity the author later claimed as his own. Canetti's father started with the boy's name, followed by the house number, the name of the street, the city, and the country, England. Elias felt compelled to add "in a loud voice": "Europe." Only this addition satisfied his concept of a complete address: "So war unsere Adresse wieder beisammen" (*GZ*, 81). In Canetti's imagination, Europe is the homeland; the existing national borders were arbitrarily created by politicians, historians, and commissions. In his notebooks Canetti suggested that all borders should be destroyed, "aus-gerottet" (*Aufz. 1942–48*, 41).

The individual chapters of *Die gerettete Zunge* provide a narrative of Canetti's inner journey in conjunction with the topographical centers of his "homeland": "Rustschuk 1905–1911," "Manchester 1911–1913," "Wien 1913–1921," "Zürich-Scheuchzerstrasse 1916–1919," "Zürich-Tiefenbrunnen 1919–1921." The second autobiographical volume, *Die Fackel im Ohr*, represents the sites, events, and people instrumental to his personal growth: "Inflation und Ohnmacht. Frankfurt 1921–1924," "Sturm und Zwang. Wien 1924–1925," "Die Schule des Hörens. Wien 1926–1928," "Das Gedränge des Hörens. Berlin 1928," "Die Flucht des Feuers 1929–1931." Canetti's topography connects cities through the travel motif.

While this motif is also central to the German *Bildungsroman* of the eighteenth and nineteenth centuries, Canetti's travels produced an ever-expanding homeland. The protagonist of a traditional *Bildungsroman*, however, would typically return home from foreign lands to his native country to assume his duties as a citizen. Canetti's outlook precludes the concept of the foreigner altogether. In addition, the motif of geographic change is tied to Jewish history and the history of the Canetti family. It is the history of a traveling nation and a traveling family on their way from fifteenth-century Spain across the Mediterranean and Bulgaria to twentieth-century Western Europe. Since elements of the larger historical experience expand the author's development at every step of his way from Bulgaria to the West, the travel motif assumes new aspects that transcend the parameters of the educational novel. Ultimately, Canetti constructs a supranational vision and topography. The images Canetti ascribes to his childhood in his autobiography function throughout his work as a network to which new images and motifs attach themselves. From the original web of images, Canetti suggests, he constructs his Europe, his *Heimat*.

Each segment of this homeland retains its cultural uniqueness and preserves a particular significance in his life and work. Rather than characterizing Canetti as an exile writer, as John Bayley does in the following statement: "[. . .] in Canettis Fall [ist] das Exil selbst eine für das Genie geschaffene Lebensform, denn seine Heimat ist die Gesamtheit der europäischen Tradition"[54] we consider Canetti a world citizen who in the course of his career found and explored his global *Heimat* beyond his family's history and the Jewish experience; his childhood experience of multiculturalism led Canetti to the discovery of the unity of the human race and he came to realize that human beings are inseparably connected. This attitude toward humanity is also present when he examines mass phenomena in Africa and South America and links them to European phenomena. While researching the crimes and defects of mankind in *Masse und Macht*, he also declares his love for human beings and his hatred of their ultimate enemy, death:

> Es ist wenig Schlechtes, was ich vom Menschen wie der Menschheit nicht zu sagen hätte. Und doch ist mein Stolz auf sie noch immer so groß, daß ich nur eines wirklich hasse: ihren Feind, den Tod. (*GZ* 13)

Canetti's hatred of death borders on denial, and reveals a fundamentally philanthropic disposition. Embedded in it is the conviction that the differences between nations do not matter; hence dying in the name of a cause is never justified. This attitude stands in sharp contrast to the views that shaped his age, and deserves serious consideration. Today, despite the Universal Declaration of Human Rights adopted by the United Nations in 1948, killing an enemy is still accepted practice, as the wars at the end of the twentieth and at the beginning of the twenty-first century have shown.

Being a Jew was a particular concern for Canetti, especially in light of Hitler's "Final Solution." Canetti's family left Roustchouk for personal reasons, but the family of Canetti's wife Veza, a native of Vienna, was immediately affected by the Holocaust, as were many of his friends and acquaintances throughout Europe. Canetti did not associate racial discrimination and persecution with his native environment, but rather with Vienna. He and his wife escaped just in time before the outbreak of the Second World War. The news about the fate of the Jews deeply concerned him, as is evident from the observations he recorded during the war years. He frequently reflected upon the relationship between Germans and Jews; however, he never wrote about the situation in Eastern Europe, and refrained from making direct reference to Bulgaria and his native city, Roustchouk.

Leaving events, personalities, and places unnamed is not unusual for Canetti. He rarely mentions Hitler and other leading National Socialists or even the National Socialist movement directly, and yet, large parts of his oeuvre seem to revolve around the trauma created by the extreme nationalist movements that emerged during his years in Frankfurt, Vienna, and Berlin. Precisely because at times he seemed to conceal the specific details informing his more abstract deliberations, it is necessary to examine the impact of the war and the genocide on his country of origin, even though he seems to ignore it in his written statements. It is also important to take a closer look at the complex Jewish-Bulgarian relations prior to the Shoah.

According to historian Vicki Tamir, Bulgarian historiography does not provide much detailed information about tensions between Bulgarians and Jews.[55] However, Meyer Weinberg, as well as Internet sources such as the *Jewish History of Bulgaria*, state that in Bulgaria, and Roustchouk in particular, anti-Semitic riots had taken place in the second half of the nineteenth century. They seem to have been sparked by "the rise of a native middle class, anchored in trade." Weinberg mentions a "bitter struggle" in 1880 that occurred over a dispute concerning market days held on the Sabbath.[56] Generally speaking, "the Bulgarian population displayed signs of resentment against the Jews. Most Bulgarian political parties were steeped in anti-Semitism. The Bulgarian peasantry did everything in their power to prevent Jews from acquiring land, and from time to time there were blood libels."[57] Historian Frederick Chary reports that in the nineteenth and early twentieth centuries several pogroms in Bulgarian cities and villages were caused by rumors of ritual murder associated with the Passover holiday. The most infamous incident occurred in 1895 in Pazardzhik, but there were others, in Sofia (1884), Vratza (1890), Lom (1903) and Kiustendil (1904). As the Jews of Bulgaria moved increasingly to the cities, where they encountered a more sophisticated social culture, these anti-Semitic outrages ceased.[58] Chary, contrary to Weinberg, does not mention anti-Jewish riots in Roustchouk. Despite certain excesses, Bulgaria seems to have retained some of the spirit of tolerance the Turks had practiced toward Jewish and other non-Muslim subjects. Chary notes that "all minorities, even nationals of countries at odds with Bulgaria, had normally been well-treated."[59] He considers the lack of economic competition between Jews and non-Jews and the rare contacts between Jews and Bulgarians the main reasons for the lack of hostility. In addition, he points out that "the leading politicians did not promote anti-Semitism as an issue, as was the case, for example, in Romania and Austria."[60] Canetti had a similar understanding of the situation. In an interview with Joachim Schickel, he refers to the tolerance with which Jews were met in the Turkish Empire.

> Viele dieser Juden [the emigrants from Spain] wurden in der Türkei gut aufgenommen. Der türkische Sultan fand nützliche Untertanen in ihnen. Sie hatten allerhand Fertigkeiten: es gab Ärzte unter ihnen, Financiers, Handwerker, die besondere Dinge beherrschten. Sie wurden gut behandelt, und sie verbreiteten sich über das ganze türkische Reich, haben aber ihre spanische Sprache behalten, und zwar das Spanisch jener Zeit. (*DgZ*, 106–7)

Here Canetti offers an explanation for the lack of anti-Semitism among the Turks: the Sultan needed Jewish businessmen and rewarded them for their contributions to the state. In an unpublished letter to Penka Angelova, Canetti furthermore mentioned that he was familiar with the tolerance with which Bulgarians treated the Jewish population. Canetti's assessment is by no means unique. Chary comments:

> As anti-Semitism grew up in Europe and became a problem of international concern for liberal and democratic societies, the Bulgarian intellectuals began to reflect upon their country's relations with its own Jewish communities. They emphasized the favorable relations, and a myth of the absence of anti-Semitisms grew up. Although this was not strictly true, the myth became as important as the fact, for a large section of the Bulgarian intelligentsia became committed to fighting the growth (or, as they preferred to think of it, the appearance) of anti-Semitism in their country. In 1937, a Jewish journalist, Buko Piti, published a book of statements of some one hundred and fifty leaders of Bulgarian society denouncing anti-Semitism and proclaiming the reasons for its absence in Bulgaria.[61]

The anything but problem-free historical record of the tenuous situation of Bulgarian Jewry puts these favorable impressions into perspective. After the liberation from Turkish rule by the Russian army the relations between Jews and non-Jews were troubled. During the Turkish-Russian war, Jewish property had been looted and in Vidin, Kazanlik, and Svishtov, where the local population suspected Jews of collaboration with the Turks, Jewish communities were plundered, and Jews expelled under appalling circumstances. Most of them fled to Adrianople and Constantinople. Prior to the Congress of Berlin in 1878, Western European Jewish organizations had tried to secure equal rights for Bulgarian, Serbian, and Romanian Jews, and the Berlin Treaty included a clause obliging the Balkan countries to grant equal rights to Jewish citizens.

In the same year, 1878, rioting, robbery, and arson erupted in Sofia, and Jews formed a militia and a fire brigade to prevent arson, and they retained the fire brigade after Bulgarian independence. Integration happened slowly and remained incomplete. In 1885, during the war between Serbia and Bulgaria, Jews were drafted into the Bulgarian Army for the first time.

Even though the principle of equality was emphasized after the First World War in the Treaty of Neuilly (1919), the principle of equal rights was repeatedly undermined. The various Bulgarian governments continued to discriminate against Jews. In secret memoranda anti-Jewish legislation was introduced. Jews were not accepted at the military academy, the state bank, or in government or municipal service. The Bulgarian national uprising in 1923 prepared the ground for the intensification of anti-Semitism. The population's frustration over economic and social hardships was frequently channeled toward minority groups and radical nationalist associations sprang up, among them the anti-Semitic Ratnik ("Warrior") association, founded in 1936. Structurally this was a fascist organization that blended the Nazi theory of race with a Bulgarian ideology.[62] Canetti never referred to specific details of this period. Indeed, the rescue of the Bulgarian Jews, explored in the 2001 documentary film *The Optimists* was relatively little known and undervalued even in Bulgaria for decades.[63] Since the 1970s extensive research about the events of 1941 to 1944 in Bulgaria has been conducted by Jewish, American, and Bulgarian scholars. Among these, two prominent intellectuals stand out, Hannah Arendt and Tzvetan Todorov.

As a journalist for the *New Yorker*, Arendt reported on the 1960 Eichmann trial. Based on her findings on the materials of the trial and the correspondence between Eichmann and the German ambassador in Bulgaria, Adolf Beckerle, she researched the sparing of Bulgaria's Jews and published her results in *Eichmann in Jerusalem: A Report on the Banality of Evil* (1963).[64] The French intellectual of Bulgarian origin, Tzvetan Todorov, published *The Fragility of Goodness: Why Bulgaria's Jews Survived the Holocaust* in 2001.[65] His study is based on documents of the Bulgarian government, written statements and protests of Bulgarian intellectuals, writers, musicians, painters, and lawyers, a statement by the Holy Synod of the Bulgarian Orthodox Church, speeches in the National Assembly, and memoirs of eyewitnesses. Prior to the Second World War, Bulgaria was home to approximately 48,000 Jews. In 1924, inspired by the Zionist movement, a major wave of emigration occurred. Canetti witnessed this during his second visit to Bulgaria the same year, and described it vividly in *Die Fackel im Ohr* (*FO*, 81–88).

The mass emigration in 1924 is rarely mentioned by historians, but it was the first Jewish mass emigration from Bulgaria. By the time Hitler's "Final Solution to the Jewish Question" was underway, most members of Canetti's family had left the country. According to Canetti, many Jews of Roustchouk, including all of his relatives, had moved to Sofia: "Alle Mitglieder der Familie waren im Lauf der Jahre nach Sofia übersiedelt, das als Hauptstadt des Landes an Bedeutung gewonnen hatte und allmählig zu einer grossen Stadt geworden war" (*FO*, 80–81). Roustchouk's importance had lessened, and now Sofia, the capital city, was a more attractive cultural center and more advantageous for business and trade. In addition, the rising anti-Semitism in the 1920s lent the Zionist movement increased credibility and urgency among Bulgarian Jews, triggering the first major wave of Jewish emigration from Bulgarian soil. As Canetti observed, it seemed that the entire Jewish community in Sofia had embraced Zionism:

> Die Familie stand vor der Auswanderung. Mit mehreren anderen Fami- lien hatten sie vor, Stadt und Land in den nächsten Wochen zu verlas- sen. Palästina, so hieß es damals, war ihr gelobtes Ziel. Die ganze Spaniolen-Gemeinde in Sofia, nicht nur in Sofia, auch überall sonst im Lande, hatte sich zum Zionismus bekehrt. Es ging ihnen nicht schlecht in Bulgarien, sie standen unter keinerlei Verfolgung, es gab keine Ghettos, auch keine drückende Armut, aber es gab Redner unter ihnen, deren Funken gezündet hatten, die die Rückkehr ins gelobte Land im- mer und immer predigten. (*FO*, 89)

This mass emigration represented to Canetti a chain of events that made him aware of a charismatic leader's impact on the masses. In this case the leader of the Jewish community was his own cousin: "Als der feurigste Redner, als einer, der wahre Wunder wirkte, galt ein Vetter von mir, Bernhard Arditti" (*FO*, 89). Arditti inspired the Jewish community and even organized the mass departure, and following his call to action, all members of the Canetti family who had remained in Bulgaria immigrated to Palestine in 1924 (*GZ*, 89–90).[66] The second wave of emigration occurred after 1947 in conjunction with the establishment of the State of Israel, coupled with anti-Jewish ten- dencies in the Communist countries of Eastern Europe. By the 1950s, over 40,000 Bulgarian Jews had moved to Israel, leaving behind a small popula- tion of 9,695 Jews. According to Oschlies, by 1965 only 5,100 Jews still lived in Bulgaria.[67]

During the Second World War Bulgaria was an ally of Nazi Germany through a pact advantageous to both parties: Germany gained control of a central Balkan country, and Bulgaria avoided the status of a conquered nation. Germany agreed to return to Bulgaria some of the territories it had ceded in the regional Balkan wars of 1912–14.[68] Hitler supported the re- annexation of some of these territories by Bulgaria, and in 1941 parts of Romania, Greece, and Macedonia were taken over by the Kingdom of Bul- garia. However, despite its alliance with Germany, Bulgaria refused to de- clare war on Russia, because it had liberated the country from Turkish occupation in 1878; and the Bulgarian Tsar Boris III of Saxe-Coburg-Gotha also refused to send soldiers to the Eastern front.

The new territories represented a strange gift. Bulgaria had a merely ad- ministrative function there, while the German army kept them under tight military control. This, together with the ambivalent position of the Bulgarian government toward the Nazi's policy on the Jewish question, caused a crisis that had serious consequences for the Jewish population. Of the Jews living in these Bulgarian territories, only the Jews of Thrace and Macedonia became victims of Hitler's "Final Solution." The Jews in the newly occupied territories were identified and singled out. Todorov states that "a governmental order dated 5 June 1942, concerning citizenship 'in lands liberated in 1941,'" decreed that "all former Yugoslavian and Greek subjects shall become Bulgarian unless they expressly request otherwise." But it was also specified that "[This measure] does not apply to individuals of Jewish origin, except for married Jewish women, to whom their husband's citizenship is given."[69] The denial of Bulgarian citizenship proved fatal to most of the Thracian and Macedonian Jews. For some reason the German authorities felt that not much could be achieved in the old Bulgarian territory. Thus their first order was to deport 20,000 Jews from the new territories. On 22, 25, and 29 March 1943, approximately 11,340 persons were deported from Thrace and Macedonia by train to Lom, a small port on the Danube near Roustchouk; they were later shipped to Austria on the Danube, and from there to the death camps of Treblinka and Auschwitz. This was the first and the only deportation of Jews from Bulgaria in the course of the three critical years.

The remaining 9,000 persons who were supposed to be deported from the old Bulgarian territories were never taken to their deaths. The public reaction to the deportations deserves special attention. Ordinary people, politicians, and members of the clergy reacted at once: they sent a delegation to parliament, met with the deputy Dimitar Peshev, who formed a parliamentarian group of forty delegates, and signed a petition to the king demanding that all deportations be stopped. Tsar Boris III approved the request. Todorov presents the report of an eyewitness, according to whom the Bulgarian metropolitan Cyril, head of the Orthodox Church in Plovdiv and future patriarch of Bulgaria, declared that he would lie down on the railroad tracks in front of the train if any Jews in his jurisdiction were to be deported. According to Todorov, this chain of actions saved the lives of about 9,000 persons from Thrace, and all the Jews in the old Bulgarian territory.[70] From that point on all deportations of Jews stopped.[71]

In Bulgaria the notion that "Jews were good and useful subjects" had outlasted Turkish rule. After the 1878 liberation Jews, as well as Turks, Armenians, and Greeks continued to form an integral part of Bulgarian society. This fact was proven again at the time of the "Final Solution." Hannah Arendt noted that Eichmann suspected Bulgaria might not understand the "Jewish Problem" as the Nazis saw it, and would not support the genocide. In January 1942 Eichmann wrote a letter to Hitler's Foreign Office declaring that "sufficient possibilities exist for the reception of Jews from Bulgaria" and that he was ready for the deportation and execution of the Bulgarian Jews.[72] However, Bulgarian politicians asserted their own policy against Nazi pressure, even feigning agreement with German policy in order to thwart it. The argument advanced by the Turkish Sultan that

"Jews are good and useful workers" was used again by the Bulgarian Prime Minister Dimitar Peshev and the Minister of Internal affairs Gabrovski when they were asked to implement the anti-Semitic policies of the Germans. They argued that "The Jews were needed for various tasks inside Bulgaria, particularly road maintenance."[73] Jewish men were put into forced labor on road crews. Another 5,000 Jews were granted special privileges. Special clauses were introduced for Jewish physicians and businessmen, as well as for Jews who had converted to Christianity. Later the government and the king evicted 20,500 Jews from Sofia, sending them into the provinces in a demonstration of support for their German allies, but none of the evictees were deported to concentration camps.[74] Arendt writes that the eviction was the last thing the Germans wanted, "since it dispersed the Jews instead of concentrating them."[75] Only now, when there were no more Jews in Sofia, were the plans for deporting the Bulgarian Jews abandoned for the time being. These events reveal that the Bulgarian government took considerable liberties in the way they responded to the German request for deportation. When the Soviet Army marched into Sofia in August-September 1944, the dispersed Jews returned to their homes in the city.

Even so, in Bulgaria as in many other European countries, anti-Semitic laws had been enacted during the war, including decrees pertaining to the confiscation of property and the wearing of the Yellow Star. A decree of August 1942 expropriated all Jewish property and ended all exemptions to anti-Jewish laws.[76] When the Red Army approached Bulgaria, government leaders distanced themselves from the racist legislation enacted earlier. On August 31, 1944, "all anti-Jewish measures were abrogated and promises were made to return confiscated property."[77] Nonetheless, in 1948 more than seventy percent of Bulgarian Jewry, alarmed at what was happening to Jews in other communist countries, left for Israel. According to Weinberg, they were at liberty to take with them their property, a rare convenience under the circumstances of the time in Eastern Europe.[78] Weinberg suggests that this decision was made under the influence of the communist leader, Georgi Dimitrov, the same person whom Hitler had accused of setting the Reichstag fire in 1933. Dimitrov had made radio broadcasts to Bulgaria from Haifa, Israel, in which he attacked Bulgarian leaders for their anti-Semitic actions.[79]

After his visit to Bulgaria in 1924, Canetti never returned to his city and country of origin, perhaps because he wanted to preserve the memories of his early years; it may be that he deliberately avoided the confrontation with places that after the exodus of the Bulgarian Jews would do little more than remind him of a tradition that had come to a tragic end. In a certain way his avoidance of Bulgaria parallels his decision not to take up permanent residence in the new German or Austrian republics. Even though he was a frequent guest in both countries, his permanent residence was in Hampstead, England. When upon his receipt of Nobel Prize, he finally acquired the means to maintain a "continental" residence, he established his second domicile in Switzerland.

Notes

[1] Elias Canetti, *Die gerettete Zunge: Geschichte einer Jugend* (Munich: Hanser, 1977), 10. Cited as *GZ*. Other works of Elias Canetti are cited as follows: *Die Fackel im Ohr: Lebensgeschichte* (Munich: Hanser, 1980), cited as *FO*; *Aufzeichnungen 1942–48* (Munich: Hanser, 1965), cited as *Aufz. 1942–48; Masse und Macht* (Munich: Hanser, 1960), cited as *MM*.

[2] The city has had many names throughout its history, and was referred to as both Roustchouk and Rousse from the liberation of Bulgaria in 1878 until the 1920s; since then, only the name Rousse has been used, but the name Roustchouk will be used in this essay, since it is the English transcription of the primary Sephardic usage during the time Canetti lived there. Canetti's own spelling is the German transcription, "Rustschuk."

[3] In the past few decades there has been an increasing interest in Bulgarian history as obvious from recent publications and new editions of older ones including: Duncan M. Perry, *Stefan Stambolov and the Emergence of Modern Bulgaria, 1870–1895* (Durham, NC: Duke UP, 1993); Philip Ward, *Sofia: Portrait of a City* (Cambridge/New York: Oleander, 1993); Gerald W. Creed, *Domesticating Revolution: From Socialist Reform to Ambivalent Transition in a Bulgarian Village* (University Park, PA: Pennsylvania State UP, 1998); R. J. Crampton, *A Concise History of Bulgaria* (Cambridge/New York: Cambridge UP, 1997); Gerald W. Creed, *Subsistence Farming and Economic Transition in Bulgaria* (Washington DC: National Council for Eurasian and East European Research, 1997).

[4] Heinrich von (Wien) Neustadt, *Apollonius von Tyrland: Nach der Gothaer Handschrift*, ed. S. Singer (Berlin: Weidmannsche Buchhandlung, 1906), 117 (verse numbers 7241 and 1760).

[5] Heinrich von Neustadt represents Apollonius as a hero and a strong and powerful enemy:

> Abacuk was auch ein helt,
> Fur den pesten gezelt
> Den indert hett Wulger landt.
> Er kam mit grymme auf in gerant
> Und sprach "der zins wart hie gegeben:
> Es giltet heut dien veiges leben."
> (Neustadt, 124, verse numbers 7665–66)

[6] Heinrich von (Wien) Neustadt, verse number 7245. Abacuck, probably the historical Bulgarian King Asparukh (around 680), and the Romanian king Nemrot, probably the historical Wallachian voivode Menumorut (around 955) are mentioned interchangeably.

[7] Wenzeslav Konstantinov. Conversation with Elias Canetti, October 18, 1992, unpublished. Cited from: "Elias Canetti — ein österreichischer Schriftsteller? Verwand-

lungen zwischen Rustschuk und Wien." *Trans: Internet-Zeitschrift für Kulturwissen-schaften* 7 (September) 1999, 4 http://www.inst.at/trans/7Nr/konstasntinov7.htm, 14.

[8] Vassil Doikov, *Rousse: Biografiata na edin grad* (= Rousse: The Biography of a City) (Rousse: Dunav Press, 2002). Vassil Doikov is historian of Roustchouk, author of more than twenty books about the city, and director of its historical museum.

[9] Doikov, 18.

[10] Doikov, 19.

[11] Vladislav was also called the Impaler and Dracula. See Elizabeth Miller, *Dracula*. Parkstone Press, 2001. See http://www.questiaonline.library/Rumania/history; see also http://parkstone on line.com.

[12] Doikov, 28–31.

[13] Doikov, 20. See also http://wickipedia.org/wiki/MihaiViteazul.

[14] Doikov, 19–20; see also http://wickipedia.org/wiki/MihaiViteazul.

[15] Doikov, 18–20.

[16] Doikov, 28.

[17] Penka Angelova and Judith Veichtbauer, eds., *Pulverfaß Balkan: Mythos oder Realität* (St. Ingbert: Röhrig Universitätsverlag, 2001), 3–7.

[18] Roberto Corcoll Calast: "Elias Canetti und Spanien." *Hüter der Verwandlung: Beiträge zum Werk von Elias Canetti,* ed. by Hanser Verlag (Munich: Hanser, 1985), 114–20. Isabella of Castile (1451–1504) was the queen who sponsored Christopher Columbus's discovery voyage to the New World. She married Ferdinand V of Aragon in 1469. They united Aragon (Northern Spain) with Castile in 1479, and in 1492 expelled all Jews who did not convert to Christianity. They are known also as the Catholic rulers who established the Inquisition in Spain. *The Columbia Encyclopedia, Sixth Edition* (New York: Columbia UP: http://www.bartleby.com/65/fe/Ferdi2Ara.html.).

[19] Elias Canetti, Interview with Joachim Schickel, *Hüter der Verwandlung,* 107.

[20] See Yonka Koksal, "The Application of Tanzimat Reforms in Bulgaria: State Bulgaria in the Ottoman Empire (1839–1878)," http://www.ksg.harward.edu/Kokkakis/GSW1/GSW11%20/Koksal.pdf.

[21] At the beginning of the nineteenth century the Turkish Empire faced serious economic problems. There were several reasons for the recession: the emancipation of Greece and Serbia and the general anarchy affecting all structures. See: History of Turkey http://www.workmall.com/wfb2001/turkey.

[22] Doikov, 30.

[23] See Barbara Sansone in Original World: http://www.originalworldjourneys.com/EUROPE/bulgariaJewish.html. In addition, Doikov states that at the end of the eighteenth century there was a wave of Jewish settlers from Belgrade, Nish, Vidin, Nikople, and Odrin. His information is based on the historical notes of Solomon Rosanes's history of Rousses Jewish community. (Solomon Rosanes, *Divrei Yemei Yisrael be-Togarmah,* the standard history of Turkish Jewry. See also: http://www.heritagefilms.com/BULGARIA.html#RABBIS%20AND%20SCHOLARS%20OF%20BULGARIA.

[24] Teodora Bakardjieva, "Jews in Bulgaria." http://www.sefarad.org/publication/lm/037/7.html.

[25] See Wenzeslav Konstantinov: "Elias Canetti — Ein österreichischer Schriftsteller? Verwandlungen zwischen Rustschuk und Wien" *Trans: Internet-Zeitschrift für Kulturwissenschaften,* September 7 (1999), 4. http://www.inst.at/trans/7Nr/konstasntinov7.htm. See also http://thefreedictionaryandthesaurus.org. See also Roberto Corcoll Calast: "Elias Canetti und Spanien," in *Hüter der Verwandlung,* 114–20.

[26] With regard to the Turkish population see Ömer Turan, *The Turkish Minority in Bulgaria, 1878–1908* (Türk Tarih Kurumu Basimevi, 1998).

[27] Salvator Israel, "Za semeistvoto i rodninite na Elias Kaneti" (About the Family and the Relatives of Elias Canetti), *Evreiski vesti,* 12/24 (1981) and research by Tzvi Keren (Doikov, 25). Insight into the Sephardic experience is also provided by Gabriel Arie, *A Sephardi Life in Southeastern Europe: The Autobiography and Journal of Gabriel Arie, 1863–1939* (Seattle: U of Washington P, 1998).

[28] See: Teodora Bakardjieva. "The Jewish Community in Rousse." http://www.sefarad.org/publication/lm/035/6.html.

[29] They are mentioned in the Constantinople newspaper *Journal israelite* in connection with the visit of Kaiser Franz Josef. Here cited from Wenzeslav Konstantinov, 3.

[30] Konstantinov, 3.

[31] See: Salvator Israel, "Za semeistvoto i rodninite na Elias Kaneti" (About the Family and the Relatives of Elias Canetti) *Evreiski vesti,* 12/24 (1981), 3.

[32] Konstantinov, 3 and Israel, 3.

[33] Doikov cites the 1910 city census, according to which there were 5790 Turks, 114 Russians, 98 Serbs, 194 other Slavic nationalities, 29 Tatars, 197 Greeks, 34 Albanians, 268 Gypsies, 3851 Jews, 1870 Armenians, 301 Romanians, 424 Germans, 55 Italians, and 32 Frenchmen among the total of 36,255 residents (69).

[34] See "The Jewish Virtual Library. Bulgaria. Independent Bulgaria." http://www.us-israel.org/source/vjw/bulgaria.html

[35] Doikov, 52–59.

[36] Ibid., 109–10.

[37] Ibid., 118.

[38] Ibid., 53–59.

[39] Ibid., 6–7.

[40] See "The Urania Idea" at http://www.urania-dresden.de/gedanke_engl.html.

[41] Ibid.

[42] This fact, not widely known to the citizens of Roustchouk, was only discovered and acknowledged by the international organizational committee on the occasion of the centennial celebration of filmmaking. Documents of the Society "Zoura," Rousse, Bulgaria.

[43] Documents of the Society "Zoura," Rousse, Bulgaria.

[44] Doikov, 56.

[45] According to the *Catholic Encyclopedia* (http://www.newadvent.org/cathen/ 03046a.htm) the population according to the census of 1900 numbered 3,744,283, divided according to religion into 3,019,296 Greek Orthodox, 28,579 Catholics of the Latin Rite and Uniat Greeks, 4524 Protestants, 13,809 Gregorian Armenians, 33,663 Jews, 643,300 (http://www.newadvent.org/cathen/10424a.htm) Mohammedans, and 1112 of other creeds; according to nationality into 2,887,860 Bulgarians, 539,656 Turks, 89,549 Gypsies, 75,223 Rumanians, 70,887 Greeks, 32,753 Jews, 18,856 Tatars, 13,926 Armenians, and 15,741 of other nationalities. The number of inhabitants in 1905 was 4,028,239.

[46] "Akustische Maske und Maskensprung. Materialien zu einer Theorie des Dramas. Ein Gespräch." Ed. Manfred Durzak, *Zu Elias Canetti* (Ernst Klett Verlag, Stuttgart 1983), 17–30.

[47] "Akustische Maske und Maskensprung, 17.

[48] Canetti, *Aufzeichnungen 1942–48*, 20–21.

[49] Extensive research on Bulgarian family life during Turkish rule was conducted by the historian Maria N. Todorova, *Balkan Family Structure and the European Pattern: Demographic Developments in Ottoman Bulgaria* (Washington, DC, Lanham, MD: American UP, 1993).

[50] Angelova has explored the correlation of particular elements such as forest, fire, rain, sea, and wind, conceived of as "the mass of nature" to the different types of masses and nations. Penka Angelova, "Über die Reconstruction des Begriffes der Nationen bei Canetti," in *Pulverfass Balkan: Mythos oder Realität. Internationales Symposium Rousse, Oktober 1998*, ed. Penka Angelova and Judith Veichtbauer (St. Ingberts: Röhrig Universitätsverlag, 2001).

[51] Grillparzer wrote: "Hast du vom Kahlenberg das Land dir rings besehn/So wirst du, was ich schrieb und wer ich bin, verstehn." Franz Grillparzer, *Sämtliche Werke*, ed. August Sauer and Reinhold Backmann (Vienna: Kunstverlag Anton Schroll & Co., 1909–1948). Here: *Gedichte* III, 153.

[52] Canetti writes: "Soll ich mich den Russen verschliessen, weil es Juden gibt, den Chinesen, weil sie ferne, den Deutschen, weil sie besessen sind? Kann ich nicht weiterhin allen gehöeren, wie bisher, und doch Jude sein?" (*Aufz. 1942–85*, 89).

[53] Dagmar C. G. Lorenz, *Keepers of the Motherland: German Texts by Jewish Women Writers* (Lincoln: U of Nebraska P, 1997), 1–13.

[54] John Bayley, "Canetti und Macht," in *Hüter der Verwandlung*, 147.

[55] Vicki Tamir, *Bulgaria and Her Jews: The History of a Dubious Symbiosis* (New York: Sepher-Hermon Press, 1979), vii.

[56] Jewish History of Bulgaria, http://www.heritagefilms.com/BULGARIA.html# Byzantine%20and%20Bulgar%20Rule. Meyer Weinberg, *Because They Were Jews: A History of Anti-Semitism* (New York/Westport: Greenwood Press, 1986), 28–29.

[57] http://www.heritagefilms.com/BULGARIA.html#Byzantine%20and%20Bulgar% 20Rule.

[58] Frederick Chary, *The Bulgarian Jews and the Final Solution 1940–1944* (Pittsburgh: U of Pittsburgh P, 1972), 32–33. See also Teodora Bakardjieva, *Jews in Bulgaria,*

http://www.sefarad.org/publication/lm/037/7.html; http://www.sefarad.org/publication/lm/035/index.html.

[59] Ibid., 33.

[60] Ibid.

[61] Buko Piti, ed. *Bulgarskata obshtestvenost za rasisma I antisemitisma* (Bulgarian Public Opinion about Racism and Anti-Semitism) (Sofia, n.p., 1937), here cited from Chary, 33.

[62] http://www.sefarad.org/publication/lm/035/6.html and http://www.heritage films.com/BULGARIA html#Byzantine%20and%20Bulgar%20Rule.

[63] *The Optimists,* dir. Jacky Comforty. Comforty Media Concepts, 2001.

[64] Hannah Arendt, *Eichmann in Jerusalem: A Report on the Banality of* Evil (New York: Viking Press, 1963).

[65] Tzvetan Todorov, *The Fragility of Goodness: Why Bulgaria's Jews Survived the Holocaust* (Princeton: Princeton UP, 2001).

[66] In this connection a statement by Elias Canetti's daughter Johanna Canetti is of interest: "So viel ich weiss, leben heute keine Verwandten mehr in Bulgarien. Die näheren Verwandten meines Vaters leben heute in Paris, sowohl Canettis als auch Ardittis. Seine beiden Brüder (verstorben) haben den grössten Teil ihres Lebens in Paris verbracht. Jacques Canetti (Nissim), der mittlere, war als Impresario tätig und gründete eine Plattenfirma; Georges, der jüngste, war Arzt und am Institut Pasteur angestellt als Lungenspezialist." From personal letter to Dagmar C. G. Lorenz, 2 March 2004.

[67] Wolf Oschlies, "Bulgarian Jewry since 1944," *Soviet Jewish Affairs,* trans. Ann Adler, May 14, 1984. Cited from Weinberg, 30.

[68] See Victor Roudometof, *Collective Memory, National Identity, and Ethnic Conflict: Greece, Bulgaria, and the Macedonian Question* (Westport, CT: Praeger, 2002).

[69] Todorov, 6.

[70] Ibid., 7.

[71] On the salvation of the Bulgarian Jews, see also Dieter Ruckhaberle and Christiane Ziesecke, *Rettung der bulgarischen Juden, 1943: Eine Dokumentation* (Berlin: Publica, 1984).

[72] Arendt treats the Bulgarian question in Chapter 11, 181 ff.

[73] Todorov 12.

[74] Ibid., 11.

[75] Arendt, 187.

[76] Weinberg 28.

[77] Ibid., 29.

[78] Ibid., 20.

[79] Ibid., 30.

Elias Canetti's Response to the Shoah: *Masse und Macht*

Michael Mack

THE WORD HOLOCAUST OR SHOAH is conspicuous in Elias Canetti's work by its absence. Why then discuss this topic in a companion volume dedicated to his oeuvre? It should be noted that, before the Eichmann trial in 1961, neither term was used to describe the Nazi genocide.[1] Both denotations are in fact problematic.[2] As this essay will examine, Canetti makes it clear that his analysis of both crowds and power goes hand in hand with an examination of the ways in which Nazism gained popular support within Germany and Austria.[3]

This essay focuses on Canetti's work that grew out of such examination of Nazism's roots. In this respect Canetti described his scholarly investigation always with a view to political and social issues. He self-consciously analyzed both *Masse* and *Macht* within this specific historical context. But why does he not specifically mention Nazi concentration camps? This avoidance in fact points to one of Canetti's intellectual goals and literary strategies. As will be discussed here, Canetti depicts humanity's constitution and history in terms of genocide. Our bodies, our language, our food habits, our everyday behavior, in short, everything that has to do with us emerges as an integral part of a huge, all-encompassing killing machine, called "society" or "civilization."

Readers might still question whether this brutal depiction of the human refers to Nazism in general and to the Shoah, in particular. There have, after all, been many writers and thinkers who had a decidedly unsavory view of humanity before they could have heard anything about what the Nazis were going to perpetrate. Canetti's response to the Shoah, by contrast, does not consist in representing a bleak worldview. His way of writing must not be confused with his anthropological and philosophical convictions. He depicts humanity qua violence, death, and survival, so as to shock his readers. In order to make this shock more efficient or, in other words, more real, Canetti employs literary devices by means of which he presents his scholarship in the light of "objective" reality.

We can thus address the hybrid position of *Masse und Macht* between literature and the social sciences: the author employs literary strategies that enhance the scientific truth claims of what he is depicting. Crucially, scientific truth here differs strikingly from positivist definitions of the same term. According to Canetti, that which is true has the capability to change the reader's life. Consequently, truth works for change, but only if its shock force persuades readers to reflect on their beliefs, assumptions, and prejudices.

One can better understand the shocking account of human nature presented by Canetti in *Masse und Macht* when we examine this work within the historical and intellectual context in which it was conceived and composed. Turning to Canetti's circle of friends, it becomes quite clear that *Masse und Macht* actually describes one historical break, that of the Shoah. It is significant that, after the publication of its first edition in 1960, Canetti dedicated a copy of *Masse und Macht* to the Holocaust survivor, poet, historian, and sociologist H. G. Adler. He wrote: "To H. G. Adler, who lived what I only thought."[4]

The first section of this essay provides an account of the intellectual and historical context of *Masse und Macht*. Crucially, Canetti developed his critique in a lively dialogue with H. G. Adler's Prague childhood friend, Franz Baermann Steiner (1909–1952). The latter was an important, if unfairly neglected, poet and anthropologist. He combined his ethnological and literary interests to develop a critique of the Western notion "civilization" against the background of the Shoah. In this context he initiated, in the 1940s, a deconstruction of what Edward Said would later call "Orientalism."[5] This deconstruction and Steiner's questioning of political and scientific categories such as taboo, slavery, and economic production anticipated intellectual trends which we now call postmodern.

Raised in Prague, Steiner survived the Holocaust, like his close intellectual friend Canetti, as an exile in England. At the University of Oxford, he strongly influenced British postwar anthropology, especially the work of Mary Douglas. In Oxford he worked on his second Ph.D. thesis (his first was completed at the German university in Prague and analyzed the linguistic roots of Semitic languages), which investigates different forms of slavery in various societies. He embedded his scholarly investigations in an overtly political and intellectual context. In his Oxford lectures titled "Taboo" (1951), he deconstructs this category and develops what he calls a "sociology of danger."[6]

Canetti frequently sought Steiner's advice and help while working on *Masse und Macht*. Each weekend Steiner would travel to London and visit his friend. The two writers would then engage in long and detailed discussions. Attention to this exchange with Steiner, among many other things, helps shed light on the historical context of Nazism in general and the Shoah in particular, against whose background Canetti spent twenty years, 1939 to 1959, composing his extensive philosophical essay *Masse and Macht*. In frequent and intensive conversations, Canetti and Steiner developed their responses to the Shoah: Canetti emphasizes power; Steiner focuses on danger. Significantly, Steiner argues that power operates through all those actions that we associate with danger. Not only was Steiner a professional anthropologist, but he also viewed his scholarly and literary work as a response to the Shoah. Steiner, in contrast to Canetti, explicitly refers to Nazi concentration camps in his poetry and in his anthropological critique of civilization.

In the second section of this essays, I will attempt to differentiate between Canetti's view of human nature and his depiction of it. Only through such a differentiation can we appreciate his literary strategies and his critique of history and civilization. That Canetti never specifically discusses Nazi concentration camps in *Masse und Macht,* where such discussion would certainly not have been out of place, emphasizes the idiosyncratic manner in which Canetti responds to the Shoah. One could define this reaction as one of "universalization." This is to say, Canetti characterizes universal human nature in terms of the crimes perpetrated in the Nazi genocide. However, Canetti did not attempt to relativize the horror of the German concentration camps. On the contrary, he tried to make it everpresent by confronting his reader's everyday life with the reality of death, killing, and survival.

The Intellectual and Historical Context of Canetti's Response to the Shoah: The Question of Genre

Canetti did preliminary work on *Masse and Macht* in Vienna and Berlin from the late 1920s until his emigration to Paris in 1938 and then to London in 1939. But he only embarked on the actual writing of *Masse und Macht* in London. He completed the work in 1959 and published it in 1960. Since then, it has posed a great challenge to Canetti scholarship.[7] The question of purview, or boundaries, is crucial in the assessment of *Masse und Macht,* but there is also a wider issue, namely, the response to Canetti himself, not least the reaction to his being awarded the Nobel Prize for Literature. While German newspapers were effusive when Canetti died in 1994, the genre-bending character of *Masse und Macht* caused some confusion with regards to the literary quality of its style immediately after he was awarded the Nobel Prize for literature. According to Manfred Durzak, German newspapers at that time failed to respond immediately to this event and he sees such failure as representative of the general difficulties critics have in dealing with Canetti, especially with *Masse und Macht.*[8]

According to Durzak, the biggest problem of Canetti criticism ensues from its failure to locate him in an intellectual and historical context. In a similar vein Dagmar Barnouw has argued that this is one of the most demanding tasks for future Canetti scholarship. Barnouw, too, focuses on *Masse und Macht.*[9]

Recently, I have attempted to address this neglect of the historical and intellectual context. It is this historical and intellectual context that can help us better understand why *Masse und Macht* was written in its highly idiosyncratic style and, indeed, why it was written at all.[10] The question of genre is best addressed when one reads *Masse und Macht* as a piece of satirical writing.

What, precisely, makes Canetti's work so difficult to assess? It is in part a question of genre. Critics have not overlooked the various influences of Musil, Kraus, and Kafka on Canetti. Yet the writings of these three authors greatly differ from that of Canetti's magnum opus, in one crucial respect: whereas all three writers abstain from scientific claims, *Masse und Macht* is undoubtedly written as a scientific work in the sense of giving the impression of representing objective truths. Critics have often found fault with this, especially with Canetti's apodictic style and his "totalitarian approach."[11]

Canetti does not wish to affirm such a totalitarian world. Rather, he wants to shock his readers into a change of social behavior through a depiction of humanity ruled by death. His one-time friend, the Austrian novelist and theorist of mass phenomena, Hermann Broch (1886–1951), speaks of a "Forschungsarbeit mit Heiltendenzen," a research project with healing tendencies,[12] and Canetti — albeit by different methods — also tries to free the reader from a damaged life. Both are convinced that scholarship is powerless against the barbarity of National Socialism. Purely imaginative texts, on the other hand, do not purport to carry the authority of objective truth that one would associate with scholarship. Fiction, according to received assumption, is a form of lying; it is true only in a literary, figurative sense, whereas scholarship purports to represent factual truth. This claim to facticity has a greater impact on the readership: it has the power to change the ethical behavior of the common reader. Having this power, Broch argues, scholarship should confront the reader with values, rather than being value-free.

In a highly individual way, Canetti takes an approach that is nonetheless related. Though he does not state it in *Masse und Macht,* his aphorisms give a clear indication that he conceives of a scholarly work that transcends the boundaries of pure scholarship in intending to have an immediate impact on the social behavior of its readership. Indeed, Canetti's idea of a new type of scholarship that serves the ethical improvement of the public is close to Broch's notion of the social sciences as laid down in his *Massenwahntheorie.* Like Broch, Canetti criticizes scholarship for scholarship's sake:

> Die Wissenschaft hat sich verraten, indem sie sich zum Selbstzweck gemacht hat. Sie ist zur Religion geworden, zur Religion des Tötens, und sie will weismachen, daß von traditionellen Religionen des Sterbens zu dieser Religion des Tötens ein Fortschritt ist. Man wird die Wissenschaft sehr bald unter die Herrschaft eines höheren Antriebs bringen müssen, der sie zur Dienerin herabdrückt, ohne sie zu zerstören.[13]

Canetti wrote this aphorism in 1943, at a time when details about the Holocaust seeped through to the German and English population. In this context, the strong word betray (*verraten*) becomes understandable: according to Canetti, standard science betrays its deadly aggression in the Nazi genocide.[14] Indeed, the Nazis called the purported inferiority of the Semitic and Slavic races a "scientific fact."[15] German science and German scholarship worked out a "scientific" theory that was supposed to prove the factual necessity for eliminating world Jewry. For Canetti, this represents science's betrayal. It is interesting that he makes no differentiation between "racial science" and "value-free" research. Indeed Canetti does not perceive of science as value-free in any respect, which is why he calls it a religion of killing. Whereas the non-secular religions of dying cheat death by establishing myths of reincarnation, the modern, scientific religion works into the hands of death, facilitating and propagating effective ways of killing. Yet the word "Selbstzweck" implies that science is an end in itself. Canetti, however, argues that when science becomes an end in itself, science is transformed into a fetish, into a religion. According to Canetti, science that is a "Selbstzweck" needs to be supervised by an ethical impulse that moves toward the overcoming of death. Science and scholarship should thus become servants of ethics. They should promote the salvation of life, rather than facilitate its destruction. This supervision of science should not destroy (zerstören) scientific procedures as such, but these methods of elucidation are to be employed to persuade the public to behave in a way that saves them from destruction.

Canetti made it clear in an interview with Horst Bienek that he wrote *Masse und Macht* as a response to fascism: "Meine Hauptarbeit in dieser Zeit war doch die Untersuchung der Wurzeln des Faschismus, das war der Sinn von 'Masse und Macht.' Um zu begreifen was geschehen war, und zwar nicht bloß als Phänomen der Zeit, sondern in seinen tiefsten Ursprüngen und Verzweigungen hatte ich mir jede literarische Arbeit verboten."[16] Canetti does not want to give an account of fascism as a phenomenon of the twentieth century because this would only explain how fascism fits into the historical context of its time. Rather than relativizing fascism by saying that it could have happened only at the time at which it happened, Canetti shows that its roots lie in certain forms of human behavior of the past as well as of the present. This means he must give an account of fascism as something that still lives with us, which indeed forms part of our daily life.

By presenting fascist behavior as something that is still with us, Canetti wants to shock the reader, and to shock the reader he needs to present a world that is factual; he achieves this by appeal to empirical scientific research. The facticity of *Masse und Macht* aims to invoke the verisimilitude of a documentary film. There are indeed many similarities between the aims of Canetti's *Masse und Macht* and those of Claude Lanzmann's film *Shoah* (1985). For Lanzmann and for Canetti, the trauma of the Nazi genocide can never be history, can never be a thing of the past. Instead — and this is the reason for Canetti's ahistorical approach — the trauma has always to be present. Like Lanzmann, Canetti wants to have nothing to do with "fiction."[17] The Holocaust and its ethical implications force Canetti, Broch, and Steiner to abstain from exclusively writing fiction, because fiction does not have the authority of truth capable of shocking the reader into a radical change of behavior.[18]

Canetti reflects on these ethical agendas that lie behind the scholarly undertaking in his aphorisms. Scholarship offers a means of gaining knowledge, which yields the possibility of improving the reader's ethical behavior. As he writes in *Die Provinz des Menschen*, knowledge is the prerequisite for human betterment: "Besser werden kann nur heißen, daß man's besser weiß. Es muß aber ein Wissen sein, das einem keine Ruhe gibt, ein hetzendes Wissen. Ein Wissen, das beruhigt, ist tödlich. Es ist wichtig, daß man manches Wissen ablehnt. Man muß den Augenblick abwarten können, in dem ein Wissen zum Stachel wird: jede Ahnung ihr eigener Schmerz" (*Aufz. 1942–85*, 344). Here we encounter the opposite of resignation, here we find a writer who wishes to employ knowledge as a means for unsettling humanity.[19] Canetti, it should be recalled, is a moralist, and like Pope and Swift before him, he employs a satirical style of writing with the aim of shocking the reader to precipitate recognition of truth.[20] As a consequence, Canetti emphasizes appalling aspects of everyday life, aspects on which we prefer not to dwell, and he does so to make his readership change in their perception of reality and then in their behavior. Canetti sometimes uses such satirical techniques to present knowledge in a way that makes the reader restless, and here we reach a point at which literature and scholarship meet. Although Canetti is learned and scholarly, he does not write for scholars only, but also for the public. He wants to evoke certain reactions in the public, and he could not achieve this if he only communicated knowledge; rather this communication of knowledge has to tease the reader; it needs to be a kind of knowledge that causes insomnia. It needs to be presented in a way that forces the reader out of all complacency; it needs to be a kind of knowledge that undermines all forms of established truths. It needs to radically question the status quo.

However, knowledge alone does not suffice to make the reader challenge commonly accepted creeds: through its literary presentation, the epistemological has to work as a sting. This sting of knowledge invokes that of death, which it opposes. What we encounter here is a modern version of Enlightenment that does not generate hope in human betterment. Instead, it shows what a dangerous route humanity has taken, and in so doing tries to make the reader create alternatives, hopeful prospects of a world that can avoid catastrophe. As I have shown elsewhere, Canetti's novel *Die Blendung* proffers a critique of a kind of Enlightenment that has turned into positivism, thus invalidating an ethical agenda.[21] Whereas eighteenth-century Enlightenment set great store by the intrinsic goodness of man, Canetti's twentieth-century version of enlightenment tries to better humanity by presenting such a bleak view of human matters that the readers are persuaded both to reflect upon an alternative state of social interaction, and, consequently, to abandon established ways of behavior. To achieve such a bleak, utterly disconcerting view of past and present societies, Canetti needs to be selective, he needs to reject knowledge of communities that inspire hope: "*Es ist wichtig, daß man manches Wissen ablehnt.*" Canetti deliberately neglects these hopeful aspects in the anthropological literature he uses, and this radical neglect is part of a satirical manner of writing that seeks to turn knowledge into a sting.

Besides knowledge and its literary presentation, Canetti develops other strategies in developing the unique genre of his work. Defamiliarization is one such upon which I shall dwell while talking about the style of *Masse und Macht*. Satire gives a one-sided,[22] topsy-turvy view of the world with which we seem to be familiar. From this perspective, it is no wonder that a sociologist like Axel Honneth is unable to understand why Canetti paid no attention both to the civilizing progress in history and to man's moral feelings.[23] If he had done so, the satirical force of *Masse und Macht* would have been lost.

Critics often take *Masse und Macht* at face value and accuse its satirist of cynicism. The opposite is the case, especially if one notes an aphorism from *Das Geheimnis der Uhr*. Here Canetti reflects on the presentation, on "die Form" of *Masse und Macht*: "Es wird die Form von *Masse und Macht* noch zu seiner Stärke werden. Mit der Fortsetzung hättest du dieses Buch durch deine Hoffnungen zerstört. So wie es jetzt ist, zwingst du die Leser dazu, *ihre* Hoffnungen zu suchen" (*Aufz. 1942–85*, 495). With "die Form," Canetti may also be referring to the satirical style in which some passages of *Masse und Macht* are written. More generally, "form" here denotes the shocking representation of anthropological material in *Masse und Macht* that has to be seen in the context of a response to the Shoah. Not a Canetti critic, but a Holocaust scholar has noticed that *Masse und Macht* depicts a *univers concentrationnaire*: Harald Kaplan is the first to point out that "*Crowds and Power* might have been written based on actual Holocaust experiences."[24]

In the following subsection, I will examine in what ways Franz Baermann Steiner's more overt response to the Nazi genocide helped to shape Canetti's work on *Masse und Macht*. The importance Canetti attributes to the intense intellectual exchange with Steiner between 1939 and 1952 can be seen in the way Canetti characterizes Steiner: "Man muß sich schon ein wenig auskennen im Geiste dieses Menschen [i.e. Steiner], um zu wissen, daß es nur um ungeheure Antworten ging. Diese sind so selten, daß ein vernünftiger Mensch sie nicht erwartet" (*Aufz. 1992–93*, 18). One of those tremendous responses was no doubt Steiner's literary-ethnological response to the Shoah.

Social Death, Danger, Civilization, and F. B. Steiner's Epistemological Response to the Shoah

While Canetti was working on *Masse und Macht*, his close intellectual friend F. B. Steiner did intensive work on a comparative study of various forms of slavery. Significantly, Steiner characterized this work on slavery as a sacrifice for surviving the Holocaust as a Jewish refugee outside of the Nazi-occupied continent.[25] Steiner's definition of the term "slave" bears a striking resemblance to the situation of European Jewry after Nazi Germany's rise to power. What makes one a slave according to Steiner's definition? Steiner defines slavery as a state in which one is cut off from any forms of kinship ties or other kinds of associations with groups in which one can command solidarity. This is a highly striking definition, not least within the context of an anthropology that was starting to define itself in terms of kinship studies. Steiner's idea is revolutionary: he defines slaves as people wholly outside society. They have no kin, nor anyone who could feel an obligation toward them. They are open to any function, manipulation, or use that their owner decides upon. They are perceived as non-human.

Dehumanization preconditioned the Nazi brand of exterminatory anti-Semitism.[26] Only after the Nazis declared the Jews to be separated from the human community could the process of deportation and murder fully begin in its highly organized and total manner. The racial laws of Nazi Germany pronounced the Jews socially dead. Steiner and Canetti were aware of what was taking place on the Nazi-occupied continent. After his family was deported to the transit-camp Theresienstadt, Steiner could only receive five words from his parents, which were delivered to him via the Red Cross in Geneva. The five-word message from his parents took up to eight months to arrive at Steiner's address in Oxford. He was literally cut off from his family. Steiner's anthropological work thus sheds light on the conditions in which Canetti was composing *Masse und Macht*. Moreover, Steiner exemplified how one could combine scholarship with intellectual critique. His case illustrates how a scholarly project can develop from a personal situation. A personal situation, moreover, that represents that of a whole community: that of European Jews during the Shoah.

Steiner's anthropological and, as we shall see, literary work has methodological significance for an understanding of Canetti's shock technique in *Masse und Macht*. Steiner emphasizes the ethical validity of a scholarly quest for a kind of truth that changes social and political ways of life by deconstructing assumptions of Western superiority. Hence, Steiner's scholarship constitutes an epistemological response to his own situation as a Jewish refugee from the Nazi-occupied continent. According to Canetti, the recognition of such shocking truth has the tendency to engender change in the behavior that helped to produce the trauma in the first place. Steiner attempted to shatter conceptions of moral superiority by radically questioning the Western myth of civilization. He does so when he argues that the West constructed the notion "slave" so as to have an excuse to enslave those it conceived as "oriental," "savage," in short, as "other."

In the first part of his study, Steiner discusses the etymology of the word "slave" in Europe. He aims to show how Europeans, from antiquity onwards, inscribed into the very word "slave" many fictions about race. According to Steiner, in ancient Greece the word *sklavenoi* and *sklabenoi,* and in ancient Rome the word *sclaveni,* closely associated the word slave with the ethnical term "slav," denoting all the peoples living north of the Balkans. This close association between the race of the "slavs" and the state of being a "slave" permeates modern English and modern German (*Sklave — Slawe*). In Steiner's account, slavery surfaces as something that voices the superiority of one race over another, as a word that has economic as well as racial connotations, and he underlines this point by claiming that the Hindi term *dasa* means both slave and the pre-Aryan race. Steiner examines how European taxonomy misrepresents particular non-European social practices: when they use the term "slavery" Westerners are actually referring to a form of social integration, in which "primitive" or "oriental" societies establish new kinship groups for those who have lost their kin. There is no intrinsic relation between European taxonomy and the non-European social reality it is supposed to denote. Steiner deconceptualizes slavery by deconstructing the Western usage of the word slave.

To prove that Western scholarship distorts particular social realities in non-European societies, Steiner examines French, German, and English encyclopedias of the eighteenth and nineteenth centuries. He argues that in these dictionary entries, the term slavery is defined in a way that fulfills the needs of contemporary ideologies. European words for slave create fictions of superiority, as do "Aryan" terms like the Hindi word *dasa* mentioned above. After the abolition of the slave trade, British encyclopedias link slavery to "savage" societies, and, following Montesquieu, European writers depict slavery as a practice only found in non-European societies.

By referring to slavery, the West shows off its moral perfection. Steiner criticizes the same European understanding in an aphorism that questions the West's insistent pride in the abolition of horror. He maintains that, rather than consider an identification with the slaveholders, Europeans assume a prideful stance, saying that they have abolished slavery.[27] Steiner points out that this position immediately stifles any self-critical approach and makes impossible any identification between the slaveholder and the European. Steiner's study of slavery, on the other hand, does precisely that, establishing a close link between European history and the evolution of servile institutions.

Steiner's critique of Western modes of thinking, in which the "other" turns into the "savage" and thus the sub-human, or worse still, non-human, partakes of his response to the Shoah. Accordingly, Western forms of making the "other" uncannily other are not radically different from anti-Semitic stereotyping. In one of his aphorisms Steiner characterizes the German reign of terror as connected to a modern European instrumentalization of reason: "Andererseits hat es das Fähnlein der Aufrechten in Westeuropa besonders beunruhigt, daß die deutsche Schreckensherrschaft so kaltblütig mechanisch mit ihren Opfern verfuhr. Derlei darf doch nicht ordentlich zugehen!"[28] Steiner mocks Europe's pride in a "systematic" way of living. In Steiner's reading, Western Europeans are not terrified by the slaughter of the Jews; the only thing that worries them is the "civilized," well-organized manner in which the killings take place. The Holocaust shows how the rationality of the West can be used for irrational ends. The systematic and well-organized extermination ultimately calls sentiments about Europe's superiority into question.

Steiner was convinced about the connection between Orientalism and anti-Semitism well before it was established by Said. In his letter to Gandhi in 1946, he sums up his position in the following manner:

> My conclusion has been that the fact of Anti-Semitism is essential for the understanding of Christian Europe, it is a main thread in that fabric. No non-European power has *ever* built a colonial empire. Do you regard the ceaseless encroachment on the life and lands of other races, that of Asia in particular as inconsistent with European civilisation? [. . .] Would you not say that European civilisation that does no more hold other cultures in tutelage or suppression ceases to be the Europe we know? And if they do so to Asiatic countries what they have done to yours, how must they treat an Oriental people which lives among them and is always at their mercy?[29]

Here Steiner establishes a connection between anti-Semitism, colonialism, and slavery. Colonialism refers to slavery via the expressions "tutelage" and "suppression": Europeans enslave and colonize Asiatic nations by erasing existing kinship ties and introducing "suppression" instead, in which an individual is deprived of his or her kinship ties. In his letter to Gandhi, Steiner restricts the practice of colonialism to Europeans, and, similarly, in his Oxford thesis he regards slavery as a purely European category. Anti-Semitism is connected to colonialism and slavery. Anti-Semitic Germans treat those whom they see as Orientals at home in a manner equal to or even worse than the way other Europeans deal with the native populations in the Orient itself.

Steiner conceived of his Jewish identity as Oriental. In his Oxford lectures on "Taboo" (1951), he identifies as a Jew with the "we" of the "primitives." In doing so he of course refers to the anti-Semitic association of the Jews with the "primitive" and "oriental" only to undermine it.[30] With this differentiation between the "primitive"/"Oriental" and the "civilized," he develops his response to the Shoah. Canetti also distinguished between the primitive and the civilized. As we will see in the following section however, in *Masse und Macht* he did not allow for any alternative to what he presented as the human killing machine.

In his exchange with Steiner, Canetti was confronted with "the sociology of danger."[31] By describing taboos as behavior by means of which one avoids danger, Steiner attempts an abstract interpretation of all primitive cultures. As we have seen, he makes it clear that the primitive also encompasses the Oriental by identifying himself as an Oriental Jew with the primitive. In this context Steiner develops his theory about power and danger. The taboo emerges as the key to solving the problems that power and danger pose to any society. Communities in which the social pressure to follow taboos embraces the whole of the society are free from violent encounters with danger and power, which Steiner explicitly pairs. He alludes to the *condicio humana,* saying that humanity has always been surrounded by danger.[32] Taboos are a part of value systems in that they prescribe the avoidance of any form of power and give instructions concerning such avoidance by indicating exactly where the danger lies:

> Danger is narrowed down by taboo. A situation is regarded as dangerous: very well, but the danger may be a socially unformulated threat. Taboo gives notice that danger lies not in the whole situation, but only in certain specified actions concerning it. These actions, these danger spots, are more challenging and deadly than the situations as a whole, for the whole situation can be rendered free from danger by dealing with or, rather, avoiding the specified danger spots completely.[33]

Steiner argues for a form of dealing with danger by avoiding it. The ethical connotation of the taboo consists precisely in this avoidance of violence. At the end of his book, primitive culture emerges as a well thought out form of establishing human relations and relations with the natural world by keeping a distance from both power and danger. Steiner theorizes the concept of taboo as a way of putting power into an intellectual framework. In *Masse und Macht,* on the other hand, the reign of power does not face any kind of circumscription. For both Steiner and Canetti, power seems to epitomize the working of the Nazi machinery. What Steiner describes as danger, Canetti calls death. By threatening opponents with infliction of danger and death, Nazism attempts to consolidate its power. Through terror, the Nazis set out to conquer the world.

In his aphoristic essay "Über den Prozess der Zivilisierung," Steiner reads this totalitarian approach in the context of Western civilization's endeavor to control danger.

> Wird jemand, der in einem Konzentrationslager gewesen ist, glauben, reißende Tiere seien ärger als die menschlichen Peiniger? Und diese Qual ist neu: dieses Fangen von Menschenmassen in dichtmaschigen Netzen, dieses Bauen von Riesenkäfigen, an denen das "gesunde" Leben vorbeiflutet.[34]

By controlling nature, civilization has not diminished violence; on the contrary, it has increased brutality, and as civilization progresses, danger increases as well. Steiner acknowledges the historical break of the Shoah. In this way he speaks of a new kind of anguish. He uses the word "Qual" (torture), thus implying that it is not only physical, but also psychological and metaphysical suffering (in the sense of anguish) that concentration camps inflict upon their victims and those who hear about the horror of the *universe concentrationnaire*. He creates the neologism "Riesenkäfig" (gigantic cage) to come to terms with the indescribable terror of the Holocaust. The process of civilization unfolds the dialectic of eradication and internalization. It removes nature's demons, but the dialectic of this process moves the demonic from the sphere of nature into the sphere of man. As a consequence, contemporary civilization does not need to be afraid so much of natural catastrophes as of manmade ones.

With the process of civilization, various types of racist and xenophobic stereotyping increase. Having controlled danger in nature, civilized society internalizes the dangerous and projects it onto those who are considered "other." This process reaches its catastrophic climax in Nazism. Here Steiner particularly discusses Nazism's opposition between the "healthy and harmless Aryan" and the "diseased Jew."[35] What in Nazi thinking is considered to be "gesund" is exactly the dangerous. The "healthy" Nazis project their danger onto the "other" of the Jew. This projection only pre-conditions the perpetration of the dangerous and the lethal on those who are equated with "danger."

Canetti could have been encouraged by Steiner's emphasis on the benefits of an epistemological approach to the Shoah. In contrast to Canetti's *Masse und Macht*, Steiner's scholarly and literary work does not primarily attempt to shock the reader. His emphasis is overtly on unveiling the horrible truth of the Shoah with a view toward a better post-Holocaust future. Significantly, Canetti's shock techniques should instigate a similar change away from death and danger, though through a different mode.

Like Canetti, Steiner forbade himself the publication of literary work during the war. Under the impact of the Shoah, both intellectuals perceived literature in terms of an epistemological quest. Steiner emphasizes this point in his poem "Gebet im Garten Am Geburtstag meines Vaters dem Ersten Oktober 1947." Steiner's concern with the epistemology of poetry is most striking in his poem "Gebet im Garten." Steiner sets out to abolish all his individual concerns, repeatedly mentioning that he is only a part of a greater whole. The horrific truth of the Nazi genocide lays open the betrayal of hope:

> Wenn die hoffnung zerbricht,
> Ist der verrat am nächsten; und die wahrheit auch.
> O daß die hoffnung nimmer aufersteh!
> O daß sie die wahrheit erleide!
> O daß die wahrheit trete aus dieser gefahr,
> Trete aus jener heimlichkeit
> Zu gepriesener stunde.[36]

The hopes of both the poet and the reader have to disappear or be effaced so that the whole truth can appear. Abolishing his individuality, the poetic voice of "Gebet im Garten" turns into the mouthpiece of those who were killed:

> Die sich in mir gefunden,
> Sind überm Meer verbunden.[37]

The poet wants to become an organ for the suffering of his people. In an attempt to record all events, Steiner moves from the sinking of the Struma (a ship filled with Jewish refugees that sunk, presumably by a German torpedo, in the presence of British and Russian warships) to the gas chambers on the continent, insisting meticulously on the exact counting of every wound:

> Keine wunde ungezählt
> An stirne oder brust,
> Nicht bruch, nicht beule ungewusst,
> Nichts, was an frauenhals und wangen
> Die starre hand begangen,
> Der kleinsten wimpern ungeschmählt.
> [. . .]
> Kein tropfen, die augen zu netzen,
> Der säuglinge augen, die gase ätzen,
> Augen der mütter, hart im entsetzen.
> Kein wundes auge ungezählt,
> Der kleinsten wimmern ungeschmält.
> Denn alles leiden auf dem meer
> Ein schmerz sei um die herrlichkeit,
> In herrlichkeit sich wandelnd,
> Alles all verwandelnd.[38]

Steiner moves from the enumeration of wounds to an acceptance of this suffering, which is, in the final part of the poem, interpreted as a basis for human existence. Does this not normalize the horrors that the poet wants to depict in detail? Does acceptance of the suffering of Nazi persecution contradict Steiner's advocacy of rejection of social structures such as national and geographical boundaries, such as in his lyrical cycle *Eroberungen*? Asking these questions might indicate a failure to understand the poem. As the discussion above has shown, Steiner is fully aware of the historical break that the Holocaust constitutes. Steiner's switching from a realistic to a metaphysical plane does not harmonize the violence described. Despite Steiner's attempt to efface his individual concerns, "Gebet im Garten" is a highly personal poem: after all, it is also a prayer for his father, who was killed presumably in Treblinka. Despite this highly personal aspect of the "Gebet," Steiner's reference to divine manifestation, or *Schechina* — of which "Herrlichkeit" is a translation — not only bespeaks a wish for comfort, but it also articulates a desire for the recognition of truth. *Schechina* is a verbal noun meaning "dwelling" and a "post biblical term particularly used for God's indwelling on earth."[39] By referring to God's presence in creation, Steiner does not idealize suffering. At the end of the poem, which describes the situation after the prayer, Steiner conceives of God's presence as pain:

> Über mein herz ist ein grosses frieren gekommen.
> Im dunkel steh ich allein, seh nichts mehr.
> Weh ist der friede, o weh,
> Weh ist der friede deiner herrlichkeit. Amen.[40]

God's presence does not cover up or aestheticize the horrors of the Nazi genocide; on the contrary, it intensifies them. The *Schechina* of Steiner's poem does not offer comfort. On the contrary, the recognition of horror coincides with the vision of divine manifestation. Love of the creator compels the poet to become the mouthpiece of horror so that the corruption of creation into a hell on earth can be witnessed. The experience of hell destroys trust in the world, as Jean Amèry so accurately describes, and as the many suicides of Holocaust survivors so overwhelmingly illustrate. Steiner's attempt at giving a voice to the witnesses ("Zeugen, zeugen, / Schließt euch in mein sagen ein, bleibt mir jetzt nah, / Laßt mich in wahrheit sprechen")[41] of this hell on earth is enabled by the abolition of selfhood that issues in a depersonalized vision of the creator and creation. Only the recognition of the utter corruption of creation makes it possible to work at changing a damaged way of life. The *Schechina* offers a view on what happened in this hell on earth, compelling humanity to prevent it from happening again. In the following I will examine how Canetti's *Masse und Macht* enacts Steiner's notion of a kind of truth that aims at changing the reader's way of life.

Truth and Metamorphosis: Canetti's Epistemological Response to the Shoah in *Masse und Macht*

The above discussion of Steiner's response to the Shoah has prepared the ground for an examination of Canetti's response. Both authors develop an understanding of truth and knowledge that should enable cultural and political change away from a "civilized" way of life in which violence has become accepted as "natural," as "normal." Whereas Steiner engages in a direct analysis of the differences between modern and primitive worlds, Canetti reads the whole of human history in terms of murder. He does so in *Masse und Macht*. His aphorisms, on the other hand, provide ample evidence that in *Masse and Macht* he deliberately excluded hopeful alternatives to a shocking representation of humanity. This is not say that *Masse und Macht* avoids an analysis of Nazi terror. Canetti in fact takes apart the totalitarian link between crowds, death, and power. In the context of this analytical move, he develops his epistemological response.

Like Steiner, Canetti strictly interdicts a confusion of truth with hope (see the above discussion of "Gebet im Garten"). Even though both writers conceive of truth in terms of social transformation, they nonetheless guard against any complacency to which one would be tempted to succumb if one hoped that such change could be easily actualized. Steiner offers the alternative of the primitive not to open up hope for return to a pre-modern way of life. Rather, this alternative reminds one of what has been lost, and thus should instigate critical reflection on the present state of affairs.

Canetti responds to the Holocaust by investigating the link between the leader, the masses, and death. In concentration camps people are coerced to work for their own destruction and the destruction of their comrades through the threat of immediate murder. One can therefore speak of a policy of "postponed death," which proves Canetti's view of the masses, death, and power right, especially in relation to the Shoah. Canetti's masses are the piles of corpses that are produced daily in the death-machineries of the Nazis.

In an aphorism, Canetti complains about all those theorists who talk about "Macht" without taking into account the interrelation between "Macht" and "Tod": "Daß die, die das Entsetzen der Macht begreifen, nicht sehen, wie sehr sie sich des Todes bedient! Ohne den Tod wäre die Macht harmlos geblieben. Da reden sie über Macht daher, meinen, gegen sie anzurennen und lassen den Tod links liegen" (*Aufz. 1942–85*, 492). According to Canetti, power employs death as its rationale. This connection between death and power is perhaps the most challenging idea developed in *Masse und Macht*.

In their respective responses to the Shoah, Canetti and Steiner examine the way in which totalitarian power works. It operates first of all as a threat, and it proves its might through the realization of this threat. Against this background, "*Macht*" would be the power of a few individuals to put numerous people to death, and "*Masse*" would be the collection of those individuals, who can be reduced to instruments, subject to arbitrary commands and ultimately killed.

This interrelation between death and power appears at various places in *Masse und Macht*. Indeed, it virtually functions as a leitmotif. We read of the desire to circumvent death as permeating the whole of human history from its beginning to the present day: "Der Inbegriff aller Gefahren ist natürlich der Tod . . . Das erste und entscheidende Merkmal des Machthabers ist sein Recht über Leben und Tod. An ihn darf niemand heran; . . . Von ihm wird der Tod planmäßig ferngehalten; er selber darf und soll ihn verhängen wie er will. Sein Todesurteil wird immer ausgeführt."[42] And: "Das Umgehen des Todes, der Wunsch, ihm auszuweichen, gehört zu den ältesten und zähesten Tendenzen aller Machthaber" (*MM*, 227). Canetti interprets the ruler's desire for power as a longing for the avoidance of death: "Der Machthaber schickt die anderen in den Tod, um selber vom Tode verschont zu bleiben: er lenkt ihn von sich ab" (*MM*, 510). *Masse und Macht* closes with an invitation to undermine power by taking away the sting of both death and the command: "Der Tod als Drohung ist die Münze der Macht. Es ist leicht, hier Münze auf Münze zu legen und enorme Kapitalien anzusammeln. Wer der Macht beikommen will, der muß den Befehl ohne Scheu ins Auge fassen und die Mittel finden, ihn seines Stachels zu berauben" (*MM*, 542–43). The image of the coin echoes Canetti's discussion of money and inflation as expressions of "mass"-feelings, and the image of coins piling up emphasizes power's close relation to the formation of crowds. Significantly, Canetti refers to the murder of European Jewry while discussing inflation in the Weimar Republic. According to Canetti, the Germans projected this experience of monetary "worthlessness" onto the life of the Jews. In the above citation, he associates the hoarding of money with power and death. Against this background, the accumulation of threats, as metaphorically described in the image of accumulated coins, proleptically points to the masses of dead bodies produced daily in Nazi concentration camps.

Engaging with Steiner's sociology of danger, Canetti argues that those who abuse power threaten those whom they dehumanize with death and violence. One could say that Canetti applies Steiner's sociology of danger to the field of *Massenpsychologie* (crowd psychology). Surely there is nothing paralleling this in the work of other writers in this field. The threat of death to individuals is supposed to testify to the potency of the ruler, and in the threat of death to many people, the ruler manifests his wished-for omnipotence. Omnipotence is the right word here, given that Canetti tries to present as a fact that someone who commands or executes people sees the probabilities of his own immortality rise in direct proportion to the increase in number of corpses.

The closing sentence of *Masse und Macht,* quoted above, urges the reader to face up to the force of commands so as to be able to rob them of their sting. However, Canetti's metaphor of death as the coin or currency of power also implies that to blunt the sting of command one has to abolish that of death. Canetti advises the reader to outdo the life-threatening operations of power. Nevertheless, he gives no indication as to how this may be possible. In an interview with the journalist Joachim Schickele, however, Canetti referred to "primitive" cultures in which death was not accepted as something "natural."[43] In not accepting death, the "primitives" undercut the workings of power, and in his conversation with Schickele, Canetti cited this attitude toward death as a possible way out of history's nightmares.

Canetti tries to persuade the reader not to accept death in a way that is related to the mode in which Steiner argues for the avoidance of danger and power. By cultivating gradually more sophisticated ways to exert power, modern society, by contrast, has supported the naturalization of death. As the desire for power increases, death is accepted as natural rather than perceived as an unnatural occurrence: as "everyone has to die some day," nothing is wrong with dying for a great ruler in war, for example.[44]

In his aphorisms Canetti questions such acceptance of death when he criticizes the eating of meat. Critics have so far belittled the significance of Canetti's pleas not to be cruel to animals. In an important article, Dagmar Lorenz has recently analyzed how Canetti "placed killing and eating into the context of power, mass-murder, survival, and the psychology of the paranoid leader."[45] In his aphorisms Canetti examines how this acceptance of death emerges from cultural rather than natural foundations. Within the satirical context of *Masse und Macht,* on the other hand, he defamiliarizes our acceptance of violence and death in our everyday lives.

By making commonly accepted forms of social behavior appear abnormal, Canetti defamiliarizes one's perception of society. We thus need to distinguish between his view of and his depiction of humanity. An examination of Canetti's literary strategies helps one understand his intellectual agenda. Through defamiliarization Canetti tries to engage the emotions of his readers on an intellectual level. This is especially the case when we encounter what I call the rhetoric of revelation or discovery, which is characterized by expressions that make the reader alert to what is to follow in the text. These markers indicate that something is going to be unveiled that was previously covered by the darkness of hypocrisy. Here Canetti discusses a reality with which most of his readers are familiar, but, as these markers indicate, by whose outward appearance they have been deceived. Canetti's use of words and phrases like "wirklich" and "in Wirklichkeit" clarify that this deception is now going to end.

In this context Canetti's discussion of skyscrapers is perhaps most striking. Canetti reveals that it is not functionality that led to the building of skyscrapers, but the longing to imitate the smoothness of teeth: "Die Gleichheit einer ganzen Reihe von Vorderzähnen, die sauberen Abstände, in denen sie eingesetzt sind, waren vorbildlich für viele Anordnungen" (*MM*, 238). Modern architecture sets out to mirror the smoothness and regularity of teeth:

> Heute hat die Glätte auch die Häuser erobert, ihre Mauern, ihre Wände, die Gegenstände, die man in sie stellt, Zierat und Schmuck sind verachtet und gelten als Zeichen schlechten Geschmacks. Man spricht von Funktion, von Klarheit und Nützlichkeit, aber was in Wirklichkeit triumphiert hat, ist die *Glätte* und das geheime Prestige der Macht, die ihr innewohnt. (*MM* 237)

Canetti debunks the myth of progress within modernity.[46] From his perspective, what is called "primitive" appears to be nothing else but an expression of aggression. If premodernism was marked by ornamentation, modernity aspires to be purely functional. However, according to Canetti, this functionality is nothing other than an indication of power in that the evenness of modern buildings copy the smoothness of teeth, which do the work of tearing apart, killing, and devouring.

By comparing modern architecture with teeth, Canetti places his argument in images, saying that modernity, rather than abolishing brutality, promotes it. He chooses two images with which everyone is acquainted, so as to be in direct rapport with his readers. The process of revelation unfolds itself via two images. First, we see modern houses and then a tooth: the one falls in place with the other. Rather than being surrounded by clarity or functionality, modern people are almost constantly confronted with teeth on a superhuman scale, which symbolize the power and the desire to eat living beings.[47]

Canetti wants to sensitize his readers to the unnaturalness of many forms of behavior that are usually taken to be natural or normal. Strikingly, before embarking on an analysis of the psychology of commands, Canetti quotes the saying "Befehl ist Befehl" (*MM*, 347), which casts the acceptance of orders as a given, something that one cannot do without: "Man nimmt ihn [den Befehl] hin als etwas, das immer so da war, er erscheint so natürlich wie unentbehrlich" (*MM*, 347).

It is one of the main aims of *Masse und Macht* to put an end to this naturalization of the culturally constructed, and Canetti does so by defamiliarizing the reader's perception of objects or forms of behavior with which he or she seems to be familiar. We have already seen an example of this in the image of modern buildings that turn out to be teeth. *Masse und Macht* abounds in such examples. After claiming that revulsion at collective killings was only born with modernity, Canetti turns this thesis on its head by arguing that reading a newspaper is a far more comfortable and effective form of participating in killings than the old one, the public execution:

> Der *Abscheu* vor dem Zusammentöten ist ganz modernen Datums. Man überschätze ihn nicht. Auch heute nimmt jeder an öffentlichen Hinrichtungen teil durch die *Zeitung.* Man hat es nur, wie alles, viel bequemer. Man sitzt in Ruhe bei sich und kann unter hundert Einzelheiten bei denen verweilen, die einen besonders erregen. Man akklamiert erst, wenn alles vorüber ist, nicht die leiseste Spur von Mitschuld trübt den Genuß. Man ist für nichts verantwortlich, nicht fürs Urteil, nicht für den Augenzeugen, nicht für seinen Bericht und auch nicht für die Zeitung, die den Bericht gedruckt hat. [. . .] Im Publikum der Zeitungsleser hat sich eine gemilderte, aber durch ihre Distanz von den Ereignissen um so verantwortungslosere Hetzmasse am Leben erhalten, man wäre versucht zu sagen, ihre verächtlichste und zugleich stabilste Form. (*MM*, 55)

The liberal, bourgeois newspaper reader suddenly appears to be a voyeuristic participant in collective killings, a participant who takes no responsibility for what he sees and hears. Rather than being a means for both enlightenment and democratic involvement of the citizen in the political affairs of the world, the newspaper is exposed as a show of factual deeds of horror that cater to the sadistic drives of its readers. The civilized newspaper reader emerges as a monster.

Defamiliarization of processes that concern the everyday life of the common reader is most striking in the chapters with the heading *"Die Eingeweide der Macht."* Here Canetti begins his discussion by claiming that eating, the acts of apprehending and devouring food, are nothing out of the ordinary for the reader: "Die Psychologie des Ergreifens und Einverleibens — wie die des Essens im allgemeinen — ist noch völlig ununtersucht; es ist uns da alles extrem verständlich" (*MM*, 231). However, by using words like "ergreifen" and "einverleiben" Canetti evokes the image of the hunt, rather than that of a civilized meal, thus defamiliarizing modern eating habits from the start. Yet Canetti does not analyze our customs of eating in great detail; instead he concentrates on the result of the devouring of food: he dwells on the importance of feces in everyday life. For Canetti feces are all-important because they represent a part of reality we wish to ignore; from Canetti's perspective, this is an indication of our guilt. According to Canetti, feces evince human cruelty. They prove that we are murderers, since they are once living beings in a lifeless form of which man frees himself by going to the toilet. As a betrayal of murder, feces also bear witness to the exertion of power in our private lives: "Aber auch abgesehen vom Machthaber, der so viel in seiner Hand zu konzentrieren versteht, gehört die Beziehung jedes Menschen zum eigenen Kot in die Sphäre der Macht" (*MM*, 239). Although feces bear witness to most atrocious crimes, although they turn the reader into a murderer, they are accepted as something self-evident.

Canetti points out the common acceptance of the criminal as natural. The exertion of power forms part of the everyday reality of the common reader, who unconsciously takes it for granted: "Er [der Vorgang der Macht] ist so selbstverständlich, selbsttätig und jenseits alles Bewußten, daß man seine Bedeutung unterschätzt. Man neigt dazu, nur die tausendfachen Späße der Macht zu sehen, die sich oberirdisch abspielen; aber sie sind ihr kleinster Teil. Darunter wird tagaus, tagein verdaut und weiterverdaut" (*MM*, 240). Behind this defamiliarization lies Canetti's aim to alert the reader to fascism in what is considered "normality." In the image of feces, Canetti presents his argument, according to which fascism still lives with us and forms part of our daily reality, and here again the reader is immediately implicated:

> Der Kot, der von allem übrigbleibt, ist mit unserer ganzen Blutschuld beladen. An ihm läßt sich erkennen, was wir gemordet haben. Er ist die zusammengepreßte Summe sämtlicher Indizien gegen uns. Als unsere tägliche, fortgesetzte, als unsere nie unterbrochene Sünde stinkt und schreit er zum Himmel. (*MM*, 240)

The "wir," "uns," and "unsere" comprises the whole of humanity. Canetti's provocative language here moves him into close proximity to Karl Kraus, one of whose satirical techniques was to contrast the criminal dirt of human legality with the purity of divine justice.[48]

As in the satire of Swift and Kraus, defamiliarization in *Masse und Macht* serves as a means of making the readers feel homeless in a world where they might have thought themselves to be at home. In general, defamiliarization, like satire, aims to make the audience restless so that they have the impetus to change aspects of their society against which an ethical sensibility revolts.[49] Canetti also focuses attention on little details like the nervous play of the hands as an unconscious urge to seize and to devour (*MM*, 242, 249), knives and forks as killing instruments (*MM*, 250), the elastic tension of the cushion on the easy chair that mirrors that of living flesh (*MM*, 447).

By defamiliarizing familiar objects and behaviors, Canetti works on the way his reader perceives reality, and in doing so opens up their perceptive faculties to the possibility of reliving what appears to be harmless normality as a shock. Such shock experiences permeate *Masse und Macht*, and to make their impact more forceful, Canetti often picks out an acceptable form of human behavior like reading the newspaper, or even endearing activities like fondling, only to reveal a dark aspect that is then described as the main motive.

To declare a shocking perspective on humanity as an objective reality, Canetti has to be selective in the employment of facts gathered from anthropological books. He reflects on this method of selection in *Nachträge aus*

Hampstead when he writes: "Ich muß weiter den Mut haben *auszuwählen,* was mir wichtig und bezeichnend erscheint. Ich muß es riskieren, von sämtlichen Spezialisten sämtlicher Gebiete als ein Ignorant verschrien zu werden."[50] Canetti uses the word courage for this attempt at selection, indicating that this selective procedure could lead to the suspicion of a non-scholarly or non-scientific method. This shows just how aware the author of *Masse und Macht* was of his preference for an ethical agenda over purely academic or literary considerations.

As another aphorism from *Nachträge aus Hampstead* illustrates, Canetti seems to have had some qualms about his shocking depiction of human nature. Does the historical break of the Shoah justify a reading of humanity as a killing machine? Clearly, his friend F. B. Steiner opted for a different approach. Canetti seems to refer to Steiner's insistence on a third approach when he questions the strategies employed while composing *Masse und Macht:* "Es hat nie größere Barbaren gegeben als uns. Man muß die Menschlichkeit in der Vergangenheit suchen ('Einwand gegen Masse und Macht')" (*NH,* 179). Humanity as depicted in *Masse und Macht* goes without *Menschlichkeit* in the sense of benevolence. Through his depiction of the human, Canetti attempts to plunge his readers into despair. As long as this experience agitates for a metamorphosis of one's way of life, it remains "truthful." Here Canetti's and Steiner's respective responses to the Shoah meet. Responding to the shock of the Nazi genocide, they both develop a notion of truth that implies a turn away from a historical development that did not preclude this catastrophe.

Notes

[1] See Peter Novick, *The Holocaust in American Life* (New York: Mariner Books, 1999), 133.

[2] As Paul Mendes-Flohr and Jehuda Reinharz have pointed out: "Holocaust is a term that has come to designate the destruction of European Jewry during World War II. The term derives from the Septuagint, the Jewish translation of the Hebrew Scripture into Greek from the third century B.C., in which *Holocaustos* (totally burnt) is the Greek rendering of the Hebrew *olah,* the burnt sacrificial offering dedicated *exclusively* to God." Mendes-Flohr and Reinharz, eds., *The Jew in the Modern World: A Documentary History* (New York: Oxford UP, 1995), 634. Novick has recently traced the transition from using the term "Holocaust" to the word "Shoah." The latter turns out to be equally problematic: "In recent years it has been said that the word [Holocaust] is hatefully inappropriate because its original meaning was a religious sacrifice consumed by fire; it thus represents a pernicious Christianization of Jewish suffering. On these grounds, as well as what might be called cultural-nationalist grounds, the Hebrew word for catastrophe, 'shoah,' is said to be superior — a purely Jewish and purely secular term, free of odious theological implications. In fact, archaic original meanings are relevant only to someone looking to pick

up a fight. [. . . But] '*shoah*,' in the Hebrew Bible, was repeatedly used to describe punishments visited by God on the Jews — hardly a more palatable connotation." Novick, 133.

[3] See Michael Mack, *Anthropology as Memory: Elias Canetti's and Franz Baermann Steiner's Responses to the Shoah* (Tübingen: Niemeyer: 2001), 32–33.

[4] Quoted from Mazel Atze, ed., *Ortlose Botschaft: Der Freundeskreis H. G. Adler, Elias Canetti und Franz Baermann Steiner: Mit Beiträgen von Jeremy Adler und Gerhard Hirschfeld. In Zusammenarbeit mit der Bibliothek für Zeitgeschichte Stuttgart* (Marbach: Deutsche Schillergesellschaft, 1998), 119.

[5] Compare Edward Said, *Orientalism: Western Conceptions of the Orient* (Harmondsworth: Penguin, 1995). Steiner's deconstruction is exemplified in the following works: "Über den Prozess der Zivilisierung," in *Akzente* 42 (1995), 213–27; and in *Taboo* (Harmondsworth: Penguin, 1967).

[6] See Franz Baermann Steiner, *Selected Writings*, vol. 1 of *Taboo, Truth and Religion*, ed. Jeremy Adler and Richard Fardon, with a memoir by Mary Douglas Steiner (New York: Berghahn, 1999).

[7] This has recently been noticed by Richard H. Lawson: "*Crowds and Power* receives surprisingly little attention from literary critics, possibly because they imagine it to be beyond their purview." Richard Lawson, *Understanding Elias Canetti* (Columbia: U of South Carolina P, 1991), 54.

[8] Manfred Durzak, "Anmerkungen zu einer Vaterfigur der deutschen Gegenwartsliteratur," in *Zu Elias Canetti*, ed. Manfred Durzak (Stuttgart: Klett, 1983), 5–8.

[9] Dagmar Barnouw, *Elias Canetti* (Stuttgart: Metzler, 1979), 112.

[10] See Mack, *Anthropology as Memory*.

[11] Hansjakob Werlen and Axel G. Steussloff have called Canetti's approach "totalinarianism." See Hansjakob Werlen "'Ohnmächtige Hoffnung.' Die Stimme des Individuums in *Masse und Macht*," in *Einladung zur Verwandlung: Essays zu Elias Canettis "Macht und Macht,"* ed. Michael Krüger (Munich: Hanser, 1995), 151–63. Here: 152; Axel G. Steussloff, *Autorschaft und Werk Elias Canettis: Subjekt. Spruche. Identität* (Würzburg: Könighausen & Neumann, 1994), 168.

[12] Hermann Broch, *Massenwahntheorie: Beiträge zu einer Psychologie der Politik* (Frankfurt: Suhrkamp, 1979), 35.

[13] Elias Canetti, *Aufzeichnungen 1942–1985* (Munich: Hanser, 1993) 36.

[14] Biagioli discusses the involvement of modern scientific methods in the experimentation on and murder of the victims in Nazi concentration camps. Mario Biagioli, "Science, Modernity, and the Final Solution," in *Probing the Limits of Representation: Nazism and the "Final Solution,"* ed. Saul Friedlander (Cambridge, MA: Harvard UP, 1992), 185–205. Kaplan calls science the Nazis' "firm and consistent authority for dealing with death." Harold Kaplan, *Conscience and Memory: Meditations in a Museum of the Holocaust* (Chicago: U of Chicago P, 1994), 65.

[15] Sander Gilman has drawn attention to racist strands within late nineteenth-century and early twentieth-century medicine. For a discussion of this point, see Gilman, *The Jew's Body* (New York: Routledge, 1991).

[16] Manfred Durzak, ed., "Elias Canetti. Horst Bienek: Ein Gespräch," in *Zu Elias Canetti* (Stuttgart: Klett, 1983), 9–16.

[17] For a discussion of how the "acting-out" of trauma abolishes the barrier between art and life, see Dominick La Capra, "Lanzmann's *Shoah:* 'Here there is no why,'" *Critical Inquiry*, 23 (1997): 231–69, 266. For a discussion of how *Shoah* depicts the present rather than the past, see Soshana Felman, "Film as Witness: Claude Lanzmann's *Shoah*," in *Holocaust Remembrance: The Shapes of Memory*, ed. Geoffrey H. Hartman (Oxford: Blackwell, 1994) 90–103.

[18] Broch alludes to Canetti's shock techniques in relation to *Die Blendung* as follows: "[. . .] indem er (Canetti) seine Gestalten und damit den Leser in die Angst des Irrsinns jagd, will er jene tiefste Zerknirschung erreichen [. . .]." Hermann Broch, *Schriften zur Literatur*, vol. 1 (Frankfurt: Suhrkamp, 1975), 61. In his review of *Masse und Macht*, Hartung hopes that a follow-up to the book might offer the reader some hope, which the present version lacks. Rudolf Hartung, "Hinweis auf Elias Canetti," in *Rudolf Hartung: Elias Canetti: Ein Rezipient und sein Autor*, ed. Bernhard Albers (Aachen: Rimbaud, 1992), 29–34. Susan Sontag has spoken of Canetti as "registering shocks." Sontag, "Mind as Passion," in *Essays in Honour of Elias Canetti*, trans. Michael Hulse (London: Deutsch, 1987), 88–107.

[19] Menke has rightly argued that for Canetti recognition of truth or epistemology is a form of practice that is able to change what it recognizes: the reality perceived in *Masse und Macht*. For discussion of this point, see Christoph Menke, "Die Kunst des Fallens. Canettis Poetik der Erkenntnis," in *Einladung zur Verwandlung: Essays zu Elias Canettis Masse und Macht*, ed. Michael Krüger (Munich: Hanser, 1995) 38–66.

[20] For a detailed discussion of Canetti's satirical style of writing, see Mack, *Anthropology as Memory*, 46–80.

[21] See Mack, *Anthropology as Memory*, 32–46.

[22] See Clifford Geertz, *Works and Lives: The Anthropologist as Author* (Cambridge: Polity, 1988), 106–7.

[23] See Axel Honneth, "Die unendliche Perpetuierung des Naturzustandes. Zur theoretischen Erkenntnis von Canettis *Masse und Macht*," in *Einladung zur Verwandlung*, 105–28.

[24] Kaplan, *Conscience and Memory*, 107.

[25] Alfons Fleischli, *Franz Baermann Steiner: Leben und Werk* (Hochdorf: Buchdruckerei Hochdorf, 1970), 24.

[26] Compare Raul Hilberg, *Perpetrators Victims, Bystanders: The Jewish Catastrophe 1933–1945* (London: Lime Tree, 1993), and Martin Gilbert, *Endlösung: Die Vertreibung und Vernichtung der Juden: Ein Atlas* (Reinbeck: Rowohlt, 1982).

[27] Like many of Steiner's other still-unpublished letters, poems, and aphoristic essays, this aphorism can be read in the Deutsche Literaturarchiv, Marbach.

[28] Franz Baermann Steiner, *Fluchtvergnüglichkeit: Feststellungen und Versuche* (Stuttgart: Flugasche, 1988), 73.

[29] Franz Baermann Steiner, "Letter to Gandhi," *Orientpolitik, Value and Civilisation* (New York: Berghahn, 1999), 132.

[30] For a detailed discussion of this point, see Mack, *Anthropology as Memory*, 126–28.

[31] Franz Baermann Steiner, *Taboo* (Harmondsworth: Penguin, 1967), 20–21.

[32] Steiner, *Taboo,* 147.

[33] Steiner, *Taboo,* 146–47.

[34] Franz Baermann Steiner "Über den Prozess der Zivilisierung," *Akzente* 42 (1995): 213–27, 218.

[35] For a discussion of this opposition, see Sander L. Gilman, *The Jew's Body* (New York: Routledge, 1991).

[36] Steiner, *Am stürzenden Pfad: Gesammelte Gedichte* (Göttingen: Wallstein, 2000), 314. Henceforth *Pfad.*

[37] Steiner, *Pfad,* 316.

[38] Steiner, *Pfad,* 316.

[39] Leo Strauss, *Liberalism Ancient and Modern* (New York: Basic Books, 1968), 160.

[40] Steiner, *Pfad,* 317.

[41] Steiner, *Pfad,* 315.

[42] Elias Canetti, *Masse und Macht* (Hamburg: Claassen, 1960), 265. Hereafter cited as *MM.*

[43] Elias Canetti, "Gespräch mit Joachim Schickele," in *Die gespaltene Zukunft* (Munich: Hanser, 1973), 104–31, Here: 124.

[44] For a detailed account of how Canetti contradicts ethnological accounts of attempts by various primitive societies to cheat both death and power, see Mack, *Anthropology as Memory,* 74–80.

[45] Dagmar C. G. Lorenz, "More than Metaphors: Animals, Gender, and Jewish Identity in Gertrud Kolmar," in *Transforming the Center, Eroding the Margins: Essays on Ethnic and Cultural Boundaries in German-Speaking Countries,* ed. Dagmar C. G. Lorenz and Renate S. Posthofen (Columbia, SC: Camden House, 1998), 21–28, Here: 21.

[46] Canetti's demystification of the "modern" as the "primitive" has an interesting parallel in Max Horkheimer, Theodor W. Adorno, and Rolf Tiedemann, *Dialektik der Aufklärung* (Frankfurt: Suhrkamp, 1981).

[47] For a similar form of the revelationary marker see Canetti's opening paragraph to the chapter "Überleben als Leidenschaft," where he is at pains to make it clear that he discovers the true motive that makes ordinary people turn into heroes (*MM, 262*); see also the revelation of the motive behind the bushmen's metamorphosis into animals (*MM, 391*), or the revelation of the melancholic's refusal to eat as driven by the fear of being eaten by the food one eats (*MM, 398*).

[48] For a discussion of how Canetti's indictment of the eating of meat harks back to the books of *Genesis* and *Leviticus,* see Mack, *Anthropology as Memory,* 149–91.

[49] For a discussion of the connection between the trope of defamiliarization and the concept of transformation see Tony Bennett, *Formalism and Marxism* (London: Routledge, 1979).

[50] Elias Canetti, *Nachträge aus Hampstead* (Zurich: Hanser, 1994), 21.

Works Cited

Adorno, Theodor W., Else Frenkel-Brunswick, Daniel J. Levinson, and Newitt R. Sanford. *The Authoritarian Personality.* New York: Harper, 1950.

Andersch, Alfred. *Efraim.* Munich: Deutscher Taschenbuch Verlag, 1971.

Angelova, Penka. "Balkanidentitäten." *Internationale Zeitschrift für transdisziplinäre Forschung* 2/3 (Elias Canetti Issue) (2000): 1–9.

———. "Canettis autobiographische Trilogie als Bildungsroman." In *Autobiographie zwischen Fiktion und Wirklichkeit,* ed. Penka Angelova and Emilia Staitscheva, 47–62. St. Ingbert: Röhrig, 1997.

Angelova, Penka, and Judith Veichtbauer, eds. *Pulverfaß Balkan: Mythos oder Realität.* St. Ingbert: Röhrig Universitätsverlag, 2001.

Ansell-Pearson, Keith. "The Significance of Michel Foucault's Reading of Nietzsche: Power, the Subject, and Political Theory." In *Nietzsche: A Critical Reader,* ed. Peter R. Sedgwick, 13–30. Oxford: Blackwell, 1995.

Arendt, Hannah. *Eichmann in Jerusalem.* New York: Viking Press, 1963.

Arens, W. *The Man-Eating Myth.* New York: Oxford UP, 1979.

Arie, Gabriel. *A Sephardic Life in Southeastern Europe: The Autobiography and Journal of Gabriel Arie, 1863–1939.* Seattle: U of Washington P, 1998.

Aschheim, Steven E. *In Times of Crisis: Essays on European Culture, Germans, and Jews.* Madison: U of Wisconsin P, 2001.

Auerbach, Erich. "The Brown Stocking." In *Mimesis: The Representation of Reality in Western Literature,* trans. Willard Trask, 463–88. New York: Doubleday, 1957.

Babel, Isaak Emmanuilovich. *Geschichten aus Odessa.* Berlin: Malik, 1926.

Baldauf, Stefan. "Die transzendentale Phänomenologie Edmund Husserls als Methode in Elias Canettis *Masse und Macht.* Diplomarbeit, University of Innsbruck, ms. 1997.

Balthasar, Hans Urs von, ed. *The Scandal of the Incarnation: Irenaeus against the Heresies.* Trans. John Saward. San Francisco: Ignatius, 1990.

Barnouw, Dagmar. "Blick, Rückblick, Verwandlung." In *Tod und Verwandlung,* ed. John Pattillo-Hess, 132–42. Vienna: Kunstverein Wien, 1990.

———. "Doubting Death: On Elias Canetti's Drama *The Deadlined.*" *Mosaic — A Journal for the Interdisciplinary Study of Literature* 7/2 (1974): 1–23.

———. *Elias Canetti*. Stuttgart: Metzler, 1979.

———. "Elias Canetti — Poet and Intellectual." In *Critical Essays on Elias Canetti*, ed. *David Darby*, 15–34. New York: G. K. Hall, 2000.

———. *Elias Canetti zur Einführung*. Hamburg: Junius, 1996.

———. "Utopian Dissent: Canetti's Dramatic Fictions." In *Critical Essays on Elias Canetti*, ed. David Darby. New York: G. K. Hall & Co., 2000.

Bartsch, Kurt, and Gerhard Melzer, eds. *Experte der Macht: Elias Canetti*. Graz: Droschl, 1985.

Bauer, Barbara. "'Unter dem Eindruck der Ereignisse in Deutschland.' Ideologiekritik und Sprachkritik in Elias Canettis *Komödie der Eitelkeit*." In *Canetti als Leser*, ed. Gerhard Neumann, 77–111. Freiburg, Rombach, 1996.

Baur, Ruprecht Slavko. "Gespräch mit Elias Canetti. Zagreb, 15 May 1972." *Literatur und Kritik* 65 (1972): 272–79.

Bayley, John. "Canetti und Macht." In *Hüter der Verwandlung: Beiträge zum Werk von Elias Canetti*, ed. Werner Hoffmann, 133–47. Munich: Hanser, 1985.

———. *Elegy for Iris*. New York: Picador/St. Martin's, 1999.

———. *Iris: A Memoir of Iris Murdoch*. London: Duckworth, 1999.

Behler, Ernst. "Nietzsche in the Twentieth Century." In *The Cambridge Companion to Nietzsche*, ed. Bernd Magnus and Kathleen M. Higgins. Cambridge: Cambridge UP, 1996.

Bell, Matthew. *Goethe's Naturalistic Anthropology: Man and Other Plants*. Oxford: Clarendon Press, 1994.

Bennett, Tony. *Formalism and Marxism*. London: Routledge, 1979.

Biagioli, Mario. "Science, Modernity, and the Final Solution." In *Probing the Limits of Representation: Nazism and the "Final Solution."* Ed. Saul Friedlander. Cambridge, MA: Harvard UP, 1992.

Birke, Lynda. *Feminism, Animals and Science: The Naming of the Shrew*. Buckingham, PA: Open UP, 1994.

Bloch, Ernst. *Das Prinzip Hoffnung*. Frankfurt: Suhrkamp, 1959.

Bollacher, Martin. "Mundus liber: Zum Verhältnis von Sprache und Judentum bei Elias Canetti." In *Elias Canettis Anthropologie und Poetik*, ed. Stefan H. Kaszyński, 60–61. Munich: Hanser, 1984.

———. "'[. . .] das Weitertragen des Gelesenen': Lesen und Schreiben in Canettis Autobiographie." In *Canetti als Leser*, ed. Gerhard Neumann, 33–48. Freiburg: Rombach Litterae, 1996.

Brecht, Bertolt. *Hauspostille*. Berlin: Propyläen, 1927.

Broch, Hermann. *Beiträge zu einer Psychologie der Politik*. Frankfurt: Suhrkamp, 1979.

———. *Kommentierte Werkausgabe*. Vol. 1. *Die Schlafwandler*, ed. Paul Michael Lützeler. Frankfurt: Suhrkamp, 1995.

———. *Schriften zur Literatur*. Frankfurt a.M.: Suhrkamp, 1975.

Browning, Christopher R. *Ordinary Men: Reserve Police Battalion 101 and the Final Solution in Poland*. New York: Harper Collins, 1992.

Brückner, Wolfgang. *"Arbeit macht frei": Herkunft und Hintergrund der KZ-Devise*. Opladen: Leske & Budrich, 1998.

Brude-Firnau, Gisela. "Wissenschaft von der Frau? Zum Einfluß von Otto Weininger 'Geschlecht und Charakter' auf den deutschen Roman." In *Die Frau als Heldin und Autorin*, ed. Wolfgang Paulsen, 136–49. Bern: A. Francke, 1979.

Burgstaller, Erich. "Zur Behandlung der Sprache in Elias Canettis frühen Dramen." In *Sprachthematik in der österreichischen Literatur des 20. Jahrhunderts*, ed. Alfred Doppler, 101–17. Vienna: Hirt, 1974.

Canetti, Veza. *Der Fund: Erzählungen und Stücke*. Munich: Hanser, 2001.

———. *Geduld bringt Rosen*. Ed. Elias Canetti. Munich: Hanser, 1992.

———. *Die gelbe Straße*. Ed. Elias Canetti. Munich: Hanser, 1990.

———. *Die Schildkröten*. Munich: Hanser, 1999.

Caplan, Caren Jane. "The Poetics of Displacement: Exile, Immigration and Travel in Contemporary Autobiographical Writing." Ph.D. diss., University of California, Santa Cruz, 1987.

Chary, Frederick. *The Bulgarian Jews and the Final Solution 1940–1944*. Pittsburgh: U of Pittsburgh P, 1972.

Cohn-Bendit, Daniel. "Die Macht der Massen und das Gewissen der Individuen." In *Der Stachel des Befehls*. IC Canetti Symposium. Ed. John Pattillo-Hess. Vienna: Löcker Verlag, 1992.

The Columbia Encyclopedia, Sixth Edition. New York: Columbia UP, 2000.

Conradi, Peter J. *Iris Murdoch: A Life*. New York: W. W. Norton, 2001.

Crampton, R. J. *A Concise History of Bulgaria*. Cambridge/New York: Cambridge UP, 1997.

Creed, Gerald W. *Domesticating Revolution: From Socialist Reform to Ambivalent Transition in a Bulgarian Village*. University Park, PA: Pennsylvania State UP, 1998.

———. *Subsistence Farming and Economic Transition in Bulgaria*. Washington DC: National Council for Eurasian and East European Research, 1997.

Curtius, Mechthild, ed. *Autorengespräche: Verwandlung der Wirklichkeit: Gespräche mit 13 Autoren.* Frankfurt: Fischer, 1991.

———. "Blendungen. Autobiographie in der Wirklichkeit." In *Autobiographie zwischen Fiktion und Wirklichkeit,* ed. Penka Angelova and Emilia Staitscheva, 91–99. St. Ingbert: Röhrig Universitätsverlag, 1997.

Darby, David. *Structures of Disintegration: Narrative Strategies in Elias Canetti's Die Blendung.* Riverside: Ariadne, 1992.

———, ed. *Critical Essays on Elias Canetti.* New York: G. K. Hall, 2000.

Darwin, Charles. *The Descent of Man, and Selection in Relation to Sex.* Princeton: Princeton UP, 1981.

———. *The Origin of Species by Means of Natural Selection, or the Preservation of Favoured Races in the Struggle for Life.* Ed. J. W. Burrow. London: Penguin, 1968.

Denby, David. "Learning to Love Canetti: The Autobiography of a Difficult Man." *The New Yorker* (May 31, 1999): 106–13.

Dennett, Daniel C. *Darwin's Dangerous Idea: Evolution and the Meanings of Life.* London: Penguin, 1995.

Di Maio, Irene Stocksieker. "'Heimat,' 'Örtlichkeiten,' and Mother-Tongue: The Cases of Jean Améry and Elias Canetti." In *Der Begriff "Heimat" in der deutschen Gegenwartsliteratur/The Concept of "Heimat" in Contemporary German Culture,* ed. in Helfried W. Seliger, 211–24. Munich: iudicium, 1987.

Dissinger, Dieter. *Vereinzelung und Massenwahn: Elias Canettis Roman "Die Blendung."* Bonn: Bouvier, 1971.

Doerr, Karin. "'To Each His Own' (*Jedem das Seine*): The (Mis-)Use of German Proverbs in Concentration Camps and Beyond." *Proverbium: Yearbook of International Proverb Scholarship* 17 (2000): 71–90.

Doikov, Vassil. *Rousse: Biografiata na edin grad.* Rousse: Dunav Press, 2002.

Donahue, William Collins. "Elias Canetti's 'Die Blendung' in Literary and Cultural Context." Dissertation Abstracts International (DAI) 56/7, Ann Arbor, MI, 1996.

———. *The End of Modernism: Elias Canetti's Auto-da-Fé.* Chapel Hill: U of North Carolina P, 2001.

Doppler, Alfred. "Gestalten und Figuren als Elemente der Zeit- und Lebensgeschichte: Canettis autobiographische Bücher." In *Autobiographien in der Österreichischen Literatur: Von Franz Grillparzer bis Thomas Bernhard,* ed. Klaus Amann and Karl Wagner, 113–23. Innsbruck: Studien, 1998.

———. "Vor- und Gegenbilder (Gestalten und Figuren als Elemente der Zeit- und Lebensgeschichte in Canettis autobiographischen Büchern." In *Elias Canetti: Londoner Symposium,* ed. Adrian Stevens and Fred Wagner, 33–44. Stuttgart: Verlag Hans-Dieter Heinz/Akademischer Verlag Stuttgart, 1991.

DuCardonnay, Eric Leroy. *Les "réflexions" d'Elias Canetti une esthétique de la discontinuité.* Bern: Lang, 1997.

Dunayer, Joan. "Sexist Words, Speciest Roots." In *Animals and Women: Feminist Theoretical Explorations,* ed. Carol J. Adams and Josephine Donovan, 11–31. Duke UP: Durham and London, 1995.

Durzak, Manfred. "The Acoustic Mask: Toward a Theory of Drama." Elias Canetti in Conversation with Manfred Durzak. In *Critical Essays on Elias Canetti,* ed. David Darby, 93–108. New York: G. K. Hall & Co., 2000.

———. "Anmerkungen zu einer Vaterfigur der deutschen Gegenwartsliteratur." In *Zu Elias Canetti,* ed. Manfred Durzak, 5–8. Stuttgart: Klett, 1983.

———. "'Die Welt ist nicht so darzustellen wie in früheren Romanen.' Gespräch mit Elias Canetti." In *Gespräche über den Roman: Formbestimmungen und Analysen,* 86–102. Frankfurt: Suhrkamp, 1976.

———, ed. *Interpretationen zu Elias Canetti,* 18–19. Stuttgart: Klett, 1983.

Durzak, Manfred, and Elias Canetti. "Akustische Maske und Maskensprung. Materialien zu einer Theorie des Dramas. Ein Gespräch." *Neue Deutsche Hefte* 22/3 (1975): 515–30. Also in *Zu Elias Canetti,* ed. Manfred Durzak, 17–30. Stuttgart: Klett 1983.

Ebner-Eschenbach, Marie von. *"Die Kapitalistinnen," und zwei andere Novellen* ["Der Muff," "Krambambuli"]. New York: F. S. Crofts, 1928.

———. *Krambambuli und andere Erzählungen.* Stuttgart: Reclam, 1965.

Eigler, Friederike. *Das autobiographische Werk von Elias Canetti: Verwandlung, Identität, Machtausübung.* Tübingen: Stauffenburg, 1988.

———. "'Fissures in the Monument': Reassessing Elias Canetti's Autobiographical Works." In *Critical Essays on Elias Canetti,* ed. David Darby, 261–75. New York: G. K. Hall & Co., 2000.

———. *Verwandlung und Machtausübung in der Autobiographie Elias Canettis: Zum Status und zur Funktion autobiographischen Schreibens.* Dissertation Abstracts International (DAI), vol. 48/7, 1782A–1783A. Ann Arbor, MI, 1988.

Elbaz, Robert, and Leah Hadomi. *Elias Canetti, or, the Failing of the Novel.* New York: Peter Lang, 1995.

———. "The Temptation of Utopia and the Problematics of Language in Canetti's *Auto da fé.*" *Orbis Litterarum* 49 (1994): 253–71.

Elias, Norbert. *The Civilizing Process.* New York: Urizen Books, 1978.

Elwood, Roger. *Six Science Fiction Plays.* New York: Pocket Books, 1967.

Engelmann, Susanna. *Babel — Bibel — Bibliothek: Canettis Aphorismen zur Sprache.* Würzburg: Königshausen & Neumann 1997.

Falk, Thomas H. *Elias Canetti.* New York: Twayne Publishers, 1993.

Felman, Soshana. "Film as Witness: Claude Lanzmann's *Shoah.*" In *Holocaust Remembrance: The Shapes of Memory,* ed. Geoffrey H. Hartman, 90–103. Oxford: Blackwell, 1994.

Feng, Guoqing. *Kreisel für Erwachsene: Zur Kurzprosa in der Gegenwartsliteratur in Österreich: Thomas Bernhard, Elias Canetti und Erich Fried,* 73–128. Bern: Lang, 1993.

Ferrara, Jenna. "Grotesque and Voiceless; Women Characters in Elias Canetti's *Die Blendung.*" In *Proceedings and Commentary: German Graduate Students Association Conference at New York University,* ed. Patricia Doykos Duquette, Mathew Griffin, and Inike Lode, 86–94. New York: n.p. 1994.

Fetscher, Iring. "Elias Canetti als Satiriker." In *Hüter der Verwandlung,* ed. Werner Hoffmann, 217–31. Munich: Hanser, 1985.

Finsen, Lawrence, and Susan Finsen. *The Animal Rights Movement in America: From Compassion to Respect.* New York: Twayne, 1994.

Flavius Josephus. *The Jewish War.* New York: Penguin Viking, 1984.

Fleischli, Alfons. *Franz Baermann Steiner: Leben und Werk.* Hochdorf: Buchdruckerei Hochdorf, 1970.

Foell, Kristie A. *Blind Reflections: Gender in Elias Canetti's Die Blendung.* Studies in Austrian Literature, Culture, and Thought. Riverside: Ariadne Press, 1994.

———. "July 15, 1927. The Vienna Palace of Justice Is Burned in a Mass Uprising of Viennese Workers, a Central Experience in the Life and Work of Elias Canetti." In *Yale Companion to Jewish Writing and Thought in German Culture,* ed. Sander L. Gilman and Jack Zipes, 464–70. New Haven: Yale UP, 1997.

Foucault, Michel. *The History of Sexuality.* Trans. Robert Hurley. New York: Vintage Books, 1990.

———. *Sexualität und Wahrheit: Der Wille zum Wissen.* Frankfurt: Suhrkamp, 1987.

Fox, Michael Allen. *Deep Vegetarianism.* Philadelphia: Temple UP, 1999.

Freud, Sigmund. *Massenpsychologie und Ich-Analyse: Gesammelte Werke: chronologisch geordnet.* Vol. 13. Ed. Anna Freud. Frankfurt: Fischer, 1968–1978.

———. *Studienausgabe.* Ed. Alexander Mitscherlich. 10 vols. Frankfurt: Fischer, 1970.

———. "Das Unbehagen in der Kultur." In *Studienausgabe.* Vol. 9, 191–270. Frankfurt: Suhrkamp, 1974.

Fricke, Harald. *Aphorismus.* Stuttgart: Metzler, 1984.

Friedrich, Peter. *Die Rebellion der Masse im Textsystem: Die Sprache der Gegenwissenschaft in Elias Canettis "Masse und Macht."* Munich: Fink, 1999.

Fuchs, Anne. "Elias Canetti's Voices of Marrakesh." In *Critical Essays on Elias Canetti,* ed. David Darby, 201–13. New York: G. K. Hall & Co. 2000.

———. "Der touristische Blick: Elias Canetti in Marrakesch. Ansatze zu einer Semiotik des Tourismus." In *Reisen im Diskurs: Modelle der literarischen Fremderfahrung von den Pilgerberichten bis zur Postmoderne,* ed. Anne Fuchs, Theo Harden, and Eva Juhl, 71–86. Heidelberg: Winter, 1995.

Fuchs, Irmgard. "Elias Canetti, ein Aristokrat der Verwandlung." In *Österreichische Literatur und Psychoanalyse,* ed. Josef Rattner and Gerhard Danzer, 295–324. Würzburg: Königshausen & Neumann, 1997.

Furness, Raymond. "Canetti the Dramatist." In *Elias Canetti, Londoner Symposium,* ed. Adrian Stevens and Fred Wagner, 75–86. Stuttgart: Akademischer Verlag Hans-Dieter Heinz, 1991.

Galton, Francis. *Inquiries into Human Faculty and its Development.* London: Dent, 1907. First published 1883.

Gass, William H. "The Road to the True Book: A Portrait of Elias Canetti." *The New Republic* (November 8, 1982): 27–34.

Gayon, Jean. "Nietzsche and Darwin." In *Biology and the Foundation of Ethics,* ed. Jane Maienschein and Michael Ruse, 154–97. Cambridge: Cambridge UP, 1999.

Geertz, Clifford. *Works and Lives: The Anthropologist as Author.* Cambridge: Polity, 1988.

Gergicov, Krum. "The szenische Interpretation des totalen apokalyptischen Bösen in zwei Aufführungen des Dramas "Die Hochzeit" von Elias Canetti auf der bulgarischen Bühne." In *Autobiographie zwischen Fiktion und Wirklichkeit,* ed. Penka Angelova and Emilia Staitscheva, 277–96. St. Ingbert: Röhrig Universitätsverlag, 1997.

Gilbert, Martin. *Endlösung: Die Vertreibung und Vernichtung der Juden: Ein Atlas.* Reinbek: Rowohlt, 1982.

Gilman, Sander L. *The Jew's Body.* New York: Routledge, 1991.

Glotz, Peter. "Der Standort daneben: Elias Canetti und die Gier der Nationen." In *Einladung zur Verwandlung: Essays zu Elias Canettis Masse und Macht,* ed. Michael Kruger, 578–80. Munich: Hanser, 1995.

Gobineau, Arthur de. *Les Religions et les philosophies dans l'Asie Centrale.* In *Oeuvres.* Ed. Jean Gaulmier. 3 vols. Paris: Gallimard, 1983. First published 1865.

Goethe, Johann Wolfgang. *West-östlicher Divan: Kritische Ausgabe der Gedichte.* Ed. Hans A. Maier. Tübingen: Niemeyer, 1965.

Goldhagen, Daniel Jonah. *Hitler's Willing Executioners: Ordinary Germans and the Holocaust.* New York: Knopf, 1996.

Goll, Claire. *Ménagerie sentimentale; Tagebuch eines Pferdes.* Thal: Pflugverlag, 1950.

———. *My Sentimental Zoo: Animal Stories.* Mount Vernon, NY: The Peter Pauper Press, 1942.

———. *Die Taubenwitwe.* St. Gallen: Pflugverlag Thal, 1952.

Göpfert, Herbert G., ed. *Canetti lesen: Erfahrungen mit seinen Büchern.* Munich: Hanser 1975.

———. "Zu den Stimmen von Marrakesch," In *Elias Canettis Anthropologie und Poetik,* ed. Stefan H. Kaszyński, 135–50. Munich: Hanser, 1984.

Grass, Günter. *Die Blechtrommel.* Luchterhand: Darmstadt and Neuwied, 1959.

Greiner, Bernhard. "Akustische Maske und Geborgenheit in der Schrift: Die Sprach-Orientierung der Autobiographie bei Elias Canetti und Walter Benjamin." *Literaturwissenschaftliches Jahrbuch im Auftrage der Görres-Gesellschaft* 34 (1993): 305–25.

Grillparzer, Franz. *Sämtliche Werke.* Ed. August Sauer and Reinhold Backmann. Vienna: Kunstverlag Anton Schroll & Co., 1909–1948.

Grosz, Elizabeth. *Sexual Subversions: Three French Feminists.* Sydney: Allen & Unwin, 1989.

Grözinger, Karl Erich. *Kafka und die Kabbala: Das Jüdische in Werk und Denken von Franz Kafka.* Frankfurt a.M.: Eichborn Verlag, 1992.

Gutmann, Thomas. "Nietzsches 'Wille zur Macht' im Werk Michel Foucaults." *Nietzsche-Studien* 27 (1998): 377–419.

Harrison, Mark. *Crowds and History: Mass Phenomena in English Towns, 1790–1835.* Cambridge: Cambridge UP, 1988.

Hartman, Geoffrey H., ed. *Holocaust Remembrance: the Shapes of Memory.* Oxford: Blackwell, 1994.

Hartung, Rudolf. "Gespräch mit Elias Canetti." In *Rudolf Hartung-Elias Canetti: Ein Rezipient und sein Autor: Eine Dokumentation.* Ed. Bernhard Albers. Aachen: Rimbaud, 1992.

———. "Hinweis auf Elias Canetti." In *Rudolf Hartung-Elias Canetti: Ein Rezipient und sein Autor.* Ed. Bernhard Albers. Aachen: Rimbaud, 1992.

Hebel, Johann Peter. *Gesammelte Werke.* Berlin: Aufbau, 1958.

———. *Schatzkästlein des rheinischen Hausfreundes.* Tübingen: Cotta, 1811.

Heiduczek, Werner. *Tod am Meer.* Halle: Mitteldeutscher Verlag, 1977.

Heine, Heinrich. *Historisch-kritische Gesamtausgabe der Werke.* Vol. 5 (*Almansor; William Ratcliff; Der Rabbi von Bacherach; Aus den Memoiren des Herren von Schnabelewopski; Florentinische Nächte*). Ed. Manfred Windfuhr. Hamburg: Hoffmann und Campe, 1994.

Heinrich von (Wien)Neustadt, *Apolonius von Tyrland: Nach der Gothaer Handschrift.* Ed. S. Singer. Berlin: Weidmannsche Buchhandlung, 1906.

Helwig, Heide. "Canetti und Nietzsche." In *"Ein Dichter braucht Ahnen": Elias Canetti und die europäische Tradition,* Proceedings of the Paris Symposium, 16–18.11.1995. *Jahrbuch für Internationale Germanistik,* ed. Gerald Stieg and Jean-Marie Valentin, 145–62. Reihe A, Akten des Pariser Symposiums/Actes du colloque de Paris. Bern etc.: Lang, 1997.

Henning-Buchmann, Claus. "Katastrophe, Massenwahn und Tabu: Zu den Dramen von Elias Canetti." *Wort in der Zeit* 10/12 (1964): 44–50.

Henninghaus, Lothar. *Tod und Verwandlung: Elias Canettis poetische Anthropologie aus der Kritik der Psychoanalyse.* Frankfurt: Peter Lang, 1984.

Herzfelde, Wieland, ed. *Junge deutsche Autoren.* Berlin: Malik, 1932.

Hilberg, Raul. *Perpetrators Victims, Bystanders: The Jewish Catastrophe 1933–1945.* London: Lime Tree, 1993.

Hobbes, Thomas. *Leviathan, or the Matter, Forme and Power of a Commonwealth Ecclesiasticall and Civill.* Ed. Michael Oakeshott. Oxford: Blackwell, 1957.

Hogen, Hildegard. *Die Modernisierung des Ich: Individualisierungskonzepte bei Siegfried Kracauer, Robert Musil und Elias Canetti.* Würzburg: Königshausen & Neumann, 2000.

Hollmann, Hans. "Arbeit an den Dramen." In *Hüter der Verwandlung, Beiträge zum Werk von Elias Canetti,* ed. Werner Hoffmann, 232–35. Munich: Hanser, 1985.

Honegger, Gitta. "Acoustic Masks — Strategies of Language in the Theater of Canetti, Bernhard, and Handke." *Modern Austrian Literature* 18/2 (1985): 57–60.

Honneth, Axel. "Die unendliche Perpetuierung des Naturzustandes. Zur theoretischen Erkenntnis von Canettis *Masse und Macht.*" In *Einladung zur Verwandlung, Essays zu Elias Canettis "Macht und Macht,"* ed. Michael Krüger, 105–27. Munich: Hanser, 1995.

Horkheimer, Max, Theodor W. Adorno, and Rolf Tiedemann. *Dialektik der Aufklärung: philosophische Fragmente.* Frankfurt: Suhrkamp, 1981.

Hrdlicka, Alfred. "Das Chaos des Fleisches." In *Graphik,* 176–77. Frankfurt: Ullstein, 1973.

Huber, Ortrun, ed. *Wortmasken: Texte zu Leben und Werk von Elias Canetti.* Munich, Vienna: Hanser, 1995.

Huntington, Samuel P. *The Clash of Civilizations and the Remaking of World Order*. New York: Simon & Schuster, 1996.

Isaacs, Jack. *An Assessment of Twentieth-Century Literature: Six Lectures Delivered in the B.B.C. Third Programme.* London: Martin Secker & Warburg, 1951.

Israel, Salvator. "Za semeistvoto i rodninite na Elias Kaneti." *Evreiski vesti,* 12/24 (1981).

Jacobs, Jürgen. "Elias Canetti." In *Deutsche Literatur der Gegenwart*. Vol. 1. ed. Dietrich Weber, 93–109. Stuttgart: Kröner, 1976.

Jonas, Hans. *The Gnostic Religion: The Message of the Alien God and the Beginning of Christianity*. Boston: Beacon Press, 1958.

Jones, Ernest. *Free Associations: Memories of a Psycho-Analyst*. London: Hogarth Press, 1959.

Kampel, Beatrix. "Ein Dichter braucht Ahnen. Canettis Begegnungen mit Literatur und Literaten im Spiegel seiner Autobiographie." In *Experte der Macht: Elias Canetti,* ed. Kurt Bartsch and Gerhard Melzer, 102–15. Graz: Droschl, 1985.

Kaplan, Harold. *Conscience and Memory: Meditations in a Museum of the Holocaust*. Chicago: U of Chicago P, 1994.

Kaszyński, Stefan H. "Im Labor der Gedanken. Zur Poetik der Aufzeichnung von Elias Canetti." In *Elias Canettis Anthropologie und Poetik*. Ed. S. Kaszyński, 151–62. Munich: Hanser, 1984.

Kenk, Françoise. "Goethe, le premier ancêtre." In *"Ein Dichter braucht Ahnen": Elias Canetti und die europäische Tradition,* Proceedings of the Paris Symposium, 16–18.11.1995. *Jahrbuch für Internationale Germanistik,* ed. Gerald Stieg and Jean-Marie Valentin, 123–43. Reihe A, Akten des Pariser Symposiums/ Actes du colloque de Paris. Bern etc.: Lang, 1997.

Kershaw, Ian. *Hitler 1889–1936: Hubris*. London: Allen Lane, 1998.

Kilcher, Andreas B., ed. *Metzler Lexikon der deutsch-jüdischen Literatur*. Stuttgart: Metzler, 2000.

Kimball, Roger. "Becoming Elias Canetti." *New Criterion* 5.1 (1986): 17–28.

Kiss, Endre. "Elias Canettis 'Masse und Macht' in methodischer Sicht. In *Autobiographie zwischen Fiktion und Wirklichkeit,* ed. Penka Angelova and Emilia Staitscheva, 223–32. St. Ingbert: Röhrig Universitätsverlag, 1997.

Klemperer, Victor. *Ich will Zeugnis ablegen bis zum letzten: Tagebücher 1933– 1945.* 2 vols. Ed. Walter Nowojski. Berlin: Aufbau Verlag, 1995.

———. *LTI: Notizbuch eines Philologen*. Cologne: Röderberg, 1987.

Knoll, Heike. *Das System Canetti: Zur Rekonstruktion eines Wirklichkeitsentwurfes*. Stuttgart: M & P, 1993.

Koeppen, Wolfgang. *Der Tod in Rom.* Stuttgart: Scherz & Goverts, 1954.

Kolmar, Gertrud. *Das lyrische Werk.* Munich: Kösel, 1960.

Kraus, Karl. *Die letzten Tage der Menschheit; Tragödie in fünf Akten.* Munich: Kösel, 1957.

Kristeva, Julia. *Powers of Horror: An Essay on Abjection.* New York: Columbia UP, 1982.

Kronauer, Brigitte, ed. *Elias Canetti über Tiere.* Munich: Hanser, 2002.

La Capra, Dominick. "Lanzmann's *Shoah:* 'Here there is no why.'" *Critical Inquiry* 23 (1997): 231–69.

Lacan, Jacques. "The Mirror Stage as Formative of the Function of the I." In *Écrits: A Selection.* New York: Norton, 1977.

Laemmle, Peter. "The Power and Powerlessness of the Earwitness: The Dramatic in Canetti's Early Plays." In *Critical Essays on Elias Canetti,* ed. David Darby, 109–20. New York: G. K. Hall & Co., 2000.

Lamping, Dieter. "'Zehn Minuten Lichtenberg.' Canetti als Leser anderer Aphoristiker." In *Canetti als Leser,* ed. Gerhard Neumann, 113–25. Freiburg, Rombach, 1996.

Lappe, Thomas. *Die Aufzeichnung: Typologie einer literarischen Kurzform im 20. Jahrhundert.* Aachen: Alano/Rader, 1991.

———. *Elias Canettis Aufzeichnungen 1942–1985: Modell und Dialog als Konstituenten einer programmatischen Utopie.* Aachen: Alano/Rader, 1988.

Largier, Niklaus, ed. *Meister Eckhart Werke.* Vol. 1. Frankfurt: Deutscher Klassiker Verlag, 1993.

Larkin, Philip. *High Windows.* London: Faber, 1974.

Lawson, Richard H. *Understanding Elias Canetti.* Columbia, SC: U of South Carolina P, 1991.

Le Bon, Gustave. *The Crowd.* London. T. Fisher Unwin, 1896.

Lessing, Theodor. *Der jüdische Selbsthaß.* Berlin: Jüdischer Verlag, 1930.

Lippit, Akira Mizuta. *Electric Animal: Toward a Rhetoric of Wildlife.* Minneapolis: U of Minnesota P, 2000.

Lorenz, Dagmar C. G. *Keepers of the Motherland: German Texts by Jewish Women Writers,* 1–13. Lincoln: U of Nebraska P, 1997.

———. "More than Metaphors: Animals, Gender, and Jewish Identity in Gertrud Kolmar." In *Transforming the Center, Eroding the Margins: Essays on Ethnic and Cultural Boundaries in German-Speaking Countries,* ed. Dagmar C. G. Lorenz and Renate Posthofen, 21–28. Columbia, SC: Camden House, 1998.

———. "Schweigen und Entfremdung. Canettis Reaktion auf Exil und Krieg." In *Das Exilerlebnis,* ed. Donald G. Daviau and Ludwig M. Fischer, 181–91. Columbia: Camden House, 1982.

———. *Verfolgung bis zum Massenmord.* New York: Peter Lang, 1992.

Macho, Thomas H. "Triumph des Überlebens," *Der Stachel des Befehls.* Ed. John Patillo-Hess, 57–64. Vienna: Löcker, 1992.

Mack, Michael. *Anthropology as Memory: Elias Canetti's and Franz Baermann Steiner's Responses to the Shoah.* Tübingen: Niemeyer: 2001.

Mack Smith, Denis. *Mussolini.* London: Weidenfeld & Nicolson, 1981.

Magris, Claudio. "The Writer in Hiding." In *Critical Essays on Elias Canetti.* Ed. David Darby. New York: G. K. Hall, 2000.

Mann, Thomas. *Der Tod in Venedig.* Frankfurt: Diesterweg, 1992.

———. *Der Zauberberg.* Berlin: Fischer, 1925.

Mariott, Emil. *Erbarm dich deines Viehes.* Innsbruck: Verlag des Thierschutzvereins, 1891.

———."Der Vogelmassenmord in Südtirol," *Neues Wiener Tagblatt,* September 22, 1892.

Mazel, Atze, ed. *Ortlose Botschaft: Der Freundeskreis H. G. Adler, Elias Canetti und Franz Baermann Steiner: Mit Beiträgen von Jeremy Adler und Gerhard Hirschfeld: In Zusammenarbeit mit der Bibliothek für Zeitgeschichte Stuttgart.* Marbach: Deutsche Schillergesellschaft, 1998.

McClelland, J. S. *The Crowd and the Mob: from Plato to Canetti.* London: Unwin Hyman, 1989.

Melzer, Gerhard. "Der einzige Satz und sein Eigentümer. Versuch über den symbolischen Machthaber Elias Canetti." In *Experte der Macht: Elias Canetti,* ed. Kurt Bartsch and Gerhard Melzer, 58–72. Graz: Droschl, 1985.

Mendes-Flohr, Paul, and Jehuda Reinharz, eds. *The Jew in the Modern World: A Documentary History.* New York: Oxford UP, 1995.

Menke, Christoph. "Die Kunst des Fallens. Canettis Poetik der Erkenntnis," In *Einladung zur Verwandlung: Essays zu Elias Canettis Masse und Macht.* Ed. Michael Krüger. Munich: Hanser, 1995.

Meyer, Christine. "Don Quichotte dans l'Auto-da-fé." In *"Ein Dichter braucht Ahnen": Elias Canetti und die europäische Tradition,* Proceedings of the Paris Symposium, 16–18.11.1995 *Jahrbuch für Internationale Germanistik.* Ed. Gerald Stieg and Jean-Marie Valentin. Reihe A, Akten des Pariser Symposiums/Actes du colloque de Paris. Bern: Lang, 1997.

———. "La Vie de Henry Brulard comme modèle pour l'autobiographie de Canetti." *Austriaca* 16 (1991): 98.

Mieder, Wolfgang. "'Die falschesten Redensarten haben den größten Reiz.' Zu Elias Canettis Sprachaphorismen." *Der Sprachdienst* 6/11–12 (1994): 173–80.

———. *"In lingua veritas": Sprichwörtliche Rhetorik in Victor Klemperers Tagebüchern 1933–1945*, 20–27. Vienna: Edition Praesens, 2000.

———. *Proverbs Are Never Out of Season: Popular Wisdom in the Modern Ages.* New York: Oxford UP, 1993.

Miller, Elizabeth. *Dracula.* New York: Parkstone Press, 2001.

Milosz, Czeslaw. *The Captive Mind.* London: Secker & Warburg, 1953.

Müller-Lauter, Wolfgang. "Der Organismus als innerer Kampf. Der Einfluß von Wilhelm Roux auf Friedrich Nietzsche." *Nietzsche-Studien* 7 (1978): 189–223.

Murdoch, Iris. *The Flight From the Enchanter.* New York: Viking, 1956.

———. "Mass, Might and Myth," *The Spectator.* September 6, 1962.

Murphy, Harriet. *Canetti and Nietzsche: Theories of Humor in Die Blendung.* Albany, State U of New York, 1996.

Neumann, Gerhard. "'Lektüren der Macht.' Elias Canetti als Leser Daniel Paul Schrebers und Franz Kafkas," In *Canetti als Leser,* ed. Gerhard Neumann, 137–59. Freiburg: Rombach, 1996.

———. "'Yo lo vi.' Wahrnehmung der Gewalt: *Canettis Masse und Macht.*" In *Einladung zur Verwandlung: Essays zu Elias Canettis Masse und Macht,* ed. Michael Krüger, 68–104. Munich: Hanser, 1995.

———, ed., *Canetti als Leser.* Freiburg, Rombach, 1996.

Nietzsche, Friedrich. *Werke.* 3 vols. Ed. Karl Schlechta. Munich: Hanser, 1966.

———. *Der Wille zur Macht: Versuch einer Umwertung aller Werte.* Stuttgart: Kröner, 1930.

Novick, Peter. *The Holocaust in American Life.* New York: Mariner Books, 1999.

The Optimists, dir. Jacky Comforty. Comforty Media Concepts, 2001.

Orlowski, Hubert. "Auf vielen Hochzeiten tanzen. Zu den Stücken von Wyspianskis *Hochzeit,* Canettis *Hochzeit* und Gombrowicz' *Die Trauung.*" In *Canettis Aufstand gegen Macht und Tod,* ed. John Pattillo-Hess and Mario L. Smole, 80–88. Vienna: Löcker, 1996.

Page, Tony. *Buddhism and Animals: A Buddhist Vision of Humanity's Rightful Relationship with the Animal Kingdom.* London: UKAVIS, 1999.

Pankau, Johannes G. "Körper und Geist. Das Geschlechterverhältnis in Elias Canettis Roman *Die Blendung.*" *Colloquia Germanica* 23/2 (1990): 146–70.

Parry, Idris. "Attitudes to Power. Canetti, Kafka, Crowds and Paranoia." *Times Literary Supplement* 15/1 (1971): 67–68. Reprinted, *TLS 10. Essays and Reviews from Times Literary Supplement 1971.* London: Oxford UP, 1971.

————. "Canetti on Kafka." *PN Review,* 31 (1983): 13–17.

————. "Elias Canetti's Novel 'Die Blendung,'" *Essays in German Literature.* Vol. 1. Ed. F. Norman, 145–66. London: University of London Institute of Germanic Studies, 1965.

Perry, Duncan M. *Stefan Stambolov and the Emergence of Modern Bulgaria, 1870–1895.* Durham, NC: Duke UP, 1993.

Petersen, Carol. *Elias Canetti.* Berlin: Colloquium, 1990.

Piel, Edgar. *Elias Canetti.* Munich: Beck, 1984.

————. "Elias Canettis Masse und Macht: Eine phantastische Anthropologie." *Literatur und Kritik* 183–84 (1984): 123–42.

Piti, Buko, ed. *Bulgarskata obshtestvenost za rasisma I antisemitisma.* Sofia, n.p., 1937.

Pöder, Elfriede. "Spurensicherung. Otto Weininger in der *Blendung.*" *Blendung als Lebensform,* ed. Friedbert Aspetsberger and Gerald Stieg, 57–72. Königstein/Ts.: Athenäum, 1985.

Quack, Josef. "Über Elias Canettis Verhältnis zu Karl Kraus: Ein kritischer Vergleich." *Internationales Archiv für Sozialgeschichte der deutschen Literatur* 23/2 (1998): 118–41.

Raddatz, Hans-Peter. *Von Gott zu Allah? Christentum und Islam in der liberalen Fortschrittsgesellschaft.* Munich: Herbig, 2001.

Razbojnikova-Frateva, Maja. "Die Essays von Elias Canetti — Eine Biographie des Geistes. Versuch einer Annäherung." In *Autobiographie zwischen Fiktion und Wirklichkeit,* ed. Penka Angelova and Emilia Staitscheva, 63–73. St. Ingbert: Röhrig, 1997.

Regan, Tom. *The Case for Animal Rights.* Berkeley: U of California P, 1983.

Reich, Wilhelm. *Massenpsychologie des Faschismus.* Frankfurt: Fischer, 1974.

Reich-Ranicki, Marcel. "Marrakesch ist überall." Rprt. in Reich-Ranicki, *Entgegnung: Zur deutschen Literatur der siebziger Jahre,* 47–54. Stuttgart: Deutsche Verlags-Anstalt, 1979.

Reiss, Hans, ed. *Kant: Political Writings.* Trans. H. B. Nisbet. *Cambridge Texts in the History of Political Thought.* Cambridge UP, 1991.

Reuth, Ralf Georg. *The Life of Joseph Goebbels.* Trans. Krishna Winston. London: Constable, 1993.

Ridley, Matt. *The Origins of Virtue.* London: Penguin, 1997.

Ritvo, Lucille B. *Darwin's Influence on Freud.* New Haven and London: Yale UP, 1990.

Robertson, Ritchie. "Between Freud and Nietzsche: Canetti's *Crowds and Power.*" *Austrian Studies* 3 (1992): 109–24.

————. "Canetti als Anthropologe." In *Einladung zur Verwandlung: Essays zu Elias Canettis Masse und Macht,* ed. Michael Kruger, 190–206. Munich: Hanser, 1995.

————. "Canetti as Anthropologist." In *Critical Essays on Elias Canetti,* ed. David Darby, 158–70. New York: G. K. Hall, 2000.

————. *The "Jewish Question" in German Literature, 1749–1939: Emancipation and its Discontents.* London: Oxford, 1999.

Rohrwasser, Michael. "Elias Canettis literarische Auseinandersetzung mit der Psychoanalyse in seinem Roman *Die Blendung.* Anmerkungen zum Verhältnis von Literatur und Psychoanalyse." In *Convivium: Germanistisches Jahrbuch Polen 2000,* 43–64. Bonn: Deutscher Akademischer Austauschdienst, 2000.

————. "Schreibstrategien. Canettis Beschreibungen von Freud." In *Psychoanalyse in der modernen Literatur: Kooperation und Konkurrenz,* ed. Thomas Anz, 145–66. Würzburg: Königshausen & Neumann 1999.

Roudometof, Victor. *Collective Memory, National Identity, and Ethnic Conflict: Greece, Bulgaria, and the Macedonian Question.* Westport, CT: Praeger, 2002.

Ruckhaberle, Dieter, and Christiane Ziesecke. *Rettung der bulgarischen Juden, 1943: Eine Dokumentation.* Berlin: Publica, 1984.

Rudé, George. *The Crowd in the French Revolution.* Oxford: Clarendon Press, 1959.

Ruppel, Ursula. *Der Tod und Canetti.* Hamburg: Europäische Verlagsanstalt, 1995.

Rushdie, Salman. "Die Schlange der Gelehrsamkeit windet sich, verschlingt ihren Schwanz und beisst sich selbst entzwei." In *Hüter der Verwandlung: Beiträge zum Werk von Elias Canetti,* ed. Werner Hoffmann, 85–89. Munich: Hanser, 1985.

Ryder, Richard. *Animal Revolution.* Oxford: B. Blackwell, 1989.

Said, Edward. *Orientalism: Western Conceptions of the Orient.* Harmondsworth: Penguin, 1995.

Sax, Boria. *Animals in the Third Reich: Pets, Scapegoats, and the Holocaust.* New York: Continuum, 2000.

Schedel, Angelika. "Nachwort." In Veza Canetti, *Der Fund: Erzählungen und Stücke,* 317–18. Munich: Hanser, 2001.

————. *Sozialismus und Psychoanalyse: Quellen von Veza Canettis literarischen Utopien.* Würzburg: Königshausen & Neumann, 2002.

Scheichl, Sigurd Paul. "Hörenlernen. Zur teleologischen Struktur der autobiographischen Bücher Canettis." In *Elias Canetti: Blendung als Lebensform.* Ed. Friedbert Aspetsberger and Gerald Stieg. Königstein/Ts.: Athenäum, 1985.

Schieth, Lydia. "Europa-Erinnerung als Rekonstruktion: Autobiographien europäischen Lebens: Elias Canetti und Manés Sperber." In *Suchbild Europa — künstlerische Konzepte der Moderne,* ed. Jürgen Wertheimer, 5–17. Amsterdam: Rodopi, 1995.

Schmidt-Dengler, Wendelin. "Ganz nah und dicht beisammen. Zum, Ohrenzeugen.' In *Blendung als Lebensform: Elias Canetti.* Ed. Friedbert Aspetsberger and Gerald Stieg. Königsstein: Athenäum, 1985.

———. "Theophrast, La Bruyére, Canetti und die Komödie." In *"Ein Dichter braucht Ahnen": Elias Canetti und die europäische Tradition,* Proceedings of the Paris Symposium, 16–18.11.1995. *Jahrbuch für internationale Germanistik,* vol. 44, ed. Gerald Stieg and Jean-Marie Valentin, 225–33. Reihe A, Akten des Pariser Symposiums/Actes du colloque de Paris. Bern etc.: Lang, 1997.

Schmidt-Rinke, Silke, and Stefan Rinke, "'Das Grundübel alles Bestehenden': Die Todesproblematik in Elias Canettis Roman Die Blendung." *Modern Austrian Literature* 31/2 (1998): 81–103.

Scholl-Latour, Peter. *Allah ist mit den Standhaften: Begegnungen mit der islamischen Revolution.* Stuttgart: Deutsche Verlags-Anstalt, 1983.

———. *Aufruhr in der Kasbah: Krisenherd Algerien.* Stuttgart: Deutsche Verlags-Anstalt, 1992.

Scholz, Hannelore. "'Keine Angst geht verloren, aber ihre Verstecke sind rätselhaft': Frauen im autobiographischen Wahrnehmungsspektrum von Elias Canetti." In *Autobiographie zwischen Fiktion und Wirklichkeit: Internationales Symposium, Russe Oktober 1992,* ed. Penka Angelova and Emilia Staitscheva, 249–68. St. Ingbert: Röhrig Universitätsverlag, 1997.

Schreber, Daniel Paul. *Denkwürdigkeiten eines Nervenkranken.* Leipzig: Oswald Mutze, 1903. Trans. Ida MacAlpine and Richard A. Hunter as *Memoirs of My Nervous Illness* (London: Dawson, 1955).

Schuh, Franz. "Schreiben gegen den Tod." In *Der Stachel des Befehls,* ed. John Patillo-Hess, 44–56. Vienna: Löcker, 1992.

Sebald, W. G. "Kurzer Versuch über System und Systemkritik bei Elias Canetti." *Etudes Germaniques* 39/3 (1984): 268–75.

Seidler, Ingo. "Bruchstücke einer großen Konfession. Zur Bedeutung von Canettis Sudelbüchern." *Modern Austrian Literature* 16/3–4 (1983): 1–21.

Shepard, Paul. *The Others: How Animals Made Us Human.* Washington: Island Press, 1966.

———. *Thinking Animals and the Development of Human Intelligence.* New York: Viking Press, 1978.

Singer, Peter. *Animal Liberation.* New York: New York Review, Random House, 1990.

Sloterdijk, Peter. *Die Verachtung der Massen: Versuch über Kulturkämpfe in der modernen Gesellschaft.* Frankfurt: Suhrkamp, 2000.

Sontag, Susan. "Mind as Passion." In *Essays in Honour of Elias Canetti.* Trans. Michael Hulse. London: Deutsch, 1987.

Sontheimer, Kurt. *Das Elend unserer Intellektuellen: Linke Theorie in der Bundesrepublik Deutschland.* Hamburg: Hoffmann und Campe, 1976.

Stammen, Theo. "Lektüre des Anderen — Elias Canettis anthropologischer Blick." In *Canetti als Leser,* ed. Gerhard Neumann, 161–76. Freiburg: Rombach, 1996.

Steiner, Franz Baermann. *Am stürzenden Pfad: Gesammelte Gedichte.* Göttingen: Wallstein, 2000.

———. *Fluchtvergnüglichkeit: Feststellungen und Versuche.* Stuttgart: Flugasche, 1988.

———. "Letter to Gandhi." *Orientpolitik, Value and Civilisation.* New York: Berghahn, 1999.

———. *Selected Writings: Franz Baermann Steiner.* Ed. Jeremy Adler and Richard Fardon. New York: Berghahn, 1999.

———. *Taboo.* Harmondsworth: Penguin, 1967.

———. "Über den Prozess der Zivilisierung." *Akzente* 42 (1995): 213–27.

Stern, J. P. "Canetti's Later Work." In *Critical Essays on Elias Canetti,* ed. David Darby, 239–48. New York: G. K. Hall, 2000.

Steussloff, Axel G. *Autorschaft und Werk Elias Canettis: Subjekt-Sprache-Identität.* Würzburg: Könighausen & Neumann, 1994.

———. "Der Reisende auf der Suche nach seiner jüdischen Vergangenheit." In *Autorschaft und Werk Elias Canettis: Subjekt-Sprache-Identität,* 98–207. Würzburg: Königshausen and Neumann, 1994.

Stevens, Adrian. "Aufzeichnungen, Menschen und Fragmente. Zur Poetik der Charakterisierung bei Canetti, Aubrey und La Bruyère." In *"Ein Dichter braucht Ahnen": Elias Canetti und die europäische Tradition,* Proceedings of the Paris Symposium, 16–18.11.1995. *Jahrbuch für Internationale Germanistik,* vol. 44, ed. Gerald Stieg and Jean-Marie Valentin, 207–24. Reihe A, Akten des Pariser Symposiums/Actes du colloque de Paris. Bern etc.: Lang, 1997.

Stevens, Adrian, and Fred Wagner, eds. *Elias Canetti: Londoner Symposium.* Stuttgart: Verlag Hans-Dieter Heinz/Akademischer Verlag Stuttgart, 1991. Concurrently available in the Publications of the Institute of Germanic Studies, University of London, vol. 48.

Stieg, Gerald. "Betrachtungen zu Elias Canettis Autobiographie." In *Zu Elias Canetti.* Ed. Manfred Durzak. Stuttgart: Ernst Klett, 1983.

———. "Canetti and Nestroy." *Nestroyana: Blätter der Internationalen Nestroy-Gesellschaft* 20/1–2 (2000): 51–64.

———. "Canetti, Elias." In *Metzler Lexikon der deutsch-jüdischen Literatur,* ed. Andreas B. Kilcher, 99–102. Stuttgart: Metzler, 2000.

———. "Canetti und die Psychoanalyse: *Das Unbehagen in der Kultur* und *Die Blendung.*" In *Elias Canetti: Londoner Symposium,* ed. Adrian Stevens and Fred Wagner, 59–73. Stuttgart: H.-D. Heinz, 1991.

———. "Canetti und die Sonne. Karl Kraus in Elias Canettis Autobiographie." In "*Ein Dichter braucht Ahnen*": *Elias Canetti und die europäische Tradition,* Proceedings of the Paris Symposium, 16–18.11.1995. *Jahrbuch für Internationale Germanistik,* ed. Gerald Stieg and Jean-Marie Valentin, 267–81. Reihe A, Akten des Pariser Symposiums/Actes du colloque de Paris. Bern etc.: Lang, 1997.

———. "Questions à Canetti." ("Homage à Canetti"). *Austriaca* 6/11 (1950): 24.

Strauss, Leo. *Liberalism Ancient and Modern.* New York: Basic Books, 1968.

Streeruwitz, Marlene. *Nachwelt.* Frankfurt: Fischer, 1999.

Strelka, Joseph. "Betrachtungen zu Elias Canettis autobiographischem Band 'Das Augenspiel,'" In *Autobiographie zwischen Fiktion und Wirklichkeit: Internationales Symposium, Russe Oktober 1992,* ed. Penka Angelova and Emilia Staitscheva. St. Ingbert: Röhrig Universitätsverlag, 1997.

Stromsik, Jiri. "'Das Eigentliche der Welt.' Menschen und Figuren in Elias Canettis Autobiographie." In *Ist Wahrheit ein Meer von Grashalmen? Zum Werk Elias Canettis,* 97–108. Bern: Lang, 1993.

Susman, Walerij. "Canetti und Kafka." In "*Ein Dichter braucht Ahnen*": *Elias Canetti und die europäische Tradition,* Proceedings of the Paris Symposium, 16–18.11.1995. *Jahrbuch für Internationale Germanistik,* ed. Gerald Stieg and Jean-Marie Valentin, 163–71. Reihe A, Akten des Pariser Symposiums/Actes du colloque de Paris. Bern etc.: Lang, 1997.

Széll, Zsuzsa. "Ist 'Wahrheit ein Meer von Grashalmen?': Zu Canettis Denkhaltung." In *Ist Wahrheit ein Meer von Grashalmen?,* ed. Joseph P. Strelka and Zsuzsa Széll, 11–16. New York: Peter Lang, 1993.

Tamir, Vicki. *Bulgaria and Her Jews: The History of a Dubious Symbiosis.'* New York: Sepher-Hermon Press, 1979.

Taylor, Ronald, ed. *Aesthetics and Politics: Ernst Bloch, Georg Lukacs, Bertolt Brecht, Walter Benjamin, Theodor Adorno.* Afterword by Fredric Jameson. London: NLB, 1980.

Teraoka, Arlene A. *EAST, WEST, and Others: The Third World in Postwar German Literature.* Lincoln: U of Nebraska P, 1996.

Theophrastus. *Characters.* Cambridge: Harvard UP, 2003.

Theweleit, Klaus. *Männerphantasien.* Frankfurt: Roter Stern, 1977–1978.

Thompson, Edward P. *The Making of the English Working Class*. London: Gollancz, 1963.

———. "The Moral Economy of the English Crowd in the Eighteenth Century." *Past and Present* 50 (1970): 76–136.

Timmermann, Harry. "Tierisches in der Anthropologie und Poetik Elias Canettis. Mit Beispielen aus dem Gesamtwerk." *Elias Canetti zu Ehren*. Ed. Walter Höllerer and Norbert Miller. *Sprache im technischen Zeitalter* 94 (1985): 99–126.

Todorov, Tzvetan. *The Fragility of Goodness: Why Bulgaria's Jews Survived the Holocaust*. Princeton: Princeton UP, 2001.

Todorova, Maria N. *Balkan Family Structure and the European Pattern: Demographic Developments in Ottoman Bulgaria*. Washington, DC, Lanham, MD: American UP, 1993.

Tönnies, Sibylle. "Die Klagemeute: Warum sich Deutsche den Opfern aufdrängen." *Frankfurter Allgemeine Zeitung*. April 23, 1996.

Trotter, Wilfred. *Instincts of the Herd in Peace and War*. London: Oxford UP, 1953.

Turan, Ömer. *The Turkish Minority in Bulgaria, 1878–1908*. Türk Tarih Kurumu Basimevi, 1998.

Völker, Klaus. *Die Dramen. Text + Kritik: Zeitschrift für Literatur* 28 (1970): 34–43.

von Matt, Peter. "Canetti and Hebbel." In *"Ein Dichter braucht Ahnen": Elias Canetti und die europäische Tradition,* Proceedings of the Paris Symposium, 16–18.11.1995. *Jahrbuch für Internationale Germanistik,* ed. Gerald Stieg and Jean-Marie Valentin, 253–63. Reihe A, Akten des Pariser Symposiums/Actes du colloque de Paris. Bern etc.: Lang, 1997.

———. "Der phantastische Aphorismus bei Elias Canetti." In *Elias Canetti: Londoner Symposium,* ed. Adrian Stevens and Fred Wagner, 9–19. Stuttgart: Heinz, 1991.

Ward, Philip. *Sofia: Portrait of a City*. Cambridge/New York: Oleander, 1993.

Weinberg, Meyer. *Because They Were Jews: A History of Anti-Semitism,* New York/Westport: Greenwood Press, 1986.

Weininger, Otto. *Geschlecht und Charakter*. Vienna: Braumüller, 1903 and 1906.

Werlen, Hansjakob. "Destiny's Herald: Elias Canetti's *Crowds and Power* and Its Continuing Influence." In *Critical Essays on Elias Canetti,* ed. David Darby, 171–85. New York: G. K. Hall, 2000.

———. *Narrative Strategies in Elias Canetti's Die Blendung and Masse und Macht*. Ph.D. diss., Stanford University, 1988.

————. "'Ohnmächtige Hoffnung.' Die Stimme des Individuums in *Masse und Macht.*" In *Einladung zur Verwandlung: Essays zu Elias Canettis "Macht und Macht.*" Ed. Michael Krüger. Munich: Hanser, 1995.

Widdig, Bernd. *Männerbünde und Massen: Zur Krise männlicher Identität in der Literatur der Moderne.* Opladen: Westdeutscher Verlag, 1992.

————. "Tägliche Sprengungen: Elias Canetti und die Inflation." In *Einladung zur Verwandlung: Essays zu Elias Canettis "Masse und Macht,"* ed. Michael Krüger, 128–50. Munich: Carl Hanser, 1995.

Wiethölter, Waltraud. "Sprechen — Lesen — Schreiben: Zur Funktion von Sprache und Schrift in Canetti's Autobiographie." *DVjS* 64/1 (1990): 149–71.

Willingham, Ralph. "Dystopian Visions in the Plays of Elias Canetti." *Science-Fiction-Studies* 19 (1992): 69–74.

Witte, Bernd. "Der Einzelne und seine Literatur. Elias Canettis Auffassung vom Dichter." *Experte der Macht: Elias Canetti.* Ed. Kurt Bartsch and Gerhard Melzer. Graz: Droschl, 1985.

————. "Elias Canetti." *Kritisches Lexikon zur deutschsprachigen Gegenwartsliteratur (KLG).* Ed. Heinz Ludwig Arnold, 11. Munich: Edition Text + Kritik, 1978.

Young, James Edward. *Writing and Rewriting the Holocaust: Narrative and the Consequences of Interpretation.* Bloomington: Indiana UP, 1988.

Contributors

PENKA ANGELOVA is Professor in Cultural Studies and Director of the Institute for European Studies at the University of Rousse; Professor in German Literature at the University of Veliko Tarnovo; Director of the Bulgarian-Romanian Inter-University Centre for Europe BRIE-Rousse; and President of the International Elias Canetti Society.

IRENE STOCKSIEKER DI MAIO is Associate Professor of German at Louisiana State University and teaches language, literature, and film. Her research interests are narrative technique, minority/majority discourses, and transcultural relations. Her studies of Wilhelm Raabe's works include *The Multiple Perspective* (1981). Currently she is annotating her translation, *Gerstaecker's Louisiana: Black, White, and Red,* for publication; is co-editing a volume, *The Louisiana Purchase: Faces and Cultures of Yesterday and Today;* and continues her project, a socio-historical comparison of the works of the nineteenth-century German-Jewish authors Berthold Auerbach and Fanny Lewald.

SVOBODA ALEXANDRA DIMITROVA studied German language, literature, and philology and Russian language at the University of Sofia, Bulgaria, and received a Ph.D. in art criticism and sociology of art from the Bulgarian Academy of Sciences. Having worked in Bulgaria as a senior researcher of contemporary culture, she is now working toward a second Ph.D. at the Department of Germanic Studies at the University of Illinois at Chicago. She has published widely on cultural and literary topics, including Elias Canetti.

WILLIAM COLLINS DONAHUE is the author of *The End of Modernism: Elias Canetti's Auto-da-Fé* (2001), which was awarded the MLA's Aldo and Jeanne Scaglione Prize for Studies in Germanic Languages and Literatures in 2002. He has written numerous articles on German literature and culture of the nineteenth and twentieth centuries as well as on contemporary literature. His research interests include German film, realism, autobiography, and Holocaust literature. He is the recipient of the Rutgers University Board of Trustees Fellowship for Scholarly Excellence (2001) and the Max Kade Prize for Best Article of the Year in *The German Quarterly* (2000). In 1999–2000, he was a fellow and Pew Scholar in the Erasmus Institute at the University of Notre Dame and in 2000–2001 a fellow at the Rutgers Center for Critical Analysis of Contemporary Culture.

Anne Fuchs is Senior Lecturer of German at University College Dublin. She has widely taught and published in the field of modern German culture and literature. Her research interests include cultural memory in postwar German discourse, modern German literature, German-Jewish literature, literary theory, and the self and the Other in travel literature and German-Jewish literature. She is the author of *Dramaturgie des Narrentums: Das Komische in der Prosa Robert Walsers* (1993), *A Space of Anxiety — Dislocation and Abjection in Modern German-Jewish Literature* (1999). Edited volumes include *Ghetto Writing: Traditional and Eastern Jewry in German-Jewish Ghetto Writing from Heine to Hilsenrath* (1999, with Florian Krobb) and *Cultural Memory: Essays on European Literature and History* (2002, with Edric Caldicott).

Helga Kraft is Professor and Head of the Department of Germanic Studies at the University of Illinois at Chicago. Her book publications include: *Writing against Boundaries: Nationality, Ethnicity and Gender in the German-speaking Context* (co-edited with Barbara Kosta, 2003); *Ein Haus aus Sprache: Dramatikerinnen und das andere Theater* (1996); and *Mütter — Töchter — Frauen: Weiblichkeitsbilder in der Literatur.*

Dagmar C. G. Lorenz, Professor of Germanic Studies at the University of Illinois at Chicago, focuses her research on Austrian and nineteenth- and twentieth-century German and German-Jewish literary and cultural issues and Holocaust Studies, with an emphasis on history and social thought and minority discourses. She was the editor of *The German Quarterly.* Recent book publications include *Keepers of the Motherland: German Texts by Jewish Women Writers* (1997), and *Verfolgung bis zum Massenmord: Diskurse zum Holocaust in deutscher Sprache* (1992). Edited volumes include *A Companion to the Works of Arthur Schnitzler* (2003), *Contemporary Jewish Writing in Austria* (1999), *Transforming the Center, Eroding the Margins: Essays on Ethnic and Cultural Boundaries in German-Speaking Countries* (co-edited with Renate S. Posthofen, 1998), and *Insiders and Outsiders: Jewish and Gentile Culture in Germany and Austria* (1994).

Michael Mack received his Ph.D. from Cambridge in 2000, with a dissertation on Franz Baermann Steiner and Elias Canetti. His book *Anthropology as Memory: Elias Canetti's and Franz Baermann Steiner's Responses to the Shoah* was published in 2001. His new book *German Idealism and the Jew: The Inner Anti-Semitism of Philosophy and German Jewish Responses* was published in 2003. The latter received an honorable mention in the Koret Jewish Book Awards 2003–2004.

Wolfgang Mieder is Professor of German and Folklore at the University of Vermont and long-time chairperson of the Department of German and Russian. He is the author of numerous books on literary and folklore studies.

Many of his publications address the use and function of proverbs in literature, the mass media, art, politics, advertising, and so forth. He is also the
founding editor of *Proverbium: Yearbook of International Proverb Scholarship*, which has been published since 1984. Among his more recent books
touching on proverbial aphorisms are: *"Sprichwort — Wahrwort!?" Studien
zur Geschichte, Bedeutung und Funktion deutscher Sprichwörter* (1992),
*Deutsche Redensarten, Sprichwörter und Zitate: Studien zu ihrer Herkunft,
Überlieferung und Verwendung* (1995), *Sprichwörtliches und Geflügeltes:
Sprachstudien von Martin Luther bis Karl Marx* (1995), *Ver-kehrte Worte:
Antizitate aus Literatur und Medien* (1997), *Verdrehte Weisheiten: An-
tisprichwörter aus Literatur und Medien* (1998), *Phrasen verdreschen: Anti-
redensarten aus Literatur und Medien* (1999), *Sprichwörtliche Aphorismen:
Von Georg Christoph Lichtenberg bis Elazar Benyoëtz* (1999), *Aphorismen,
Sprichwörter, Zitate: Von Goethe und Schiller bis Victor Klemperer* (2000).

HARRIET MURPHY teaches in the Department of German Studies at the
University of Warwick. She specializes in nineteenth- and twentieth-century
German, Austrian, and comparative European literatures and cultures and
has widely published on authors in these fields including Canetti, Kleist,
Nietzsche, Gogol, Kafka, Stendhal, and Julian/Jutta Schutting. She is the
author of *Canetti and Nietzsche: Theories of Humor in Die Blendung* (1996),
and is editor of *Critical Essays on Julian Schutting* (2000).

JOHANNES G. PANKAU received the Ph.D. in 1982 at the University of
Freiburg. He has been a Professor of German at the University of Olden-
burg since 1987, with a specialization in literary studies and rhetoric. He has
produced numerous publications on Romanticism, culture and literature of
fin-de-siècle Germany and Austria (Wedekind, Schnitzler), rhetoric, twentieth-century literature, exile literature, and media.

JULIAN PREECE was educated at the universities of Oxford and Münster, and
the Free University, Berlin. After appointments in London and Hudders-
field, he joined the School of European Culture and Language at the University of Kent in 1996, where he teaches German and Comparative Literary
Studies. In addition to articles on Elias and Veza Canetti, he has written
about Bernhard, Fontane, and Brecht; memoirs from the former GDR;
Kafka's letters; and the Gruppe 47. He is the author of *The Life and Work
of Günter Grass: Literature, History, Politics* (2001), and has recently edited
the *Cambridge Companion to Kafka* (2002).

HANS REISS was born in Mannheim, Germany, and emigrated to Ireland in
1939. He attended Wesley College and Trinity College, University of Dublin, where he obtained a B.A. (Gold Medallist), an M.A., and a Ph.D. He has
published twelve books and editions, including *Franz Kafka; The Political
Thought of the German Romantics; Goethes Romane; Goethe's Novels; Kant:*

Political Writings; The Writer's Task from Nietzsche to Brecht; Formgestaltung und Politik: Goethe Studien, and numerous articles on German literature, history, political theory, and aesthetics. He has been Professor of German at McGill University, Montreal, and in Bristol, where he is now an Emeritus Professor and a Senior Research Fellow. He has received research awards from the Rockefeller Foundation, the British Academy, and the Deutsche Akademische Austauschdienst as well as the Officer's Cross of the Order of Merit of the Federal Republic of Germany and the Gold Medal of the Goethe Gessellschaft in Weimar, and has been Visiting Professor at McGill, Middlebury College, and the universities of Munich and Heidelberg.

RITCHIE ROBERTSON teaches German language and literature at St. John's College, Oxford. He has published *Kafka: Judaism, Politics, and Literature* (1985; German translation published by Metzler, 1988); *Heine* (1988; German translation published by Eichbauer, 1997); *The "Jewish Question" in German Literature, 1749–1939* (1999); and, as editor, *The Cambridge Companion to Thomas Mann* (2002), in addition to several translated volumes, most recently *The German-Jewish Dialogue: An Anthology of Literary Texts, 1749–1993* (1999). He has written articles on many subjects in German and Austrian literature from the Enlightenment to the present day.

SIGURD PAUL SCHEICHL is Professor for Austrian literary history and literature at the Institute of German Language, Literature, and Literary Criticism at the University of Innsbruck. He specializes in Austrian literature of the nineteenth and twentieth centuries. He has also published on Tyrolian literature and on Jewish culture and literary anti-Semitism, and conducted research on journals and Austrian German. He has widely published in scholarly journals, anthologies, and yearbooks, and is the co-editor of the collection of essays *Literatur über Literatur: Eine österreichische Anthologie* (1995, together with Petra Nachbaur).

Index

acoustic mask, 55, 96, 139, 144–45, 154n, 184, 223, 270, 317

Adams, Carol, 244, 254n, 257n, 317

Adler, H. G., 8, 96, 225, 290, 310n, 324

Adorno, Theodor, 14, 21n, 153n, 171, 173n, 232, 250, 312n, 313, 321, 330

Afghanistan, 149–50

Agee, Joel, x

Aleichem, Sholem, 5

Alexander von Battenberg. *See* Battenberg

Altenberg, Peter, 65, 223

Altvater, Christiane, 119n

Ammann, Egon, 27

Andersch, Alfred, 109, 119n, 313

Angelova, Penka, viii, 18, 135n, 153n, 196n, 236n, 237n, 261–88, 313, 316, 319, 321, 326, 328, 330, 333

Animal Liberation (Peter Singer), 240, 254n, 257n, 328

animal rights, 160, 254n

Animal Rights Movement, 244, 252, 318

animals, 18, 26, 113, 129, 160–62, 201–7, 212–20, 239–57, 306

Anschluß, 8, 69, 77

Ansell-Pearson, Keith, 215n, 313

anthropocentrism, 239–40, 243, 248–50, 252

anthropology, 241, 254n, 290, 296

anti-Semitism, 4, 8, 119n, 207, 277–80, 282, 296, 298, 334

aphorisms, vii, x, 11, 16, 27, 31, 33–34, 56, 75, 89, 107–21, 124, 127, 131–34, 143, 179, 225, 228, 244–49, 292–98, 303, 305, 309, 311n, 335

Arafat, 208, 211

Arbeiter-Zeitung (newspaper), 8, 20n, 54

Arditti, Bernhard, 180–81, 280

Arditti, Mathilde, 2, 101, 261, 263, 265. *See also* Canetti, Mathilde

Arendt, Hannah, 14, 279, 281–82, 287n

Arens, W., 215n, 313

Arie, Gabriel, 285n

Aristophanes, 15, 65, 85n

Aristotle, 126, 129, 138

Armenia, 185, 261

Arnold, Fritz, 30, 38n, 39n, 40n

Arnold, Heinz Ludwig, 238n, 332

Arnold, Matthew, 171

Ashkenazic Jews, 4, 179

Asparukh, 283n

Aspetsberger, Friedbert, 154n, 196n, 237n, 326, 327, 328

assimilated Jews, 4

Atze, Mazel, 310n, 324

Aubrey, John, 65, 75, 82–83, 85n, 103n, 329

Auerbach, Erich, 95, 102n, 313

Auffermann, Verena, 36n, 41n

Aufklärung. See Enlightenment

Auschwitz, 8, 281. *See also* Shoah

Austria, 2, 3, 7, 11, 16, 28, 72, 77, 79, 92, 101, 137–40, 154n, 222, 232, 265–68, 273–74, 277, 281, 282, 289

Austrian Cultural Forum, 87
Austrofascism, 6
Austro-Hungarian empire, 37,
 263, 264, 267
Austro-Hungarian Jews, 4
authoritarian personality, 14
autobiography, 4, 7, 6, 11, 12–19,
 29, 30–33, 37n, 38n, 45–60,
 62–65, 71–72, 77, 85n, 89–92,
 94–96, 96, 99–101, 123, 173–
 97, 204, 217–38, 261–62, 269,
 273–76
avant-garde (postwar), 4, 11, 190,
 271

Babel, Isaac, 6, 36, 65, 99, 177–
 78, 189, 196n, 313
Bad Reichenhall, 3
Bakardjieva, Teodora, 285n, 286n
Baker, Geoff, 37
Baldauf, Stefan, 134n, 313
Balkans, 3, 37, 100, 178–79, 261,
 263, 297
Balthasar, Hans Urs von, 172n,
 313
barbarism, 159
Barnouw, Dagmar, 30, 39n, 59n,
 123, 125, 137, 151, 153n,
 220–21, 291, 313
Bartsch, Kurt, 38n, 59n, 314
Bastille, 208, 211
Battenberg, Alexander von, 263,
 265–66
Batuta, Ibn, 208
Bauer, Barbara, 85n, 236n
Bauer, Felice, 1, 11, 77, 221,
 229, 230
Baur, Ruprecht Slavko, 84n, 314
Bayley, John, 10, 30, 38n, 221,
 236n, 276, 314
Beckerle, Adolf, 279
Bell, Matthew, 214n, 314
ben Yitzchak, Abraham, 7, 57
Bender, Hans, 10
Benedikt, Ernst, 8, 188

Benedikt, Moritz, 8
Benjamin, Walter, 41n, 159, 255n,
 320, 330
Bennett, Tony, 312n, 314
Benyoëtz, Elazar, 109, 119n, 335
Berlin, 6, 76–77, 100, 159, 176–
 78, 189–90, 233, 263, 265–66,
 268, 275, 277, 278, 291
Bienek, Horst, 90, 102n, 180,
 274, 293, 311n
Bildungsroman, 101, 196n, 275
Birke, Lynda, 243, 256n, 314
Bischoff, Alfons-M., 120n
Bismarck, Otto von, 263
Blake, William, 82
Bloch, Ernst, 173n, 314
Bollacher, Martin, 45, 59n, 180,
 197n, 314
book burning, 64, 149
Bradley, F. H., 82
Brecht, Bertolt, 6, 7, 20n, 36, 63,
 65, 76–77, 99, 138, 160, 172n,
 228, 314
Brief Lives (John Aubrey), 83,
 103n
Broch, Hermann, 7, 12, 20n, 28,
 36, 52, 56, 61, 63, 65, 76, 90,
 93, 102n, 153n, 172, 217, 226,
 241, 268, 292, 294, 311n, 315
Brod, Max, 100
Browning, Christopher, 207,
 215n, 315
Brückner, Wolfgang, 119n, 315
Brude-Firnau, Gisela, 237n, 315
Bruno, Giordani, 75
Buber, Martin, 5
Büchner, Georg, 5, 15, 63, 65,
 73, 90, 91, 132, 138, 147, 187,
 197n, 232
Büchner Prize, 11, 197n
Buddhism, 245, 249, 256n
Bulgaria, xiii, 1–5, 12, 18, 19,
 100, 179, 181, 186, 261–87
Burckhardt, Jakob, 70
Burgtheater, 2, 48, 65, 268

Calast, Roberto Corcoll, 284n
Camartin, Iso, 41n
Canetti, Abraham, 264, 265
Canetti, Elias, works by:
  *Alle Vergeudete Verehrung:
  Aufzeichnungen 1949–1960*
  (1970), x, xiii, 11, 126, 133
  Aufzeichnungen 1942–1948
  (1965), x, xiii, 134n, 271,
  273, 275. *See* ix–x for full
  titles in German of remaining
  Aufzeichungen
  *Aufzeichnungen 1942–1985:
  Die Provinz des Menschen;
  Das Geheimherz der Uhr*
  (1993), xiii, 240, 241, 244–
  53, 294, 295, 303. *See* ix–x
  for full titles in German of
  remaining *Aufzeichungen*
  *Das Augenspiel: Lebensgeschichte
  1931–1937* (1985; *The Play of
  the Eyes,* 1986), x, xiii, 7, 12,
  37n, 46–47, 52–53, 55, 57,
  64, 90, 93, 96, 100, 101,
  176, 184, 193, 217, 234
  *Das Geheimherz der Uhr:
  Aufzeichnungen 1973–1985*
  (1987; *The Secret Heart of
  the Clock: Notes, Aphorisms,
  Fragments, 1973–1985,*
  1991), x, xiii, 12, 64, 72, 75,
  77–78, 126, 130–32
  Das Gewissen der Worte: Essays
  (1976; *The Conscience of
  Words,* 1979), x, xiii, 11, 62,
  69, 90, 98–99, 128
  *Der andere Prozeß: Kafka's
  Briefe an Felice* (1965; *Kafka's
  Other Trial: The Letters to
  Felice,* 1974), ix, xiv, 11, 18,
  78, 99, 100, 229–31
  Der Beruf des Dichters (1976),
  x, 11.
  *Der Ohrenzeuge: Fünfzig
  Charaktere* (1964; *The

  Earwitness,* 1979), ix, xiv, 11,
  90, 91, 98, 103n, 123, 140
  Die Befristeten (written 1952,
  published 1964; *The
  Numbered: A Play,* 1984), ix,
  10, 11, 12, 16, 89, 137, 141,
  146, 148–52
  Die Blendung (1935; *Auto-da-
  fé,* 1946), ix, xiii, 4–9, 11, 16,
  18, 19, 25, 29–33, 47, 54–55,
  64, 71, 73, 79, 82–84, 87–95,
  98–99, 105, 115, 140, 142,
  145, 163, 175, 177, 183–84,
  188, 193, 225–35, 248–49,
  270, 273, 294
  *Die Fackel im Ohr:
  Lebensgeschichte 1921–1931*
  (1980; *The Torch in My Ear,*
  1982), x, xiii, 6, 12, 45–47,
  52, 55, 90, 92–93, 99–100,
  176, 222–23, 233, 275, 279
  *Die Fliegenpein:
  Aufzeichnungen 1973–1985*
  (1992; *The Agony of Flies:
  Notes and Notations,* 1994),
  x, xiii, 12, 33, 126–27, 245,
  247, 250
  *Die gerettete Zunge: Geschichte
  einer Jugend* (1977; *The
  Tongue Set Free:
  Remembrance of a European
  Childhood,* 1979), x, xiii, 2,
  11, 19, 46–47, 52, 54, 62,
  100, 175–76, 231, 250, 261,
  269, 271, 273, 275
  *Die gespaltene Zukunft:
  Aufsätze und Gespräche*
  (1972), x, xiii, 11, 90, 263,
  278
  *Die Provinz des Menschen:
  Aufzeichnungen 1942–1972*
  (1973; *The Human Province,*
  1978), x, xiv, 11, 56, 68, 70,
  73–74, 76–80, 90, 100, 107,
  124–33, 138, 294

Canetti, Elias, works by (continued):

Die Stimmen von Marrakesch (1967; *The Voices of Marrakesh,* 1978), x, xiii, 1, 10, 11, 17, 52, 57–58, 90–91, 95–98, 123, 157–60, 164–65, 167, 171–72, 243–44, 253

Fritz Wotruba (1955), ix, xiii, 16, 89

Hochzeit (1932; *The Wedding,* 1986), ix, 7, 10, 18, 19, 31, 34, 37n, 89, 137, 139, 141–55, 175, 184, 188, 232–34

Hochzeit, Komödie der Eitelkeit, Die Befristeten (1964), ix, 7, 10, 11, 69, 89, 90, 137, 139, 141–42, 145, 148–52, 234, 314

Masse und Macht (1960; *Crowds and Power,* 1962), viii, ix, xiii, 1, 10, 13, 14, 16, 17, 18, 27, 28, 29, 31–37, 69, 74, 83, 89, 91–93, 96–100, 107, 123, 125–26, 129, 133, 141–43, 149, 159, 175, 177, 183, 201–16, 217–19, 221, 223–26, 228–30, 250, 252–53, 272–73, 276, 289–312

Nachträge aus Hampstead: Aus den Aufzeichnungen 1954–1971 (1994, *Notes from Hampstead: The Writer's Notes 1954–1971,* 1998), xi, xiv, 73, 74, 125, 126, 127, 130, 244, 309

Welt im Kopf (1962), ix, xiv

Canetti, Jacques, 2, 3, 263, 275

Canetti, Johanna, 11, 19, 87n, 125, 387n

Canetti, Mathilde (née Arditti), 2–6, 12, 74, 191–92, 194, 263, 265, 267

Canetti, Moiss, 264

Canetti, Nissim, 3, 188, 191, 263

Canetti, Veza (Venetiana Taubner-Calderon), xi, 5–8, 10, 12, 20n, 52, 53–55, 72, 98, 103n, 178, 183–84, 186–88, 191, 193–95, 221–22, 231–32, 252, 276, 315

Canetti Gesellschaft, 29, 103n

capitalism, 18, 159, 171, 213, 227

Caplan, Caren Jane, 172n, 315

Catholicism, 2

Central European Jews, 1, 19, 291–308

Cerha, Michael, 38n, 40n

Cervantes, 15, 65, 74, 133

Chaplin, Charlie, 146

Chargaff, Erwin, 109

China, 97, 180

Chiusano, Italo, 33, 40n

civil society, 150, 168, 268

Clarendon, Edward Hyde, 66, 83

Cohn-Bendit, Daniel, 150, 155n, 315

Cold War, 101, 110, 117

communication, 55, 108, 115, 117–18, 127, 131, 147, 217, 234, 245, 249–51, 267, 271, 294

communism, 3, 13, 213, 280, 282

Conradi, Peter J., 38n, 315

Constantine, David, 33, 40n

Constantinople, 265, 278, 285n

Coriolanus, 74

Corriere della sera (newspaper), 36, 37n, 38n, 40n, 41n

Crampton, R. J., 283n

Creed, Gerald W., 283n

crowds, 7, 8, 12, 14, 18, 63, 69, 74, 92, 98, 126, 133, 181–83, 190, 203, 208, 210, 212, 213, 217–20, 225–26, 229, 272, 289, 303–4. *See also Masse und Macht* (*Crowds and Power*)

Curtius, Mechthild, 229, 238n, 316

Danube monarchy, 4, 217
Danube region, 4, 175, 178, 180, 186, 262–69
Darby, David, 39n, 255n
Darwin, Charles, 202, 214n, 252, 316
Darwinism, 17, 201, 214
Das Urteil (Franz Kafka), 78
Dawkins, Richard, 202
de Beauvoir, Simone, 27
de Maistre, 70
de Rothermann, x
death, 1, 9, 16, 50, 53, 56, 62–70, 80, 94, 101, 123, 127–29, 151–52, 168–70, 188, 191–92, 194, 197n, 205–7, 218, 220, 224, 241, 245, 246, 250, 276, 289–309
Defoe, Daniel, 65
Denby, David, 192, 197n, 316
Denkwürdigkeiten eines Nervenkranken (Daniel Paul Schreber), 100, 215n
Dennett, Daniel, 202, 214n, 316
Der ewige Jude (Fritz Hippler dir.), 242
Der jüdische Selbsthaß (Theodor Lessing), 12, 323
Der Mann ohne Eigenschaften (Robert Musil), 79, 93
Der Prozeß (Franz Kafka), 77
Der Spiegel (magazine), 32, 39n, 237n
Der Zauberberg (Thomas Mann), 93, 324
Descartes, René, 241, 256n
Deutsche Grammaphongesellschaft, 11
Deutscher Kritikerpreis, 11
Dickens, Charles, 16, 65, 75, 189
Die Blechtrommel (Günter Grass), 94, 320
Die Fackel (journal, Karl Kraus), 5
Die Letzten Tage der Menschheit (Karl Kraus), 5, 323

Die Schildkröten (Veza Canetti), 8, 252, 315
Die Schlafwandler (Hermann Broch), 7, 93, 315
die tageszeitung (newspaper), 38n, 40n
Die Woche (newspaper), 41n
Die Zeit (newspaper), 32, 39n, 40n, 70, 173n
Di Maio, Irene Stocksieker, viii, 17, 175–200, 316
Dimitrov, Georgi, 282
Dimitrova, Svoboda Alexandra, viii, 18, 261–83, 333
Dissinger, Dieter, 29, 38n, 316
Doerr, Karin, 119n, 316
Dollfuss, Engelbert, 77
Don Quixote, 65, 91, 173n
Donahue, William Collins, vii, 14–15, 25–41, 142, 147, 316, 333
Doppelmasse (dual mass), 223–24, 228–29, 253
Doppler, Alfred, 29, 316
Dostoyevsky, Feodor, 16, 65, 75
Douglas, Mary, 290
Dubrovnik, 262
DuCardonnay, Eric Leroy, 123, 134n, 317
Dunayer, Joan, 244, 251
Durzak, Manfred, 138, 145, 146, 154n, 270–71, 291, 317

Eastern European Jews, 4, 261–83
Ebner-Eschenbach, Marie, von, 109, 252, 317
Ecce homo (George Grosz), 233
Efraim (Alfred Andersch), 109, 313
Eichmann, Adolf, 14, 279, 281, 289
Eichmann in Jerusalem: A Report on the Banality of Evil (Hannah Arendt), 279, 281
Eigler, Friederike, 59n, 197n, 317

Ein Dichter gegen Macht und Tod (Erich Fried), 30

Eine feste Burg ist unser Gott (Martin Luther), 45

El País (newspaper), 38

Elbaz, Robert, 142, 317

Elias, Norbert, 224, 317

Eliot, T. S., 81–82, 86n

Empson, William, 81

Engelmann, Susanna, 134n, 318

England. *See* Great Britain

Enlightenment, 145, 201–202, 218, 220, 228, 239, 294–95, 307

environmentalists, 246

Estermann, Josef, 36

ethnicity, 176, 185, 241, 270

fascism, 3, 6–8, 13, 18, 28, 145, 179, 213, 227, 232, 234, 239, 279, 293, 308

Feldmann, Arthur, 109

Felman, Shoshana, 318

feminist scholarship, 18, 29, 148, 221, 229, 243–44, 251–52

Feng, Guoqing, 103n, 318

Ferdinand of Aragon, 263, 284n

Ferrara, Jenna, 148, 318

Fetscher, Iring, 138, 318

feuilleton, 26, 31, 33–36

Final Solution, 265, 276, 279, 281

Finsen, Lawrence, and Susan Finsen, 244, 318

First World War, 4, 13, 69, 72, 182, 193, 210, 222, 250, 253, 268, 279

flâneur, 157, 184

Flaubert, Gustav, 65

Fleischli, Alfons, 318

Foell, Kristie, 155n, 196n, 318

Foucault, Michel, 173n, 203, 215n, 232, 238n, 313, 318, 320

Fox, Michael A., 244, 245, 254n, 318

France, 9, 10, 91, 263, 267

Frankfurt Institute for Social Research, 34

Frankfurt School, 12

Frankfurter Allgemeine Zeitung (newspaper), 37n, 39n, 40n, 331

Franz Josef, 93, 265, 285n

Franz Nabl Prize, 11

Freies Theater Heidelberg, 153n

French classicism, 98

French Revolution, 33, 74, 208, 216n, 327

Frenkel-Brunswik, Else, 21n, 313

Freud, Sigmund, 5, 17, 75, 92, 141–42, 172, 182–83, 190, 201–2, 209–10, 217–18, 222, 223–37, 253, 318, 326, 327

Fricke, Harald, 120n, 124, 127, 319

Fried, Erich, 25, 30, 98, 103n, 229

Friedell, Egon, 4

Friedrich, Peter, 218, 236n, 319

Fuchs, Anne, 15, 45–60, 243, 319

Fuchs, Irmgard, 235n, 319

Galton, Francis, 209, 319

Gass, William, 35, 41n, 319

Geertz, Clifford, 311n, 319

gender relations, 11, 14, 18, 147–48, 217–34, 253, 318

genocide, 1, 63, 248, 277, 281, 289–309

Gergicov, Krum, 153n, 319

Geschichten aus Odessa (Isaac Babel), 177–78, 313

Gilbert, Martin, 311n, 319

Gilman, Sander L., 310n, 319

globalization, 37

Gnosticism, 158–59, 168, 171

Gobineau, Arthur de, 212, 216n, 319

Goebbels, Joseph, 168, 209, 326

Goethe, Johann Wolfgang, von, 65, 74, 82–83, 86n, 90, 132, 187, 319

Gogol, Nikolai, 65, 74, 75, 138, 335
Goldhagen, Daniel, 207, 320
Goll, Claire, 252, 257n, 320
Gorky, Maxim, 65
Gottfried Keller Prize, 11
Gotthelf, Jeremias, 65, 112, 119n
Grass, Günter, 94, 102n, 275, 320
Great Britain, 1, 3, 8, 9, 18, 73, 77, 80–83, 94, 133, 164, 176, 180, 252, 261, 263, 267, 271, 273, 275, 282, 290
Greece, 10, 129, 266, 280, 284n, 297, 327
Greene, Graham, 81
Großer Österreichischer Staatspreis, 11
Grosz, Elizabeth, 50, 60n, 320
Grosz, George, 6, 233
Grözinger, Karl Erich, 255n, 320
Grünanger, Franz, 265
Guardian (newspaper), 33, 40n
Gulf War, 37
Gutmann, Thomas, 215n, 320

Habsburg monarchy, 2, 93
Hadomi, Leah, 142, 154n, 317
Halter, Martin, 32, 39n
Hampstead, England, 8, 10, 25, 27, 221, 282
Handke, Peter, 11, 321
Hanuschek, Sven, 37
Hargraves, John, xi
Harrison, Mark, 216n, 320
Hartung, Rudolf, 64, 84–85n, 172n, 311n, 320
Hasidic Jews, 5
Hebbel, Friedrich, 65, 75, 85n, 124
Hebel, Johann Peter, 63, 65, 74–75, 178, 197n, 320
Hebel Prize. *See* Johann Peter Hebel Prize
Hegel, Georg Wilhelm Friedrich, 75, 160, 171

Hegelianism, 82
Heilig, Barbara Villiger, 38n
Heine, Heinrich, 16, 21n, 54, 65, 77, 321
Heine und die Folgen (Karl Kraus), 77
Heinrich von Neustadt, 261, 283n, 321
Helwig, Heide, 85n, 321
Helwig, Werner, 172
Henninghaus, Lothar, 236n, 321
Heraclitus, 75, 129
Herder, Johann Gottfried, 186, 187
Higgins, Kathleen M., 214n, 314
Hilberg, Raul, 311n, 321
Hinduism, 245, 249
Hippler, Fritz, 256n
Hiroshima, 9, 21n
History of the Great Rebellion (Edward Hyde, Earl of Clarendon), 66, 83
Hitler, Adolf, 14, 40n, 69, 91, 92, 98, 99, 119n, 124, 144, 149, 204, 209, 220, 226, 276, 277, 279–82
Hobbes, Thomas, 65–71, 82, 201, 203–6, 210, 215n, 224, 227, 237n, 321
Hofmannsthal, Hugo von, 61–62, 65
Hollmann, Hans, 27, 137, 153n, 321
Holocaust. *See* Shoah
Honegger, Gitta, ix, 144, 154n, 321
Honneth, Axel, 203, 215n, 235n, 236n, 237n, 295, 321
Hörisch, Jochen, 41n
Horkheimer, Max, 171, 250, 321
Hoyer, Gisela, 37n
Hrdlicka, Alfred, 98, 103n, 321
Hsün-Tse, 76
Huber, Ortrun, 86n, 321

Huntington, Samuel P., 171, 173n, 322
Hurley, Robert, 238n, 318

Iden, Peter, 40n
individualism, 3, 13, 143, 205, 210, 219, 225
Innsbrucker Zeitungsarchiv, 37
intertextuality, 132
Isaacs, Jack, 80–81, 86n, 322
Isabella the Catholic, 263
Islam, 149, 161, 165–72, 211–12
Israel, 26, 37, 274, 280, 282
Israel, Salvator, 285n, 322
Italian Europa Prize, 12
Italy, 10, 28, 252, 266–67

Jaccard, Roland, 32, 39n
Jacobs, Jürgen, 118n, 322
Jameson, Frederic, 173n, 330
Japan, 9, 180, 247
Jelinek, Elfriede, 16, 139, 271
Jensen, Katherine A., 197n
Jerusalem, 2, 180, 205, 211
Jewish authors, 13, 16, 35, 41n, 65, 81, 275
Jewish identity, 1, 5, 16, 19, 35, 41n, 65, 81, 94, 96–97, 101, 157–59, 168–72, 176–80, 192, 196n, 242, 261–83, 293, 299
Jewish law, 2
Jewish resistance, 205
Jewish Socialists, 5
Jivaros, 1
Johann Peter Hebel Prize, 12, 74
Jonas, Hans, 158, 172n, 322
Jones, Ernest, 209, 215n, 322
Josephus, Flavius, 1, 20n, 205–6, 318
Joubert, 85n, 124
Joyce, James, 12, 25, 37n, 79–80, 95
Juvenal, 116

Kafka, Franz, 1, 11, 39n, 63, 74–79, 90–93, 99–100, 113–14, 133, 142, 151, 221, 229–32, 242, 249, 252–53, 255–56n, 292, 320, 325
Kafka Prize, 12
Kalahari Desert, 91, 213
Kampel, Beatrix, 85n, 322
Kant, Immanuel, 68, 74, 326
Kaplan, Harald, 295, 310n, 322
Karbala, Iraq, 1, 211
Kaszyński, Stefan H., 118n, 322
Keller, Gottfried, 11, 65
Kenk, Françoise, 85n, 322
Keren, Tzvi, 285n
Kimball, Roger, 35, 41n, 322
King Lear (Shakespeare), 53, 63
Kirkup, James, 38n
Kiss, Endre, 237n, 322
Kleist, Heinrich von, 16, 65, 160
Klemperer, Viktor, 109, 119n, 322
Knoll, Heike, 236n, 322
Koksal, Yonka, 284n
Kolmar, Gertrud, 252, 257n, 312n, 323
König, Otto, 8
Konstantinov, Wenzeslav, 262, 283–85n
Kraft, Helga, vii, 17, 137–56, 334
Kraus, Karl, 4–12, 16, 28, 30, 36, 41n, 47, 52–55, 63, 65, 76–77, 85n, 90, 91, 101, 107, 109–10, 116, 119n, 133, 138, 144, 193, 222, 223, 230, 241, 255n, 268, 292, 308, 323
Kristallnacht. See Night of Broken Glass
Kristeva, Julia, 50, 57, 60n, 323
Kronauer, Brigitte, 239, 241, 254n, 323
Krüger, Michael, 27, 34, 38n, 40n
Kunert, Günter, 35, 41n
Küng, Luzie, 41n

La Bruyére, Jean de, 65, 75, 103n
La Capra, Dominick, 311n, 323
La Chartreuse de Parme
   (Stendhal), 72, 73
La Jornado (newspaper), 32
La Mettrie, Julien Offroy de, 241,
   255n
La Rochefoucault, François Duc
   de, 124
Lacan, Jacques, 150, 155n, 238n,
   323
Lachaise, Père, 184
Laemmle, Peter, 141, 144, 154n,
   323
Lang, Fritz, 138
languages, 1–2, 9, 13, 15, 16, 45–
   106, 140–47, 166, 172, 185,
   231, 245–50, 256n, 289, 308
   Arabic, 58, 96, 166, 179
   Armenian, 265
   Bulgarian, 2, 185, 262–63, 271
   Chinese, 83
   English, 3, 65, 94, 115, 181,
      265, 283n, 297
   French, 65, 96, 157, 180, 297
   German, 1, 9, 13–15, 18, 21n,
      45–59, 172, 180, 271, 273–75
   Greek, 265, 309n
   Hebrew, 7, 57, 179, 180, 265,
      309n
   Ladino, 2, 179–80, 185–86,
      263–64, 271, 274
   Moldavian, 262
   Russian, 265
   Turkish, 185, 265
   Wallachian, 262, 265
   Welsh, 83–84, 96
   Yiddish, 4, 265
Lanzmann, Claude, 293–94,
   311n, 318, 323
Lappe, Thomas, 113, 120n,
   121n, 123, 125, 323
Larkin, Philip, 206, 215n, 323
Law of the Father, 51

Lawson, Richard H., 124, 134n,
   137, 145, 310n, 323
Le Bon, Gustave, 92, 208–10,
   218, 226, 323
Le Monde (newspaper), 27, 32,
   39n, 85n
Le Rouge et Le Noir (Stendhal),
   73
Leavis, F. R., 171
Lec, Stanisław Jerzy, 109
Lenz, J. M. R., 65, 187
Lessing, Theodor, 12, 21n, 323
Leviathan, 67, 215n, 227, 321
Levinson, Daniel J., 21n, 313
liberalism, 18, 213
Lichtenberg, Georg Christoph, 16,
   65, 75, 107, 109, 124, 132, 335
Lippit, Akira Mizuta, 249, 256n,
   323
Literaturpreis der Bayerischen
   Akademie der Schönen Künste,
   11
Literaturpreis der Stadt Wien, 11
Loetscher, Hugo, 35, 41n
Lorenz, Dagmar C. G., 1–24, 87n,
   239–60, 287n, 305, 323–24
Luther, Martin, 45

Macedonia, 280–91, 327
Machiavelli, 34, 67
Macho, Thomas H., 197n, 324
Mack, Michael, viii, 19, 36, 41n,
   289–310, 324
Mack Smith, Denis, 215n, 324
Magnus, Bernd, 214n, 314
Magris, Claudio, 25, 27, 30–31,
   35, 38n, 39n, 59n, 324
Mahler, Anna, 7, 12, 193
Mahler-Werfel, Alma, 7, 59n,
   187, 197n, 221
Manheim, Ralph, x
Mann, Heinrich, 65
Mann, Thomas, 65, 79, 93, 99,
   188, 324

Männerphantasien (Klaus Theweleit), 12, 21n, 330
Mariott, Emil, 257n, 324
Marti, Urs, 40n
Marx, Karl, 160, 171, 213
Masken. See masks
Maskensprung. See masks
masks, 47–48, 55, 144–52, 212–13, 218, 223, 270, 317
mass psychology, 12–13, 14, 241
Masse, Michelle, 197
Mataja, Emilie, 252
materialism, 67, 165, 201
Mayröcker, Friederike, 27
McClelland, J. S., 92, 102n, 215n, 324
Melzer, Gerhard, 38n, 59n, 175, 196n, 314, 322, 324
Menachemoff, 178, 180
Mendes-Flohr, Paul, 309n, 324
Metropolis, 138
Meyer, Christine, 85n, 324
Meyer, Conrad Ferdinand, 65
Midgley, Mary, 254n
Mieder, Wolfgang, vii, 16, 107–22, 325
Milosz, Czeslaw, 212, 216n, 325
misogyny, 18, 29, 54, 59n, 147–48, 220–23, 227–30
Mitsch, Werner, 109
modernity, vii, 17, 25, 28, 30, 41n, 91, 137–56, 190, 208, 217–18, 223–26, 234, 306
monotheism, 149, 245
Morocco, 10, 96–97, 158, 244. *See also Die Stimmen von Marrakesch*
mother tongue, vii, 13, 15, 45–60, 316
Muchnik, Mario, 27, 38n
Müller-Lauter, Wolfgang, 214n, 325
Müller-Steiger, Hans Ruedi, 61
Mulot, Sibylle, 236n

Murdoch, Iris, 10, 21n, 29–30, 38n, 83, 221, 314, 315, 325
Murphy, Harriet, viii, 17, 157–74, 325, 335
Musil, Robert, 28, 36, 52, 55–56, 65, 76, 79–80, 93, 226, 292, 321
Mussolini, Benito, 209, 215n, 324

Nardo, Anna, 197
National Socialism, 3, 7, 14, 18, 69, 109, 177, 261, 277, 292. *See also* Nazism
nationalism, 13, 77, 244, 250, 274, 277, 279, 309n
Nazism, 7, 8, 9, 13, 19, 64, 109–14, 131, 137, 242, 265, 267, 279–82, 289–313. *See also* National Socialism
Nelly Sachs Prize, 11
Nestroy, Johann Nepomuk, 76, 86n, 140, 330
Neue Freie Presse (newspaper), 8
Neue Rundschau (newspaper), 99, 119n
Neue Subjektivität. See New Subjectivity
Neue Züricher Zeitung (newspaper), 28, 38n, 41n
Neues Deutschland (newspaper), 37n
Neugroschel, Joachim, ix, x, xi
Neumann, Gerhard, 41n, 230
New Criterion (journal), 41n, 322
New Republic (magazine), 41n, 172n, 319
New Subjectivity, 233
New Yorker (magazine), 35, 41n, 197n, 279, 316
Newkirk, Ingrid, 254n
Nietzsche, Friedrich, viii, 17, 32, 70, 79, 160, 201–16, 241, 253, 313, 314, 319, 320, 321, 325
Night of Broken Glass (*Kristallnacht*), 69, 149

Nobel Prize, 12, 14, 27, 28, 30, 31, 76, 81, 82, 100, 187, 274–75, 282, 291
Norris, Christopher, 173n
Novick, Peter, 309–10n, 325

Occident, 1, 17, 240. *See also* Western culture
Orient, 1, 95, 171, 175, 178–80, 184, 265–70, 273, 290, 297–99, 329
Orientalism: Western Conceptions of the Orient (Edward Said, 1978), 171, 327
Orlowski, Hubert, 238n, 325
Oschlies, Wolf, 280, 287n

Pacheco, Alex, 254
Page, Tony, 256, 325
Palestine, 179–80, 280
Pankau, Johannes G., viii, 18, 217–37, 325, 335
Parry, Idris, 10, 61, 72, 73, 75, 77–79, 84n, 87n, 325, 326
Pasha, Midhad, 263–64
Patillo-Hess, John, 10
Perry, Duncan M., 283n, 326
Peshev, Dimitar, 281–82
Petersen, Carol, 21n, 326
Piel, Edgar, 173n, 256n, 326
Pollak, Felix, 109
Pound, Ezra, 83
Pour le Mérite, 12
Powell, Enoch, 81
Prague, 8, 96, 192, 290
Preece, Julian, vii, 16, 89–106, 335
Pressburger, Giorgio, 36, 41n
primitive cultures, 2, 151, 171, 202, 208, 224, 297, 299, 303–6, 312n
Prix International, 9
proverbs, 16, 108–18, 120n, 316, 325
Pueblo Indians, 1–2

Pundt, Michael, 154n

Quevedo, 41n, 65, 133

Raddatz, Hans-Peter, 173n, 326
Raimund, Ferdinand, 140
Ranke, Friedrich, 155n
Rathenau, Walter, 73, 183
Razbojnikova-Frateva, Maja, 103n, 326
Real Presences (George Steiner, 1989), 158
Regan, Tom, 255n, 256n, 326
Reich, Wilhelm, 14, 326
Reich-Ranicki, Marcel, 10, 157, 172n, 326
Reigen (Arthur Schnitzler, 1896–97), 232
Reinharz, Jehuda, 309n, 324
Reiss, Hans, vii, 15–16, 61–88, 326, 335–36
Renard, Jules, 124
Ridley, Matt, 202, 214n, 326
Rinke, Stefan, 254n, 328
Ritvo, Lucille B., 214n, 326
Robertson, Ritchie, viii, 17–18, 29, 31, 35, 39n, 102n, 196n, 201–16, 326–27
Röhrich, Lutz, 120n
Roth, Josef, 5
Rothstein, Edward, 172
Roustchouk, Bulgaria (also Russe, Rustschuk), 1, 2, 18–19, 175–78, 181–88, 191, 194, 261–88
Roux, Wilhelm, 202, 214n, 325
Ruckhaberle, Dieter, 287n, 327
Rudé, George, 216n, 327
Rushdie, Salman, 145, 155n, 327
Russell, Bertrand, 81
Ryder, Richard, 244, 254n, 327

Sachs, Nelly, 12
Said, Edward, 17, 171, 290, 298, 327
Sansone, Barbara, 284n

Sartre, Jean Paul, 27
satire, 5, 7, 11, 47, 52, 55, 69,
    76, 91, 98, 107, 109–10, 114,
    116, 123, 128, 130–33, 138,
    144, 211, 228, 232–33, 292,
    294–95, 305, 308
Sax, Boria, 242, 256n, 327
Scheichl, Sigurd Paul, vii, 16,
    123–36, 196, 327
Schickele, Joachim, 305, 312n
Schieth, Lydia, 255n, 328
Schiller, Friedrich, 51, 160
Schmidt-Dengler, Wendelin,
    103n, 140, 154n, 328
Schmidt-Rinke, Silke, 254n, 328
Schneider, Manfred, 41n
Schneider, Robert, 27, 32
Schnitzer, Vivian, 38n, 41n
Schnitzler, Arthur, 5, 61, 95, 223,
    232, 334, 335
Scholem, Gershom, 5
Scholl-Latour, Peter, 17, 173n,
    328
Scholz, Hannelore, 60n, 197n,
    222, 328
Schreber, Daniel Paul, 14, 100,
    204–6, 230, 325, 328
Schuh, Franz, 197n, 328
Sebald, W. G., 41n, 141, 154n,
    328
Second World War, 62, 110, 117,
    146, 261, 268, 276, 279–80
Seidler, Ingo, 118n, 133, 328
Serbia, 267, 278, 284n
sexuality, 52, 101, 147, 168,
    217–18, 232–34
Shakespeare, William, 51, 53, 65,
    74, 82, 132, 207
Shepard, Paul, 245, 246, 256n,
    328
Shepardic Jews, 1, 2, 179, 261–83
Shi'ites, 1
Shoah, viii, 8, 9, 14, 18, 19, 36,
    101, 109, 114, 117, 179, 193,
    207, 250, 261, 275–79, 289–
    313, 318, 320, 322, 325, 327,

13, 318, 320, 322, 325, 327,
    331, 332, 333, 334
subjectivity, vii, 15, 45–60, 145,
    150
Singer, Isaac Bashevis, 5, 12
Singer, Peter, 240, 254, 328
Skibra, Daniel, 37
slavery, 148, 202, 209, 213, 296–
    97
Sloterdijk, Peter, 171, 173n, 220,
    236n, 329
Sobieski, Janet, 120n
socialism, 3, 18, 252
Sokel, Walter, 29
Sonne, Abraham, 7, 12, 47, 52–
    53, 55–57, 65, 72, 79, 180,
    194–95
Sonnheimer, Kurt, 173n
Sontag, Susan, 29, 222, 236n,
    311n, 329
Sorin, Raphael, 85
Soviet Union, 14, 212, 213
Spain, 65, 179, 180, 263–64,
    267, 274, 275, 278, 284n
Spanish Civil War, 101, 179
Sperber, Manés, 5, 255n, 275
Spiegel, Marjory, 254
Staatstheater Braunschweig, 10
Stalinism, 13, 14
Steiner, Franz Baermann, 19, 36,
    83, 124, 290–313, 329
Steiner, George, 158
Steinhof asylum, 6, 188, 193
Stendhal, Henry Brulard de, 65,
    71–76, 93, 127–28, 132, 185,
    335
Steussloff, Axel Gunther, 103n,
    173n, 310n, 329
Stevens, Adrian, 329, 38n, 85n
Stieg, Gerald, 20n, 27, 35, 40n,
    76, 175, 329–30
Stockholm, Sweden, 76, 78
Storm and Stress, 187
Strassburg, Gottfried von, 146,
    155n

Streeruwitz, Marlene, 12, 16, 21n, 139, 330
Strelka, Joseph, 57, 59n, 330
Strindberg, August, 189, 227, 232
Stromsik, Jiri, 103n, 330
Sturm und Drang. *See* Storm and Stress
Surrealism, 160, 162
Susman, Walerij, 85n, 330
Swift, Jonathan, 65, 69, 76, 82, 294, 308
Switzerland, 3, 4, 11, 18, 61, 72, 77, 139, 154n, 176, 274, 283
Széll, Zsuzsa, 196n, 330

taboo, 52, 191, 290, 299
Taliban, 149–50
Tallis, Raymond, 173n
Tamir, Vicki, 277, 286n, 330
Tauber, Reinhold, 41n
Taubner-Calderon, Veza. *See* Canetti, Veza
Teraoka, Arlene A., 103n, 330
terrorism, 13
The Great Dictator (Charlie Chaplin), 146
theater of cruelty, 160
Theophrastus, 75, 98, 140, 330
Theweleit, Klaus, 12, 21n, 330
Thompson, Edward P., 216n, 331
Timmermann, Harry, 120n, 238n, 331
Todorov, Tzvetan, 279, 281, 287n, 331
Todorova, Maria, 286n, 331
Tolstoy, Leo, 16, 63, 65
Tönnies, Sibylle, 39n, 159, 331
transformation, 91–92, 100–101, 112, 125, 127, 142, 208, 212–13, 240, 241–42, 248, 250, 253, 274
Trotter, Wilfred, 209–10, 215n, 331

Turan, Ömer, 285n, 331
Turrini, Peter, 139
Twain, Mark, 124

Uhlenbruck, Gerhard, 109

Veichtbauer, Judith, 284n, 286n, 313
Venice, 262
Verfremdungseffekt, 111
Verwandlung. See transformation
Vie de Henry Brulard (Stendhal), 71–73, 85n, 324
Vienna, 2, 7, 8, 11, 28, 50, 54, 61, 65, 69, 79, 94, 96, 100–101, 176, 178, 180, 183, 186, 188, 190, 215, 218, 224, 233, 264, 266–67, 276, 291; anti-Semitism in, 4; *Burgtheater,* 2, 48, 65, 268; Justizpalast, 72, 226, 270; Leopoldstadt, 4–5; University of, 6; *Urania,* 10, 268
Vietnam War, 10, 97
Villa Yalta, Zurich, 182, 186, 190
Viteazul, Michail (Michael the Brave), 262, 284n
Völker, Klaus, 144, 154n, 331
von Matt, Peter, 32–35, 39n, 40n, 85n, 119n, 130–31, 135n, 331

Wagner, Richard, 79, 146
Waldinger, Ernst, 13
Waldinger, Fred, 5, 21n, 242
Walser, Robert, 65, 78, 79
Ward, Philip, 283
Wedekind, Frank, 65, 223, 232
Weimar Republic, 6, 176, 187, 304
Weininger, Otto, 59n, 222–26, 230, 235, 237n, 253, 315, 326, 331
Weiss, Peter, 53, 77
Werfel, Franz, 7, 65

Werlen, Hansjakob, 33–34, 39n, 40n, 237n, 310n, 331

Western culture, 2, 17, 33, 56, 64, 96–97, 127, 133, 142–43, 148, 151, 157, 159, 167–68, 172, 178, 241, 243, 245, 250, 290, 296–300. *See also* Occident

Widdig, Bernd, 177, 186, 196n, 197n, 226, 237n, 238n, 332

Widmer, Urs, 41n

Wiese, Benno von, 119n

Wiethölter, Waltraut, 53, 59n, 60n, 332

Willi Weismann Verlag, 9

Williams, Raymond, 171

Willingham, Ralph, 140, 152n, 332

Witte, Bernd, 57, 59n, 60n, 229, 239n, 332

Wolf, Christa, 53

women, portrayal of, 96, 128, 147–50, 161, 163–70, 194, 208, 217–38

Woolf, Virginia, 82–83, 95

World War I. *See* First World War

World War II. *See* Second World War

Wotruba, Fritz, 7, 10, 98, 190, 194–95. *See also* Canetti, Elias, works by: *Fritz Wotruba*

Woyzeck (Georg Büchner), 138, 147, 232

xenophobia, 37, 300

Yeats, William Butler, 83

Zepesh, Vladislav, 262

Ziesecke, Christiane, 287n

Zionism, 13, 180, 280

Zipes, Jack, 197n, 255n, 318

Zuckmayer, Carl, 65

Zurich, 69, 83, 101, 176–77, 181–82, 186, 189, 192, 273

Zweig, Stefan, 65

(*Compiled by Lilian Friedberg*)